Cloud Computing: Automating the Virtualized Data Center

Venkata Josyula
Malcolm Orr
Greg Page

Cisco Press

800 East 96th Street

Indianapolis, IN 46240

Cloud Computing: Automating the Virtualized Data Center

Venkata Josyula
Malcolm Orr
Greg Page

Published by:
Cisco Press
800 East 96th Street
Indianapolis, IN 46240 USA

Printed in the United States of America 1 2 3 4 5 6 7 8 9 0

First Printing December 2011

Library of Congress Cataloging-in-Publication Number is on file.

ISBN-13: 978-1-58720-434-0

ISBN-10: 1-58720-434-7

Warning and Disclaimer

This book is designed to provide information about cloud computing. Every effort has been made to make this book as complete and as accurate as possible, but no warranty or fitness is implied.

The information is provided on an "as is" basis. The authors, Cisco Press, and Cisco Systems, Inc., shall have neither liability nor responsibility to any person or entity with respect to any loss or damages arising from the information contained in this book or from the use of the discs or programs that may accompany it.

The opinions expressed in this book belong to the authors and are not necessarily those of Cisco Systems, Inc.

Trademark Acknowledgments

All terms mentioned in this book that are known to be trademarks or service marks have been appropriately capitalized. Cisco Press or Cisco Systems, Inc. cannot attest to the accuracy of this information. Use of a term in this book should not be regarded as affecting the validity of any trademark or service mark.

Corporate and Government Sales

The publisher offers excellent discounts on this book when ordered in quantity for bulk purchases or special sales, which may include electronic versions and/or custom covers and content particular to your business, training goals, marketing focus, and branding interests. For more information, please contact: U.S. Corporate and Government Sales 1-800-382-3419 corpsales@pearsontechgroup.com

For sales outside of the U.S., please contact: International Sales international@pearsoned.com

Feedback Information

At Cisco Press, our goal is to create in-depth technical books of the highest quality and value. Each book is crafted with care and precision, undergoing rigorous development that involves the unique expertise of members from the professional technical community.

Readers' feedback is a natural continuation of this process. If you have any comments regarding how we could improve the quality of this book, or otherwise alter it to better suit your needs, you can contact us through email at feedback@ciscopress.com. Please make sure to include the book title and ISBN in your message.

We greatly appreciate your assistance.

Publisher: Paul Boger

Associate Publisher: Dave Dusthimer

Executive Editor: Mary Beth Ray

Managing Editor: Sandra Schroeder

Project Editor: Mandie Frank

Editorial Assistant: Vanessa Evans

Cover Designer: Sandra Schroeder

Book Designer: Gary Schroeder

Business Operation Manager, Cisco Press: Anand Sundaram

Manager Global Certification: Erik Ullanderson

Senior Development Editor: Christopher Cleveland

Copy Editor: John Edwards

Technical Editors: Krishna Arji, Eric Charlesworth

Proofreader: Sheri Cain

Indexer: Erika Millen

Composition: Mark Shirar

Americas Headquarters
Cisco Systems, Inc.
San Jose, CA

Asia Pacific Headquarters
Cisco Systems (USA) Pte. Ltd.
Singapore

Europe Headquarters
Cisco Systems International BV
Amsterdam, The Netherlands

Cisco has more than 200 offices worldwide. Addresses, phone numbers, and fax numbers are listed on the Cisco Website at **www.cisco.com/go/offices.**

About the Authors

Venkata (Josh) Josyula, Ph.D., CCIE No. 13518, is a distinguished services engineer (DSE) and lead solutions architect in Cisco Services Technology Group (CSTG). He has more than 25 years of diverse experience in network management for telecommunications and IP in a variety of positions, including systems engineering, technical marketing, consulting, customer management, and deployment.

Josh has been with Cisco for 11 years and, prior to that, worked at Bell Laboratories as a distinguished engineer. Josh has written and/or contributed to key ITU-T network management documents and served as advisory director for the TMF board. Josh has published more than 60 technical papers, reports, articles, and books and is frequently called upon by Cisco customers and internal Cisco engineers around the world for advice and presentations and to perform OSS assessment on OSS/BSS architecture and products.

Malcolm Orr (B.S.) is an enterprise architect within the Cisco Services Division. Malcolm focuses on advising telecommunication companies and large enterprise clients on how to architect, build, and operate NGN and cloud platforms. Malcolm has more than 18 years in the IT industry, of which the past 5 years he has spent at Cisco involved in architecting and delivering complex solutions to various clients. He currently is the lead architect for a number of Tier 1 public cloud projects within Cisco. Prior to joining Cisco, Malcolm was a principal consultant at AMDOCS, working on the BT 21CN transformation, and he was one of the founders and the technical director of Harbrook Consultants, a consulting firm specializing in network and system management.

Greg Page (B.A. (Hons.)) is a solutions architect for Cisco Systems within the presales Data Center architecture team. Greg has been working in the IT industry for 16 years (the last 11 with Cisco Systems) in a variety of technical consulting roles specializing in data center architecture and technology in addition to service provider security (CISSP #77673).

About the Technical Reviewers

Krishna Arji is a senior manager at Cisco. In this role, he is responsible for the development of technology that enables delivery of Cisco Services. Krishna has held various positions in the Services Technology Group at Cisco. Most recently, he played a key role in evaluating and developing technologies required for the delivery of cloud planning, design, and implementation services. Under his leadership, his team has developed several tools to perform routing, switching, data center, security, and WLAN assessments of customers' infrastructure. His areas of expertise include networking, software design and development, and data center technologies such as virtualization. Krishna holds a bachelor's degree in electronics and communications engineering, and he has a master's degree in enterprise software technologies. He has a patent pending with USPTO for Automated Assessments of Storage Area Networks (Serial No. 13/115,141).

Eric S. Charlesworth is a Technical Solutions Architect in the WW Data Center/Virtualization & Cloud architecture organization at Cisco Systems. Eric has more than 20 years of experience in the Data Center/Networking field and is currently focused on Cloud Computing and Data Center management. Formerly, he worked in various technical leadership positions at companies such as BellSouth and IBM. Eric is also a member of the review board for the Cloud Credential Council (www.cloudcredential.org) and helped to develop and approve the material in the program, as well as for the Cloud Challenge (www.cloudchallenge.com). As a technical editor, Eric has provided technical edits/reviews for major publishing companies, including Pearson Education and Van Haren Publishing.

Dedications

Venkata (Josh) Josyula Thanks to my family, colleagues, and my management for all the support.

Malcolm Orr To G for all the support, to mum and dad, finally something to make up for my 11+.

Greg Page To SGAL, my family and friends. Thanks for all your support and love over the years.

Acknowledgments

Venkata (Josh) Josyula I want to thank my family for the support at home and also like to thank my manager Sunil Kripalani for the encouragement. In addition, I'd like to thank the reviewers Krishna Arji and Eric Charlesworth. Also, I'd like to thank Charles Conte (now at Juniper), Jason Davis, Gopal Renganathan, Manish Jain, Paul Lam, and many other project members who were part of the DC/V project. Also special thanks to Chris, Mary Beth, and Mandie, from Cisco Press.

Malcolm Orr I would like to thanks James Urquart for his advice around cloud maturity, Aaron Kodra for his support in getting this done, and all my colleagues for putting up with me.

Greg Page I would like to thank my Cisco colleagues for their support, in particular my co-authors Malcolm and Josh, as well as John Evans, Thomas Reid, Eric Charlesworth, Uwe Lambrette, Wouter Belmans; and related to my early years at Cisco, Mark Grayson. Finally, thanks to Wendy Mars for giving me the opportunity and freedom to focus on the then emerging topic of 'Cloud'/IaaS.'

Contents at a Glance

Contents

Introduction

Cloud computing is a paradigm shift in the IT industry similar to the displacement of local electric generators with the electric grid, providing utility computing, and it is changing the nature of competition within the computer industry. There are over a hundred companies that claim they can provide cloud services. However, in most cases, they discuss server provisioning or data center automation.

Many leading IT vendors, such as Amazon, Google, Microsoft, IBM, HP, and Cisco, to name a few, believe that cloud computing is the next logical step in controlling IT resources, as well as a primary means to lower total cost of ownership. More than just an industry buzzword, cloud computing promises to revolutionize the way IT resources are deployed, configured, and managed for years to come. Service providers stand to realize tremendous value from moving toward this "everything as a service" delivery model. By expanding and using their infrastructure as a service, instead of dealing with a number of disparate and incompatible silos or the common single-tenant hosting and colocation model, service providers can offer high value to their customers.

This book provides a practical approach for building an architecture for providing virtualized/cloud services and Infrastructure as a Service (IaaS) specifically. Based on our experiences of working with many industry-leading management software vendors and system integrators, we have provided the most comprehensive knowledge that details how to manage the cloud architecture and provide cloud services. This book details management steps with practical example use cases and best practices to build a cloud that can be used by cloud consumers and providers.

Objectives of This Book

Cloud Computing: Automating the Virtualized Data Center provides exhaustive information on how to build and implement solution architectures for managing the cloud from start to finish. For novice users, this book provides information on clouds and a solution architecture approach for managing the cloud. For experienced, hands-on operations folks, this book provides information on how to set up and provision the Infrastructure as a Service (IaaS). For product specialists, this book covers what service providers look for in their products and discuss how their systems need to interact with other systems to provide an integrated solution that meets end-user needs.

This book evolved as we started working in the lab with major management software vendors to provision an end-to-end cloud infrastructure that consisted of compute, network, and storage resources. During the process, we found that most of the independent software vendors (ISV) could not meet the challenges of provisioning an end-to-end cloud infrastructure. This led us to work with the various Cisco software vendor partners to develop end-to-end integrated solutions for cloud management using Cisco and partner products. The solutions and the best practices in this book provide end-to-end architecture solutions and can be replicated and used in any lab and/or production network for the scenarios described in this book.

How This Book Is Organized

The book is divided into four parts:

Part I: Introduction to Managing Virtualization and Cloud Computing Environments

- **Chapter 1, "Cloud Computing Concepts":** This chapter illustrates the virtualization and cloud concepts. Virtualization and cloud computing are dovetailed, and vendors and solution providers are increasingly using virtualization to build private clouds. This chapter will discuss public, private, and hybrid clouds, as well as the benefits of on-site computing to cloud computing. This chapter will also provide information on types of services that can be provided on top of clouds, such as Infrastructure as a Service (IaaS), Software as a Service (SaaS), barriers to cloud adoption, and cloud benefits and return on investment (ROI).

- **Chapter 2, "Cloud Design Patterns and Use Cases":** This chapter illustrates typical application design patterns and use cases found in most enterprises today and discusses how these can be transitioned into the cloud.

- **Chapter 3, "Data Center Architecture and Technologies":** This chapter provides an overview of the architectural principles and the infrastructure designs needed to support a new generation of "real-time" managed IT service use cases. This chapter focuses on the building blocks, technologies, and concepts that help simplify the design and operation of the data center.

- **Chapter 4, "IT Services":** This chapter describes the classification of IT services from both a business-centric and a technology-centric perspective. In addition, this chapter looks at the underpinning economics of IaaS and the contextual aspects of making a "workload" placement in the cloud, that is, risk versus cost.

- **Chapter 5, "The Cisco Cloud Strategy":** This chapter discusses Cisco Systems' corporate strategy, focusing on the technological, system, and service developments related to the cloud. This chapter also briefly covers the technology evolution toward the cloud to understand how we got to where we are today as an IT industry.

Part II: Managing Cloud Services

- **Chapter 6, "Cloud Management Reference Architecture":** This chapter discusses various industry standards and describes how they can be used to build a reference architecture. This chapter discusses ITIL, TMF, and ITU-TMN standards, and uses these standards to build a cloud reference architecture for process models, cloud frameworks, and management models. It gives recommendations on integration models between various management layers.

- **Chapter 7, "Service Fulfillment":** This chapter describes the details of cloud service fulfillment, also referred to as cloud service provisioning. Service fulfillment is responsible for delivering products and services to the customer. This includes order handling, service configuration and activation, and resource provisioning. Chapter 6 provided two reference architectures from a management perspective. This chapter builds on Chapter 6 and provides details on cloud service fulfillment and an end-to-end logical functional architecture for managing clouds. The end-to-end logical functional architecture is built based on the Tele-Management Forum (TMF) eTOM (enhanced Telecom Operations Map) and Information Technology Infrastructure Library (ITIL) V3 life cycle.

- **Chapter 8, "Service Assurance":** This chapter describes how infrastructure can be automated and how services can be provisioned from the time a customer orders a service to the time the service is provisioned. These services need to be monitored to provide high-quality services to the customers. This chapter discusses proactive and reactive maintenance activities, service monitoring (SLA/QoS), resource status and performance monitoring, and troubleshooting. This includes continuous resource status and performance monitoring to proactively detect possible failures, and the collection of performance data and analysis to identify and resolve potential or real problems.

- **Chapter 9, "Billing and Chargeback":** The ultimate goal of cloud computing is to provide a set of resources on demand when required and to provide an accurate usage of data. The choice to bill/charge or simply show this data to the consumer depends on many factors, all of which are discussed in this chapter. This chapter introduces cloud billing/charging terminology; billing considerations for IaaS, PaaS, and SaaS; process flow from Order-to-Cash (OTC); and the billing/charging architecture for cloud services.

Part III: Managing Cloud Resources

- **Chapter 10, "Technical Building Blocks of IaaS":** This chapter describes how to design and build an IaaS service starting with the basic building blocks and evolving into a full-service catalogue. This chapter also discusses how service data is persisted in the cloud management systems and provides some thoughts on where cloud solutions will challenge traditional CMDB implementations.

- **Chapter 11, "Automating and Orchestration Resources":** Building on Chapter 10, this chapter explores how the service catalogue offers can be realized in the cloud infrastructure and describes best practices around provisioning, activating, and managing cloud services throughout their lifetime.

- **Chapter 12, "Cloud Capacity Management":** Optimizing any infrastructure is challenging, let alone when you factor in the sporadic, real-time demand that the cloud generates. This chapter outlines some of the key capacity challenges, describes the process around developing a capacity model, and discusses deploying tools to support this model.

- **Chapter 13, "Providing the Right Cloud User Experience":** The cloud fundamentally changes the way IT is consumed and delivered, and the key to being a successful cloud provider is the user experience. This chapter defines the typical roles that will interact with the cloud, their requirements, and some typical integration patterns that should be considered to achieve a consistent user experience.

- **Chapter 14, "Adopting Cloud from a Maturity Perspective":** Building and deploying a cloud will, in most cases, touch on organizational, process, and technology areas. Assessing where you as a potential cloud consumer or provider are in these three areas is a critical first step. This chapter provides a simple, extensible framework for assessing cloud maturity.

Part IV: Appendixes

- **Appendix A, "Case Study: Cloud Providers - Hybrid Cloud":** This case study brings together the concepts outlined in the book with an illustrative example showing the choices an IT and a telecommunications company make when considering the cloud from the consumer and provider perspectives. Although it is a fictional example, the case study is drawn from real-world experiences.

- **Appendix B, "Terms and Acronyms":** This appendix lists common acronyms, their expansions, and definitions for the cloud terminology used throughout this book.

Chapter 1

Cloud Computing Concepts

Upon completing this chapter, you will be able to understand the following:

- Virtualization and types of virtualization
- Cloud computing and types of cloud computing
- Cloud service models
- Cloud adoption and barriers
- Cloud return on investment (ROI) and benefits

This chapter provides virtualization and cloud computing concepts. Virtualization and cloud computing are dovetailed, and vendors and solution providers are increasingly using virtualization to build clouds. This chapter will discuss various types of virtualization and cloud computing, and the benefits of on-site computing to cloud computing. This chapter will also provide information on types of services that can be provided on top of clouds, such as Software as a Service (SaaS), Platform as a Service (PaaS), and Infrastructure as a Service (IaaS). Also, cloud adoption and barriers, ROI for cloud computing, and cloud benefits are covered in this chapter.

Virtualization

Virtualization has become a technical necessity these days, and the trend is continuing for a good reason because when implemented, it provides many benefits such as the following:

- Access to server, network, and storage resources on demand
- Energy savings for a greener earth
- Physical space reduction
- Hard-to-find people resource savings
- Reduction in capital and operational costs

The sum of these savings can be huge, depending on the size of the enterprise.

Virtualization is the creation of a virtual version of something such as an operating system, computing device (server), storage device, or network devices. Server virtualization changes the rules by breaking the traditional mold of one physical server playing host to a single operating system by creating several virtual machines on top of a single server using hypervisor technology. Cloud computing and virtualization are used interchangeably, but this is incorrect. For example, server virtualization provides flexibility to enable cloud computing, but that does not make virtualization the same as cloud computing. There are many technologies that enable cloud computing, and virtualization is one of them; however, it is not absolutely necessary to have virtualization for cloud computing. For example, Google and others have demonstrated clouds without using virtual servers, and using other techniques that achieve similar results. You read more on cloud computing later in the chapter.

It's hard to define virtualization because there are many flavors of it. There's usually a one-to-many or many-to-one aspect to it. In a one-to-many approach, virtualization enables you to create many virtualized resources from one physical resource. This form of virtualization allows data centers to maximize resource utilization. Virtual resources hosting individual applications are mapped to physical resources to provide more efficient server utilization.

With a many-to-one approach, virtualization enables you to create a virtual (logical) resource from multiple physical resources. This is especially true in the context of cloud computing—multiple physical resources are grouped together to form one *cloud*. Virtualization is not cloud as explained before, but rather an enabler for establishing and managing clouds. Virtualization here refers to OS virtualization (as supported by VMware, Xen, or other hypervisor-based technologies). In the Cisco cloud concept, virtualization is extended to incorporate various types of virtualization, such as network, compute, storage, and services. These are explained in the next section.

Virtualization can be defined as a layer of abstraction, and it can exist in parts of or throughout the entire IT stack. In other words, virtualization could be restated from the data center and IT perspective as "the process of implementing a collection of technological capabilities required to hide the physical characteristics of server resources, network resources, and storage resources from the way in which systems, applications, or end users interact with those resources."

Virtualization Types

Virtualization can mean many things to many people. This chapter covers the following virtualization types:

- Server virtualization
- Storage virtualization
- Network virtualization
- Service virtualization

Figure 1-1 shows server virtualization, network virtualization, storage virtualization, and service virtualization that can exist in a data center and be managed using virtualization management. There can be other types of virtualization, but this is a start for virtualization technology in the data centers.

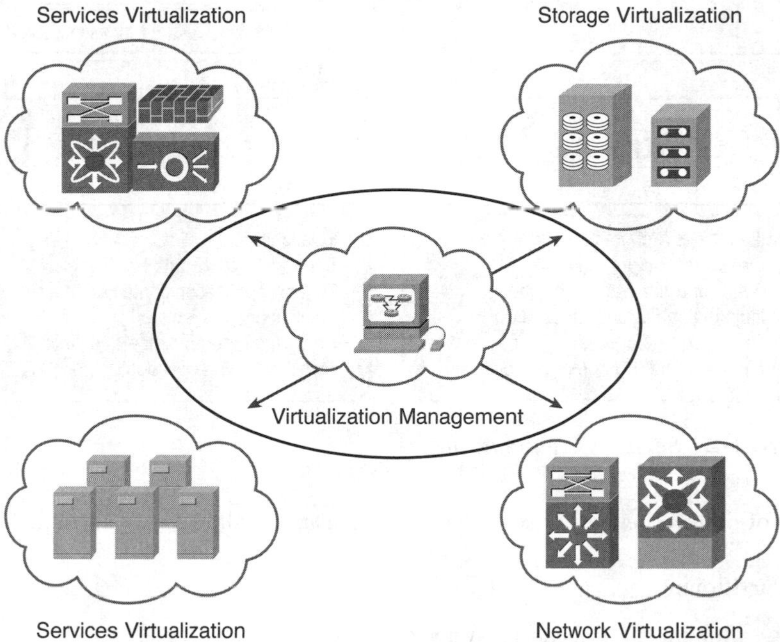

Figure 1-1 *Virtualization Types*

Server Virtualization

Server virtualization (also referred as hardware virtualization) is the best known application for hardware virtualization today. Today's powerful x86 computer hardware was designed to run a single operating system and a single application. This leaves most machines vastly underutilized. Virtualization lets you run multiple virtual machines on a single physical machine, sharing the resources of that single computer across multiple environments. Different virtual machines can run different operating systems and multiple applications on the same physical computer. Figure 1-2 shows how a virtualized server looks against a physical server without virtualization.

The hypervisor software enables the creation of a virtual machine (VM) that emulates a physical computer by creating a separate OS environment that is logically isolated from the host server. A hypervisor, also called a virtual machine manager (VMM), is a program that allows multiple operating systems to share a single hardware host. A single physical machine can be used to create several VMs that can run several operating systems independently and simultaneously. VMs are stored as files, so restoring a failed system can be as simple as copying its file onto a new machine.

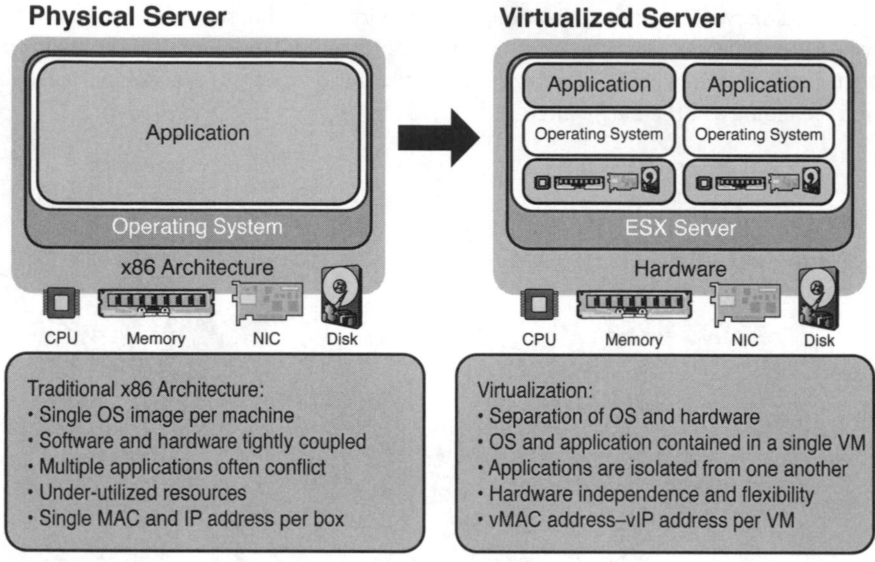

Figure 1-2 *Server Virtualization*

Some of the key benefits of server virtualization are as follows:

- **Partitioning**
  - Run multiple operating systems on one physical machine.
  - Divide the physical system resources among virtual machines.
  - One VM does not know the presence of the other.
- **Management**
  - Failure of one VM does not affect other VMs.
  - Management agents can be run on each VM separately to determine the individual performance of the VM and the applications that are running on the VM.
- **Encapsulation**
  - The entire VM state can be saved in a file.
  - Moving and copying VM information is as easy as copying files.
- **Flexibility**
  - Allows provisioning and migration of any VM to a similar machine on any physical server.
  - Usage of multiple OS platforms, for example, Windows, Linux.
  - Allows VM configuration changes without actually bringing the VM down.

Server virtualization is a key driving force in reducing the number of physical servers and hence the physical space, cooling, cabling, and capital expenses in any data center consolidation projects.

Storage Virtualization

Storage virtualization refers to providing a logical, abstracted view of physical storage devices. It provides a way for many users or applications to access storage without being concerned with where or how that storage is physically located or managed. It enables physical storage in an environment to be shared across multiple application servers, and physical devices behind the virtualization layer to be viewed and managed as if they were one large storage pool with no physical boundaries. The storage virtualization hides the fact there are separate storage devices in an organization by making all the devices appear as one device. Virtualization hides the complex process of where the data needs to be stored and bringing it back and presenting it to the user when it is required.

Typically, storage virtualization applies to larger storage-area network (SAN) arrays, but it is just as accurately applied to the logical partitioning of a local desktop hard drive and Redundant Array of Independent Disks (RAID). Large enterprises have long benefited from SAN technologies, in which storage is uncoupled from servers and attached directly to the network. By sharing storage on the network, SANs enable scalable and flexible storage resource allocation, efficient backup solutions, and higher storage utilization.

Virtualizing storage provides the following benefits:

- **Resource optimization:** Traditionally, the storage device is physically tied and dedicated to servers and applications. If more capacity is required, more disks are purchased and added to the server and dedicated to the applications. This method of operation results in a lot of storage not being used or wasted. Storage virtualization enables you to obtain the storage space on an as-needed basis without any wastage, and it allows organizations to use existing storage assets more efficiently without the need to purchase additional assets.
- **Cost of operation:** Adding independent storage resources and configuring for each server and application is time-consuming and requires a lot of skilled personnel that are hard to find, and this affects the total cost of operation (TCO). Storage virtualization enables adding storage resources without regard to the application, and storage resources can be easily added to the pool by a drag-and-drop method using a management console by the operations people. A secure management console with a GUI would enhance the security and allows operations people to add the storage resources easily.
- **Increased availability:** In traditional storage applications, the scheduled downtime for maintenance and software upgrades of storage devices and unplanned downtime because of virus and power outages could result in application downtimes to the customers. This results in not being able to meet the service-level agreements (SLA) offered to customers, resulting in customer dissatisfaction and loss of customers.

Storage virtualization provisions the new storage resources in a minimal amount of time, improving the overall availability of resources.

- **Improved performance:** Many systems working on a single task can overwhelm a single storage system. If the workload is distributed over several storage devices through virtualization, the performance can be improved. In addition, security monitoring can be implemented in the storage such that only authorized applications or servers are allowed to access the storage assets.

Network Virtualization

Network virtualization might be the most ambiguous virtualization of all virtualization types. Several types of network virtualization exist, as briefly described here:

- A VLAN is a simple example of network virtualization. VLANs allow logical segmentation of a LAN into several broadcast domains. VLANs are defined on a switch on a port-by-port basis. That is, you might choose to make ports 1–10 part of VLAN 1 and ports 11–20 part of VLAN 2. There's no need for ports in the same VLAN to be contiguous. Because this is a logical segmentation and not physical, workstations connected to the ports do not have to be located together, and users on different floors in a building or different buildings can be connected together to form a LAN.
- Virtual Routing and Forwarding (VRF), commonly used in Multi-Protocol Label Switching (MPLS) networks, allows multiple instances of a routing table to coexist within the same router at the same time. This increases the functionality by allowing network paths to be segmented without using multiple devices. Because traffic is automatically segregated, VRF also increases network security and can eliminate the need for encryption and authentication.
- Another form of network virtualization is the aggregation of multiple physical network devices into a virtualized device. An example of this is the Virtual Switching System (VSS) feature for the Catalyst 6500 switches. This feature is a virtual combination of two separate chassis into one bigger and faster Catalyst switch.
- Virtual device contexts (VDC), a data center virtualization concept, can be used to virtualize the device itself, presenting the physical switch as multiple logical devices. Within that VDC, it can contain its own unique and independent set of VLANs and VRFs. Each VDC can have physical ports assigned to it, thus allowing the hardware data plane to be virtualized as well. Within each VDC, a separate management domain can manage the VDC itself, thus allowing the management plane itself to also be virtualized. Each VDC appears as a unique device to the connected users.
- Virtual networks (VN) represent computer-based networks that consist, at least in part, of VN links. A VN link does not consist of a physical connection between two resources, but is implemented using methods of network virtualization. Cisco VN link technology was developed to bridge server, storage, and network management domains to help ensure that changes in one environment are communicated to the others. For example, when a customer in a VMware vSphere environment uses vCenter to initiate VMotion to move a VM from one physical server to another, that

event is signaled to the data center network and SAN, and the appropriate network profile and storage services move with the VM.

Figure 1-3 illustrates how virtualized network, compute, and storage interact with each other in the infrastructure.

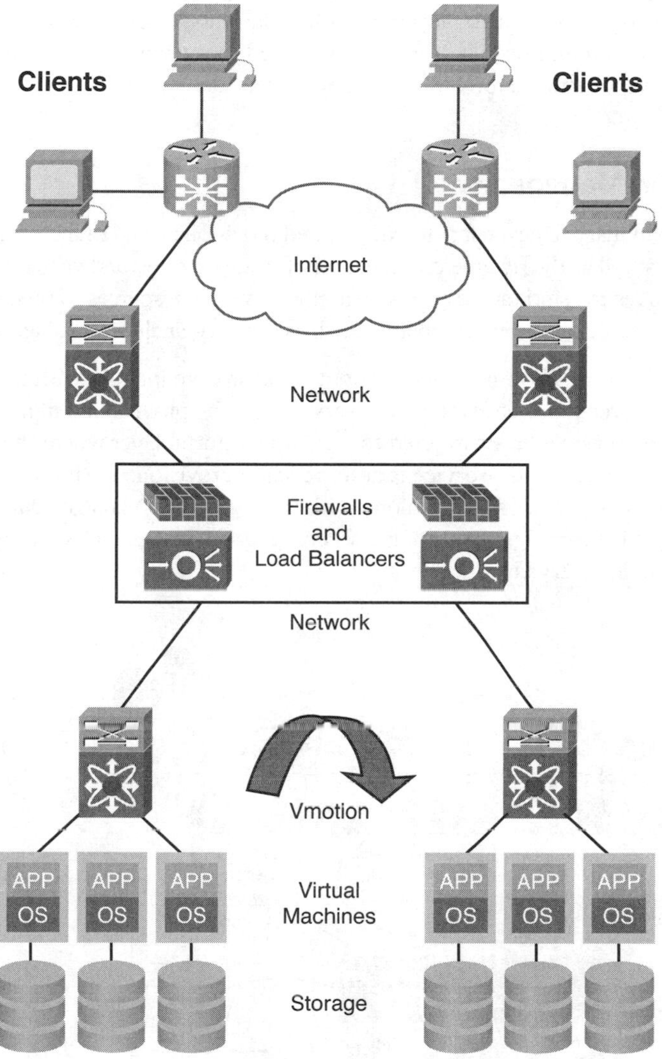

Figure 1-3 *Network Virtualization*

In a broad sense, network virtualization, when properly designed, *is* similar to server virtualization or hypervisor, in that a common physical network infrastructure is securely shared among groups of users, applications, and devices.

Service Virtualization

Service virtualization in data centers refers to the services such as firewall services for additional security or load-balancing services for additional performance and reliability. The virtual interface—often referred to as a virtual IP (VIP)—is exposed to the outside world, representing itself as the actual web server, and it manages the connections to and from the web server as needed. This enables the load balancer to manage multiple web servers or applications as a single instance, providing a more secure and robust topology than one allowing users direct access to individual web servers. This is a one-to-many virtualization representation. One server is presented to the world, hiding the availability of multiple servers behind a reverse proxy appliance.

Virtualization Management

Virtualization management refers to coordinated provisioning and orchestration of virtualized resources, as well as the runtime coordination of resource pools and virtual instances. This feature includes the static and dynamic mapping of virtual resources to physical resources, and also overall management capabilities such as capacity, analytics, billing, and SLAs.

Figure 1-4 illustrates how network, compute, and storage interact with the management/orchestration layer, so the services can be provisioned in near real time. Typically, the services are abstracted to a customer portal layer where the customer selects the service, and the service is automatically provisioned using various domain and middleware management systems along with Configuration Management Database (CMDB), service catalog, accounting, and chargeback systems; SLA management; service management; and service portal.

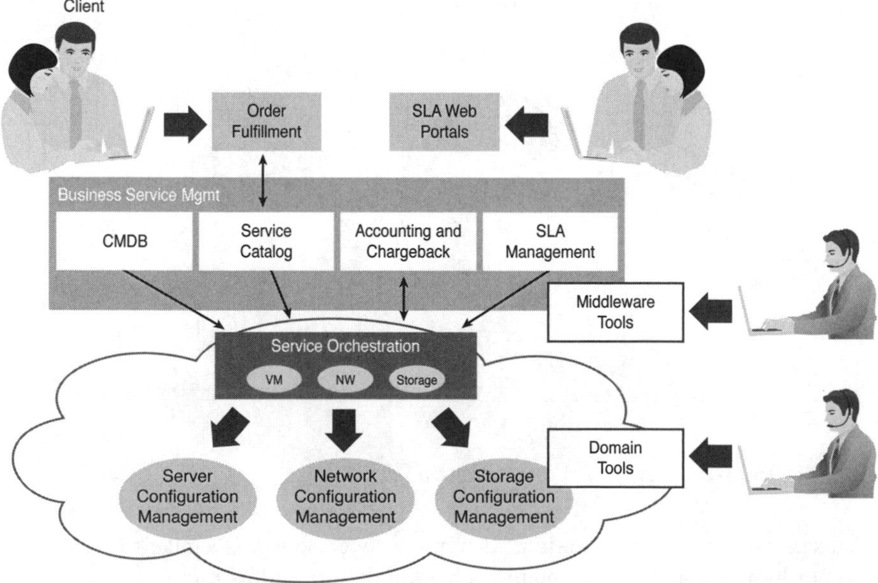

Figure 1-4 *Management Virtualization*

Network, compute, and storage virtualization is impacting IT significantly by providing flexible and fault-tolerant services that are decoupled from fixed technology assets. No longer do you need to take maintenance windows and offline applications to service or upgrade underlying hardware. The hardware can be repaired or upgraded and the applications moved back onto the newly enhanced infrastructure without a maintenance window. Other benefits of virtualization include more efficient use of underused resources, reduction of managed hardware assets, and consolidation of hardware maintenance agreements.

Although virtualization brings great flexibility, it also increases the need for monitoring and management services to provide greater situational awareness. In the past, an administrator could state definitively, "My database is run on server X, which is connected to switch B and uses storage array C." Virtualization decouples that relationship and allows those infrastructure resources to be used in a more scalable and performance-oriented way. An application can reside on any compute node in a cluster of servers, can use storage space in any storage devices, can use a virtualized network, and can be moved to suit performance or operational needs. It is now even more important to understand the interdependencies before doing maintenance.

So, what is the difference between virtualization and cloud computing? This is a common question. The answer is simply that virtualization is a technology, and when you run software in a VM, the program instructions run through the hypervisor as if it were a dedicated server. The hypervisor is the heart and soul of server virtualization. Cloud computing, on the other hand, is an operational model. When you run a cloud, there is no layer like the hypervisor layer, where the data would have to go through. To have a cloud, server virtualization probably will be there, but that alone will not be able to run a cloud. In a cloud, the resources involved are abstracted to deliver services to customers on demand, at scale, and in a multitenant environment. It is how you use the technologies involved. For the most part, cloud computing uses the same infrastructure, service catalog, service management tools, resource management tools, orchestration systems, CMS/CMDB, server platforms, network cabling, storage arrays, and so on. Typically, the customer is provided with a self-service portal where he can order service and hide all the physical complexity of the infrastructure and management. The next section covers the specifics of cloud computing in more detail.

Cloud Computing

Cloud is the most hyped word in the world, and everyone in the industry has his own definition. In our opinion, the National Institute of Technology and Standards (NIST) provides the simplest definition for a cloud:

> Cloud computing is a model for enabling convenient, on-demand network access to a shared pool of configurable computing resources (e.g., networks, servers, storage, applications, and services) that can be rapidly provisioned and released with minimal management effort or service provider interaction.[1]

Gartner defines cloud computing as

> A style of computing where massively scalable IT-related capabilities are provided 'as a service' using Internet technologies to multiple external customers.[2]

So, what is cloud computing? From a "utility" perspective, cloud could be considered as the fourth utility (after water, electricity, and telephony), which, as we and many others believe, is the ultimate goal of cloud computing. Consider electricity and telephony (utility) services. When we come home or go to the office, we plug into the electric outlet and get electricity as much and as long as we want without knowing how it is generated or who the supplier is (we only know that we have to pay the bill at the end of each month for the consumption). Similarly for telephony, we plug in, dial, and talk as long as we want without knowing what kind of networks or service providers the conversation is traversing through. With cloud as the fourth utility, we could plug in a monitor and get unlimited computing and storage resources as long and as much as we want. In the next phase of the Internet called *cloud computing*, where we will assign computing tasks to a "cloud"—a combination of compute, storage, and application resources accessed over a network—we will no longer care where our data is physically stored or where servers are physically located, as we will only use them (and pay for them) just when we need them. Cloud providers deliver applications through the Internet that are accessed from a web browser, while the business software and data are stored on servers at a remote location. Most cloud computing infrastructures consist of services delivered through shared data centers. The cloud appears as a single point of access for consumers' computing needs, and many cloud service providers provide service offerings on the cloud with specified SLAs.

The cloud will offer all of us amazing flexibility as we can specify the exact amount of computing power, data, or applications we need for each task we are working on. It will be inexpensive because we won't need to invest in our own capital and, with a network of proven data centers and a solid infrastructure, it will be reliable. We will be able to literally "plug into" the cloud instead of installing software to run on our own hardware. Table 1-1 highlights some of the key cloud characteristics/features.

Table 1-1 *Key Cloud Characteristics/Features*

Characteristic	Explanation
On-demand self-service through a secure portal	On-demand self-service provisioning is done unilaterally by the cloud service user for server, network, and storage capabilities, without interacting with the service providers.
Scalability and elasticity	Rapidly scale the computing capabilities up or down, always elastically to maintain cost efficiencies.
Pay per use	Capabilities are charged using a metered, fee-for-service or advertising-based billing model to promote optimization of resource use.
Ubiquitous access	Capabilities are available over the network and accessed through standard mechanisms that promote use by heterogeneous thick, thin, or mobile client platforms. Security must be everywhere in the cloud, and the access to the cloud through Internet devices must be secured to ensure data integrity and authenticity.

Table 1-1 *Key Cloud Characteristics/Features*

Characteristic	Explanation
Location-independent resource pooling	Computing resources of the provider(s) are pooled to serve all users using a multitenant model, with different physical and virtual resources dynamically assigned and reassigned according to user demand. No control or knowledge over the exact location of the provided resources is needed.

Table 1-2 outlines the various cloud deployment models, their characteristics, and a brief description of each.

Table 1-2 *Cloud Delivery Model*

Cloud Model	Characteristics	Description
Public cloud	Cloud infrastructure made available to the general public	Public cloud or external cloud describes cloud computing in the traditional mainstream sense. Public clouds are open to the general public or a large industry group and are owned and managed by a cloud service provider.
Private cloud	Cloud infrastructure operated solely for an organization	Private cloud and internal cloud have been described as offerings that emulate cloud computing on private networks. Private clouds are operated solely for one organization. They can be managed by the organization itself or by a third party, and they can exist on premises or off premises. They have been criticized on the basis that users "still have to buy, build, and manage them" and as such, do not benefit from lower up-front capital costs and less hands-on management.
Hybrid cloud	Cloud infrastructure comprised of two or more public and private clouds that interoperate through technology	Combines two or more private and public clouds by technology that enables data and application portability. The goal of a hybrid cloud is that as you run out of capacity in a private cloud, you can quickly reach out to the public cloud for additional resources to continue to operate your business.
Community cloud	Cloud infrastructure shared by several organizations and supporting a specific community	Features infrastructure that is shared by several organizations and supports a specific community. They can be managed by the organizations or a third party and can exist on premises or off.

Service Models

Figure 1-5 shows service models and delivery models. All the services can be delivered on any of the cloud delivery models.

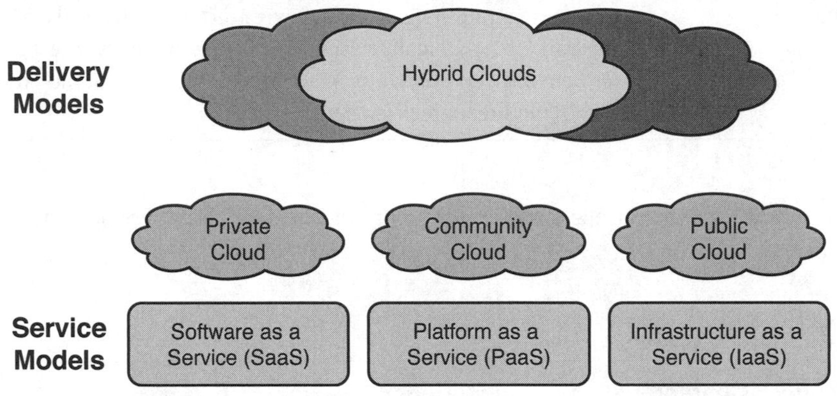

Figure 1-5 *Service Delivery Models (Source: NIST)*

Table 1-3 provides a brief description of the service models.

Table 1-3 *Cloud Services Model*

Service Description	Characteristic	Example
Software as a Service (SaaS)	The customer accesses the provider's application running on the provider's servers.	Sales force.com, Google Apps
Platform as a Service (PaaS)	The customer runs its applications on the provider's servers using the provider's operating systems and tools.	Google's App Engine, Force.com, MS Azure
Infrastructure as a Service (IaaS)	The customer uses, administers, and controls its operating system and applications running on providers' servers. It can also include operating systems and virtualization technology to manage the resources.	Amazon AWS, Savvis Symphony, Terremarks Vcloud Express, and Enterprise Cloud

Figure 1-6 shows the service models and IT foundation, along with the major players. Additional descriptions of the services are given in the list that follows.

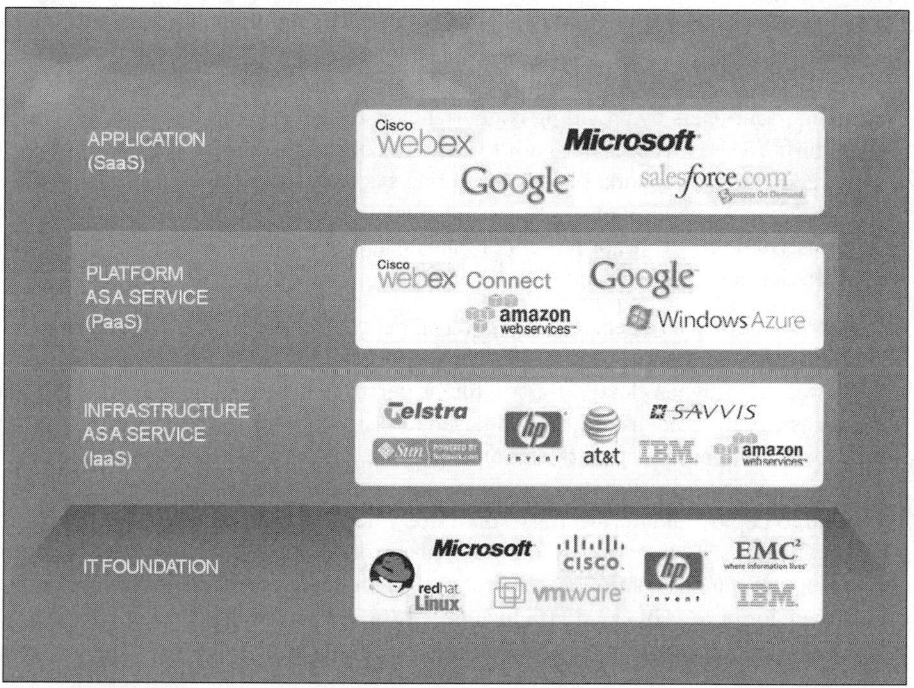

Figure 1-6 *Services Model and Major Players*

The following list provides a description of the SaaS, PaaS, and IaaS services shown in Figure 1-6:

- **Software as a Service (SaaS):** SaaS is common in the IT industry. Usually, software companies that provide SaaS host their software and then upgrade and maintain it for their customers. SaaS in a cloud combines this hosting practice with the cloud and helps the demands of the businesses by enabling the software to be run on the cloud without the need for installation on the local machines. This capability is provided to the consumer by the vendor's applications running on a cloud infrastructure. The applications are easily accessible from various client devices through a thin-client interface, such as a web browser (for example, web-based email). The consumer is transparent to the underlying cloud infrastructure, including network, servers, operating systems, storage, or even individual application capabilities, with the possible exception of limited user-specific application configuration settings. Some of the major players of SaaS include Cisco (WebEx), Microsoft, Google, and Salesforce.com.
- **Platform as a Service (PaaS):** In computing terminology, a platform typically means hardware architecture and a software framework (including applications) that allows software to run. A common platform in computing is the Linux, Apache, MySQL, and PHP (LAMP) stack. The PaaS that runs on a cloud supplies these familiar

platform stacks to users and facilitates the deployment of applications without the cost and complexity of buying and managing the underlying hardware and software. The PaaS offerings typically attempt to support the use of the application by many concurrent users by providing concurrency management, scalability, failover, and security. The consumer does not manage or control the underlying cloud infrastructure, including network, servers, operating systems, or storage, but has control over the deployed applications and possibly application hosting environment configurations. Some of the major players of PaaS include Cisco (WebEx connect), Amazon Web Services, Google, and Windows Azure.

- **Infrastructure as a Service (IaaS):** When people think about infrastructure, they think of items such as network devices, servers, storage devices, links, and cooling systems. But when cloud infrastructure is purchased, none of these components are necessary; instead, users of cloud-based infrastructure only need to concern themselves with developing platforms and software. The IaaS capability provided to the consumer includes network, compute, and storage resources, where the consumer is able to deploy and run arbitrary software, which can include operating systems and applications. The consumer does not manage or control the underlying cloud infrastructure but has control over operating systems and deployed applications. Some of the major players of cloud IaaS include Telstra, AT&T, Savvis, Amazon Web Services, IBM, HP, Sun, and others.

The IT foundational hardware and software resources include items such as networks comprised of switches, routers, firewalls, load balancers, and so on; server and storage farms; and the software. Typically, the IT foundation is comprised of multivendor devices and software. Some of the major players that supply IT foundational hardware and software include Cisco, HP, IBM, Dell, VMware, Red Hat, Microsoft, and others.

Cloud Adoption and Barriers

Most company C-level executives no longer need to be sold on the benefits of cloud—they get it. They understand that cloud computing creates significant simplicity, cost savings, and efficiencies. But they do have concerns regarding the cloud.

The data from various surveys shows that key factors in the minds of IT personnel for cloud adoption are security and integration. Although security and integration issues are clearly users' biggest fears about cloud computing, these concerns have not stopped companies from implementing cloud-based applications within their organizations. Seventy percent of IT decision makers using cloud computing are planning to move additional solutions to the cloud within the next 12 months, recognizing the benefits of cloud, ease of implementation, and security features and cost savings of cloud computing.[3]

Based on many discussions with customers and surveys, the following security and integration issues seem to be on many customers' minds:

- How the cloud will keep data secure and available
- How to comply with current and future security and risk management compliance

- What type of security services are available through the cloud
- How to perform internal and external audits of cloud security
- How to automate network, compute, and storage provisioning
- How to do on-demand provisioning in near real time from a customer portal to all the infrastructure devices
- How to orchestrate among many new cloud tools and existing legacy tools

Although most of the surveys show that most customers are concerned about security and integration, most of the successful organizations are taking calculated risks and implementing the cloud with appropriate security measures. As many of you know, nothing can be 100 percent secure, but by knowing the current state, one can apply appropriate security measures to mitigate the risk and grow the business. More details on security and integration are discussed in later chapters.

Return on Investment and Cloud Benefits

The return on investment is shown through the capacity/utilization curve published by Amazon Web Services.[4]

Figure 1-7 shows the capacity-versus-usage curve as an example in a typical data center and a cloud IT IaaS on demand versus the resource usage. There is excess capacity because of unnecessary capital expenditure early in the life cycle, and there is a shortage of resources later in the life cycle. Without cloud IT IaaS, the planned resources are either being wasted because the actual usage is less than the planned resources or there are not enough resources available to meet the customer demand, resulting in customer dissatisfaction and lost customers.

Figure 1-7 is a clear indication of why cloud IaaS is beneficial in preventing either overprovisioning or underprovisioning to improve cost, revenue, and margins and provide the required resources to match the dynamic demands of the customer. With cloud IaaS, the provisioning of resources follows the demand curve (see the curves illustrated in Figure 1-7), and there is no wastage or shortage of resources.

Based on the capacity-versus-usage curve and the cloud IaaS technological merits, some of the economic benefits of cloud IaaS are outlined as follows:

- Pay-per-usage of the resources. The end user investment cost is only for the duration of the connection and has no up-front cost.
- The abstraction of infrastructure devices is typically done by the cloud provider, and the end user is not locked into any physical devices. The end user gets the infrastructure required at the time of usage, through on-demand provisioning.

- The end user gets service on demand and will be able to scale up or down, with no planning cost or physical equipment cost. The cloud vendor that will be providing the infrastructure will also have the benefit of using the spare capacity from the devices anywhere under its control.
- The end user access to applications, compute, and storage is unlimited and can be from anywhere.
- The end user capacity is unlimited, and the performance remains the same and is only dictated by the agreed-upon SLAs.

You can find additional detailed information on ROI analysis from the white paper "Building Return on Investment from Cloud Computing," by the Open Group.[5]

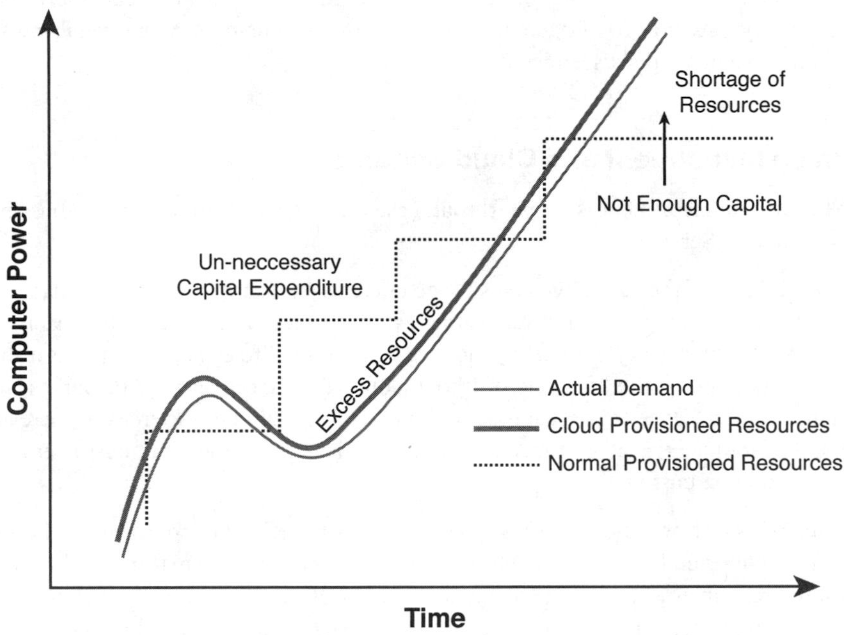

Figure 1-7 *Capacity Utilization Curve (Source: AWS[4])*

Summary

Virtualization is already taking place in most of the enterprises and service provider environments, and cloud computing in the form of IaaS is taking place to a limited extent in large enterprises and some service provider environments. Virtualization allows creating virtual (logical) resources from multiple physical resources. Virtualization can be done in compute (server) networks, router and switching networks, storage networks, and firewall and load-balancing services, and management of virtualized resources can be done using management tools such as provisioning, orchestration, and middleware tools. Cloud computing and virtualization are used interchangeably, but that is incorrect. For example, server virtualization provides flexibility to enable cloud computing, but that does not make virtualization the same as cloud computing. There are many technologies that enable cloud computing, and virtualization is one of them.

Cloud computing is the abstraction of underlying applications, information, content, and resources, which allows resources to be provided and consumed in a more elastic and on demand manner. This abstraction also makes the underlying resources easier to manage and provides the basis for more effective management of the applications themselves. Clouds can provide an almost immediate access to hardware resources without incurring any up-front capital costs. This alone will provide incentive for many enterprises and service providers to move to clouds, because it provides a quick return on investment.

References

[1] The NIST Definition of Cloud Computing; refer to http://csrc.nist.gov/groups/SNS/cloud-computing.

[2] The Gartner Definition of Cloud Computing; refer to http://www.gartner.com/it/page.jsp?id=707508.

[3] www.mimecast.com/News-and-views/Press-releases/Dates/2010/2/70-Percent-of-Companies-Using-Cloud-Based-Services-Plan-to-Move-Additional-Applications-to-the-Cloud-in-the-Next-12-Months.

[4] Amazon Web Services, AWS Economic Center, at http://aws.amazon.com/economics.

[5] Building Return on Investment from Cloud Computing by the Open Group, at www.opengroup.org/cloud/whitepapers/ccroi/index.htm.

Chapter 2

Cloud Design Patterns and Use Cases

Upon completing this chapter, you will be able to understand the following:

- Typical application design patterns and business functions found in most enterprises today
- Which deployment model is most suitable for a given design patterns
- Typical cloud use cases
- How IaaS can be used by SaaS and PaaS services to provide greater agility and management consistency
- How to describe how IaaS forms a foundation for other cloud services models
- What a cloud consumer operating model looks like

This chapter provides an overview of the components that make up a cloud deployment, with particular emphasis on the Infrastructure as a Service (IaaS) service model.

Typical Design Patterns and Use Cases

Chapter 1, "Cloud Computing Concepts," discussed the standard definition of a cloud and, to some extent, explained why it is becoming such an important technology strand for both consumers and providers. From the viewpoint of the cloud service consumer, you should understand that cloud in all its service models (Infrastructure as a Service [IaaS], Platform as a Service [PaaS], and Software as a Service [SaaS]) should not be seen as a new service; it does not introduce any new design patterns or software by itself. Instead, it should be seen as a new way to consume compute, storage, network, and software resources in a much more dynamic fashion. From the perspective of the cloud provider, cloud service models offer a new way for the provider to offer a well-defined solution in a more dynamic manner and bill or charge for these services based on their consumption. This, in turn, allows the consumers of these services to implement different business models for their products and the way they use IT.

Think about an example from the perspective of the consumer. Consumer A wants to deploy a service to host content, whatever that might be. He can buy it as part of a new hosting contract where he is simply given a space to upload files and manage the content and charged on a monthly basis for that space. Changes to that content can happen in real time; however, if for example, the consumer needed to add server-side processing or a backend database to persist data, he might have to wait several days for his provider to revise the contract to add this to his current service. In this example, you as a service consumer will be charged regardless of the activity of the web server, and you will typically enter into a contract that requires you to pay for six months to a year.

Alternatively, you could purchase a virtual instance from Amazon (EC2) that provides a basic machine with set CPU, RAM, and disk size; deploy a standard web server image; and modify content as required. When you need additional functionality, you could deploy additional software or instances. If this isn't what you need, you can simply destroy the instance and stop paying.

The major difference between the traditional hosting model and the cloud, therefore, is the fact that the consumer will be charged only for what he uses rather than a fixed fee. If the web-hosting service is not busy, the consumer will potentially pay less. So, cloud is not really offering a new service in this case. The service is still hosting, but the offering and consumption models are different, potentially allowing the consumer to do more with his money. A more topical example is the content provider Netflix, which to scale with the expected demand, uses Amazon to host its platform. **This means Netflix** can increase **its** capacity pretty much in real time and with minimal disruption. Had it needed to add more physical capacity or renegotiate its existing hosting contract, it might not have been able to meet the demand in the time frames it needed to. So, cloud itself does not in itself increase the range of what is possible to do, but it does change what is practical to do.

So, what is an IT service? Many definitions exist, but for the purposes of this chapter, an IT service is defined as a set of IT resources organized in a specific topology providing or supporting a specific business function. The decision to move a particular service into the cloud should first be assessed to ensure that the cloud can support the topology and the business can risk the function of being hosted in the cloud. Furthermore, you need to assess what cloud deployment model best suits the use case for cloud adoption that is being proposed.

Design Patterns

Figure 2-1 illustrates the typical design patterns found in the large enterprise today across its application base.

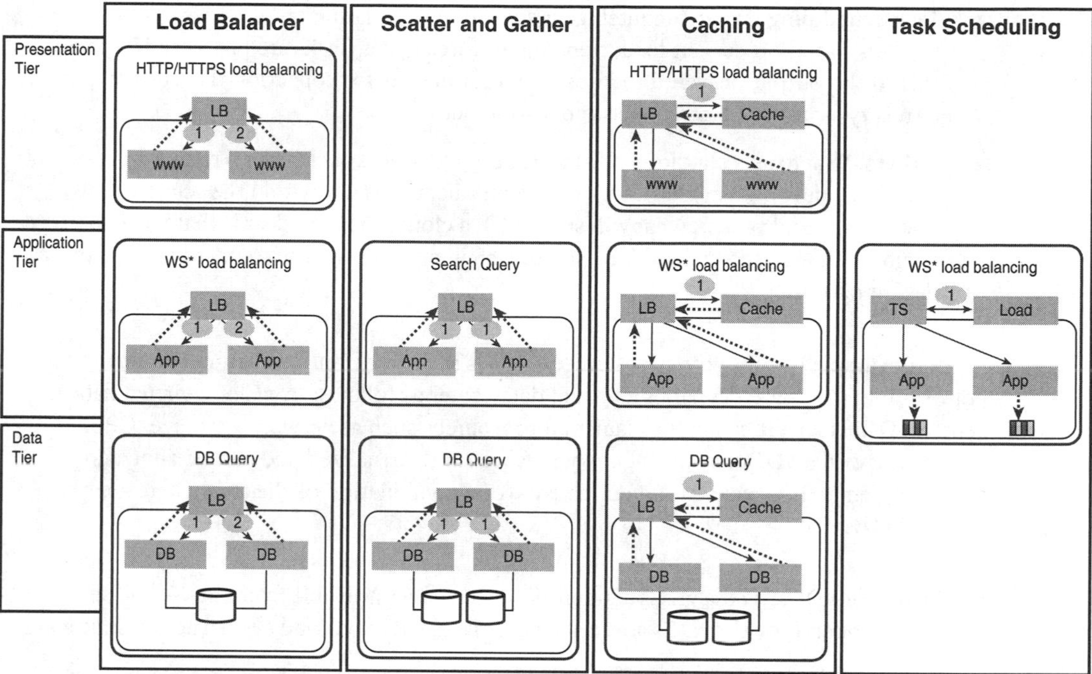

Figure 2-1 *Typical Design Patterns*

The tiering of applications is common in most enterprises, which separates presentation, application, and data often from a security standpoint onto different platforms within the data center. Therefore, at a minimum, a cloud solution (IaaS) must support the concept of *zoning*—allowing different virtual machines to reside in different security and/or availability zones to meet the application-tiering requirement. Within a tier, different design patterns exist to provide solutions to different problems:

- **Load balancer:** Where many instances/workers do the same job and a request is distributed among them using a load balancer that allocates requests and responds to the requestor. This design pattern is common across all three tiers and is often used to implement websites and or business applications.
- **Scatter and gather:** Where a request can be broken down into a number of separate requests, distributed among a number of workers, and then the separate worker responses consolidated and returned to the requestor. Search engines often use this pattern, and it is common across application and database tiers.
- **Caching:** Where prior to a request being allocated using either load balancer or scatter and gather patterns, a cache is consulted that has stored all previous queries. If no match is found, a request is issued to the workers. This design pattern is common across all three tiers.

- **Task scheduling:** Where an intelligent scheduler is initiating tasks across a set of workers based on current load, trending, or forecasting. Tasks are processed in parallel and the output delivered to a set of output queues for collection. This design pattern is typically used across the application tier.
- **Others:** Where as technology advances, design patterns such as map reduce, blackboarding, and so on might become more prevalent. It is not within the scope of this book to try and predict what will succeed in a cloud. What is clear is that where horizontal scaling based on load is required, IaaS is a good platform to host this type of design pattern.

A good example of these other design patterns is the use of "infrastructure containers." For example, VMware describes a virtual data center as follows: "A vCloud virtual datacenter (vDC) is an allocation mechanism for resources such as networks, storage, CPU, and memory. In a vDC, computing resources are fully virtualized and can be allocated based on demand, service-level requirements, or a combination of the two. There are two kinds of vDCs:

- **Provider vDCs:** These vDCs contain all the resources available from the vCloud service provider. Provider vDCs are created and managed by vCloud system administrators.
- **Organization vDCs:** These vDCs provide an environment where virtual systems can be stored, deployed, and operated. They also provide storage for virtual media, such as floppy disks and CD-ROMs.

An organization administrator specifies how resources from a provider vDC are distributed to the vDCs in an organization."

VMware vDCs offer a good way to abstract out the complexities of a tenant-specific topology, such as Layer 2 separation and firewalls, as well as provide a way to manage resources. Another variation on this theme are Cisco Network Containers that have been submitted to OpenStack as the basis for Network as a Service, a further abstraction of the IaaS service model that will allow complex network topologies to be hidden for the end user and consumed as part of a larger design pattern. In Figure 2-2, you can see that the three load balancer design patterns have been instantiated. However, the load-balancing capability, Layer 2 isolation and security, and Layer 3 isolation have all been instantiated in a network container that runs on a set of physical network devices. This allows the application developer to concentrate on the application capabilities and not worry about the network topology implementation specifics. The application developed simply connects his virtual machines to a specific zone in a specific network container, and now load balancing, firewalling, addressing, and so on will all be handled by the network container.

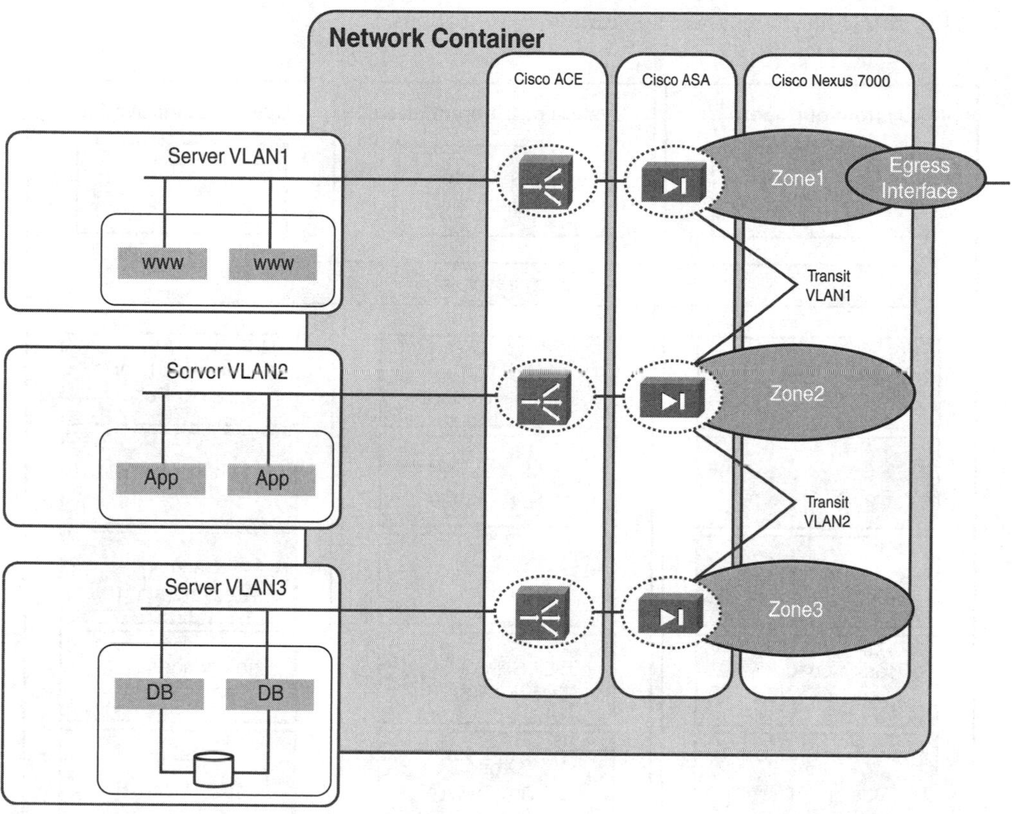

Figure 2-2 *Network Container Design Pattern*

Understanding what design patterns are being used in the enterprise will allow you to understand the application topology and the basic building blocks required to support those topologies in the cloud. A broader question, however, is do I want to risk moving my application and its data into the cloud?

Gartner defines three classifications of applications:

- *Systems of record* that record data about the business and business interactions.
- *Systems of differentiation* that differentiate how a business is perceived and operates.
- *Systems of innovation* can offer real value to businesses. Systems of innovation can benefit from the elasticity and rapid provisioning capabilities provided by cloud, but the dynamic and unfiltered nature of the data can make it unwise to host these applications outside the corporate boundary.

Figure 2-3 illustrates these application classifications.

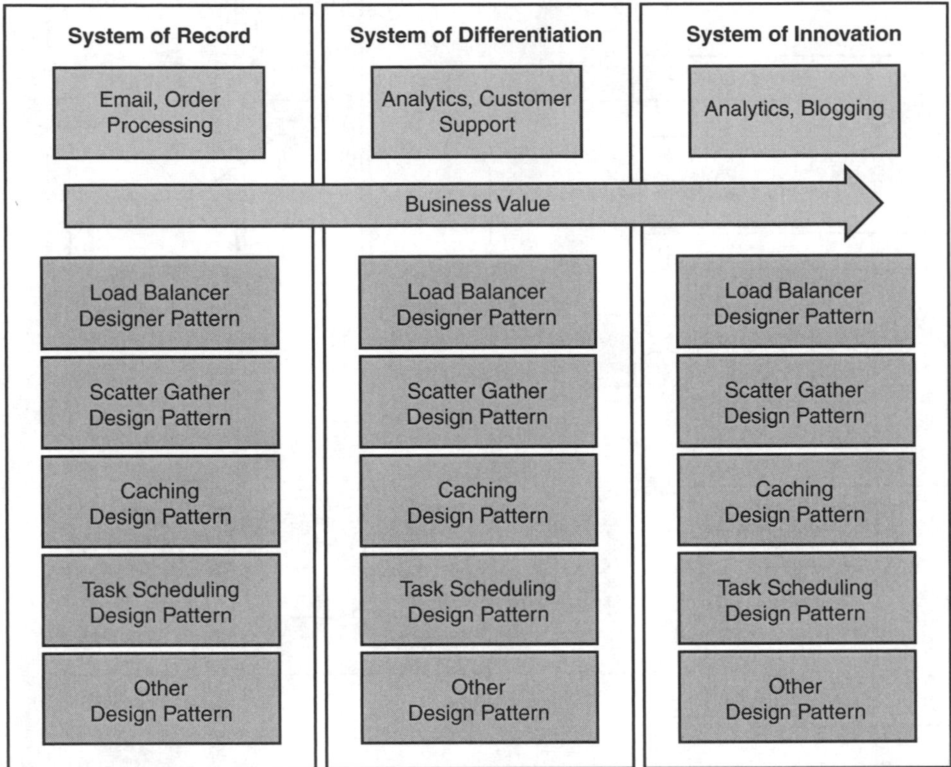

Figure 2-3 *Application Functional Classifications*

Cloud Use Cases

So, what is currently impractical or cost-prohibitive for most large enterprises? We will focus on large enterprises as they are by far the most likely candidates for the adoption of private, public, or hybrid cloud solutions. Most cloud technology is still fairly immature when compared to mainstream IT technology, and the processes of adoption of a cloud solution remains a risk, but substantial rewards can be forthcoming if the adoption of the cloud solution is successful by allowing enterprises to become more agile and cost-effective. Given the maturity of the cloud market today and concerns about security, it is unlikely that large enterprises will choose to deploy their business-critical applications into a cloud (IaaS, PaaS) in the short term. Of course, SaaS offerings today around Customer Relationship Management (CRM) and sales tools clearly are being adopted, but these applications tend to be fairly standalone and require little integration into the existing business's processes or technology and so adoption is simpler. A number of typical use cases have been identified that allow enterprises to "dip their toe" into the cloud (IaaS/PaaS/SaaS) while gaining some significant business benefit. Table 2-1 illustrates the typical use cases found in the large enterprise today.

Table 2-1 *Cloud Use Cases*

Use Case	Reasons for Moving to the Cloud	Service Models
Development and Test	High capital outlay, cyclical usage	IaaS, PaaS
Business Continuity	High criticality, low usage	SaaS, IaaS
Usage Monitoring	Centralized IT/public cloud needs cost allocation	IaaS
Desktop Management	Automated desktop delivery and management	IaaS
Storage	Low utilization	IaaS
Compute on Demand	Long procurement cycles and VM sprawl	IaaS

The setup and maintenance of corporate *development and test environments* is both labor- and cost-intensive, and given the cyclical nature of application development and hardware refreshes, it means that often these environments were underused for a large portion of time and out of date when they were required. Virtualization has helped in reducing the hardware refresh requirements as virtual machines can have memory and CPU added on the fly and ported relatively seamlessly among hardware platforms; however, hardware is still required and will be underutilized. In addition, how does the enterprise cope with a pizza- and Coke-fueled developer who has suddenly had a eureka moment and understands how he can make a company application run three times faster and wants to start working on it at 3 a.m. but needs a new database server? Cloud (IaaS and PaaS) offers the enterprise the ability to meet these requirements of flexibility, on-demand self-service, and utilization. (The question about which deployment model to use—private or public—will be discussed in the next section.)

Business continuity and *disaster recovery* are two key areas that are critical to any enterprise. Business continuity can be seen as the processes and tools that allow critical business functions to be accessed by customers, employees, and staff at any time and encompass, among other things, service desk, change management, backup, and disaster recovery. In the same way the development and test environments can be underutilized, the systems that support the business continuity processes can also be underutilized when a business is operating normally; however, in the case of a failure, for example, the help desk might experience much greater demand. In the case of a major outage or "disaster," moving or switching these applications to a secondary site to ensure that users can still access applications, raise cases, or access backup data is critical. Cloud can clearly assist with enhanced utilization through its use of virtualization technology or reduce cost by using a SaaS "pay as you use" model for help desk or change management software. The horizontal scaling of applications by creating new instances of a particular application to cope with demand is something that IaaS will support, along with the failover to a backup or secondary application hosted on a second public or private cloud, or even splitting loads across both in a hybrid cloud model.

As internal IT begins to centralize its functions in a shared service model, it becomes more important to track and allocate costs to different lines of business or business units. If that service is moved off-premises by a SaaS or IaaS provider, the capability to track and allocate cost based on usage becomes a critical capability for businesses to manage costs. Hosting a service in a cloud (IaaS) can mean that the inherent mechanisms in an IaaS solution can be used to calculate and present a variety of billing, chargeback, and showback data.

Desktop management is a well-known issue within large enterprises with a large amount of operational resources being deployed to troubleshoot, patch, modify, and secure a variety of desktop configurations. The introduction and benefits of Virtual Desktop Infrastructure (VDI), which allow a user to connect to a centrally managed desktop, is well known and will not be discussed here, but cloud (IaaS) can assist with the self-management of that desktop, the cloning of new desktops, and the management of the master image. In addition, charging and billing of the use of VDI resources can also be provided by utilizing a cloud-based VDI solution.

Pure *storage-based services*, such as file backup, image backup, and .ISO storage, are typically required in any large enterprise and consume a vast amount of terabytes. When funded and allocated at the line of business (LOB) or business unit (BU) level, this again can lead to a large capital outlay and underutilization. A cloud (subset of IaaS) solution can help drive higher utilization but still provide the same level of flexibility and self-service that would be available if the resources were allocated to an individual LOB or BU. In addition, the storage cloud can utilize other cloud use cases such as disaster recovery and chargeback to provide a more comprehensive service.

Compute-on-demand services are the foundation for any IaaS cloud, regardless of the use case. The consumer simply wants to increase business agility by being able to either supplement existing services to cope with demand or to support new ventures quickly for a period of time. All the IaaS use cases depend on the ability of the cloud provider to support compute on demand; however, the solution to this should not simply be seen as deploying server virtualization technologies, such as VMware ESX or Microsoft HyperV. Many applications cannot or will not be virtualized; therefore, the need to include physical compute-on-demand services in any cloud offering is often overlooked. Although the provision of physical servers will not be as common as virtual ones, it is a necessary capability and requires the supporting capabilities to provision physical storage and networking that is no longer being encapsulated at the hypervisor level as well as the physical server and its operating systems and applications.

Deployment Models

So far, this chapter focused on use cases and design patterns that could exist within a private cloud hosted with an enterprise data center or on a public cloud accessed publicly through the Internet or privately through a corporate IP VPN service provided by a telecommunications (telco) company. Chapter 1 discussed these models; Table 2-2 describes the most prevalent models.

Table 2-2 *Private and Public Clouds*

	Public[1]	Hosted (Private)	Private[1]
Access	Internet-connected data centers/private IP-VPN	Internet-connected data centers/ corporate data center	Corporate data center
Tenancy model	Multiple clients	Single company	Single company
Infrastructure type	Shared infrastructure	Shared or dedicated infrastructure	Dedicated infrastructure
Security model is	Common across all customers, with limited configurability	Based on the infrastructure type choice	Unique to the customer
Cloud managed by	Provider	Provider or IT ops	IT ops
Billed by	Consumption	Monthly for dedicated infra-structure; excess billed by con-sumption. Spare capacity can be used by the provider and a discount applied.	Consumption-based metering for BU chargeback or allocation

Public cloud, or virtual private cloud as it's sometimes offered by service providers, supports a set of standard design patterns and use cases. For example, Amazon Web Services (AWS) EC2 supports a load balancing design pattern within, arguably, a single tier. With its use of availability zones and autoscaling, it would support compute-on-demand, usage monitoring, and business continuity use cases, but the specific requirements for a given use case would need to be evaluated. A key principle of a public cloud is that it uses a shared infrastructure to host multiple tenants with the provider's own data center and uses a common security model to provide isolation among these tenants. All management of the cloud is performed by the provider, and the consumer is simply billed on usage.

A private cloud is built and operated by IT operations, so it will support any use cases that the internal consumer wants to describe as part of the overall cloud reference model. Although multiple LOBs or BUs might use the same infrastructure, the security model might not need to be as complex as a public cloud as the cloud infrastructure is hosted on-premises and data is typically stored within the enterprise. Building a private cloud does require the enterprise to build or already have significant technical capabilities in virtualization, networking, storage, and management (to name a few), but it will mean that that enterprise can fully leverage the cloud and potentially develop new revenue opportunities or business models. In addition, the enterprise must invest in the initial infrastructure to support the cloud services and sustain the investment as capacity is exhausted and new infrastructure is required.

The third option is to allow a service provider to build and run a private cloud hosted either in its data center or on-premises. A hosted cloud is an ideal solution to those enterprises that want to leverage cloud services with low investment and meet any security or compliance concerns. This is unlike a public cloud, where the infrastructure in a hosted cloud is dedicated to a specific tenant during normal operational hours. There is an option to lease back resources during off-peak hours to the service provider, which might allow the application of discounts to the overall bill; however, some tenants might feel uncomfortable with different workloads running in their data center. Hosted cloud does mean that the enterprise doesn't have to build or invest in a cloud competency center, and if the provider does offer public cloud services, it might be possible to migrate workloads between a low-cost public cloud and a higher-cost private cloud as required and vice versa. Figure 2-4 illustrates this concept.

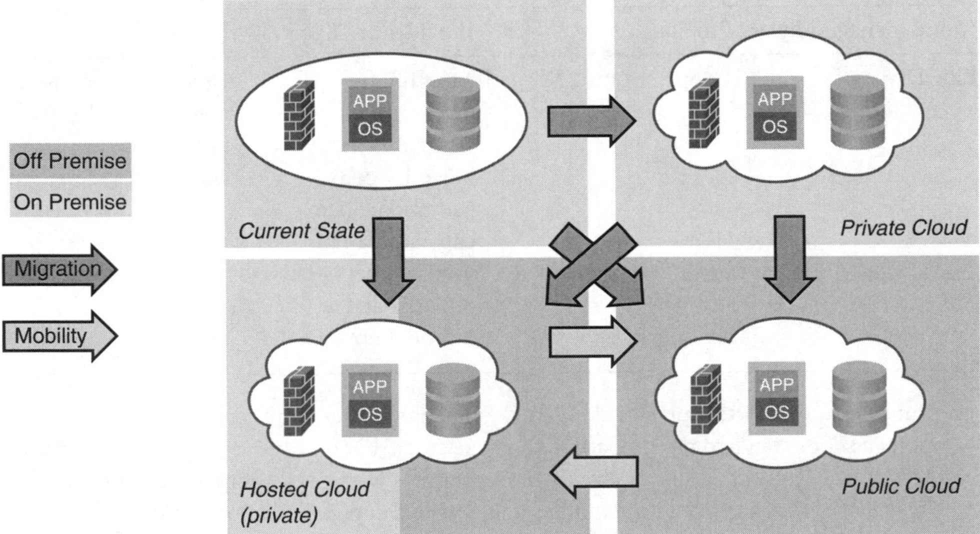

Figure 2-4 *Cloud Deployment Models and Mobility*

IaaS as a Foundation

So far, we've looked at the components that make up a cloud service from the consumer viewpoint—the use case, design patterns, and deployment models they can consider when using or deploying cloud. Chapter 1 also looked at the different cloud service models: Infrastructure, Platform, and Software as a Service. This section describes the why, for the service provider, IaaS[1] is a foundation for the other two service models and describes the components that are required in IaaS[1] to support the typical use cases and design patterns described. Review the SaaS[1] and PaaS[1] definitions from Chapter 1:

- **SaaS:** The capability provided to the consumer to use the provider's applications running on a cloud infrastructure

- **PaaS:** The capability provided to the consumer to deploy onto the cloud infrastructure consumer-created or -acquired applications created using programming languages and tools supported by the provider

Both SaaS and PaaS increase the provider's responsibility for a service over and above that of IaaS. Given that the provider still needs to provide the same type of characteristics of self-service and elasticity to fulfill basic cloud requirements, it makes sense to deploy SaaS and PaaS on top of an IaaS solution to leverage the capabilities, systems, and processes that are fundamental to IaaS. This doesn't mean that it is obligatory for a SaaS or PaaS provider to deploy IaaS first; however, it will allow a SaaS and PaaS solution to scale more easily. The rest of this section takes a high-level look at what components make up the different service models; Figure 2-5 describes the components from both a consumer and provider perspective.

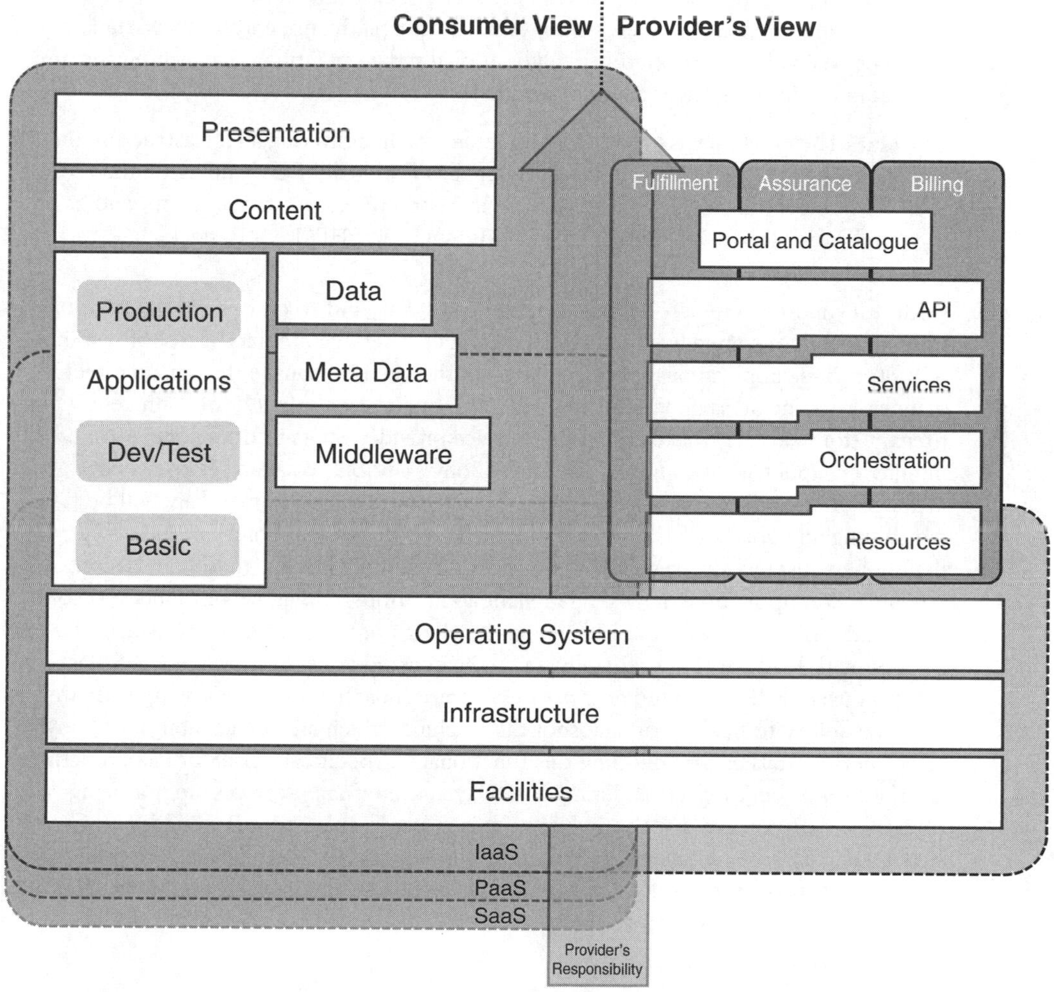

Figure 2-5 *High-Level Component View*

One of the major points to note about Figure 2-5 is that the application stack is included in all service models. From a standard definition perspective, IaaS is often seen as pure infrastructure, so no operating system or applications are provided on the servers, but in practice, most cloud providers will include applications as a service option. However, the nature of the applications within each service model is different as discussed in the list that follows:

- **SaaS:** The consumer is only really interested in using the finished application, so content and data are paramount. Presentation might also be a significant contributing factor if multiple devices (smartphones, laptops, and so on) are used to access the application. Metadata might also be relevant at this level if different tenants are given different application "skins."
- **PaaS:** The consumer is predominantly interested in developing and testing applications in this environment, so the application use here might be integrated development environments (IDE), test tools, middleware platforms, and so on. Metadata schemas will be developed here and optionally the operating systems (OS) and any required libraries might also be managed.
- **IaaS:** The consumer is predominantly interested in delivering an infrastructure on which he can add applications for which he is responsible. Depending on the scope of the service, this might include network infrastructure, operating systems, and basic applications such as a Linux, Apache, MySQL, and PHP (LAMP) stack.

Both SaaS and PaaS require servers, operating systems, and so on to support the applications that are consumed by the service users. As the service provider's level of responsibility for those applications increases, so does the need to manage them in an effective manner. Looking at SaaS, specifically where the application might not be inherently multitenant (for example, where a managed service provider wants to offer some form of monitoring application on top of an IP telephony solution), you can see that a new instance of an application must be created per tenant. Doing this manually will be time-consuming and costly for the service provider, so using an IaaS solution to quickly deploy new instances makes a lot of business sense. It also means that there is a process available to support other new single-tenant applications, adding new instances to cope with load (horizontal scaling) or changing the vRAM or vCPU of an existing application to cope with load (vertical scaling) in an automated and consistent manner. IaaS/PaaS solution users will often need access to OS libraries, patches, and code samples as well as have the ability to back up or snapshot the machine, which are key capabilities of any IaaS solution. Rather than building this functionality, specifically SaaS or PaaS functionality, the idea of building a foundational IaaS layer, even if IaaS services are not being offered directly, means that the architecture is more flexible and agile. Building the infrastructure in a consistent manner also means that it is possible to manage, bill, or charge in a consistent manner, regardless of whether the infrastructure is being used for IaaS, PaaS, SaaS, or a combination of all of them.

A cloud consumer will typically not care how a service is fulfilled or managed and will look for the provider to maintain responsibility for the service levels, governance, change, and configuration management throughout the lifetime of his service instance, regardless of whether it's just for the infrastructure, the platform, or the software. Therefore, the service provider needs to manage the fulfillment, assurance, and optionally billing/chargeback of that service consistently. In addition, if the provider offers more than one service model (for example, SaaS + PaaS), these functions ideally will be offered by an integrated management stack rather than different silos.

Regardless of the application design pattern, use case, or deployment model required by the cloud consumer, the consumer operating model chosen for the cloud is critical and forms the basis for the cloud reference architecture discussed in the next chapter.

Cloud Consumer Operating Model

An operating model describes how an organization designs, creates, offers, and supplies a product to consumers. Within the context of a cloud, the operations model describes how the cloud consumer will offer cloud-based IT services to his IT users. The model shown in Figure 2-6 shows the operating model from the cloud consumer's perspective. A similar model will exist for the cloud provider that illustrates how the provider offers and manages cloud services, but this will need to take into account many different consumers and markets and will therefore be more complex.

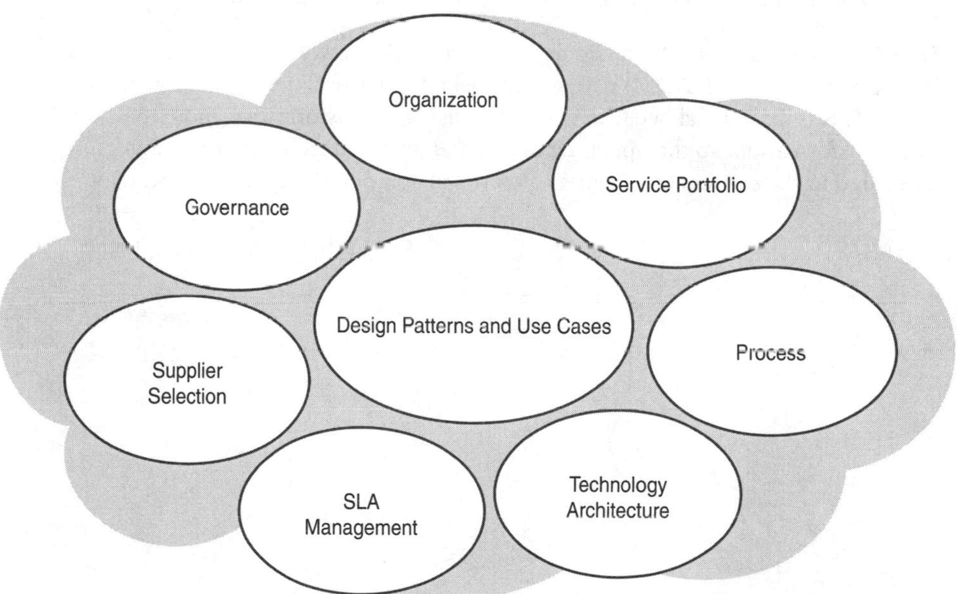

Figure 2-6 *Cloud Consumer Operating Model*

Central to all operating models is an understanding of the use cases and design patterns that will be hosted in the cloud solution. After these two things are understood and agreed upon, the following areas must be addressed:

- **Organization:** How the consumer structures and organizes his IT capabilities to support a more on-demand, utility model when resources can be hosted off-site or by a third party.
- **Service portfolio:** What services will be offered internally and to whom, and how new services will be created.
- **Processes:** What processes are changed by the move to utility computing and what those changes are.
- **Technology architecture:** What systems or technology needs to be deployed, modified, or purchased to support the agreed-upon use cases and deployment models.
- **SLA management:** What service-level agreement (SLA) will be provided to the end user and therefore needs to be provided between the organization and the cloud provider (which can be the IT department in the case of private cloud).
- **Supplier management:** What cloud provider or tool vendor will be selected, the selection criteria, the type of licensing, and contractual models that will be used.
- **Governance:** How the consumer makes, prioritizes, and manages decisions about cloud and mitigates risk as a utility computing model is introduced.

Those familiar with The Open Group Architecture Framework (TOGAF) Architecture Development Method (ADM) will see some similarities between Figure 2-6 and the ADM. This is intentional because cloud is a business transformation more than a technology transformation, so the operating model and management reference architecture described in the subsequent chapters are critical components of a cloud strategy.

Summary

The adoption of cloud is a business transformation first and a technology one second. When looking at adopting a cloud consumption model, the following aspects should be well understood:

- What design patterns and use cases need to be supported in the cloud?
- What deployment model provides the best business advantage while still conforming to any regulatory or security requirements?

The way to answer these questions is through the development of a cloud operating model that encompasses the organizational, process, and technology changes required to adapt to utility computing.

References

[1] The NIST Definition of Cloud Computing, at http://csrc.nist.gov/groups/SNS/cloud-computing.

[2] The Open Group TOGAF ADM, at www.opengroup.org/architecture/togaf8-doc/arch/chap03.html.

[3] VMware vCloud API, at www.vmware.com/pdf/vcd_10_api_guide.pdf.

[4] Cisco Network Containers @ Openstack, at http://wiki.openstack.org/NetworkContainers.

Chapter 3

Data Center Architecture and Technologies

In this chapter, you will learn the following:

- How to articulate what is meant by "architecture" in relation to IT design
- Describe the data center architectural building blocks
- Describe the evolution of the data center network design with the impact of virtualization
- Describe the cloud Infrastructure as a Service (IaaS) solution and its functional components
- Describe the network services that are necessary to deliver an "end-to-end" service-level agreement

This chapter provides an overview of the architectural principles and infrastructure designs needed to support a new generation of real-time-managed IT service use cases in the data center. There are many process frameworks and technologies available to architects to deliver a service platform that is both flexible and scalable. From an operational perspective, maintaining visibility and control of the data center that meets the business's governance, risk, and compliance needs is a must. This chapter will discuss the building blocks, technologies, and concepts that help simplify the design and operation, yet deliver real IT value to the business, namely, business continuity and business change.

Architecture

Architecture is a borrowed term that is often overused in technology forums. The Oxford English Dictionary defines architecture as "the art or practice of designing and constructing buildings" and further, "the conceptual structure and logical organization of a computer or computer-based system."

In general, outside the world of civil engineering, the term *architecture* is a poorly understood concept. Although we can understand the concrete concept of a building and the process of building construction, many of us have trouble understanding the more abstract concepts of a computer or a network and, similarly, the process of constructing an IT system like a service platform. Just like buildings, there are many different kinds of service platforms that draw upon and exhibit different architectural principles.

As an example of early architectural prinicples, requirements and/or guidelines (also known as *artifacts*), Figure 3-1 depicts the the famous drawing of Leonardo Da Vinci's "Vitruvian Man." We are told that the drawing is based on the ideas of a Roman Architect Marcus Vitruvius Pollio that a "perfect building" should be based on the fact (the mainly Christian religious idea) that man is created in the image of God and thus provides the blueprint of "proportional perfection" (that is, the relationship between the length of one body part to another is a constant fixed ratio). It was believed that these ratios can serve as a set of architectural principles when it comes to building design; thus, a "perfect building" can be acheived. Obviously, our ideas on architecture and design are much more secular and science-based today. That said, the Vitruvian Man provides a good a example of the relationship of architecture to design and its implimentation.

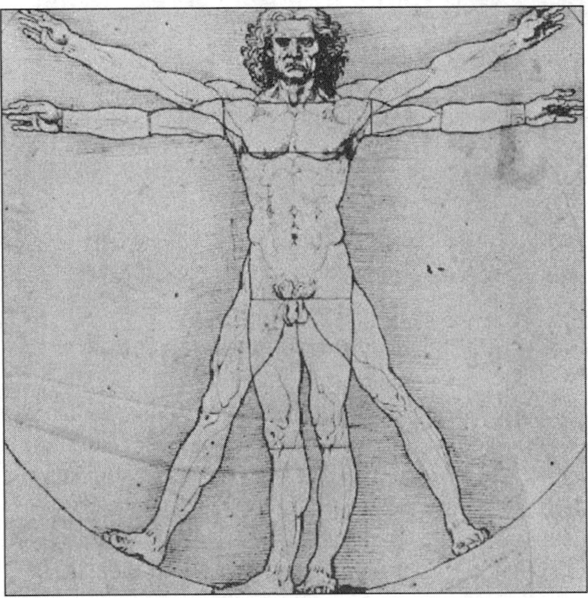

Figure 3-1 *Leonardo da Vinci's Vitruvian Man (Named After the Ancient Roman Architect Vitruvius)*

Even though architecture involves some well-defined activities, our first attempt at a definition uses the words *art* along with *science*. Unfortunately, for practical purposes, this definition is much too vague. But, one thing the definition does indirectly tell us is that architecture is simply part of the process of building things. For example, when building a new services platform, it is being built for a purpose and, when complete, is expected to have certain required principles.

The purpose of a "service delivery platform" is usually described to an architect by means of requirements documents that provide the goals and usage information for the platform that is to be built. Architects are typically individuals who have extensive experience in building IT systems that meet specific business requirements and translating those business requirements into IT engineering requirements. It is then up to subject matter experts (for example, server virtualization, networking, or storage engineers) to interpret the high-level architectural requirements into a low-level design and ultimately implement (build) a system ready for use. Figure 3-2 shows the many-to-one relationship among architecture, design, and implementations. Note that clear and well-understood communication among all stakeholders is essential throughout the project delivery phases to ensure success.

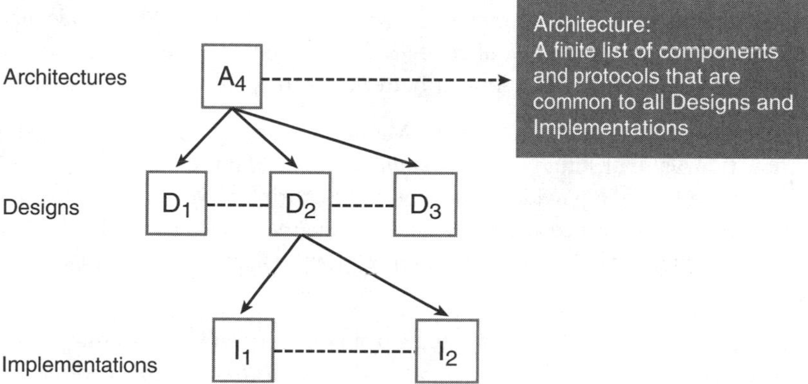

Figure 3-2 *Architecture Shapes the Design and Implementation of a System and/or Service*

Therefore, architecture is primarily used to communicate future system behavior to stakeholders and specify the building blocks for satisfying business requirements (this data is normally referred to as *artifacts*). A stakeholder is usually a person who pays for the effort and/or uses the end result. For example, a stakeholder could be the owner or a tenant of a future service platform, or a business owner or user of an anticipated network. Architecture blueprints are frequently used to communicate attributes of the system to the stakeholders before the system is actually built. In fact, the communication of multiple attributes usually requires multiple architecture documentation or blueprints. Unfortunately, architecture diagrams (usually multiple drawings) are often used incorrectly as design diagrams or vice versa.

With regard to cloud services, architecture must extend beyond on-premises (private cloud) deployments to support hybrid cloud models (hosted cloud, public cloud, community cloud, virtual private cloud, and so on). Architecture must also take into consideration Web 2.0 technologies (consumer social media services) and data access ubiquity (mobility).

Architectural principles that are required for a services platform today would most likely include but not be limited to efficiency, scalability, reliability, interoperability, flexibility, robustness, and modularity. How these principles are designed and implemented into a solution changes all the time as technology evolves.

With regard to implementing and managing architecture, process frameworks and methodologies are now heavily utilized to ensure quality and timely delivery by capitalizing of perceived industry best practices. Chapter 6, "Cloud Management Reference Architecture," covers frameworks in detail.

At this point, it is worth taking a few moments to discuss what exactly "IT value" is from a business perspective. Measuring value from IT investments has traditionally been an inexact science. The consequence is that many IT projects fail to fulfill their anticipated goals. Thus, many CIOs/CTOs today do not have much confidence in the accuracy of total cost of ownership (TCO), or more so, return on investment (ROI) modeling related to potential IT investments. A number of academic research projects with industry partnership have been conducted to look at better ways to approach this challenge.

One example would be the IT Capability Maturity Framework (IT-CMF), developed by the Innovation Value Institute (http://ivi.nuim.ie/ITCMF/index.shtml) along with Intel. Essentially, the IT-CMF provides a "capabilities maturity curve" (five levels of maturity) with a number of associated strategies aimed at delivering increasing IT value, thus ultimately supporting the business to maintain or grow sustainable differentiation in the marketplace.

The concept of *capability maturity* stems from the Software Engineering Institute (SEI), which originally developed what is known as the *Capability Maturity Model Integration (CMMI)*. In addition to the aforementioned IT-CMF, organizations can use the CMMI to map where they stand with respect to the best-in-class offering in relation to defined IT processes within Control Objectives for Information and Related Technology (COBIT) or how-to best practice guides like ITIL (Information Technology Infrastructure Library provides best practice for IT service management). Chapter 4, "IT Services," covers COBIT in detail.

Architectural Building Blocks of a Data Center

Data center design is at an evolutionary crossroads. Massive data growth, challenging economic conditions, and the physical limitations of power, heat, and space are exerting substantial pressure on the enterprise. Finding architectures that can take cost, complexity, and associated risk out of the data center while improving service levels has become a major objective for most enterprises. Consider the challenges facing enterprise IT organizations today.

Data center IT staff is typically asked to address the following data center challenges:

- Improve asset utilization to reduce or defer capital expenses.
- Reduce capital expenses through better management of peak workloads.

- Make data and resources available in real time to provide flexibility and alignment with current and future business agility needs.
- Reduce power and cooling consumption to cut operational costs and align with "green" business practices.
- Reduce deployment/churn time for new/existing services, saving operational costs and gaining competitive advantage in the market.
- Enable/increase innovation through new consumption models and the adoption of new abstraction layers in the architecture.
- Improve availability of services to avoid or reduce the business impact of unplanned outages or failures of service components.
- Maintain information assurance through consistent and robust security posture and processes.

From this set of challenges, you can derive a set of architectural principles that a new services platform would need to exhibit (as outlined in Table 3-1) to address the aforementioned challenges. Those architectural principles can in turn be matched to a set of underpinning technological requirements.

Table 3-1 *Technology to Support Architectural Principles*

Architectural Principles	Technological Requirements
Efficiency	Virtualization of infrastructure with appropriate management tools. Infrastructure homogeneity is driving asset utilization up.
Scalability	Platform scalability can be achieved through explicit protocol choice (for example, TRILL) and hardware selection and also through implicit system design and implementation.
Reliability	Disaster recovery (BCP) planning, testing, and operational tools (for example, VMware's Site Recovery Manager, SNAP, or Clone backup capabilities).
Interoperability	Web-based (XML) APIs, for example, WSDL (W3C) using SOAP or the conceptually simpler RESTful protocol with standards compliance semantics, for example, RFC 4741 NETCONF or TMForum's Multi-Technology Operations Systems Interface (MTOSI) with message binding to "concrete" endpoint protocols.
Flexibility	Software abstraction to enable policy-based management of the underlying infrastructure. Use of "meta models" (frames, rules, and constraints of how to build infrastructure). Encourage independence rather than interdependence among functional components of the platform.

Table 3-1 *Technology to Support Architectural Principles*

Architectural Principles	Technological Requirements
Modularity	Commonality of the underlying building blocks that can support scale-out and scale-up heterogeneous workload requirements with common integration points (web-based APIs). That is, integrated compute stacks or infrastructure packages (for example, a Vblock or a FlexPod). Programmatic workflows versus script-based workflows (discussed later in this chapter) along with the aforementioned software abstraction help deliver modularity of software tools.
Security	The appropriate countermeasures (tools, systems, processes, and protocols) relative to risk assessment derived from the threat model. Technology countermeasures are systems based, security in depth. Bespoke implementations/design patterns required to meet varied hosted tenant visibility and control requirements necessitated by regulatory compliance.
Robustness	System design and implementation—tools, methods, processes, and people that assist to mitigate collateral damage of a failure or failures internal to the administratively controlled system or even to external service dependencies to ensure service continuity.

Industry Direction and Operational and Technical Phasing

New technologies, such as multicore CPU, multisocket motherboards, inexpensive memory, and Peripheral Component Interconnect (PCI) bus technology, represent an evolution in the computing environment. These advancements, in addition to abstraction technologies (for example, virtual machine monitors [VMM], also known as hypervisor software), provide access to greater performance and resource utilization at a time of exponential growth of digital data and globalization through the Internet. Multithreaded applications designed to use these resources are both bandwidth intensive and require higher performance and efficiency from the underlying infrastructure.

Over the last few years, there have been iterative developments to the virtual infrastructure. Basic hypervisor technology with relatively simple virtual switches embedded in the hypervisor/VMM kernel have given way to far more sophisticated third-party distributed virtual switches (DVS) (for example, the Cisco Nexus 1000V) that bring together the operational domains of virtual server and the network, delivering consistent and integrated policy deployments. Other use cases, such as live migration of a VM, require orchestration of (physical and virtual) server, network, storage, and other dependencies to enable uninterrupted service continuity. Placement of capability and function needs to be carefully considered. Not every capability and function will have an optimal substantiation as a virtual entity; some might require physical substantiation because of performance or compliance reasons. So going forward, we see a hybrid model taking shape, with each capability and function being assessed for optimal placement with the architecture and design.

Although data center performance requirements are growing, IT managers are seeking ways to limit physical expansion by increasing the utilization of current resources. Server consolidation by means of server virtualization has become an appealing option. The use of multiple virtual machines takes full advantage of a physical server's computing potential and enables a rapid response to shifting data center demands. This rapid increase in computing power, coupled with the increased use of VM environments, is increasing the demand for higher bandwidth and at the same time creating additional challenges for the supporting networks.

Power consumption and efficiency continue to be some of the top concerns facing data center operators and designers. Data center facilities are designed with a specific power budget, in kilowatts per rack (or watts per square foot). Per-rack power consumption and cooling capacity have steadily increased over the past several years. Growth in the number of servers and advancement in electronic components continue to consume power at an exponentially increasing rate. Per-rack power requirements constrain the number of racks a data center can support, resulting in data centers that are out of capacity even though there is plenty of unused space.

Several metrics exist today that can help determine how efficient a data center operation is. These metrics apply differently to different types of systems, for example, facilities, network, server, and storage systems. For example, Cisco IT uses a measure of power per work unit performed instead of a measure of power per port because the latter approach does not account for certain use cases—the availability, power capacity, and density profile of mail, file, and print services will be very different from those of mission-critical web and security services. Furthermore, Cisco IT recognizes that just a measure of the network is not indicative of the entire data center operation. This is one of several reasons why Cisco has joined The Green Grid (www.thegreengrid.org), which focuses on developing data center–wide metrics for power efficiency. The power usage effectiveness (PUE) and data center efficiency (DCE) metrics detailed in the document "The Green Grid Metrics: Describing Data Center Power Efficiency" are ways to start addressing this challenge. Typically, the largest consumer of power and the most inefficient system in the data center is the Computer Room Air Conditioning (CRAC). At the time of this writing, state-of-the-art data centers have PUE values in the region of 1.2/1.1, whereas typical values would be in the range of 1.8–2.5. (For further reading on data center facilities, check out the book *Build the Best Data Center Facility for Your Business*, by Douglas Alger from Cisco Press.)

Cabling also represents a significant portion of a typical data center budget. Cable sprawl can limit data center deployments by obstructing airflows and requiring complex cooling system solutions. IT departments around the world are looking for innovative solutions that will enable them to keep up with this rapid growth with increased efficiency and low cost. We will discuss Unified Fabric (enabled by virtualization of network I/O) later in this chapter.

Current Barriers to Cloud/Utility Computing/ITaaS

It's clear that a lack of trust in current cloud offerings is the main barrier to broader adoption of cloud computing. Without trust, the economics and increased flexibility of cloud computing make little difference. For example, from a workload placement perspective, how does a customer make a cost-versus-risk (Governance, Risk, Compliance [GRC]) assessment without transparency of the information being provided? Transparency requires well-defined notations of service definition, audit, and accountancy. Multiple industry surveys attest to this. For example, as shown in Figure 3-3, Colt Technology Services' CIO Cloud Survey 2011 shows that most CIOs consider security as a barrier to cloud service adoption, and this is ahead of standing up the service (integration issues)! So how should we respond to these concerns?

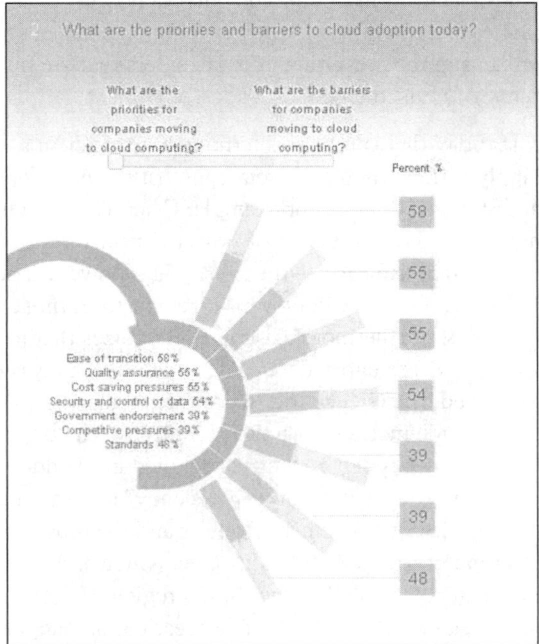

Figure 3-3 *CTS' CIO Cloud Survey 2011 (www.colt.net/cio-research)*

Trust in the cloud, Cisco believes, centers on five core concepts. These challenges keep business leaders and IT professionals alike up at night, and Cisco is working to address them with our partners:

- **Security:** Are there sufficient information assurance (IA) processes and tools to enforce confidentiality, integrity, and availability of the corporate data assets? Fears around multitenancy, the ability to monitor and record effectively, and the transparency of security events are foremost in customers' minds.

- **Control:** Can IT maintain direct control to decide how and where data and software are deployed, used, and destroyed in a multitenant and virtual, morphing infrastructure?
- **Service-level management:** Is it reliable? That is, can the appropriate Resource Usage Records (RUR) be obtained and measured appropriately for accurate billing? What if there's an outage? Can each application get the necessary resources and priority needed to run predictably in the cloud (capacity planning and business continuance planning)?
- **Compliance:** Will my cloud environment conform with mandated regulatory, legal, and general industry requirements (for example, PCI DSS, HIPAA, and Sarbanes-Oxley)?
- **Interoperability:** Will there be a vendor lock-in given the proprietary nature of today's public clouds? The Internet today has proven popular to enterprise businesses in part because of the ability to reduce risk through "multihoming" network connectivity to multiple Internet service providers that have diverse and distinct physical infrastructures.

For cloud solutions to be truly secure and trusted, Cisco believes they need an underlying network that can be relied upon to support cloud workloads.

To solve some of these fundamental challenges in the data center, many organizations are undertaking a journey. Figure 3-4 represents the general direction in which the IT industry is heading. The figure maps the operational phases (Consolidation, Virtualization, Automation, and so on) to enabling technology phases (Unified Fabric, Unified Computing, and so on).

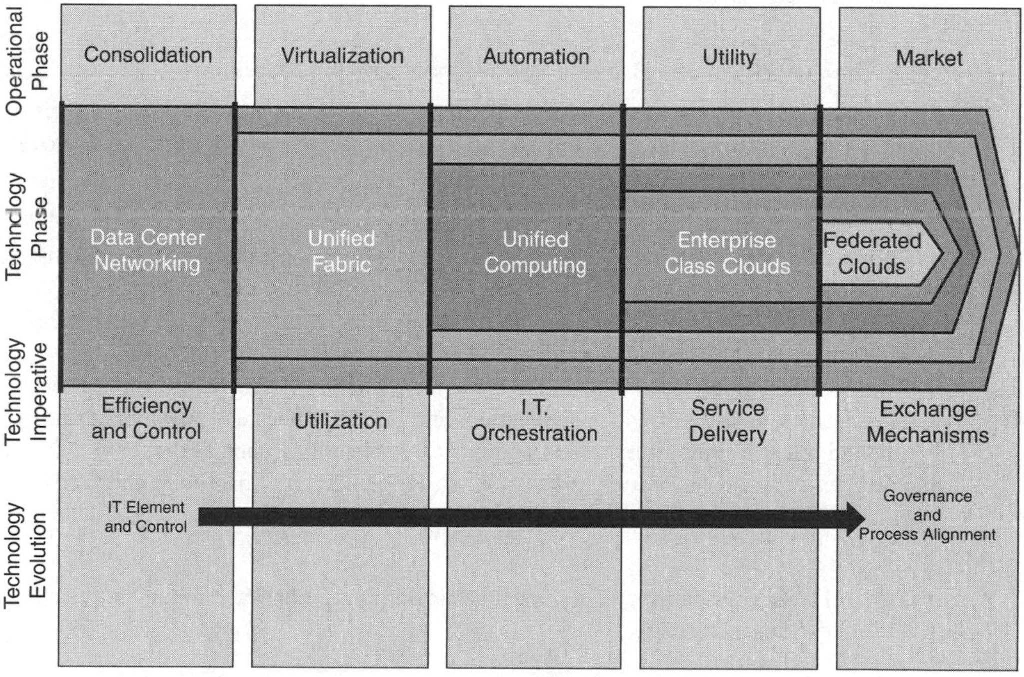

Figure 3-4 *Operational and Technological Evolution Stages of IT*

Organizations that are moving toward the adoption and utilization of cloud services tend to follow these technological phases:

1. Adoption of a broad IP WAN that is highly available (either through an ISP or self-built over dark fiber) enables centralization and consolidation of IT services. Application-aware services are layered on top of the WAN to intelligently manage application performance.
2. Executing on a virtualization strategy for server, storage, networking, and networking services (session load balancing, security apps, and so on) enables greater flexibility in the substantiation of services in regard to physical location, thereby enabling the ability to arrange such service to optimize infrastructure utilization.
3. Service automation enables greater operational efficiencies related to change control, ultimately paving the way to an economically viable on-demand service consumption model. In other words, building the "service factory."
4. Utility computing model includes the ability meter, chargeback, and bill customer on a pay-as-you-use (PAYU) basis. Showback is also a popular service: the ability to show current, real-time service and quota usage/consumption including future trending. This allows customers to understand and control their IT consumption. Showback is a fundamental requirement of service transparency.
5. Market creation through a common framework incorporating governance with a service ontology that facilitates the act of arbitrating between different service offerings and service providers.

Phase 1: The Adoption of a Broad IP WAN That Is Highly Available

This connectivity between remote locations allows IT services that were previously distributed (both from a geographic and organizational sense) to now be centralized, providing better operational control over those IT assets.

The constraint of this phase is that many applications were written to operate over a LAN and not a WAN environment. Rather than rewriting applications, the optimal economic path forward is to utilize application-aware, network-deployed services to enable a consistent Quality of Experience (QoE) to the end consumer of the service. These services tend to fall under the banner of Application Performance Management (APM) (www.cisco.com/go/apm). APM includes capabilities such as visibility into application response times, analysis of which applications and branch offices use how much bandwidth, and the ability to prioritize mission-critical applications, such as those from Oracle and SAP, as well as collaboration applications such as Microsoft SharePoint and Citrix.

Specific capabilities to deliver APM are as follows:

- **Performance monitoring:** Both in the network (transactions) and in the data center (application processing).

- **Reporting:** For example, application SLA reporting requires service contextualization of monitoring data to understand the data in relation to its expected or requested performance parameters. These parameters are gleaned from who the service owner is and the terms of his service contract.
- **Application visibility and control:** Application control gives service providers dynamic and adaptive tools to monitor and assure application performance.

Phase 2: Executing on a Virtualization Strategy for Server, Storage, Networking, and Networking Services

There are many solutions available on the market to enable server virtualization. Virtualization is the concept of creating a "sandbox" environment, where the computer hardware is abstracted to an operating system. The operating system is presented generic hardware devices that allow the virtualization software to pass messages to the physical hardware such as CPUs, memory, disks, and networking devices. These sandbox environments, also known as virtual machines (VM), include the operating system, the applications, and the configurations of a physical server. VMs are hardware independent, making them very portable so that they can run on any server.

Virtualization technology can also be applicable to many different areas such as networking and storage. LAN switching, for example, has the concept of a virtual LAN (VLAN) and routing with Virtual Routing and Forwarding (VRF) tables; storage-area networks have something similar in terms of virtual storage-area networks (VSAN), vFiler for NFS storage virtualization, and so on.

However, there is a price to pay for all this virtualization: management complexity. As virtual resources become abstracted from physical resources, existing management tools and methodologies start to break down in regard to their control effectiveness, particularly when one starts adding scale into the equation. New management capabilities, both implicit within infrastructure components or explicitly in external management tools, are required to provide the visibility and control service operations teams required to manage the risk to the business.

Unified Fabric based on IEEE Data Center Bridging (DCB) standards (more later) is a form of abstraction, this time by virtualizing Ethernet. However, this technology unifies the way that servers and storage resources are connected, how application delivery and core data center services are provisioned, how servers and data center resources are interconnected to scale, and how server and network virtualization is orchestrated.

To complement the usage of VMs, virtual applications (vApp) have also been brought into the data center architecture to provide policy enforcement within the new virtual infrastructure, again to help manage risk. Virtual machine-aware network services such as VMware's vShield and Virtual Network Services from Cisco allow administrators to provide services that are aware of tenant ownership of VMs and enforce service domain isolation (that is, the DMZ). The Cisco Virtual Network Services solution is also aware of the location of VMs. Ultimately, this technology allows the administrator to tie together service policy to location and ownership of an application residing with a VM container.

The Cisco Nexus 1000V vPath technology allows policy-based traffic steering to "invoke" vApp services (also known as *policy enforcement points [PEP]*), even if they reside on a separate physical ESX host. This is the start of *Intelligent Service Fabrics (ISF)*, where the traditional IP or MAC-based forwarding behavior is "policy hijacked" to substantiate service chain–based forwarding behavior.

Server and network virtualization have been driven primarily by the economic benefits of consolidation and higher utilization of physical server and network assets. vApps and ISF change the economics through efficiency gains of providing network-residing services that can be invoked on demand and dimensioned to need rather than to the design constraints of the traditional traffic steering methods.

Virtualization, or rather the act of abstraction from the underlying physical infrastructure, provides the basis of new types of IT services that potentially can be more dynamic in nature, as illustrated in Figure 3-5.

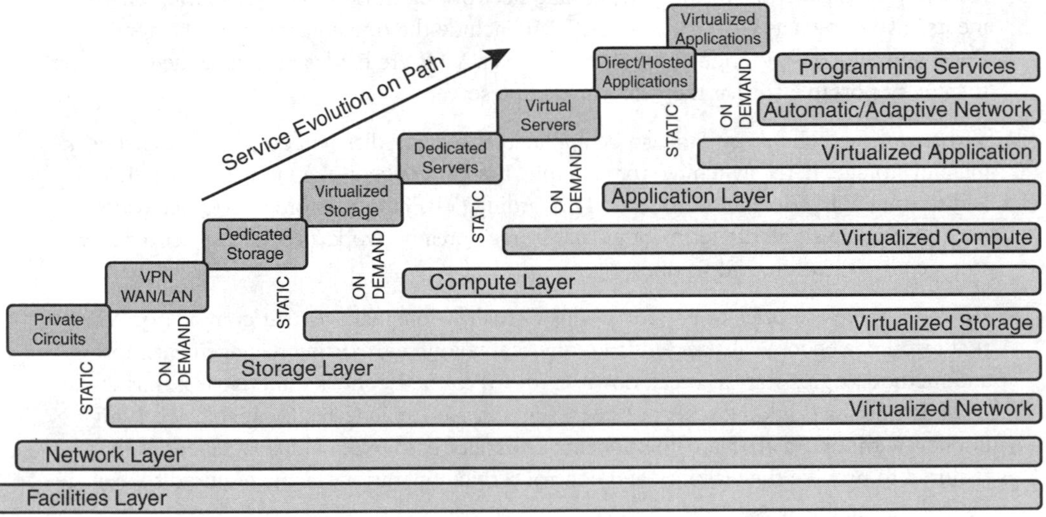

Figure 3-5 *IT Service Enablement Through Abstraction/Virtualization of IT Domains*

Phase 3: Service Automation

Service automation, working hand in hand with a virtualized infrastructure, is a key enabler in delivering dynamic services. From an IaaS perspective, this phase means the policy-driven provisioning of IT services though the use of automated task workflow, whether that involves business tasks (also known as Business Process Operations Management [BPOM]) or IT tasks (also known as IT Orchestration).

Traditionally, this has been too costly to be economically effective because of the reliance on script-based automation tooling. Scripting is linear in nature (makes rollback challenging); more importantly, it tightly couples workflow to process execution logic to assets. In other words, if an architect wants or needs to change an IT asset (for example, a server type/supplier) or change the workflow or process execution logic within a workflow step/node in response to a business need, a lot of new scripting is required. It's like building a LEGO brick wall with all the bricks glued together. More often than not, a new wall is cheaper and easier to develop than trying to replace or change individual blocks.

Two main developments have now made service automation a more economically viable option:

- Standards-based web APIs and protocols (for example, SOAP and RESTful) have helped reduce integration complexity and costs through the ability to reuse.
- Programmatic-based workflow tools helped to decouple/abstract workflow from process execution logic from assets. Contemporary IT orchestration tools, such as Enterprise Orchestrator from Cisco and BMC's Atrium Orchestrator, allow system designers to make changes to the workflow (including invoking and managing parallel tasks) or to insert new workflow steps or change assets through reusable *adaptors* without having to start from scratch. Using the LEGO wall analogy, individual bricks of the wall can be relatively easily interchanged without having to build a new wall.

Note that a third component is necessary to make programmatic service automation a success, namely, an *intelligent infrastructure* by which the complexity of the low-level device configuration syntax is abstracted from the northbound system's management tools. This means higher-level management tools only need to know the *policy semantics*. In other words, an orchestration system need only ask for a chocolate cake and the element manager, now based on a well-defined (programmatic) object-based data model, will translate that request into the required ingredients and, furthermore, how they those ingredients should be mixed together and in what quantities.

A practical example is the Cisco Unified Compute System (UCS) with its single data model exposed through a single transactional-based rich XML API (other APIs are supported!). This allows policy-driven consumption of the physical compute layer. To do this, UCS provides a layer of abstraction between its XML data model and the underlying hardware through *application gateways* that do the translation of the policy semantics as necessary to execute state change of a hardware component (such as BIOS settings).

Phase 4: Utility Computing Model

This phase involves the ability to monitor, meter, and track resource usage for chargeback billing. The goal is for self-service provisioning (on-demand allocation of compute resources), in essence turning IT into a utility service.

In any IT environment, it is crucial to maintain knowledge of allocation and utilization of resources. Metering and performance analysis of these resources enable cost efficiency, service consistency, and subsequently the capabilities IT needs for trending, capacity management, threshold management (service-level agreements [SLA]), and pay-for-use chargeback.

In many IT environments today, dedicated physical servers and their associated applications, as well as maintenance and licensing costs, can be mapped to the department using them, making the billing relatively straightforward for such resources. In a shared virtual environment, however, the task of calculating the IT operational cost for each consumer in real time is a challenging problem to solve.

Pay for use, where the end customers are charged based on their usage and consumption of a service, has long been used by such businesses as utilities and wireless phone providers. Increasingly, *pay-per-use* has gained acceptance in enterprise computing as IT works in parallel to lower costs across infrastructures, applications, and services.

One of the top concerns of IT leadership teams implementing a utility platform is this: If the promise of pay-per-use is driving service adoption in a cloud, how do the providers of the service track the service usage and bill for it accordingly?

IT providers have typically struggled with billing solution metrics that do not adequately represent all the resources consumed as part of a given service. The primary goal of any chargeback solution requires consistent visibility into the infrastructure to meter resource usage per customer and the cost to serve for a given service. Today, this often requires cobbling together multiple solutions or even developing custom solutions for metering.

This creates not only up-front costs, but longer-term inefficiencies. IT providers quickly become overwhelmed building new functionality into the metering system every time they add a service or infrastructure component.

The dynamic nature of a virtual converged infrastructure and its associated layers of abstraction being a benefit to the IT operation conversely increase the metering complexity. An optimal chargeback solution provides businesses with the true allocation breakdown of costs and services delivered in a converged infrastructure.

The business goals for metering and chargeback typically include the following:

- Reporting on allocation and utilization of resources by business unit or customer
- Developing an accurate cost-to-serve model, where utilization can be applied to each user
- Providing a method for managing IT demand, facilitating capacity planning, forecasting, and budgeting
- Reporting on relevant SLA performance

Chargeback and billing requires three main steps:

Step 1. Data collection

Step 2. Chargeback mediation (correlating and aggregating data collected from the various system components into a billing record of the service owner customer)

Step 3. Billing and reporting (applying the pricing model to collected data) and generating a periodic billing report

Phase 5: Market

In mainstream economics, the concept of a market is any structure that allows buyers and sellers to exchange any type of goods, services, and information. The exchange of goods or services for money (an agreed-upon medium of exchange) is a transaction.

For a marketplace to be built to exchange IT services as an exchangeable commodity, the participants in that market need to agree on common service definitions or have an ontology that aligns not only technology but also business definitions. The alignment of process and governance among the market participants is desirable, particularly when "mashing up" service components from different providers/authors to deliver an end-to-end service.

To be more detailed, a *service* has two aspects:

- **Business:** The business aspect is required for marketplace and a technical aspect for exchange and delivery. The business part needs product definition, relationships (ontology), collateral, pricing, and so on.
- **Technical:** The technical aspect needs fulfillment, assurance, and governance aspects.

In the marketplace, there will be various players/participants who take on a variety and/or combination of roles. There would be exchange providers (also known as *service aggregators* or *cloud service brokers*), service developers, product manufacturers, service providers, service resellers, service integrators, and finally consumers (or even prosumers).

Design Evolution in the Data Center

This section provides an overview of the emerging technologies in the data center, how they are supporting architectural principles outlined previously, how they are influencing design and implementation of infrastructure, and ultimately their value in regard to delivering IT as a service.

First, we will look at Layer 2 physical and logical topology evolution. Figure 3-6 shows the design evolution of an OSI Layer 2 topology in the data center. Moving from left to right, you can see the physical topology changing in the number of active interfaces between the functional layers of the data center. This evolution is necessary to support the current and future service use cases.

Virtualization technologies such as VMware ESX Server and clustering solutions such as Microsoft Cluster Service currently require Layer 2 Ethernet connectivity to function properly. With the increased use of these types of technologies in data centers and now even across data center locations, organizations are shifting from a highly scalable Layer 3 network model to a highly scalable Layer 2 model. This shift is causing changes in the technologies used to manage large Layer 2 network environments, including migration away from Spanning Tree Protocol (STP) as a primary loop management technology toward new technologies, such as vPC and IETF TRILL (Transparent Interconnection of Lots of Links).

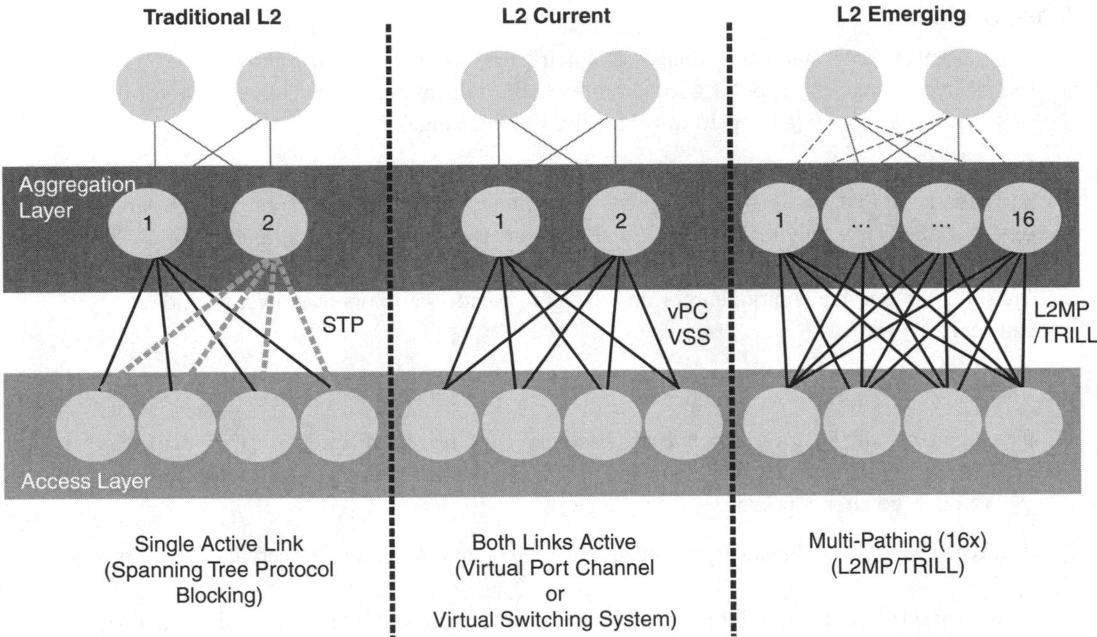

Figure 3-6 *Evolution of OSI Layer 2 in the Data Center*

In early Layer 2 Ethernet network environments, it was necessary to develop protocol and control mechanisms that limited the disastrous effects of a topology loop in the network. STP was the primary solution to this problem, providing a loop detection and loop management capability for Layer 2 Ethernet networks. This protocol has gone through a number of enhancements and extensions, and although it scales to very large network environments, it still has one suboptimal principle: To break loops in a network, only one active path is allowed from one device to another, regardless of how many actual connections might exist in the network. Although STP is a robust and scalable solution to redundancy in a Layer 2 network, the single logical link creates two problems:

- Half (or more) of the available system bandwidth is off limits to data traffic.
- A failure of the active link tends to cause multiple seconds of system-wide data loss while the network reevaluates the new "best" solution for network forwarding in the Layer 2 network.

Although enhancements to STP reduce the overhead of the rediscovery process and allow a Layer 2 network to reconverge much faster, the delay can still be too great for some networks. In addition, no efficient dynamic mechanism exists for using all the available bandwidth in a robust network with STP loop management.

An early enhancement to Layer 2 Ethernet networks was PortChannel technology (now standardized as IEEE 802.3ad PortChannel technology), in which multiple links between two participating devices can use all the links between the devices to forward traffic by using a load-balancing algorithm that equally balances traffic across the available Inter-Switch Links (ISL) while also managing the loop problem by bundling the links as one logical link. This logical construct keeps the remote device from forwarding broadcast and unicast frames back to the logical link, thereby breaking the loop that actually exists in the network. PortChannel technology has one other primary benefit: It can potentially deal with a link loss in the bundle in less than a second, with little loss of traffic and no effect on the active STP topology.

Introducing Virtual PortChannel (vPC)

The biggest limitation in classic PortChannel communication is that the PortChannel operates only between two devices. In large networks, the support of multiple devices together is often a design requirement to provide some form of hardware failure alternate path. This alternate path is often connected in a way that would cause a loop, limiting the benefits gained with PortChannel technology to a single path. To address this limitation, the Cisco NX-OS Software platform provides a technology called virtual PortChannel (vPC). Although a pair of switches acting as a vPC peer endpoint looks like a single logical entity to PortChannel-attached devices, the two devices that act as the logical PortChannel endpoint are still two separate devices. This environment combines the benefits of hardware redundancy with the benefits of PortChannel loop management. The other main benefit of migration to an all-PortChannel-based loop management mechanism is that link recovery is potentially much faster. STP can recover from a link failure in approximately 6 seconds, while an all-PortChannel-based solution has the potential for failure recovery in less than a second.

Although vPC is not the only technology that provides this solution, other solutions tend to have a number of deficiencies that limit their practical implementation, especially when deployed at the core or distribution layer of a dense high-speed network. All multi-chassis PortChannel technologies still need a direct link between the two devices acting as the PortChannel endpoints. This link is often much smaller than the aggregate bandwidth of the vPCs connected to the endpoint pair. Cisco technologies such as vPC are specifically designed to limit the use of this ISL specifically to switch management traffic and the occasional traffic flow from a failed network port. Technologies from other vendors are not designed with this goal in mind, and in fact, are dramatically limited in scale especially because they require the use of the ISL for control traffic and approximately half the data throughput of the peer devices. For a small environment, this approach might be adequate, but it will not suffice for an environment in which many terabits of data traffic might be present.

Introducing Layer 2 Multi-Pathing (L2MP)

IETF Transparent Interconnection of Lots of Links (TRILL) is a new Layer 2 topology-based capability. With the Nexus 7000 switch, Cisco already supports a prestandards version of TRILL called *FabricPath*, enabling customers to benefit from this technology before the ratification of the IETF TRILL standard. (For the Nexus 7000 switch, the migration from Cisco FabricPath to IETF TRILL protocol, a simple software upgrade migration path is planned. In other words, no hardware upgrades are required.) Generically, we will refer to TRILL and FabricPath as "Layer 2 Multi-Pathing (L2MP)."

The operational benefits of L2MP are as follows:

- Enables Layer 2 multipathing in the Layer 2 DC network (up to 16 links). This provides much greater *cross-sectional bandwidth* for both client-to-server (North-to-South) and server-to-server (West-to-East) traffic.
- Provides built-in loop prevention and mitigation with no need to use the STP. This significantly reduces the operational risk associated with the day-to-day management and troubleshooting of a nontopology-based protocol, like STP.
- Provides a single control plane for unknown unicast, unicast, broadcast, and multicast traffic.
- Enhances mobility and virtualization in the FabricPath network with a larger OSI Layer 2 domain. It also helps with simplifying service automation workflow by simply having less service dependencies to configure and manage.

What follows is an amusing poem by Ray Perlner that can be found in the IETF TRILL draft that captures the benefits of building a topology free of STP:

I hope that we shall one day see,

A graph more lovely than a tree.

A graph to boost efficiency,

While still configuration-free.

A network where RBridges can,

Route packets to their target LAN.

The paths they find, to our elation,

Are least cost paths to destination!

With packet hop counts we now see,

The network need not be loop-free!

RBridges work transparently,

Without a common spanning tree.

(Source: Algorhyme V2, by Ray Perlner from IETF draft-perlman-trill-rbridge-protocol)

Network Services and Fabric Evolution in the Data Center

This section looks at the evolution of data center networking from an Ethernet protocol (OSI Layer 2) virtualization perspective. The section then looks at how network services (for example, firewalls, load balancers, and so on) are evolving within the data center.

Figure 3-7 illustrates the two evolution trends happening in the data center.

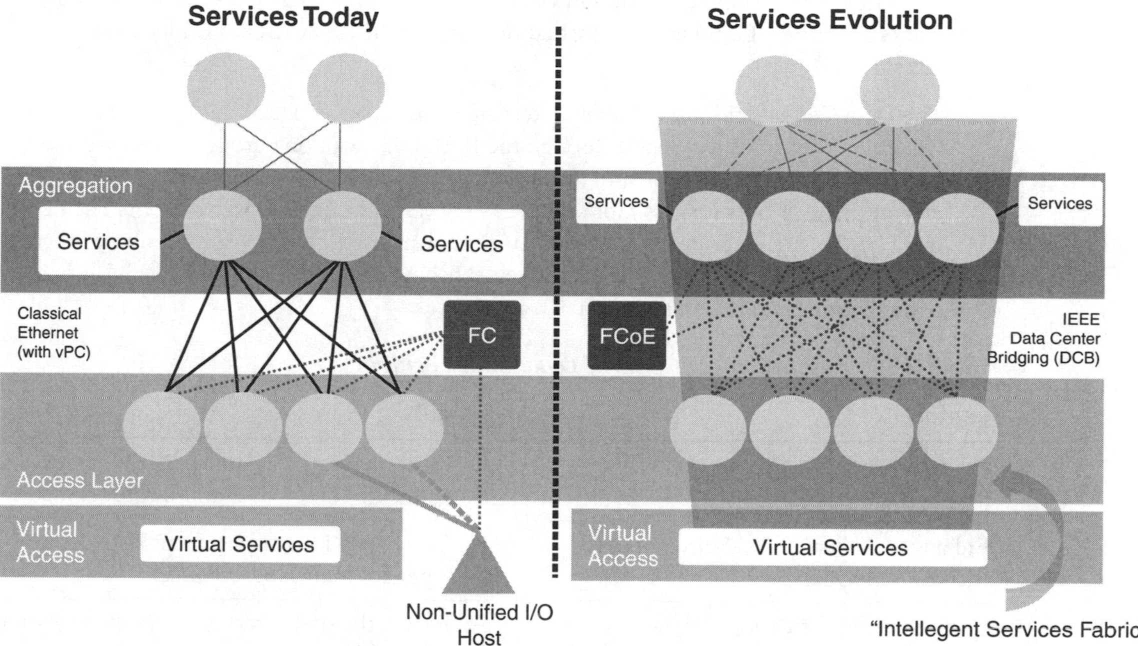

Figure 3-7 *Evolution of I/O Fabric and Service Deployment in the DC*

1. Virtualization of Data Center Network I/O

From a supply-side perspective, the transition to a converged I/O infrastructure fabric is a result of the evolution of network technology to the point where a single fabric has sufficient throughput, low-enough latency, sufficient reliability, and lower-enough cost to be the economically viable solution for the data center network today.

From the demand side, multicore CPUs spawning the development of virtualized compute infrastructures have placed increased demand of I/O bandwidth at the access layer of the data center. In addition to bandwidth, virtual machine mobility also requires the flexibility of service dependencies such as storage. Unified I/O infrastructure fabric enables the abstraction of the overlay service (for example, file [IP] or block-based [FC] storage) that supports the architectural principle of flexibility: "Wire once, any protocol, any time."

Abstraction between the virtual network infrastructure and the physical networking causes its own challenge in regard to maintaining end-to-end control of service traffic from a policy enforcement perspective. Virtual Network Link (VN-Link) is a set of standards-based solutions from Cisco that enables policy-based network abstraction to recouple the virtual and physical network policy domains.

Cisco and other major industry vendors have made standardization proposals in the IEEE to address networking challenges in virtualized environments. The resulting standards tracks are IEEE 802.1Qbg Edge Virtual Bridging and IEEE 802.1Qbh Bridge Port Extension.

The Data Center Bridging (DCB) architecture is based on a collection of open-standard Ethernet extensions developed through the IEEE 802.1 working group to improve and expand Ethernet networking and management capabilities in the data center. It helps ensure delivery over lossless fabrics and I/O convergence onto a unified fabric. Each element of this architecture enhances the DCB implementation and creates a robust Ethernet infrastructure to meet data center requirements now and in the future. Table 3-2 lists the main features and benefits of the DCB architecture.

Table 3-2 *Features and Benefits of Data Center Bridging*

Feature	Benefit
Priority-based Flow Control (PFC) (IEEE 802.1 Qbb)	Provides the capability to manage a bursty, single-traffic source on a multiprotocol link
Enhanced Transmission Selection (ETS) (IEEE 802.1 Qaz)	Enables bandwidth management between traffic types for multiprotocol links
Congestion Notification (IEEE 802.1 Qau)	Addresses the problem of sustained congestion by moving corrective action to the network edge
Data Center Bridging Exchange (DCBX) Protocol	Allows autoexchange of Ethernet parameters between switches and endpoints

IEEE DCB builds on classical Ethernet's strengths, adds several crucial extensions to provide the next-generation infrastructure for data center networks, and delivers unified fabric. We will now describe how each of the main features of the DCB architecture contributes to a robust Ethernet network capable of meeting today's growing application requirements and responding to future data center network needs.

Priority-based Flow Control (PFC) enables link sharing that is critical to I/O consolidation. For link sharing to succeed, large bursts from one traffic type must not affect other traffic types, large queues of traffic from one traffic type must not starve other traffic types' resources, and optimization for one traffic type must not create high latency for small messages of other traffic types. The Ethernet pause mechanism can be used to control the effects of one traffic type on another. PFC is an enhancement to the pause mechanism. PFC enables pause based on user priorities or classes of service. A physical link divided into eight virtual links, PFC provides the capability to use pause frame on a single virtual link without affecting traffic on the other virtual links (the classical Ethernet pause option stops all traffic on a link). Enabling pause based on user priority allows administrators to create lossless links for traffic requiring no-drop service, such as Fibre Channel over Ethernet (FCoE), while retaining packet-drop congestion management for IP traffic.

Traffic within the same PFC class can be grouped together and yet treated differently within each group. ETS provides prioritized processing based on bandwidth allocation, low latency, or best effort, resulting in per-group traffic class allocation. Extending the virtual link concept, the network interface controller (NIC) provides virtual interface queues, one for each traffic class. Each virtual interface queue is accountable for managing its allotted bandwidth for its traffic group, but has flexibility within the group to dynamically manage the traffic. For example, virtual link 3 (of 8) for the IP class of traffic might have a high-priority designation and a best effort within that same class, with the virtual link 3 class sharing a defined percentage of the overall link with other traffic classes. ETS allows differentiation among traffic of the same priority class, thus creating priority groups.

In addition to IEEE DCB standards, Cisco Nexus data center switches include enhancements such as FCoE multihop capabilities and lossless fabric to enable construction of a Unified Fabric.

At this point to avoid any confusion, note that the term *Converged Enhanced Ethernet (CEE)* was defined by "CEE Authors," an ad hoc group that consisted of over 50 developers from a broad range of networking companies that made prestandard proposals to the IEEE prior to the IEEE 802.1 Working Group completing DCB standards.

FCoE is the next evolution of the Fibre Channel networking and Small Computer System Interface (SCSI) block storage connectivity model. FCoE maps Fibre Channel onto Layer 2 Ethernet, allowing the combination of LAN and SAN traffic onto a link and enabling SAN users to take advantage of the economy of scale, robust vendor community, and road map of Ethernet. The combination of LAN and SAN traffic on a link is called unified fabric. Unified fabric eliminates adapters, cables, and devices, resulting in savings that can extend the life of the data center. FCoE enhances server virtualization initiatives with the availability of standard server I/O, which supports the LAN and all forms of Ethernet-based storage networking, eliminating specialized networks from the data center. FCoE is an industry standard developed by the same standards body that creates and maintains all Fibre Channel standards. FCoE is specified under INCITS as FC-BB-5.

FCoE is evolutionary in that it is compatible with the installed base of Fibre Channel as well as being the next step in capability. FCoE can be implemented in stages nondisruptively on installed SANs. FCoE simply tunnels a full Fibre Channel frame onto Ethernet. With the strategy of frame encapsulation and deencapsulation, frames are moved, without overhead, between FCoE and Fibre Channel ports to allow connection to installed Fibre Channel.

For a comprehensive and detailed review of DCB, TRILL, FCoE and other emerging protocols, refer to the book *I/O Consolidation in the Data Center*, by Silvano Gai and Claudio DeSanti from Cisco Press.

2. Virtualization of Network Services

Application networking services, such as load balancers and WAN accelerators, have become integral building blocks in modern data center designs. These Layer 4–7 services provide service scalability, improve application performance, enhance end-user productivity, help reduce infrastructure costs through optimal resource utilization, and monitor quality of service. They also provide security services (that is, policy enforcement points [PEP] such as firewalls and intrusion protection systems [IPS]) to isolate applications and resources in consolidated data centers and cloud environments that along with other control mechanisms and hardened processes, ensure compliance and reduce risk.

Deploying Layer 4 through 7 services in virtual data centers has, however, been extremely challenging. Traditional service deployments are completely at odds with highly scalable virtual data center designs, with mobile workloads, dynamic networks, and strict SLAs. Security, as aforementioned, is just one required service that is frequently cited as the biggest challenge to enterprises adopting cost-saving virtualization and cloud-computing architectures.

As illustrated in Figure 3-8, Cisco Nexus 7000 Series switches can be segmented into virtual devices based on business need. These segmented virtual switches are referred to as *virtual device contexts (VDC)*. Each configured VDC presents itself as a unique device to connected users within the framework of that physical switch. VDCs therefore deliver true segmentation of network traffic, context-level fault isolation, and management through the creation of independent hardware and software partitions. The VDC runs as a separate logical entity within the switch, maintaining its own unique set of running software processes, having its own configuration, and being managed by a separate administrator.

The possible use cases for VDCs include the following:

- Offer a secure network partition for the traffic of multiple departments, enabling departments to administer and maintain their own configurations independently
- Facilitate the collapsing of multiple tiers within a data center for total cost reduction in both capital and operational expenses, with greater asset utilization
- Test new configuration or connectivity options on isolated VDCs on the production network, which can dramatically improve the time to deploy services

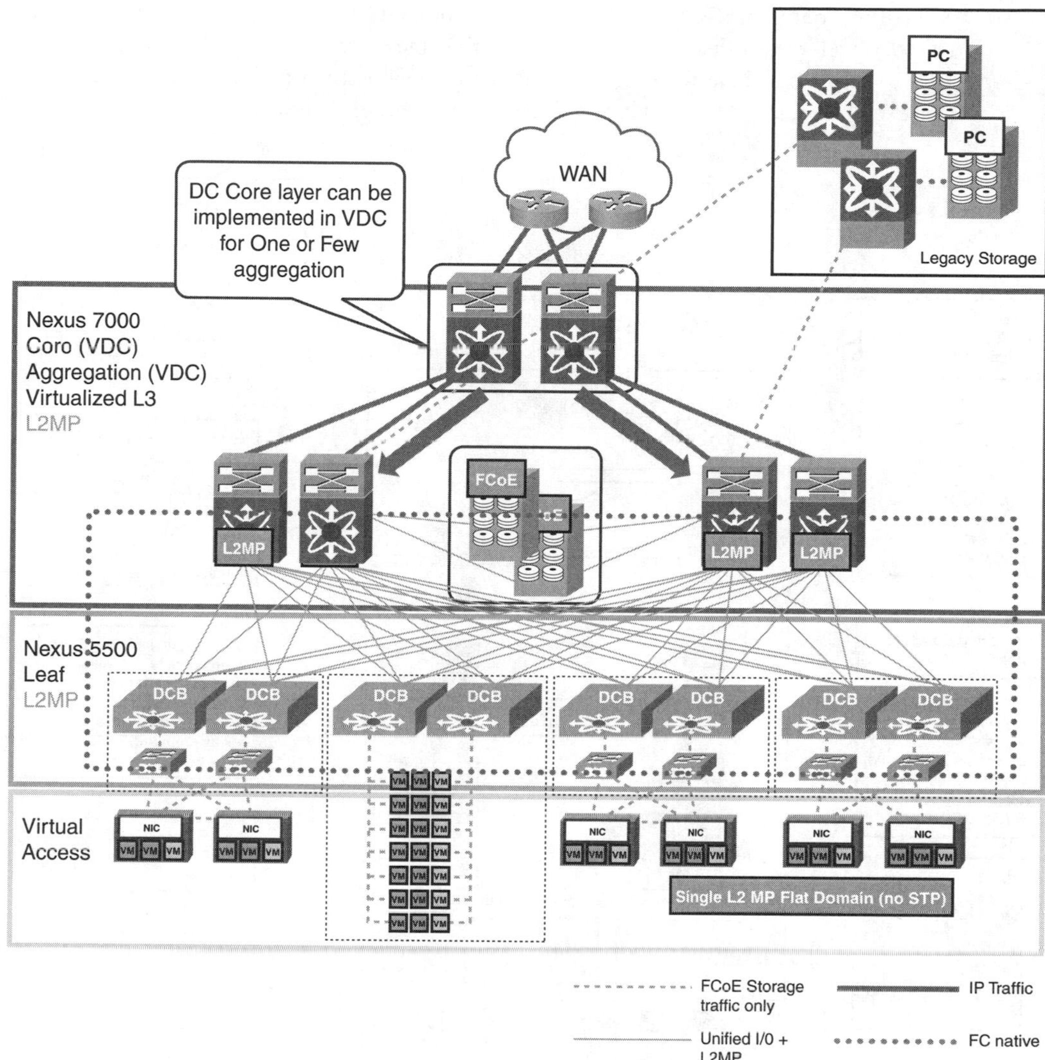

Figure 3-8 *Collapsing of the Vertical Hierarchy with Nexus 7000 Virtual Device Contexts (VDC)*

Multitenancy in the Data Center

Figure 3-9 shows multitenant infrastructure providing end-to-end logical separation between different tenants and shows how a cloud IaaS provider can provide a robust end-to-end multitenant services platform. *Multitenant* in this context is the ability to share a single physical and logical set of infrastructure across many stakeholders and customers. This is nothing revolutionary; the operational model to isolate customers from one another has been well established in wide-area networks (WAN) using technologies such as

Multi-Protocol Label Switching (MPLS). Therefore, multitenancy in the DC is an evolution of a well-established paradigm, albeit with some additional technologies such as VLANs and Virtual Network Tags (VN-Tag) combined with virtualized network services (for example, session load balancers, firewalls, and IPS PEP instances).

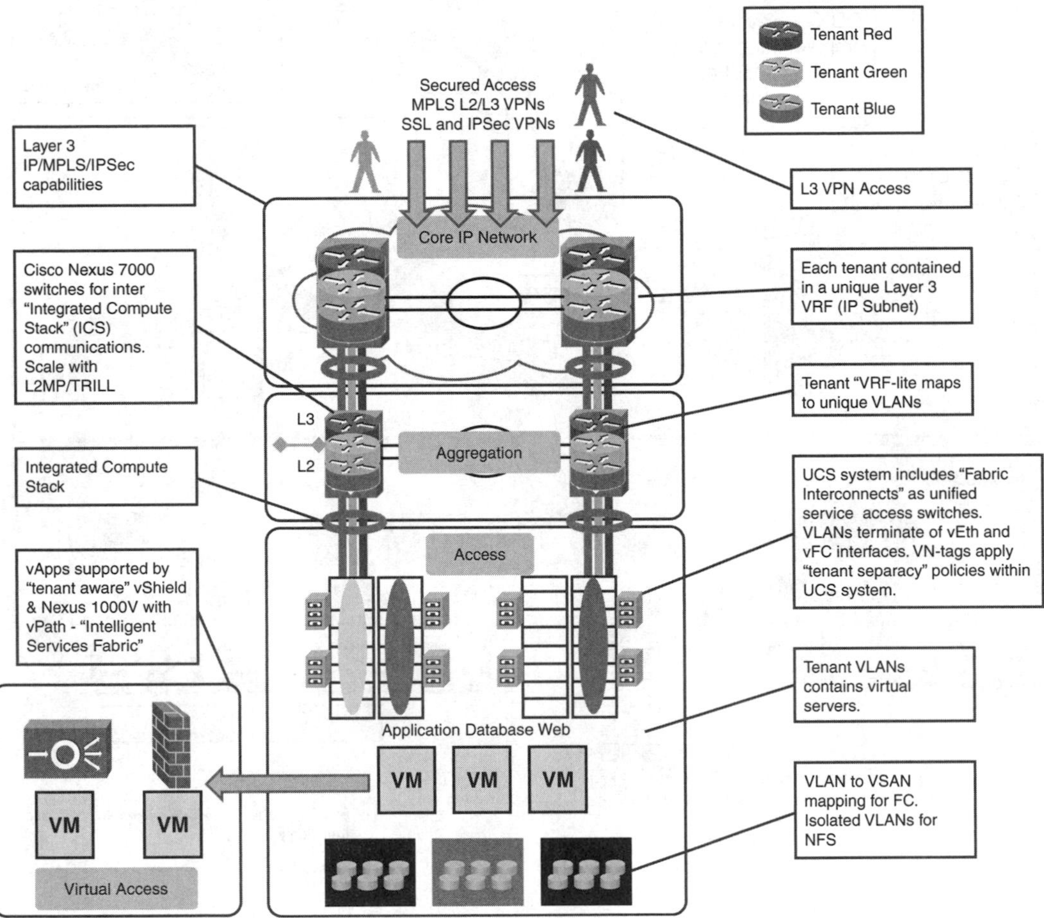

Figure 3-9 *End-to-End "Separacy"—Building the Multitenant Infrastructure*

In addition to multitenancy, architects need to think about how to provide multitier applications and their associated network and service design, including from a security posture perspective a multizone overlay capability. In other words, to build a functional and secure service, one needs to take into account multiple functional demands, as illustrated in Figure 3-10.

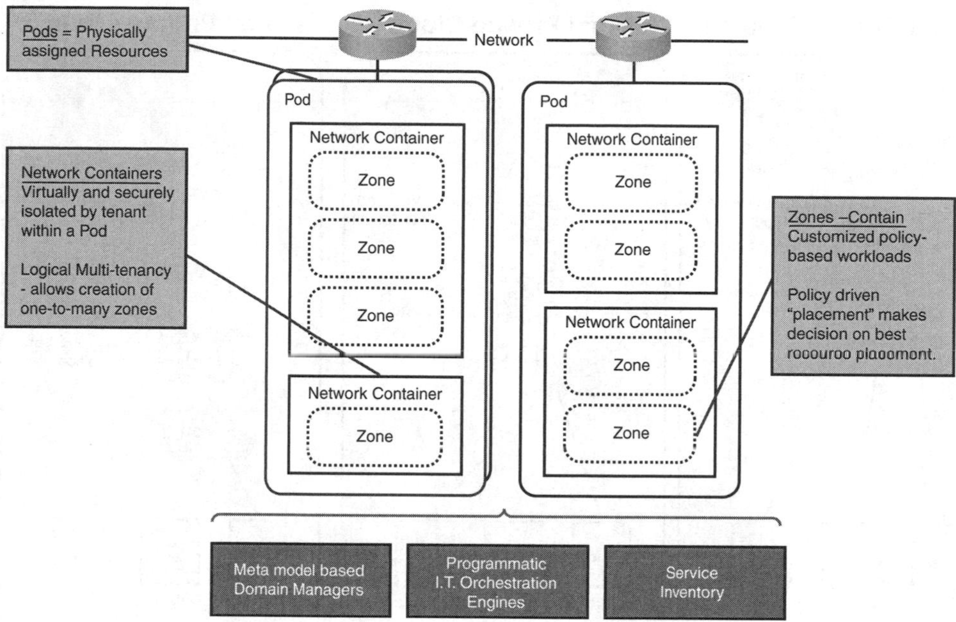

Figure 3-10 *Example of a Hierarchical Architecture Incorporating Multitenancy, Multitier, and Multizoning Attributes for an IaaS Platform (Source: Cisco Systems VMDC 2.0 Solution)*

The challenge is being able to "stitch" together the required service components (each with their own operational-level agreement (OLAs underpin an SLA) to form a service chain that delivers the end-to-end service attributes (legally formalized by a service-level agreement [SLA]) that the end customer desires. This has to be done within the context of the application tier design and security zoning requirements.

Real-time capacity and capability posture reporting of a given infrastructure are only just beginning to be delivered to the market. Traditional ITIL Configuration Management Systems (CMS) have not been designed to run in real-time environments. The consequence is that to deploy a service chain with known quantitative and qualitative attributes, one must take a structured approach to service deployment/service activation. This structured approach requires a predefined infrastructure modeling of the capacity and capability of service elements and their proximity and adjacency to each other. A predefined service chain, known more colloquially as a network container, can therefore be activated on the infrastructure as a known unit of consumption. A service chain is a group of technical topology building blocks, as illustrated in Figure 3-11.

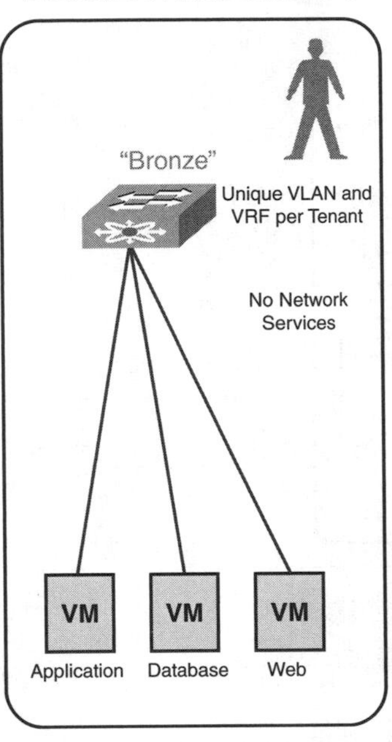

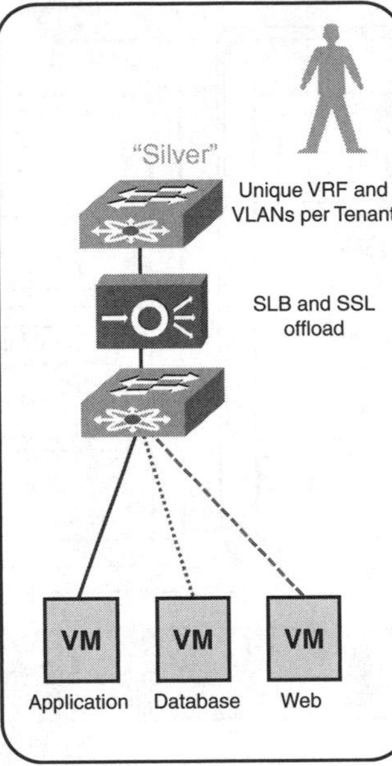

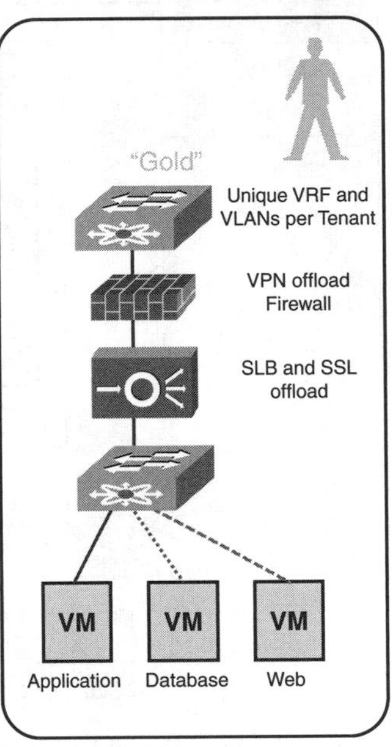

Figure 3-11 *Network Containers for Virtual Private Cloud Deployment*

As real-time IT capacity- and capability-reporting tooling becomes available, ostensibly requiring autodiscovery and reporting capabilities of all infrastructure in a addition to flexible meta models and data (that is, rules on how a component can connect to other components—for example, a firewall instance can connect to a VLAN but not a VRF), providers and customers will be able to take an unstructured approach to service chain deployments. In other words, a customer will be able to create his own blueprint and publish within his own service catalogue to consume or even publish the blueprint into the provider's service portfolio for others to consume, thereby enabling a "prosumer" model (*prosumer* being a portmanteau of producer and consumer).

Service Assurance

As illustrated in Figure 3-12, SLAs have evolved through necessity from those based only on general network performance in Layers 1 through 3 (measuring metrics such as jitter and availability), to SLAs increasingly focused on network performance for specific applications (as managed by technologies such as a WAN optimization controller), to SLAs based on specific application metrics and business process SLAs based on key performance indicators (KPI) such as cycle time or productivity rate. Examples of KPIs are the number of airline passengers who check in per hour or the number of new customer accounts provisioned.

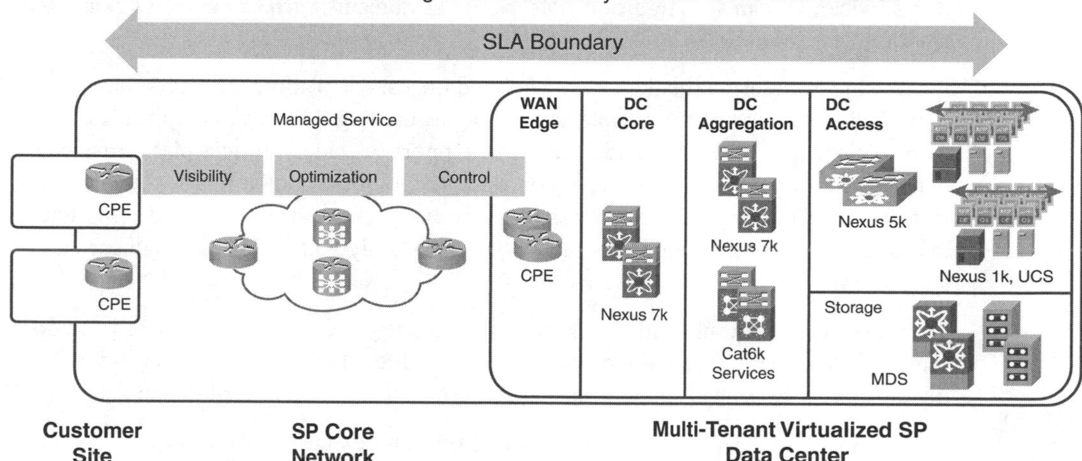

Figure 3-12 *Expanding the SLA Boundary*

Customers expect that their critical business processes (such as payroll and order fulfillment) will always be available and that sufficient resources are provided by the service provider to ensure application performance, even in the event that a server fails or if a data center becomes unavailable. This requires cloud providers to be able to scale up data center resources, ensure the mobility of virtual machines within the data center and across data centers, and provide supplemental computer resources in another data center, if needed.

With their combined data center and Cisco IP NGN assets, service providers can attract relationships with independent software vendors with SaaS offerings, where end customers purchase services from the SaaS provider while the service provider delivers an assured end-to-end application experience.

In addition to SLAs for performance over the WAN and SLAs for application availability, customers expect that their hosted applications will have security protection in an external hosting environment. In many cases, they want the cloud service provider to improve the performance of applications in the data center and over the WAN, minimizing application response times and mitigating the effects of latency and congestion.

With their private IP/MPLS networks, cloud service providers can enhance application performance and availability in the cloud and deliver the visibility, monitoring, and reporting that customers require for assurance. As cloud service providers engineer their solutions, they should consider how they can continue to improve on their service offerings to support not only network and application SLAs but also SLAs for application transactions and business processes.

Service assurance solutions today need to cope with rapidly changing infrastructure configurations as well as understand the status of a service with the backdrop of ever-changing customer ownership of a service. The solution also needs to understand the context of a service that can span traditionally separate IT domains, such as the IP WAN and the Data Center Network (DCN).

Ideally, such a solution should ideally be based on a single platform and code base design that eliminates some of the complexities of understanding a service in a dynamic environment. This makes it easier to understand and support the cloud services platform and also eliminates costly and time-consuming product integration work. However, the single-platform design should not detract from scalability and performance that would be required in a large virtual public cloud environment and obviously with an HA deployment model supported.

Northbound and southbound integration to third-party tools, with well-defined and documented message format and workflow that allow direct message interaction and web integration APIs, is an absolute basic requirement to build a functional system.

An IaaS assurance deployment requires a real-time and extensible data model that can support the following:

- Normalized object representation of multiple types of devices and domain managers, their components, and configuration
- Flexible enough to represent networking equipment, operating systems, data center environmental equipment, standalone and chassis servers, and domain managers such as vSphere, vCloud Director, and Cisco UCS
- Able to manage multiple overlapping relationships among and between managed resources
- Peer relationships, such as common membership in groups
- Parent-child relationships, such as the relationship between a UCS chassis and blade
- Fixed dependency relationships, such as the relationship between a process and an operating system
- Mobile dependency relationships, such as the relationship between a VM and its current host system
- Cross-silo discovered relationships, such as the relationship between a virtual host and a logical unit number (LUN) that represents network attached logical storage volume
- Linkages between managed objects and management data streams, such as event database and performance metrics
- Security boundaries between sets of managed objects and subsets of users to enable use in multitenant environments
- Developer-extensible to allow common capabilities to be developed for all customers
- Field-extensible to enable services teams and customers to meet uncommon or unique requirements

The ability to define logical relationships among service elements to represent the technical definition of a service is a critical step in providing a service-oriented impact analysis.

Service elements include

- **Physical:** Systems, infrastructure, and network devices
- **Logical:** Aspects of a service that must be measured or evaluated
- **Virtual:** Software components, for example, processes
- **Reference:** Elements represented by other domain managers

In addition, to understand the service components, the service element relationships are both fixed and dynamic and need to be tracked. Fixed relationships identify definitions, such as the fact that this web application belongs to this service. Dynamic relationships are managed by the model, such as identifying as an example which Cisco UCS chassis is hosting an ESX server where a virtual machine supporting this service is currently running.

Service policies evaluate the state of and relationships among elements and provide impact roll-up so that the services affected by a low-level device failure are known. They assist in root cause identification so that from the service a multilevel deep failure in the infrastructure can be seen to provide up, down, and degraded service states. (For example, if a single web server in a load-balanced group is down, the service might be degraded.) Finally, service policies provide event storm filtering, roll-up, and windowing functions.

All this information, service elements, relationships, and service policies provide service visualization that allows operations to quickly determine the current state of a service, service elements, and current dynamic network and infrastructure resources, and in addition allow service definition and tuning. A good example of a service assurance tool that supports these attributes and capabilities can be found at www.zenoss.com.

Evolution of the Services Platform

Organizations tend to adopt a phased strategy when building a utility service platform. Figure 3-13 shows a four-step approach that actually is a simplification of the actual journey to be undertaken by the end customer. How such a goal is realized does heavily depend on the current state of the architecture. For example, are we starting from a greenfield or brownfield deployment? What services are to be offered to whom, at what price and when? All these factors need decided up front during the service creation phase.

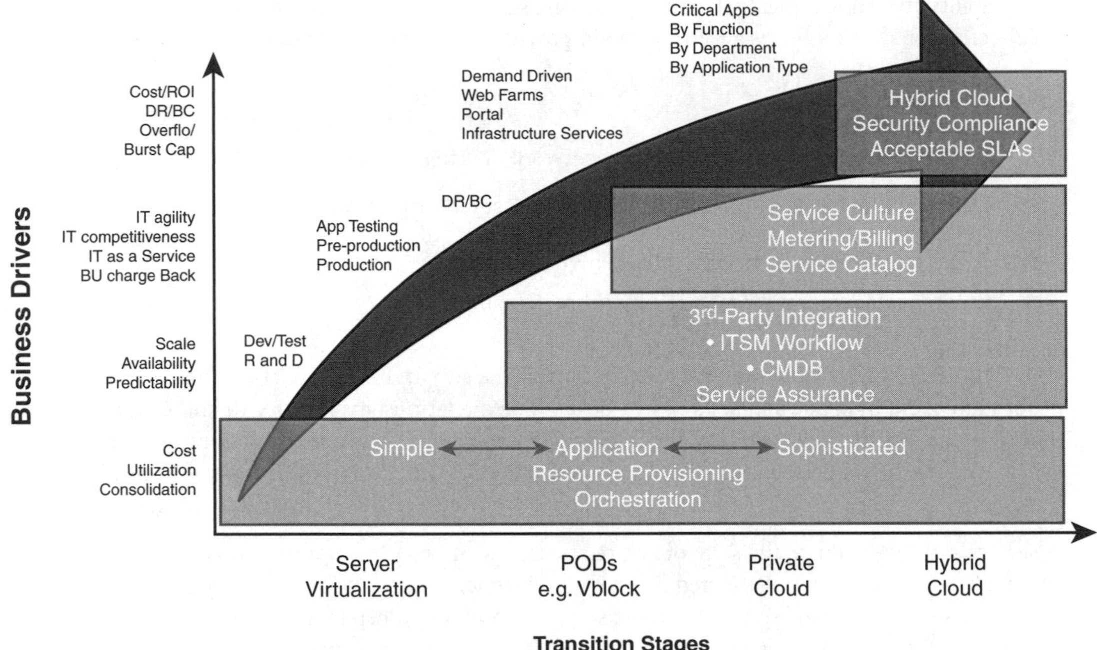

Figure 3-13 *Evolving Customer Needs from Service Platform*

The phasing closely maps to the IT industry evolution we discussed earlier in this chapter:

1. Virtualization of the end-to-end infrastructure
2. Automation of the service life cycle from provisioning to assurance
3. Deployment and integration of the service infrastructure, that is, customer portal, billing, and CRM
4. Deployment of intercloud technologies and protocols to enable migration of workloads and their dependencies

Migration of existing applications onto the new services platform requires extensive research and planning in regard not only to the technical feasibility but also the feasibility in regard to current operational and governance constraints which, with this authors' experience to date, prove to be the most challenging aspects to get right. It is essential that technical and business stakeholders work together to ensure success.

Building a virtualization management strategy at tool set is key to success for the first phase. The benefits gained through virtualization can be lost without an effective virtualization management strategy. Virtual server management requires changes in policies surrounding operations, naming conventions, chargeback, and security. Although many server and desktop virtualization technologies come with their own sets of management capabilities, businesses should also evaluate third-party tools to plug any gaps in management. These tools should answer questions such as, "How much infrastructure capacity and capability do I have?" or "What are the service dependencies?" in real time.

Virtualization, as discussed earlier, helps to deliver infrastructure multitenant capability. This means the ability to group and manage a set of constrained resources (normally virtual) that can be used exclusively by a customer and is isolated from other customer-assigned resources at both the data and management planes (for example, customer portal and life cycle management tools). A good example of a tool that can achieve this level of abstraction is the Cisco Cloud Portal (CCP) that provides RBAC-based entitlement views and management or, from a service activation approach example, network containers as aforementioned in this chapter.

The second phase is to introduce service automation through (ideally) end-to-end IT orchestration (also known as Run Book Automation) and service assurance tools. This phase is all about speed and quality of IT service delivery at scale, with predictability and availability at lower change management costs. In short, this is providing IT Service Management (ITSM) in a workflow-based structured way using best-practice methodologies.

This second phase is a natural progression of software tool development to manage data center infrastructure, physical and virtual. This development timeline is shown in Figure 3-14. The IT industry is now adopting 'programmatic' software to model underlying infrastructure capability and capacity. Within these software models, technology and business rules can be built within to ensure compliance and standardization of IT infrastructure. We discuss an example of this type programmatic model tooling in Chapter 5 when we discuss the 'Network Hypervisor' product.

The third phase is building and integrating service capabilities. Service-enabling tools include a customer portal and a service catalogue in conjunction with SLA reporting and metering, chargeback, and reporting. (*Service catalogue* is often an overused term that actually consists of multiple capabilities, for example, portfolio management, demand management, request catalogue, and life cycle management). From an operational perspective, integration of IT orchestration software (for example, Cisco Enterprise Orchestrator) along with smart domain/resource management tools completes the end-to-end service enablement of infrastructure. This third phase is about changing the culture of the business to one that is service lead rather than product lead. This requires organizational, process, and governance changes within the business.

Technology to support the fourth phase of this journey is only just starting to appear in the marketplace at the time of this writing. The ability to migrate workloads and service chains over large distances between (cloud) service providers requires an entire range of technological and service-related constraints that are being addressed. Chapter 5, "The Cisco Cloud Strategy," will discuss some of these constraints in detail.

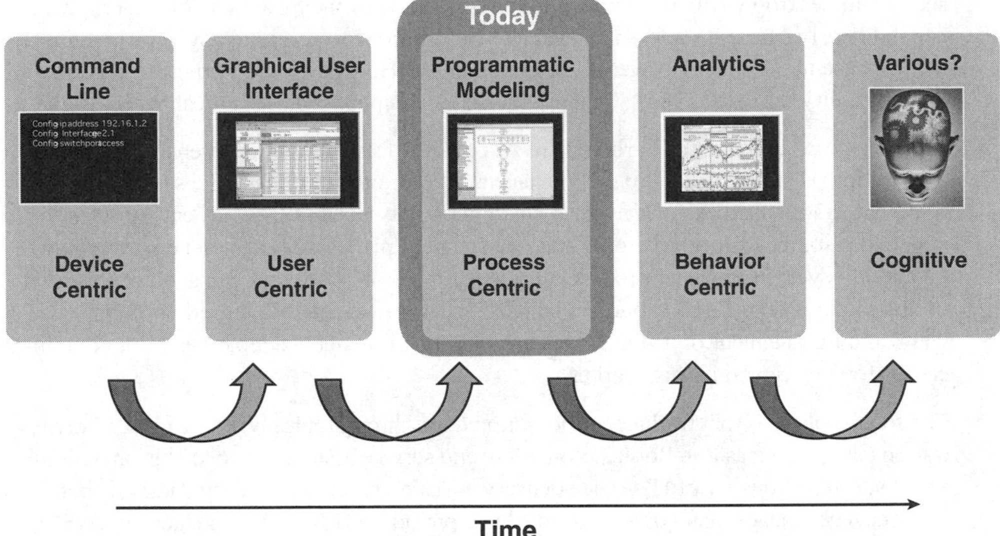

Figure 3-14 *Evolution of Data Center Management Tools*

Summary

Cisco believes that the network platform is a foundational component of a utility service platform as it is critical to providing intelligent connectivity within and beyond the data center. With the right built-in and external tools, the network is ideally placed to provide a secure, trusted, and robust services platform.

The network is the natural home for management and enforcement of policies relating to risk, performance, and cost. Only the network sees all data, connected resources, and user interactions within and between clouds. The network is thus uniquely positioned to monitor and meter usage and performance of distributed services and infrastructure. An analogy for the network in this context would be the human body's autonomic nervous system (ANS) that acts as a system (functioning largely below the level of consciousness) that controls visceral (inner organ) functions. ANS is usually divided into sensory (afferent) and motor (efferent) subsystems that is analogous to visibility and control capabilities we need from a services platform to derive a desired outcome. Indeed, at the time of this writing, there is a lot of academic research into managing complex network systems, might they be biological, social, or traditional IT networking. Management tools for the data center and wider networks have moved from a user-centric focus (for example, GUI design) to today's process-centric programmatic capabilities. In the future, the focus will most likely shift toward behavioral- and then cognitive-based capabilities.

The network also has a pivotal role to play in promoting resilience and reliability. For example, the network, with its unique end-to-end visibility, helps support dynamic orchestration and redirection of workloads through embedded policy-based control capabilities. The network is inherently aware of the physical location of resources and users. Context-aware services can anticipate the needs of users and deploy resources appropriately, balancing end-user experience, risk management, and the cost of service.

Chapter 4

IT Services

Upon completing this chapter, you should be able to understand the following:

- How and why IT services and data are classified
- Service roles, function, and value within a business
- The four cornerstones of cloud economics
- Contextualization of workload placement

This chapter describes the classification of Information Technology (IT) services from both business-centric and technology-centric perspectives. This chapter looks at the underpinning economics of Infrastructure as a Service (IaaS) and the contextual aspects of making a "workload" placement in the cloud, that is, risk versus cost.

Classification of IT Services and Information

Workload placement, or rather IT service placement, becomes a critical decision point when managing cloud-based services. The challenge is a simple one: Should an application or IT service be placed on the private cloud or in a hosted cloud environment? The result of this decision can be simplified to a cost-versus-risk equation. Like all decision-making processes, the quality and/or reliability of the outcome of a decision is heavily dependent on the information provided in forming that decision. Hence, there is a lot of discussion regarding the *transparency* of an operational service from the provider to the customer and how this could be achieved through standardization of classification and notification methodologies.

We will first discuss the concept of *risk* (defined in this context as the exposure to the chance of financial loss) and how can this be classified and quantified (qualitative and quantitative), and then we will discuss the *cost* within the context of cloud economic fundamentals.

Classification of IT services (information and information systems) is mainly associated with classes or tranches of risk related to the loss or theft of information and the criticality (potential impact) of the service in performing the work of the enterprise (that is, make money).

Put another way, the purpose of classification is to ostensibly protect information and information services from being able to degrade or endanger the function of the enterprise through leakage or failure.

Risk Assessment and Classification of Information

Security risk analysis, otherwise known as *risk assessment*, is fundamental to the security of any corporation. It is essential in ensuring that controls and expenditures are fully commensurate with the risks to which the corporation is exposed. Risk analysis is normally conducted in either a qualitative (looks at vulnerabilities, threats, and controls) or quantitative (probability [per annum] * single loss expectancy = annualized loss expectancy) manner.

Figure 4-1 shows a high-level view of a *security-profiling model* used to classify data and its information security controls.

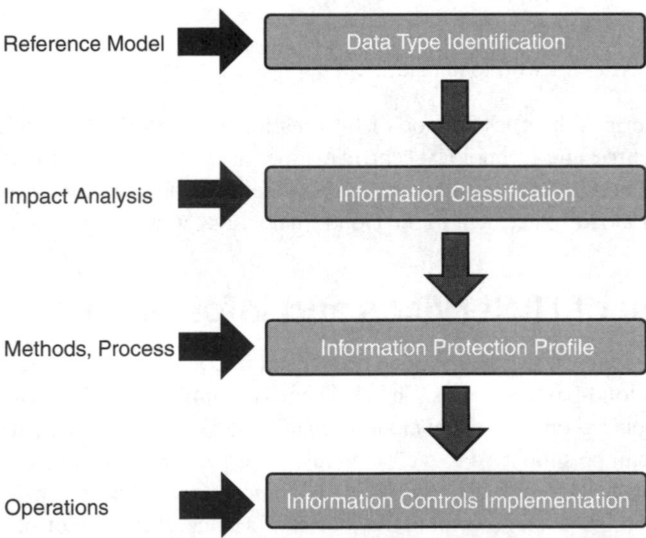

Figure 4-1 *Security Profiling Model for Classifying Data and Assessing Its Security Controls*

As a first step, an organization needs a reference model to identify the different types of data that might exist. (Data is the lowest level of abstraction; by itself, it carries no meaning, whereas information does convey meaning. Knowledge is the highest form of abstraction, carrying meaning as well as conveying application value.) Customer data is an example that is heavily protected by law in many countries. Customer information and knowledge—when, where, and what he purchased, for example—would be of great value to a corporation for analytics and marketing purposes.

As an example of classification of risk, governments convey the potential impact of information misuse through unambiguous classifications known as *Information Assurance Levels (IAL)* that correspond to a set of countermeasures and controls that are designed to mitigate the risk of such an exposure. Although classification systems vary from country to country, most have IALs that correspond in a similar fashion to the following British government definitions (from the highest level to lowest) called *Business Impact Levels (BIL)*:

- **BIL6, Top Secret (TS):** The highest level of classification of material on a national level. Such material would cause "exceptionally grave damage" to national security if made publicly available.
- **BIL5, Secret:** Such material would cause "grave damage" to national security if it were publicly available.
- **BIL4, Confidential:** Such material would cause "damage" or be "prejudicial" to national security if made publicly available.
- **BIL3, Restricted:** Such material would cause "undesirable effects" if made publicly available. Some countries do not have such a classification.
- **BIL2, Protect:** Information or material that if compromised, would likely cause substantial distress to individuals or, for example, breach statutory restrictions on the disclosure of information.
- **BIL1, Protect:** Technically not a classification level, but is used for government documents that do not have a classification listed previously. Such documents can sometimes be viewed by those without security clearance.
- **BIL0, Unclassified:** Information that is available to the general public and would not cause any harm or infringe any law were it to be intentionally or accidentally disclosed to the general public.

Further details are publicly available at www.cesg.gov.uk/policy_technologies/policy/media/business_impact_tables.pdf.

This document provides useful contextual guidance through *subcategories* (use cases for public sector bodies). We will discuss BILs in more detail later in this chapter.

Similarly, for the U.S. government, information classification levels are set out in Executive Order 13526 (amended in 2009). In Section 1.2, Classification Levels information can be classified at one of three levels:

- **"Top Secret"** shall be applied to information, the unauthorized disclosure of which reasonably could be expected to cause exceptionally grave damage to the national security that the original classification authority is able to identify or describe.

- **"Secret"** shall be applied to information, the unauthorized disclosure of which reasonably could be expected to cause serious damage to the national security that the original classification authority is able to identify or describe.
- **"Confidential"** shall be applied to information, the unauthorized disclosure of which reasonably could be expected to cause damage to the national security that the original classification authority is able to identify or describe. (The U.S. government classifies NATO partner information as Restricted as Confidential.)
- **"Unclassified"** is technically not a classification level.

Governance, Risk, and Compliance in the Enterprise

As IT architects and systems designers, we tend to think of *risk* in terms of IT *security* controls (for example, AAA, firewalls, and so on). However, we must first of all consider the business aspects of risk that relate to governance and compliance (also known as Governance, Risk, Compliance [GRC]). As IT becomes more critical to the business and in many cases counts for more than 50 percent of capital budget, business leaders will subject IT to more oversight, so it is important to understand the role and function of the various frameworks available to deliver effective oversight. The sections that follow (Governance, Risk, and Compliance) cover some relevant frameworks and methodologies to help us deal with corporate oversight.

Governance

Corporate governance consists of the set of internal processes, policies, and external laws and institutions that influence the way people administer a corporation. Corporate governance also includes the relationships among the many actors involved (the stakeholders) and the corporate goals. The main actors include the shareholders, management, and the board of directors, as well as external actors such as regulatory bodies.

IT governance is to assure the investment in IT generate real business value and mitigate the risks that are associated with IT projects.

The sections that follow examine some of the governance frameworks in more detail.

As a side note, for all frameworks and methodologies, there are champions and detractors of each. What you and your corporation will utilize or how it is implemented is down to individuals and the corporate culture that exists.

COBIT (Control Objectives for Information and Related Technology)

COBIT is positioned as the overarching governance framework. COBIT is readily accessible to both business and IT professionals, containing a wealth of supporting documentation and tools that assist in enabling adoption. COBIT was originally developed by the Information Systems Audit and Control Association (ISACA) in 1996 and is today owned by the IT Governance Institute (ITGI).

The ITGI has also developed and built into the COBIT framework a set of management guidelines for COBIT that consist of maturity models, critical success factors (CSF), key goal indicators (KGI), and key performance indicators (KPI).

Thus, COBIT addresses the full spectrum of IT governance processes, but only from a high-level business perspective, emphasizing audit and control. Other frameworks address a subset of processes in more detail, including ITIL for IT service management and delivery and ISO 17799 for IT security.

ITIL (Information Technology Infrastructure Library)

ITIL is a series of eight books that provide best practices for IT service management and delivery. ITIL provides the foundation for quality IT service management. ITIL was initially developed and published by the British Office of Government Commerce (OGC). In 2000, it was revised in conjunction with the British Standards Institute (BSI) and incorporated within BS15000. ITIL V3 is the current incarnation.

The eight ITIL books include the following:

1. Planning to Implement Service Management
2. The Business Perspective
3. Software Asset Management
4. Service Support
5. Service Delivery
6. Security Management
7. ICT Infrastructure Management
8. Application Management

TOGAF (The Open Group Architecture Framework)

TOGAF is a methodology to develop an enterprise architecture. The purpose of an enterprise architecture is to optimize across the enterprise the often-fragmented legacy of processes (both manual and automated) into an integrated environment that is responsive to change and supportive of the delivery of the business strategy (that is, increase the likelihood of project delivery and thus reduce risk).

TOGAF (v9 is the latest) has at its core the *Architecture Development Method (ADM)*. The purpose of the preliminary phase of the ADM is to define how architecture is developed within an enterprise, that is, the actual framework to work within and architectural principles. It is in this phase that IT governance is incorporated and adhered to. In other words, develop an IT architectural vision that aligns with the business architecture, drivers, and goals.

Risk

In an enterprise, risk management requires a thorough understanding of business requirements, potential threats, and vulnerabilities that might be exploited, along with an evaluation of the likelihood and impact of a risk being realized. Some corporations might issue a risk appetite statement that allows it to communicate the overall level of risk that they are prepared to tolerate to achieve their business aims.

A Business Impact Analysis (BIA) report will identify the corporation's most crucial systems and processes and the effect an outage would have on the organization and classify them within *Business Impact Levels (BIL)*. The greater the potential impact, the more money a company should spend to restore a system or process quickly. For example, a large hedge fund might decide to pay for completely redundant IT systems that would allow it to immediately start processing trades at another location if the primary location fails. A BIA will help companies set a restoration sequence to determine which parts of the business should be restored first.

Enterprises in larger organizations have a dedicated *Risks Assessment Team (RAT)* to undertake the risk assessment process on a regular basis. During this process, three types of qualitative and quantitative tests can typically be employed:

- **Penetration testing:** Penetration testing tests for the *depth* of vulnerabilities in specific applications, hosts, or systems. This type of testing poses the greatest risk to the resource and should be used sparingly.
- **Vulnerability Analysis (VA):** A vulnerability analysis considers the *breadth* of scope and might include testing methods ranging from simple network scanning using automated or manual tools to complex testing through automated electronic means.
- **Risk Assessment Model (RAM):** A RAM combines the requirements of ISO 27001:2005 with an enterprise's information security requirements using various frameworks (standardized or in-house). This tends to lead to a process that is organization unique, having its own scoring model to identify strengths and weaknesses in the overall information security posture.

ISO 27001

According to www.27001-online.com, "the basic objective of the [ISO 27001] standard is to help establish and maintain an effective information management system, using a continual improvement approach ['Plan-Do-Check-Act']. It implements OECD (Organization for Economic Cooperation and Development) principles, governing security of information and network systems." It includes an information classification taxonomy that is similar to the national government information classification models we discussed at the beginning of this chapter. However, this taxonomy is more focused for use in the corporate enterprise and is shown in Table 4-1.

Table 4-1 *ISO 27001:2005 A.7.2.1 Information Classification Policy*

Information Category	Description	Examples
Unclassified Public	Information is not confidential and can be made public without any implications for the company. Loss of availability because of system downtime is an acceptable risk. Integrity is important but not vital.	Product brochures widely distributed Information widely available in the public domain, including publicly available company website areas Sample downloads of company software that is for sale Financial reports required by regulatory authorities Newsletters for external transmission
Proprietary	Information is restricted to management-approved internal access and protected from external access. Unauthorized access could influence the company's operational effectiveness, cause an important financial loss, provide a significant gain to a competitor, or cause a major drop in customer confidence. Information integrity is vital.	Passwords and information on enterprise security procedures Know-how used to process client information Standard operating procedures used in all parts of the enterprise's business All enterprise-developed software code, whether used internally or sold to clients
Client Confidential Data	Information received from clients in any form for processing in production by the company. The original copy of such information must not be changed in any way without written permission from the client. The highest possible levels of integrity, confidentiality, and restricted availability are vital.	Client media Electronic transmissions from clients Product information generated for the client by company production activities as specified by the client

Table 4-1 *ISO 27001:2005 A.7.2.1 Information Classification Policy*

Information Category	Description	Examples
Company Confidential Data	Information collected and used by the company in the conduct of its business to employ people, to log and fulfill client orders, and to manage all aspects of corporate finance. Access to this information is very restricted within the company. The highest possible levels of integrity, confidentiality, and restricted availability are vital.	Salaries and other personnel data Accounting data and internal financial reports Confidential customer business data and confidential contracts Nondisclosure agreements with clients/vendors Company business plans / long-range planning

Compliance

From the Society of Corporate Compliance and Ethics (SCCE), *compliance* is defined simply as "the process of meeting the expectations of others." (Source: www.corporatecompliance.org.)

There is a raft of different regulations that require compliance depending on geography and industry, for example, legal compliance by the enactment or enforcement of laws of a particular jurisdiction.

Data privacy laws directly impact how IT infrastructure is configured and operated. Data has legal protection that is in the form of privacy laws. For example, Germany has the Bundesdatenschutzgesetz (BDSG), and the U.K. has the Data Protection Act 1998 (DPA).

In addition to national data privacy laws, industry verticals also have their own regulatory bodies. Popular examples include Sarbanes-Oxley (SOX), Payment Card Industry Data Security Standard (PCI DSS), and Health Insurance Portability and Accountability Act (HIPAA). Corporations that are subject to these regulatory frameworks have to consider the level of internal controls (IT and non-IT) necessary to protect the identified data against compromise and inappropriate use, that is, protect its confidentiality, integrity, and availability.

Regulatory regimes and legal and taxation jurisdictions tend to be, because of their providence, geographically bound, and thus the physical location of a service or the workload will determine the controls needed to be compliant. Accordingly, when making a *workload* placement decision (*workload* is a business term for a virtual machine [VM] containing one or more applications coupled with supporting services, for example, storage and security), the data owner or custodian must be cognizant of the regulatory requirements of a given geographic location of the service versus the corresponding compliance of the offered service in addition to the standard IT capabilities and their capacity (vCPU, memory, I/O, IOPS) offered as part of the SLA.

Furthermore, end customers will potentially be evaluating service offers from different providers. To enable efficient arbitrage between competing offers within any marketplace, a common ontology is required. Simply put, the industry needs standards to provide service transparency, not only from the perspective of the offer (ontology describing the SLA) but also in terms of the operational status of active services (that is, if an infrastructure component fails causing a breech of the SLA, the incident needs to be reported and, if applicable, penalties or reparations made).

Service providers have been looking at ways by which they standardize information regarding the cloud service SLA that incorporates capabilities related to risk management.

An example of an industry body defining standards would be the Cloud Security Alliance, which has developed the *GRC Stack* (www.cloudsecurityalliance.org/grcstack.zip). The GRC Stack provides a tool kit for enterprises, cloud service providers, security solution providers, IT auditors, and other key stakeholders to instrument and assess both private and public clouds against industry-established best practices, standards, and critical compliance requirements.

The Cloud Security Alliance GRC Stack is an integrated suite of three CSA initiatives:

- **CSA CloudAudit:** Allows cloud service providers to automate the process of audit, assertion, assessment, and assurance.
- **CSA Controls Matrix:** Provides fundamental security principles to guide cloud vendors and to assist prospective cloud customers in assessing the overall security risk of a cloud provider—categorized into 11 control areas from compliance to security architecture.
- **CSA Consensus Assessment Initiative:** The Cloud Security Alliance Consensus Assessments Initiative (CAI) was launched to perform research, create tools, and create industry partnerships to enable cloud-computing assessments.

Assessment and Classification of Services

Referring to Figure 4-2, we can categorize (simplified for illustrative purposes) a service or application within the contextualization of the enterprise's value needs. A *core* service or application helps the enterprise sustain a competitive advantage in the marketplace. In other words, if a core application fails, it will inhibit the capability of the enterprise to differentiate itself and therefore compete effectively. Examples of a core application can include, but not be limited to Enterprise Resource Planning (ERP) systems or collaboration systems and their implementation.

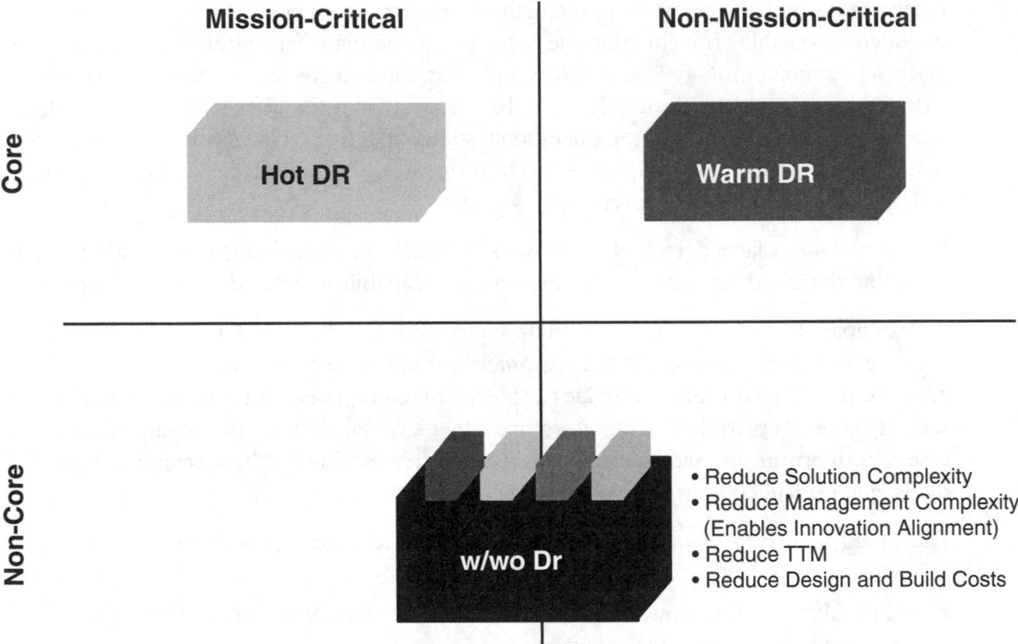

Figure 4-2 *IT Service Mapping: A Simplified View*

A method to define the value of an IT service or application is to categorize it from the perspective of its *service role* (see Table 4-2). This process allows a better understanding of whether an IT service or application is core or context to the enterprise, but with more granularity. Therefore, this provides a simple way to plan future investments, moving away from *systems of record* toward more *core* service classes, namely, *systems of differentiation* and *systems innovation*. Keep in mind that these systems still need to work together in a cohesive and efficient way as possible. Thus meta-frameworks, meta-models, and meta-data alongside governance standards and architectural principles are also required.

Table 4-2 *System Value Classification*

	System of Record	System of Differentiation	System of Innovation
Definition	Foundational, standardized, repeatable, structured	Value added, autonomous, more dynamic, less structured	Step change in behavior or function

Table 4-2 *System Value Classification*

Example	Core ERP (for example, employee, asset, and order supplier databases) Core IT (for example, CMDB)	Market analytics system Talent management/ HR systems R&D systems Intellectual property life cycle management systems Customer service systems (for example, customer care, billing)	Service development systems Predictive forecast modeling systems Collaboration tools and systems
Analytics	Reporting, historical	Planning, budgeting	Predictive, scenario-based
Content	Static/stable	Both	Dynamic
Strategic Focus	Improve execution	Better design	New idea
Summary	"I know what I want, and it doesn't have to be unique."	"I know what I want, but it needs to be different from everyone else's."	"I don't know exactly what I want. I need to experiment."

*Source: ERP Strategies: Exploit Innovations in Enterprise Software, by Jim Shepherd, VP & Distinguished Analyst, Gartner

Referring to Figure 4-2 again, on the horizontal axis, *mission-critical* provides a temporal contextualization, that is, the *criticality* of the application or service in relation to the operational execution of the business. Put simply, how long can the enterprise cope without a particular IT service being operational? What is the maximum permissible *downtime* of a service?

This directly relates to both the high-availability (HA) capabilities built into each service component and its dependencies. Further, this relates to disaster recovery (DR) investments required to manage the Recovery Point Objective (RPO)—how frequently to back up data as well as the Recovery Time Objective (RTO) and how long will it take to get the service back up and running—of a particular IT service or services because of an unplanned outage. In other words, how often is a system backed up or the state of the system replicated? How quickly can the IT system be brought back into operation after failure? As a practical example, Cisco IT uses a criticality index to classify its business services that are made up of the application(s) and supporting dependencies, for example, network, network services, database, storage, and so on, as outlined in Table 4-3.

These classifications might also aid in determining whether an enterprise wants to consume a "black box" solution from a third-party vendor. In-house applications that contain intellectual property of the enterprise, normally viewed as a core application (a system of differentiation or innovation), would require *characterization* (base lining, benchmarking) and interoperability testing for a third-party organization to develop an SLA to manage the in-house application or service either *on-prem* or *off-prem* (private or hosted cloud—also known as a hybrid cloud model).

Table 4-3 *Resiliency Framework: Service Criticality Levels, Cisco IT*

C-Level	Term	Impact Description
C1	Mission Imperative	Any outage results in the immediate cessation of a primary function,* equivalent to the immediate and critical impact to revenue generation, brand name, and/or customer satisfaction; no downtime is acceptable under any circumstances.
C2	Mission Critical	Any outage results in the immediate cessation of a primary function, equivalent to a major impact to revenue generation, brand name, and/or customer satisfaction.
C3	Business Critical	Any outage results in the cessation over time or an immediate reduction of a primary function, equivalent to a minor impact to revenue generation, brand name, and/or customer satisfaction.
C4	Business Operational	A sustained outage** results in the immediate cessation of a primary function.
C5	Business Administrative	A sustained outage has little or no impact on a primary function.

*Primary function: A function (for example, a business process) that is directly aligned with the organization's top-level objective. For Cisco, the top-level objective is to generate revenue, be profitable, and grow.

**Sustained: 24 hours or more.

From an infrastructure resource perspective, when planning to place a workload on a cloud service platform, you need to map the baseline performance and scalability requirements to infrastructure capabilities. Figure 4-3 provides an abstract representation of this concept. This enables an administrator to see quickly whether a particular Integrated Compute Stack (ICS) or point of delivery (POD) can support certain application workloads or whether enhancements need to be made to the infrastructure to meet those requirements.

When thinking about *consuming* a cloud service, in this case IaaS, you need to take into account an application's or a service's criticality level to the business, how *core* or *context* it is, and also what information assurance level it requires in addition to IT-centric metrics like performance and scalability.

If you look at Figure 4-4, you will see a three-dimensional model with the three axes representing criticality, role, and information assurance. The sphere represents a service or an application (let's call it Service A). So from this model, any workload that is mapped in the near upper left would be "business imperative" (taking the Cisco IT definition as an example) as well as being core to the business (that is, enabling the business to differentiate itself in the marketplace). Finally, the data the workload contains is company confidential and so requires a high security posture level (referring to confidentiality and integrity).

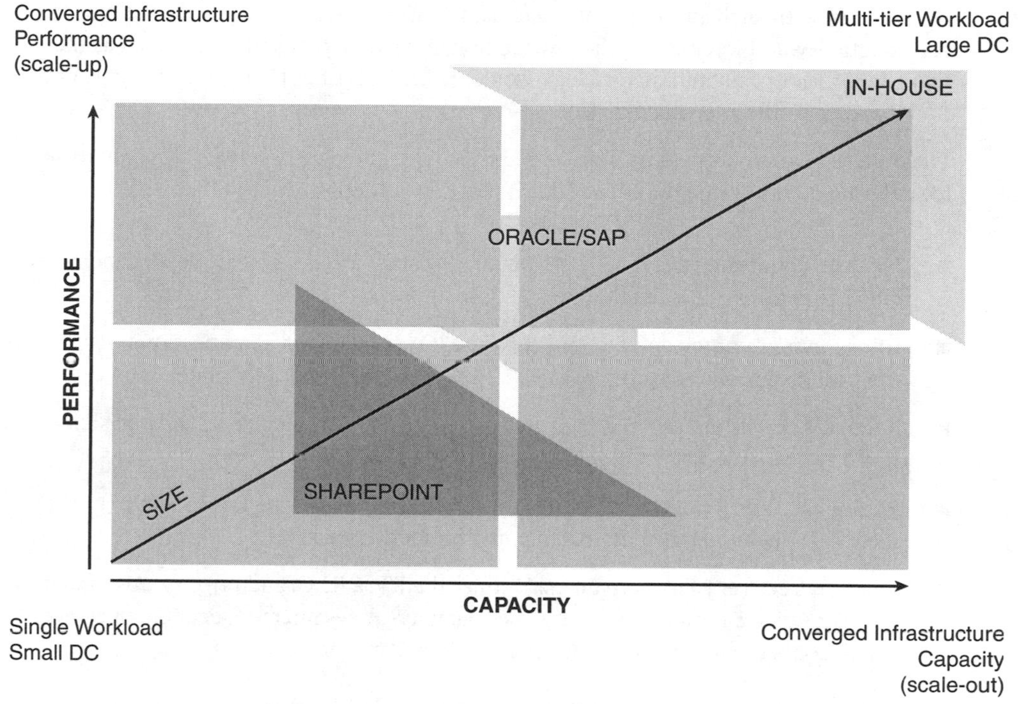

Figure 4-3 *Application Mapping to Infrastructure Capability and Capacity*

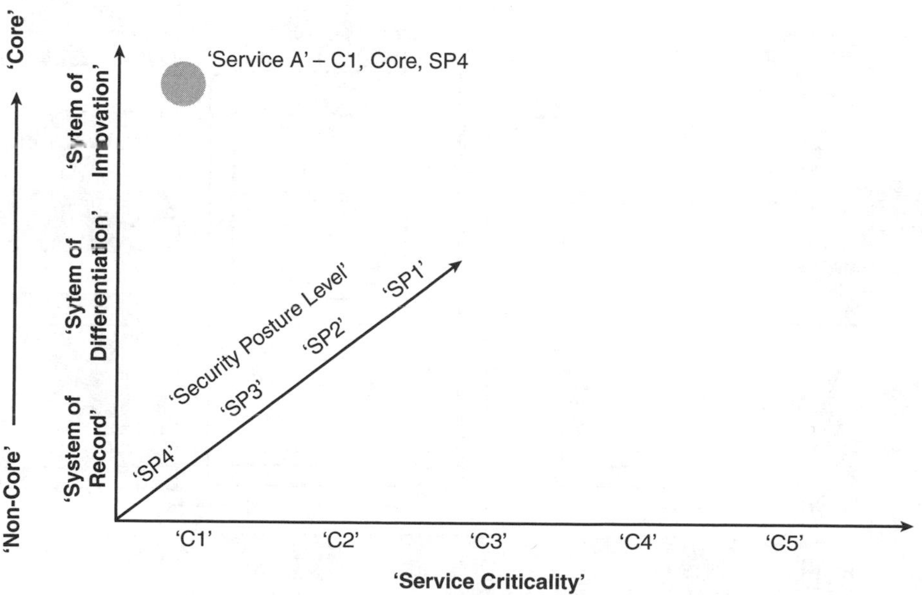

Figure 4-4 *Three-Dimensional Service/Application Mapping*

A workload with such an aforementioned classification cannot have any downtime. The confidentiality and integrity of the information must at all times be maintained as the financial impact of an information leak would be critical if not terminal to the corporation if either of these events did occur.

These service attributes would help to determine the correlation service mapping to service offering attributes (in the case of IaaS) that can be defined by the following:

- **Network containers:** Defines performance, scalability, and service dependencies (attributes and variables, qualitative and quantitative).
- **Interconnect containers:** Defines the type (OSI Layer 2 or 3), connectivity type, and method protocol (for example, LISP, VPLS, OTV, and so on) to remote data centers.
- **Security zones:** Defines the security posture, policy enforcement, and decision point types, as well as their implementation and operation.
- **High-availability domains:** Defines the application or service HA model (for example, N+1), including the data backup and protection services.
- **Disaster recovery link activators:** Defines the RTO, RPO, and priority class and initiates DR service between two network containers. Uses interconnect containers for WAN connectivity to remote disaster recovery data center sites.

Figure 4-5 illustrates the aforementioned service capabilities that form the services architecture building blocks.

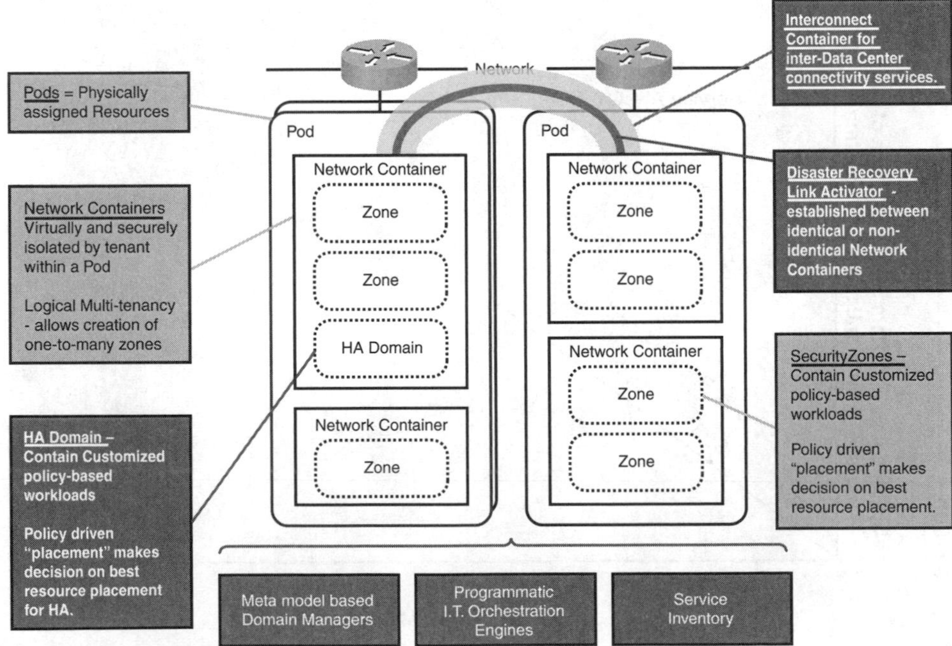

Figure 4-5 *Service Architecture Capability Building Blocks*

The trick is being able to translate and correlate the service offering (service [level] description) to the desired service requirements for a particular workload. As previously mentioned, nonstandard definitions and a lack of normative references make this an odious task today. Recently, the Tele-Management Forum (TMF) has been doing some work on standardized service definitions. We will discuss the development of the marketplace in Chapter 5, "The Cisco Cloud Strategy."

These required service attributes might also differ during the life cycle of a particular service or application. This process can be described as the *service gestation* period. As an example, Cisco IT would typically move an application through multiple proving stages called alpha, ACE, and production. Each of these stages has certain governance rules associated with them. More typical naming conventions would be research and development (R&D), alpha and beta (trial), and then finally general availability (GA) or production.

All this complexity is down to the fact that we are mapping traditional enterprise-class Service Orientated Architecture (SOA) onto the new web/cloud horizontal service platforms. This legacy will be with us for some time just as many mainframe applications are still with us today. The laws of "Cloudonomics" and its associated *scale-out* architectural principles such as *designed to fail* will take some time to realize as a new wave of applications that are built for the cloud model slowly supersede existing application workloads. In the intervening period, we have to operationalize these existing applications into our new cloud operational paradigm, achieving the bipolar goals of standardization and flexibility.

Four Cornerstones of Cloud Economics

When making a workload placement decision, we also need to look at the costs as well as the risks, as we have just been discussing. The fundamentals of cloud economics can be summarized to four different areas:

- Cost per unit of IT service
- Financing of workload variability
- Time value of money
- Innovation

Figure 4-6 depicts the first two of the four cornerstones, unit service costs and financing the variability or workload (peak, trough, frequency).

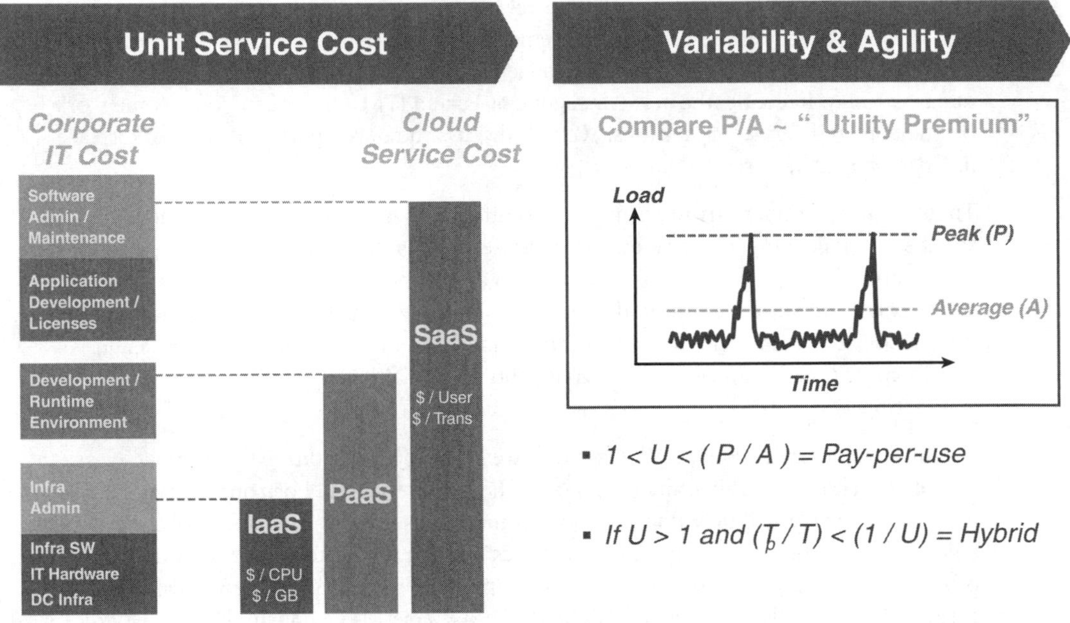

Figure 4-6 *Cloud Economics: Unit Cost and Financing Variability*

Sources: Cisco IBSG, Wouter Belmans

Let's look at the costs associated with Infrastructure as a Service (IaaS). It is assumed that because of scale and the complexity in building automated workflows that public cloud providers can offer IT services at a lower cost per unit than can be achieved by an enterprise offering in-house service. However, a number of studies have shown this not to be true in all cases. Economies of scale start to show diminishing returns after an enterprise has reached a certain consumption volume, thus enabling better buying power for IT resources.

Counterintuitively, a pure "pay as you use" solution also makes sense, even if unit costs are higher than can be achieved by in-house IT. This is because you have to take into account the cost of financing the workload variability, both from a peak-to-average ratio workload perspective and from a temporal/frequency perspective (that is, how often the workload peaks are reached).

The reason for this is straightforward. The fixed-capacity dedicated solution must be built to the peak workload, whereas the cloud service provider needs to build a capacity to the average of the peaks (this obviously assumes a good level of distribution of the total workloads placed on the infrastructure to reduce the variability).

However, some cloud services are required to be metered and billed in fractal units of time for consumers so that they can benefit from the utility nature of the service (near-real-time service activation and teardown). Typically, utility services would be billed on an hourly basis or even by the minute. This utility service example directly relates to the our third area of cloud economics, the time value of money.

If an enterprise can leverage extra processing capacity when needed, faster than it can deliver it itself, the enterprise would be willing to pay a premium for that capability. Fundamentally, it is about reaching business decisions quicker with greater accuracy. This concept is depicted in Figure 4-7 along with the concept of innovation.

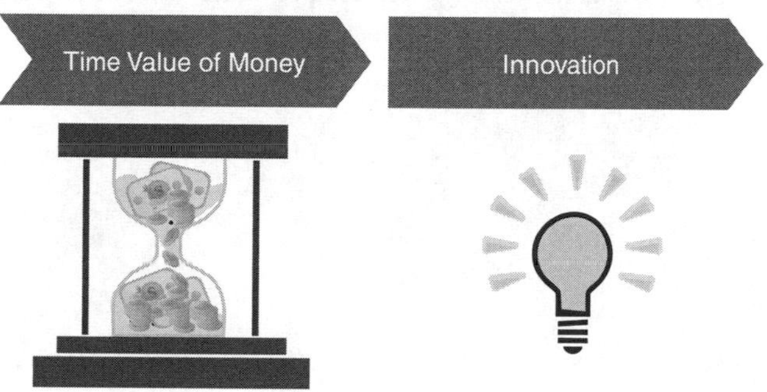

Figure 4-7 *Cloud Economics: Time Value of Money and Innovation*

The fourth and final cornerstone of cloud economics is probably the least realized. The cloud is essentially predicated on web applications that have undergone a major shift in thinking regarding scaling. *Scale-up* (vertical scaling, that is, adding more resources to a single node in a system) enterprise-type architectures are limited in growth capability versus *scale-out* (a.k.a. horizontal scaling, that is, adding more nodes). Horizontal scaling coupled with the utility delivery model of IT services (the theoretical capability to burst for additional capacity in real time) somewhat change the landscape of resource availability to developers.

For example, if for the same cost, rather than having ten CPUs available for 10,000 hours, a developer could procure 10,000 CPUs for ten hours. This paradigm shift in IT resource consumption benefits a subset of use cases such as large scale-out "big data" application research and development projects that require lots of computational power if only for a short period of time (for example, Monte Carlo trading algorithms, geological analysis programs, and so on). The real-time consumption model removes the economic barrier to such application development requirements.

Summary

In the end, it boils down to the simple yet well-known trade-off: cost versus risk. Understanding what risks are associated with the consumption of a particular service is not an easy task, as we have discussed throughout this chapter. To avoid too much cost associated with classification of data and the search for the right service offer, the industry needs clear, easy-to-implement models and service descriptions within an agreed-upon service framework and ontology. Service providers will continue to develop risk profiles for customer workloads as the industry matures.

Chapter 5

The Cisco Cloud Strategy

"Simplicity and Flexibility through Abstraction"

Upon completing this chapter, you should be able to understand the following:

- How Cisco views the "cloud"
- How the Cisco approach to developing new technology, systems, and solutions is related to the cloud
- How Cisco is helping partners and customers deliver on the promises of the cloud

This chapter describes the Cisco Systems strategy regarding technological, system, and service developments related to the cloud. The chapter also briefly covers the technology evolution toward the cloud to understand how we got to where we are today.

A Brief History of IT Service Delivery

With hindsight, it is easy to see that cloud computing is simply the next big step in the evolution of the Internet. We, as consumers of information services, have moved from mainframes to desktops to mobile devices, such as tablets. On the web, we have moved from the delivery of content and applications to today, where it is now possible to even rent virtualized computing, network, and storage resources. This is actually quite remarkable and a real tribute to the original architects of the Internet to be able to have grown to the size it is today and thus be able to support these new Web 2.0–based models. The purpose of the original ARPANET was to provide remote access to other computers, so in many ways, we have come full circle.

We are reminded of an alleged quote (or more likely a misquote) by Thomas J. Watson of IBM fame in 1943: "*I think there is a world market for maybe five computers.*" This apparent misquote might be closer to the truth than anyone realized until now!

Nicolas Carr published a book in 2008 titled *The Big Switch: Rewiring the World from Edison to Google* (published by W.W. Norton & Co.). In the book, Nicholas Carr compares the starting transition in the IT industry with the evolution of the electrical power generation industry toward a utility model. The idea is simple—pay only for what you use, just as we do with electricity. The efficiency and cost savings of such a model are clear to understand, as we discussed in Chapter 4, "IT Services," in the section, "Four Cornerstones of Cloud Economics." However, efficiency and cost savings are not the only reasons why cloud computing is proving popular.

Figure 5-1 depicts an analogy of two boxers representing seemingly opposing approaches to the delivery and provision of information services to end users. The boxer on the left represents the disruption of the cloud model on more traditional enterprise information services delivery.

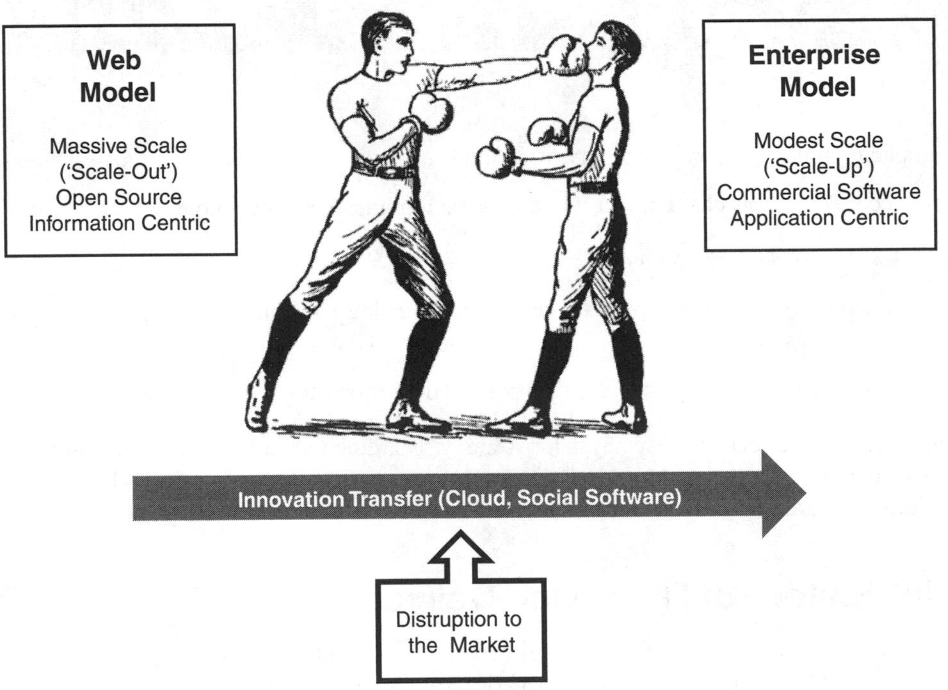

Figure 5-1 *Enterprise Versus the Web—The Web Wins Today's Battle*

If you compare and contrast the typical enterprise IT model of the last decade versus the recent emergence of the Web 2.0 model, you can see a number of bipolar approaches. The enterprise model was based on specific applications or service-oriented infrastructures featuring a vertical scale model (also known as scale-up) with per-application-based high availability (N+1) failover capabilities. This architectural approach achieved only modest scalability.

Contrast this with the web model's architectural principles and proven design capabilities: horizontal scaling (also known as scale-out), multilayer caching, eventual consistency, information-centric, shared infrastructure, and open APIs.

Note *Eventual consistency* is a form of weak consistency whereby an information update, a "write," is not immediately available for subsequent "reads." This relates to the CAP theorem (Consistency, Availability and Partition tolerance) introduced by Eric Brewer (University of California, Berkley) in 2000 whereby data consistency, systems availability (think scale and performance), and tolerance to network partitions are three competing properties of a system, of which only two can be achieved at any one time. In other words, for social networking services or even the Domain Name System (DNS) to scale on a global network basis, immediate global data consistency has to give way.

The web model is no accident. It has evolved to solve technological problems of the day; a good example is "big data." Large organizations increasingly face the need to maintain large amounts of structured and unstructured data to comply with government regulations. Recent court cases have legally mandated corporations in certain industry verticals (for example, the healthcare industry) to retain large masses of documents, email messages, and other forms of electronic communication that might be required in the event of possible litigation.

"Big data" is a (marketing) term applied to data sets whose size is beyond the capability of commonly used enterprise software tools to capture, manage, and process within a tolerable elapsed time. Big data sizes are a constantly moving target currently ranging from a few dozen terabytes to many petabytes of data in a single data set. Recently, new technologies being applied to big data include massively parallel processing (MPP) databases, compute grids, map-and-reduce file systems (inspiring commercialized applications like Apache Hadoop), along with cloud computing platforms coupled with the power of the Internet to help us to manage the "big data" challenge.

In short, enterprises are now adopting the web model, first pioneered mainly in the consumer social-media market and now adopted to solve or enhance the enterprise's capabilities, for example, to foster collaboration between employees as well as speed data processing and result accuracy. Essentially, enterprises need a model that provides capabilities that deliver IT value to the business in today's global marketplace.

Note that the new cloud paradigm does not negate the need for enterprise requirements such as regulatory adherence. As an example, corporations that are subject to the Sarbanes-Oxley (SOX) regulation are required to keep data archives (active or inactive) for up to seven years. Other than the commoditization of storage media prices, there is little room to maneuver to reduce costs.

In some cases, the nature of where the data is held in the cloud might require the customer to implement extra regulatory compliance.

Market and Technology Development

In planning any strategy regarding technology development, one needs to understand what the potential market demands are.

A *megatrend* is a major trend (a prevailing tendency) that is predicted to happen in the future with some degree of certainty because of the weight of historical and empirical evidence supporting it. Manufacturing moving from the Western world to China and other Far Eastern countries in the last couple of decades is an example of a megatrend. The interaction between megatrends is as important as each individual megatrend. That is why organizations of all kinds (commercial, governmental, and others) use megatrends when they develop working scenarios. The intersection of megatrends can be a starting point for analyzing what could be "market adjacencies," in other words, a major shift in how technology is delivered and how usage (consumption) patterns can change.

Megashocks, on the other hand, are the antithesis of megatrends—hard-to-predict risks defined by sudden and significant events, such as the earthquake and subsequent tsunami that tragically hit northeast Japan in March 2011. Japan supplies about 40 percent of the world's NAND memory (NAND is a specific type of flash memory based on the 'Not AND' logic gate) that is used in products such as Apple's iPad. The earthquake affected Toshiba's and SanDisk's factory in Yokkaichi, Mie Prefecture. Toshiba, by itself, supplies more than a third of the world's NAND memory chips. The collateral damage of such an event, therefore, can be far-reaching and pronounced.

The World Economic Forum publishes a "Global Risks Network" report on a yearly basis (www.weforum.org/issues/global-risks). As the world becomes more interconnected, the greater the impact of a megashock will be.

Information Growth and Complexity

The Cisco Virtual Networking Index (VNI) usage research provides quantitative insights into current activity on service provider networks and qualitative samples of consumers' online behavior. In this cooperative program, more than 20 global service providers share anonymous, aggregate data with Cisco to analyze current network usage trends and gauge future infrastructure requirements. Participating service providers serve millions of subscribers from around the world. They represent the mobile, wireline, and cable segments throughout North America, Latin America, Europe, Asia-Pacific, and various emerging markets.

The Cisco VNI also utilizes information in part upon data published by Informa Telecoms and Media, Strategy Analytics, Infonetics, Datamonitor, Gartner, IDC, Dell'Oro, Synergy, Nielsen, comScore, and the International Telecommunications Union (ITU). This helps provide what has proved to be a reliable indicator of future information growth on the Internet.

Using Cisco VNI, if you look at the growth in the amount of information that is being created and managed worldwide, measured by how much data is flowing across the network on a monthly basis, you can see that in 2010, there were approximately 21 exabytes of traffic crossing the Internet each month (approximately 4.8 billion DVDs), up from 5 exabytes of information in 2007, more than quadrupling (approximately a 400 percent increase) the amount of information in three years. Table 5-1 provides more everyday examples to convey the type of data set sizes characterized by the standard International System of Units used by the IT industry.

Table 5-1 *International System of Units (SI Prefixes)*

Name	Decimal Value	Binary Value	Example
Megabyte (MB)	10^6	2^{20}	1 MB is 0.16 hours (6 seconds) of CD-quality audio.
Gigabyte (GB)	10^9	2^{30}	1 GB is 1.9 hours (114 minutes) of CD-quality audio.
Terabyte (TB)	10^{12}	2^{40}	1 TB is 2000 hours of CD-quality audio.
Petabyte (PB)	10^{15}	2^{50}	1 PB is approximately 228 years of CD-quality audio.
Exabyte (EB)	10^{18}	2^{60}	1 EB is approximately 2280 centuries of CD-quality music.
Zettabyte (ZB)	10^{21}	2^{70}	It is a lot of music. Put another way, 66 ZB is the amount of visual information conveyed from the eyes to the brain of the entire human race in a single year.

By 2013, it is estimated that the flow of information globally is going to increase dramatically again to roughly 13 billion DVDs crossing the Internet on a monthly basis.

If you look at this picture as a whole, it's not a story about slow, predictable growth. We are talking about truly exponential growth in the amount of information that's flowing around the world. This presents both a challenge and an opportunity. In the midst of this deluge of data, the advantage goes to the organizations that can help individuals and businesses find the most relevant information. Speed and accuracy are king.

The makeup of Internet traffic itself is also changing. Historically, we mostly had FTP, HTTP, and peer-to-peer traffic. Today, video is already dominating the mix, and by 2013, it is estimated that video will represent more than 90 percent of all consumer Internet traffic.

This shift has broad implications. In the past, the IT department's job was to build a data and voice network that carried some video. But from now on, the IT department's job is to build a video network that might carry some data and some voice traffic. Safe to say, video not only changes the shape and behavior of traffic on networks, but video is forcing us to change the way we think, design, and operate networks.

To serve and manage the number of users searching through enormous amounts of data, we are now building vast data centers—industrial-scale machines. In fact, you could argue that cloud computing started with the needs of the largest Internet companies having to manage tens of thousands of servers. At this scale, you can begin to view large data centers or even multiple data centers as a single operational system, with many parts, running a highly distributed scale-out application. Because of the scale and complexity, the process of IT industrialization could only be accomplished with almost fully automated management systems. Given the numbers involved, failure of individual components becomes an everyday occurrence, and applications need to be designed in such a way as to be able to survive despite such failures. System management is still being improved and honed today. Having said this, aspects of cloud computing have actually been around for some time; it has just been called different things. We have been talking about the concept of *utility computing* for at least 20 years, and virtualization goes back to the mainframe era.

Added to the large number of Internet users and information growth, in 2010, approximately 35 billion devices are connected to the Internet (Source: Cisco IBSG). It is important to note that the aforementioned 35 billion devices go far beyond devices that we hold in our hands. It includes device-to-device and machine-to-machine communications, what is often referred to as the "Internet of Things."

Examples of machine-to-machine communications include everything from radio frequency ID (RFID) tags to wireless sensors now being deployed as part of SmartGrids to distribute energy more effectively. By 2013, it is estimated that the device total will grow to 50 billion devices, or approximately seven devices per person on earth. By 2020, it is estimated that there will be a trillion devices connected to the Internet. This has profound consequences on how we collaborate as communication devices, coverage, and channels become ubiquitous. The challenge becomes how to best manage all of these communication options and distributed data. In doing so, you need to think of the end user. The so-called Generation X people (born from 1965 to 1980) have very different perspectives on technology usage from the Generation Y (also known as millennials) end users. The millennials have no issues with blurring the distinction between personal and corporate usage of multitasking end devices. In fact, many business users do not see an issue using multifunctional devices for both personal and professional tasks; however, for IT departments charged with protecting corporate information assets, this is a perennial nightmare. Corporations need to develop new information assurance methodologies to embrace consumerization to enable the business to manage its risk profile in this new borderless world.

The Cisco Cloud Strategy: An Overview

In this chapter so far, we have discussed the major trends such as information growth and "consumerization" (consumer devices being used in the workplace) of IT and some of the challenges this presents information service management and delivery. In this section, we discuss what the Cisco Systems strategy is in response to those challenges, helping partners and customers build solutions (see Figure 5-2).

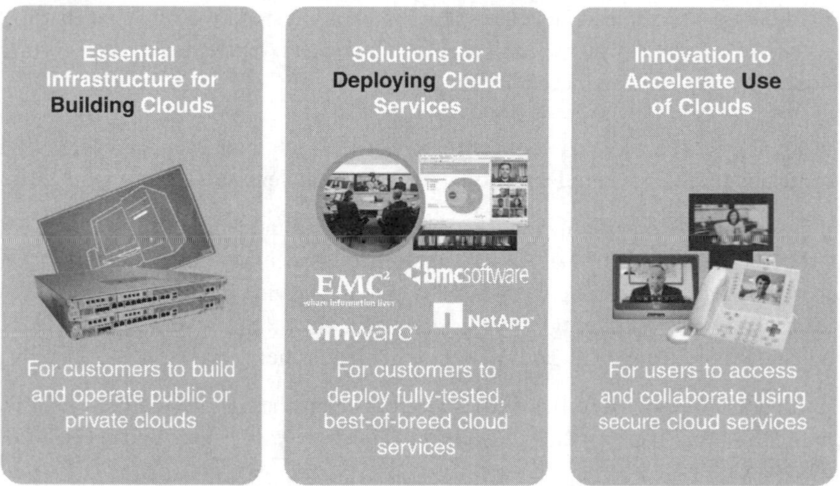

Figure 5-2 *Cisco Cloud Computing Strategy*

The Cisco cloud computing strategy has three core elements:

1. Essential infrastructure for building clouds: Cisco develops technology, both software and hardware, to create products and solutions to address customer needs that, for example, assist cloud builders deliver innovative and flexible service platforms. This technology applies to an enterprise building a private cloud or a service provider building a virtual private cloud or a public cloud infrastructure. Cisco is investing heavily to advance the market for the cloud by driving technology innovation that is based on open standards (addressing vendor and service provider lock-in concerns) alongside ecosystem development.

2. Solutions for deploying cloud services: Cisco is delivering systems and service platforms to organizations so that they can deliver their own secure cloud services capable of supporting enterprise-class service-level agreements (SLA), of which security is a core component. Cisco is enabling service providers and enterprises to deliver secure cloud solutions with end-to-end, top-to-bottom validated designs coupled with world-class professional services that are aligned to partner and end customer business goals. Cisco partners both on an engineering/technology research and development level as well as on a system build level with "best of breed" technology vendors to provide partners and customers with a choice in how they consume and deliver IT services.

3. Innovation to accelerate the use of clouds: Cisco is investing in services and solutions that can be delivered in a multitenant and utility-based cloud form, offered by

Cisco Service Provider partners, that combine collaboration and mobility capabilities with security. It is important to note that a central tenant of Cisco Systems' cloud strategy is its support for an indirect "go-to-market" model. In other words, Cisco Systems does not intend to offer Infrastructure as a Service (IaaS) directly from its own data centers to end customers. Rather, Cisco Systems would prefer that its service provider partners provide this service (and others) bundled with their own value-added services (mainly network [WAN] derived).

The following sections look at some examples of the technologies, products, systems, and solutions that Cisco can deliver today that help deliver the IT utility model, ITaaS.

Cisco Systems, unlike its main competitors, supports an indirect, partnership-based go-to-market (GTM) model for IaaS. Cisco Systems fundamentally believes that service providers can leverage their network assets as the underlying platform for cloud-based services, whereas systems integration partners have the more traditional IT skill sets that can be augmented through an addition of an intelligent network.

To reinforce this approach to the market, Cisco Systems has developed the Cloud Partner Program (CPP) that is specifically designed to assist the enablement and acceleration of cloud services for

- **Cloud builders:** Partners that sell infrastructure and professional service capabilities
- **Cloud providers:** Partners that build, operate, and run cloud service platforms
- **Cloud resellers:** Partners that OEM or resell cloud services of cloud providers (typically do not own the infrastructure assets)

Each of these defined partner roles can leverage the benefits of certification and go-to-market programs designed specifically around cloud-based services.

More information on the CPP framework and program kits can be found at www.cisco.com/web/partners/partner_with_cisco/cloud_partner.html.

Technology and Products

Chapter 3, "Data Center Architecture and Technologies," discussed the architectural trends and the corresponding design and implementation changes that are affecting the data center today. The following sections provide some examples of how Cisco is delivering cloud-ready service platforms by building on the technology and products developed by Cisco and its technology partners.

Unified Network Services

Application networking services, such as load balancers and WAN accelerators, have become integral building blocks in modern data center designs. These Layer 4 through 7 services provide service scalability, improve application performance, enhance end-user productivity, help reduce infrastructure costs through optimal resource utilization, and monitor quality of service (QoS). They also provide security services (that is, policy enforcement points [PEP] such as firewalls and intrusion protection systems [IPS]) to isolate applications and resources in consolidated data centers and cloud environments that, along with other control mechanisms and hardened processes, ensure compliance and reduce risk.

Deploying Layer 4 through 7 services in virtual data centers has however been extremely challenging. Traditional service deployments are completely at odds with highly scalable virtual data center designs that have mobile workloads, dynamic networks, and strict SLAs. Security is just one required service frequently cited as the biggest challenge to enterprises adopting cost-saving virtualization and cloud-computing architectures.

When services could be deployed effectively, they frequently undermined the benefits of virtualization by adding cost and complexity to the infrastructure build, thus reducing flexibility. Network-based services also tended to conflict with each other, with poor integration and completely separate policy management platforms, further increasing costs and management overhead.

One of the greatest design challenges is how to "steer" application traffic flows through the physical and virtual infrastructure so that network services can be applied. Traditionally, engineers have used utilities such as Policy-Based Routing (PBR) and Web Cache Communications Protocol (WCCP) in conjunction with Network Address Translation (NAT). Although all these technologies have been valuable in given use cases, in general, they do not enable the efficient (flexible) invocation of network services to build, in effect, a dynamic service chain that is policy based in its construction.

In other words, this strategy works well in traditional data centers but not in the cloud computing world, where (nearly) everything is virtual. To adapt to this change, Cisco developed the UNS strategy.

Cisco Unified Network Services (UNS) brings together an intelligent solution set that secures and optimizes the delivery of applications across the distributed enterprise. UNS addresses the requirements of dynamic, on-demand service delivery with consistently managed, policy-based provisioning, bringing integrated application delivery and security services to highly scalable, virtualized data centers and cloud environments.

UNS enables customers to

- Transparently insert application and security services into the network
- Dynamically steer traffic to appropriate services on a per–virtual machine (VM) basis
- Provide an extensible policy management architecture across products

A new concept of steering the traffic had to be developed for the virtual environment. Cisco developed a protocol called *vPath*. The Cisco Nexus 1000V switch's vPath functionality provides a single architecture supporting multiple Layer 4–7 network services in virtualized environments with service policy–based traffic steering capabilities. In other words, it provides an "intelligent services fabric" that allows a service designer to place virtual service nodes (VSN) adjacent to the application VMs it is serving (that is, on the same ESX host or physical server) or place the VSNs on a separate and dedicated "service" ESX host (physical server). In effect, this provides a greater degree of flexibility in where and when to place VSNs. VSNs can support a variety of network services, such as virtual firewalls or WAN acceleration. Figure 5-3 illustrates the Nexus 1000V distributed virtual switch running across three VMware ESX servers (each a separate physical server), supporting the VSNs with the vPath policy-based traffic steering capability.

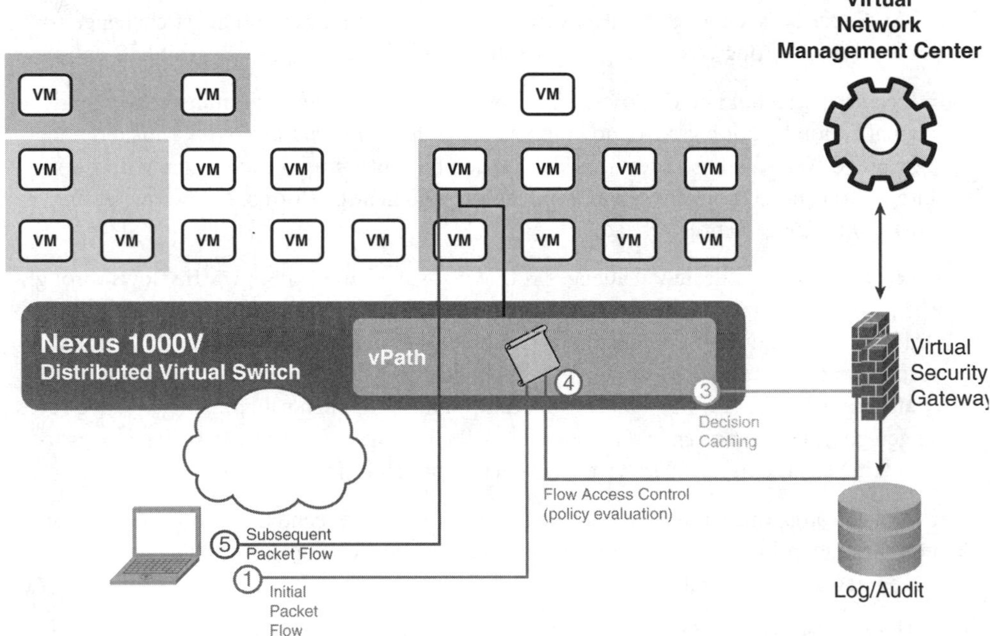

Figure 5-3 *Policy-Based Traffic Steering with the Nexus 1000V's vPath*

At press time, the Nexus 1000V virtual distributed virtual switch supports VMware ESX, KVM, and Microsoft's Hyper-V hypervisor/virtual machine monitor (VMM) software.

Today, Cisco offers a virtual form factor of a network security service running in a VM. The Cisco Virtual Security Gateway (VSG) for the Cisco Nexus 1000V virtual switch is an example of a VSN, enabling service policy creation and enforcement at the VM level (Cisco Systems also supports virtual wide-area application services [vWAAS] as a virtual appliance at the time of this writing, with other virtual appliances to be announced shortly). Integrated with the Cisco Nexus 1000V in a virtual host, a VSN provides

- **VM-level granularity:** Apply, manage, and audit policy at the VM context level
- **Support for vMotion:** Policy stays intact across manual and automated vMotion events
- **Nondisruptive operations:** Server administrators apply the policy to VMs through vCenter; ownership of the security policy stays with the security team

In addition, Cisco UNS also consists of physical services, that is, traditional network service appliances and modules. The combination of VSNs and dedicated appliances or servers provides customers with the flexibility to take full advantage of existing resource investments and to scale easily as new capacity is required while leveraging a common operational model and management toolset. Cisco UNS thus provides the capability to integrate and manage both virtual and physical services into a common, consistent framework. Integration of policy-based, traffic-steering capabilities for both physical and virtual network services is seen as the next logical step forward, but it is not supported today.

Virtual Extensible Local-Area Network

Virtual extensible local-area network (VXLAN) is a new standard to help cloud data centers scale beyond current technology limits.

The (802.1Q) VLAN has been the traditional mechanism for providing logical network isolation. Because of the ubiquity of the IEEE 802.1Q standard, numerous switches and tools provide robust network troubleshooting and monitoring capabilities, enabling mission-critical applications to depend on the network. Unfortunately, the IEEE 802.1Q standard specifies a 12-bit VLAN identifier that hinders the scalability of cloud networks beyond 4K VLANs.

Some vendors in the industry have proposed incorporation of a longer logical network identifier in a MAC-in-MAC or MAC in Generic Route Encapsulation (MAC-in-GRE) as a way to scale. Unfortunately, these techniques cannot make use of all the links in a port channel between switches, that is often found in the data center network or in some cases does not behave well with Network Address Translation (NAT). In addition, because of the encapsulation, monitoring capabilities are lost, preventing troubleshooting and monitoring. Hence, customers are not confident in deploying Tier 1 applications or applications requiring regulatory compliance in the cloud.

VXLAN solves these challenges with a MAC in User Datagram Protocol (MAC-in-UDP) encapsulation technique. VXLAN uses a 24-bit segment identifier to scale. In addition, the UDP encapsulation enables the logical network to be extended to different subnets and helps ensure high utilization of port channel links.

Cisco and VMware, along with other networking and server virtualization companies, proposed and submitted a new LAN segmentation technology proposal, "VXLAN," to the Internet Engineering Task Force (IETF) in August 2011 for standardization. The IETF draft submission is available at http://datatracker.ietf.org/doc/draft-mahalingam-dutt-dcops-vxlan.

Data Center Interconnect Evolution

Globalization, business process optimization, and the need for continuous computing operations motivate businesses to seek solutions that can both distribute and unite data centers over geographically dispersed locations. Geographically distributed data centers are desired for mutual backup to reduce interruption from a local disaster and also to facilitate data center maintenance. Ideally, computing operations can switch transparently between sites, maintaining user sessions, application availability, and access to data resources. VM technology is increasingly used for distributed data center operations.

Organizations need to have technology options that allow Layer 2 extensions over dark fiber links or over Layer 3 WANs if they use packet-based (IP) or label-based (Multi-Protocol Label Switching [MPLS]) solutions. Cisco offers a range of multisite Data Center Interconnect (DCI) solutions for redundant, scalable, and secure LAN extension across WAN networks based on dark fiber, MPLS, and IP technologies. Table 5-2 summarizes many of the different protocol solution options for extending Layer 2 (also known as *Extended Subnet mode*) between data centers.

Table 5-2 *Cisco DCI LAN Extension Technologies*

Requirement	Solution
Layer 2 over fiber	Virtual switching system (VSS) and MEC Virtual PortChannel (vPC) FabricPath (and future TRILL)
Layer 2 over MPLS	Ethernet over MPLS (EoMPLS) Virtual Private LAN Service (VPLS) Advanced VPLS (A-VPLS) Provider Backbone Bridge (802.1ah) VPLS (PBB-VPLS) – (planned future support)
Layer 2 over IP	EoMPLS over GRE (EoMPLSoGRE) A-VPLS over GRE (A-VPLSoGRE)
Dynamic Layer 2 over IP or MPLS (also known as MAC routing)	Overlay Transport Virtualization (OTV) ("MAC Routing" [IS-IS]) Ethernet Virtual Private Network (EVPN) PBB-EVPN ("MAC Routing" [BGP]) – (planned future support)
Encryption	IEEE 802.1ae and IP Security (IPsec)

Layer 2 extensions between data centers have traditionally been driven by high-availability service use cases, for example, stateful replication between active, standby firewalls; session load balancers; or synchronous data storage replication. This means relatively short geographic distances between paired data centers. With the adoption of virtual machines, the ability to execute a live migration from one physical server to another situated in either the same or a geographically dispersed data center for workload balancing, driving up asset utilization or for disaster recovery (DR) purposes is now a viable technical use case. The latter case is driving up the bandwidth requirements (today, a recommended minimum of 622 Mbps) required for VMware's VMotion/Site Recovery Manager (SRM) service. Technologies like Cisco virtual Port Channel (vPC) is ideal for Layer 2 deployments over dark fiber. Layer 2 extension technologies need to guarantee the basic operational principles of Ethernet, loop-free forwarding, no packet duplication, and MAC address table stability. In addition, the solution should provide the following:

- Flooding minimization (ARP broadcast, some unknown unicast)
- MAC mobility
- Ease of management and provisioning
- Multicast optimization

In this challenging environment, Layer 3 overlay solutions that enable fast, reliable, high-capacity, and highly scalable DCI are also essential. Such a solution is available with virtual private LAN service (VPLS), a technology that provides Ethernet connectivity over packet-switched WANs. VPLS supports the connection of multiple sites in a single bridged domain over a managed IP or IP and MPLS (IP/MPLS) network. VPLS presents an Ethernet interface, simplifying the LAN and WAN boundary for enterprise customers and helping enable rapid and flexible service provisioning. Data centers, each having their own Ethernet LAN, can be united in a VLAN over a WAN by using VPLS.

The Advanced VPLS (A-VPLS) feature introduces the following enhancements to VPLS:

- Capability to load-balance traffic across multiple core interfaces using equal-cost multipathing (ECMP)
- Support for redundant DCI and provider-edge switches

One of the most recent innovations for Layer 2 extension over IP (or MPLS) is Overlay Transport Virtualization (OTV). OTV provides Layer 2 connectivity between remote network sites by using MAC address–based routing and dynamic IP-encapsulated forwarding across a Layer 3 transport network to provide support for applications that require Layer 2 adjacency, such as clusters and virtualization. OTV is deployed on the edge devices in each site. OTV requires no other changes to the sites or the transport network. OTV builds Layer 2 reachability information by communicating between edge devices with the overlay protocol. The overlay protocol forms adjacencies with all edge devices. After each edge device is adjacent with all its peers on the overlay, the edge devices share MAC address reachability information with other edge devices that participate in the same overlay network.

OTV discovers edge devices through dynamic neighbor discovery that can leverage the multicast support of the core. This means efficient multisite Layer 2 extensions, which are ideal for the VM live migration use case. It is important to note that OTV is aimed at private cloud scenarios, as the protocol does not explicitly support per-tenant semantics. In other words, one can dedicate an overlay to a customer (maximum overlays supported today is three on a Nexus 7000), but it cannot provide per-tenant isolation (for example, VPN). Figure 5-4 illustrates the simplified view of the OTV dynamic encapsulation of Layer 2 frames in a Layer 3 (pseudo-GRE) header for transport across a Layer 3 (IP) network.

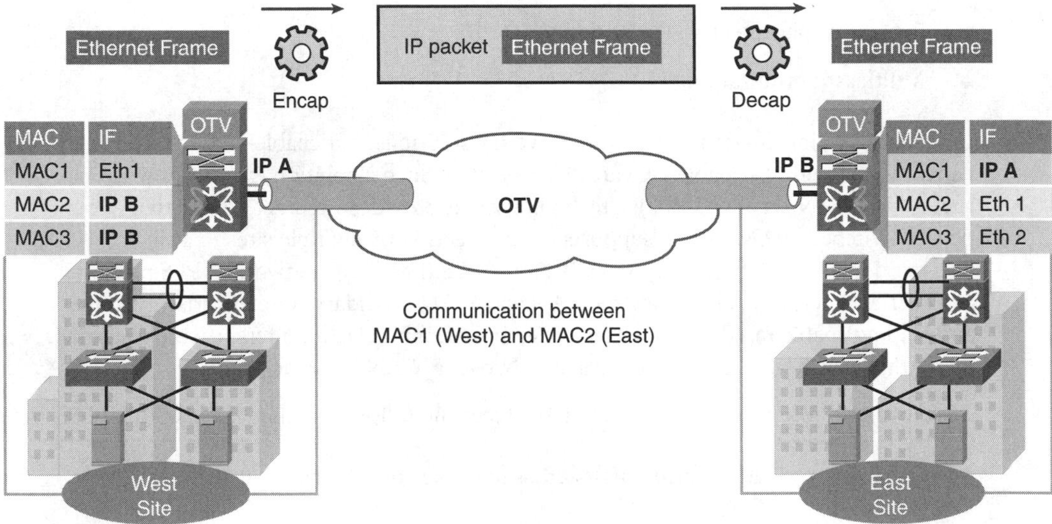

Figure 5-4 *Overlay Transport Virtualization Overview*

Enabling Machine Mobility Across Layer 3 Boundaries

The vision of the cloud for many is the ability to instantaneously "burst" into (and retract from) third-party clouds when additional infrastructure resources are needed. However, there are large parts that need to be adapted for the mechanisms to be ready to support "cold" and ultimately "live" VM migrations.

Today, if an administrator wants to spin up VMs in a cloud, he would use an API to manage the life cycle of that VM. There are plenty of cloud OS/cloud stacks that have been built to support these APIs. Examples of cloud APIs (normally using the RESTful protocol) include but are not limited to the following:

- **OCCI:** www.ogf.org/gf/group_info/view.php?group=occi-wg
- **VMware vCD API:** www.vmware.com/pdf/vcd_10_api_guide.pdf
- **Amazon EC2 (AWS) API:** http://aws.amazon.com/developertools/Amazon-EC2/351
- **ElasticHosts API:** www.elastichosts.com/cloud-hosting/api

- **FlexiScale API:** www.flexiant.com/reference/api
- **GoGrid API:** www.gogrid.com/cloud-hosting/cloud-api.php
- **Sun Cloud API:** http://kenai.com/projects/suncloudapis/pages/Home
- **OpenStack:** Using nova-manage (https://launchpad.net/openstack-dashboard) and Euca2ools (http://open.eucalyptus.com/wiki/Euca2oolsGuide_v1.1) APIs

Use of these APIs is suitable for cold VM migration from one (for example, private) cloud to another (for example, public) cloud managed and operated separately. Because each cloud has its own administrative ambience and methods, this is one of the many challenges today that restricts live VM migration between clouds. Each cloud requires unique machine images (for example, Amazon Machine Image [AMI]). There are companies that specialize in converting machine images, such as CohesiveFT. (AWS also has its own conversion service called VM Import.)

The Distributed Management Task Force (DMTF) is working on something called the Open Virtualization Format (OVF). From www.dmtf.org/standards/ovf:

> DMTF's Open Virtualization Format (OVF) is a packaging standard designed to address the portability and deployment of virtual appliances. OVF enables simplified and error-free deployment of virtual appliances across multiple virtualization platforms.
>
> OVF is a common packaging format for independent software vendors (ISV) to package and securely distribute virtual appliances, enabling cross-platform portability. By packaging virtual appliances in OVF, ISVs can create a single, prepackaged appliance that can run on customers' virtualization platforms of choice.

Note that OVF v1.1.0 supports both standard single VM packages (VirtualSystem element) and packages containing complex, multitier services consisting of multiple interdependent VMs (VirtualSystemCollection element). OVF v1.1.0 supports virtual hardware descriptions based on the Common Information Model (CIM) classes to request the infrastructure to support the running of the virtual machine(s) or appliance(s). The XML representation of the CIM model is based on the WS-CIM mapping.

Some cloud service providers offer their own CloudOS as Software as a Service (SaaS) to manage the private cloud on the end customer's premises or expose APIs, as previously mentioned.

From a "live" machine migration point of view, solving this problem at the management plane is only the first step before moving onto another challenge at the data plane (network and storage). Let's briefly discuss the challenge of OSI Layer 3 boundaries related to this goal and how Cisco is innovating with new technology, Locator/Identifier Separation Protocol (LISP), to address, at least in part, the challenge.

LISP is a "map-and-encapsulate" protocol that is currently being developed by the IETF LISP Working Group. The basic idea behind the separation is that the Internet architecture combines two functions, routing locators (where you are attached to the network) and identifiers (who you are) in one number space: the IP address (see Figure 5-5).

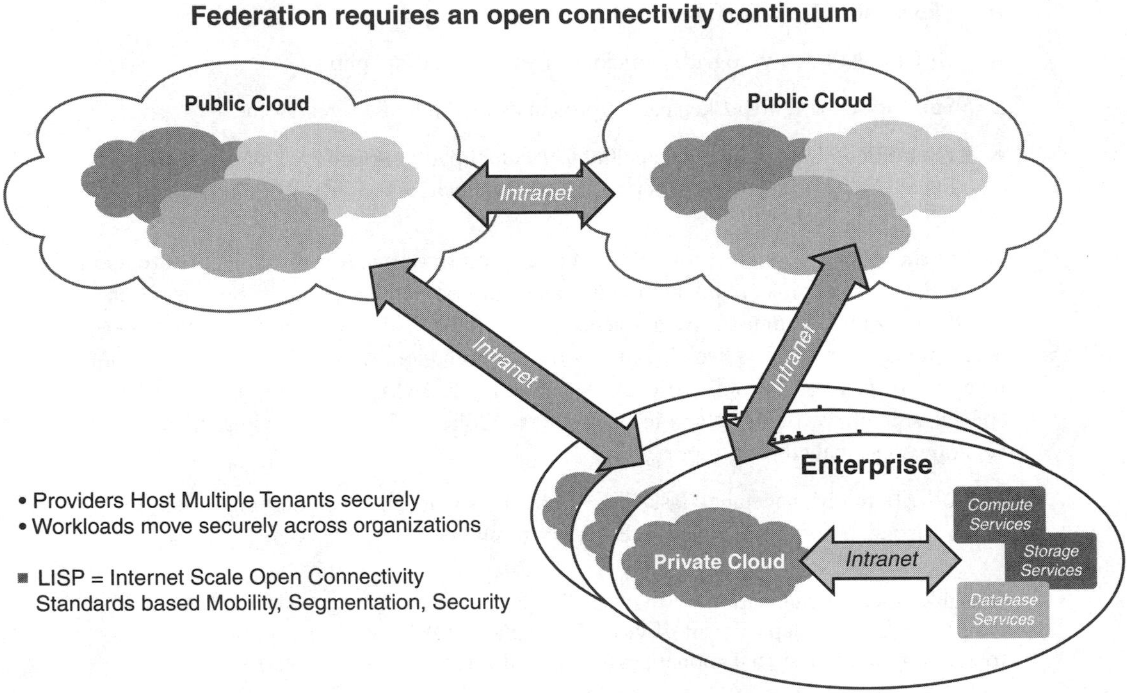

Figure 5-5 *Path from Hybrid Cloud to Federation with LISP*

Layer 3 routing has been developed over time to incorporate interadministrative domain interface points. Exterior gateway protocols like Border Gateway Protocol (BGP) have been specifically developed for this purpose. For Layer 2 connectivity between administrative domains, this is more problematic and as such is not considered as a viable option. So we need to look at Layer 3 options that can support the live VM migration use case.

A basic observation, made during early network research and development work, is that the use of a single address field for both device identification and routing is problematic. To effectively identify a device as a network session endpoint, an address should not change, even if the device moves, such as from a home to a work location, or if the organization with which the device is associated changes its network connectivity, perhaps from one cloud service provider to another. However, it is not feasible for the routing system to track billions of devices with such flexibly assigned addresses, so a device needs an address that is tightly coupled to its topological location to enable routing to operate efficiently.

To provide improved routing scalability while also facilitating flexible address assignment for multihoming, provider independence, and mobility, LISP was created. LISP describes a change to the Internet architecture in which IP addresses are replaced by routing locators (RLOC) for routing through the global Internet and by endpoint identifiers (EID) for identifying network sessions between devices. Essentially, LISP introduces a new hierarchy (also known as "jack up") to the forwarding plane, allowing the separation of location and identity.

> **Note** You can find more information about LISP capabilities, use cases, and deployments at www.cisco.com/go/lisp, http://lisp4.cisco.com, and http://lisp6.cisco.com.
>
> Cisco Systems Nexus 7000 now supports LISP VM-Mobility mode (see www.cisco.com/en/US/docs/switches/datacenter/sw/5_x/nx-os/lisp/configuration/guide/NX-OS_LISP_Configuration_Guide_chapter2.html).

LISP VM-Mobility provides adaptable and comprehensive first-hop router functionality to service the IP gateway needs of the roaming devices that relocate in addition to being able to control which VMs can move through dynamic-EID prefix lists. This capability works in both Extended Subnet Mode (ESM), extending Layer 2 connectivity between data centers, and Across Subnet Mode (ASM), which allows a Layer 3 hop between data centers.

Policy Management of the Data Center Network and Services

For some time now, architects have looked at ways to try and automate the activation and change management of Data Center Networks (DCN) and network service in IaaS environments. Thus far, it has proven a difficult challenge because of the frequency and complexity of changes through traditional per-device management using scripting tools and Secure Shell command-line interface (SSH CLI) access (or even XML-based RFC 4741 NETCONF). Per-device knowledge (syntax) adds complexity, and SSH CLI access methods are serial in nature, thus causing the queuing of orchestration tasks in system management tools, which in turn slows change management tasks.

What is needed is a way to abstract from the low-level "concrete" configuration tasks to more policy-based, high-level ("abstract") system change management tasks.

The Cisco Network Hypervisor product has been designed specifically for highly virtualized environments and cloud delivery models and does for the network infrastructure what server virtualization has done for the data center—provide efficiency, elasticity, automation, and control. The virtualization capabilities provided by Network Hypervisor facilitate the transformation of static, rigid networks into a dynamic infrastructure that responds automatically to the demands of virtual and cloud environments based on the rules and business policies defined by administrators.

The network services orchestration capabilities of Network Hypervisor allow physical or virtualized computing/storage resources to be combined with network access and security models into a single service chain—a cloud service—that is fully automated and can be deployed, on demand, to selected end users. Network Hypervisor business policies define and capture the discrete elements of a cloud service and translate those elements into actual device services and configuration syntax that is automatically disseminated to the appropriate devices across the network to initiate the requested service.

From the activation of a business policy that defines a new cloud service, Network Hypervisor automatically initiates the creation of the required VMs. As the VMs are coming online, Network Hypervisor defines and deploys the network access and security models across all required infrastructure devices (routers, switches, and firewalls) as needed to deliver the cloud service to the defined end users. The entire process is completed in seconds and can include the setup and deployment of network routes, Virtual Private Networks (VPN), VLANs, and access control lists (ACL); the deployment of security certificates; and the configuring of firewall rules and DNS entries, all of which are defined through the business policy and deployed automatically without any chance of command-line mistakes.

Cisco Network Hypervisor virtualizes network services by creating or abstracting a logical network in concordance with the physical network that it also manages. It controls the physical network by virtualizing hardware switches and routers to create subnets of network addressing space, typically VPNs, that also enable and orchestrate clouds and VMs.

The logical network is driven by policies that control network access for individuals to resources. The policies specify high-level resource sharing. They can be created externally or using the Network Hypervisor Command Center as documents that can be imported, exported, and edited within the center. At the XML level, they comprise elements that model all the specifications (and more) that can be expressed using a grammar of variable and parameter substitutions that let admins and network configurators easily specify individual and multiple models that Network Hypervisor can express. For this reason, they are called metamodel files.

Figure 5-6 depicts the functional subcomponents of the Network Hypervisor and shows how it logically connects to the northbound ITSM (Information Technology Service Management) tools shown on the left and to the southbound underlying infrastructure shown on the right.

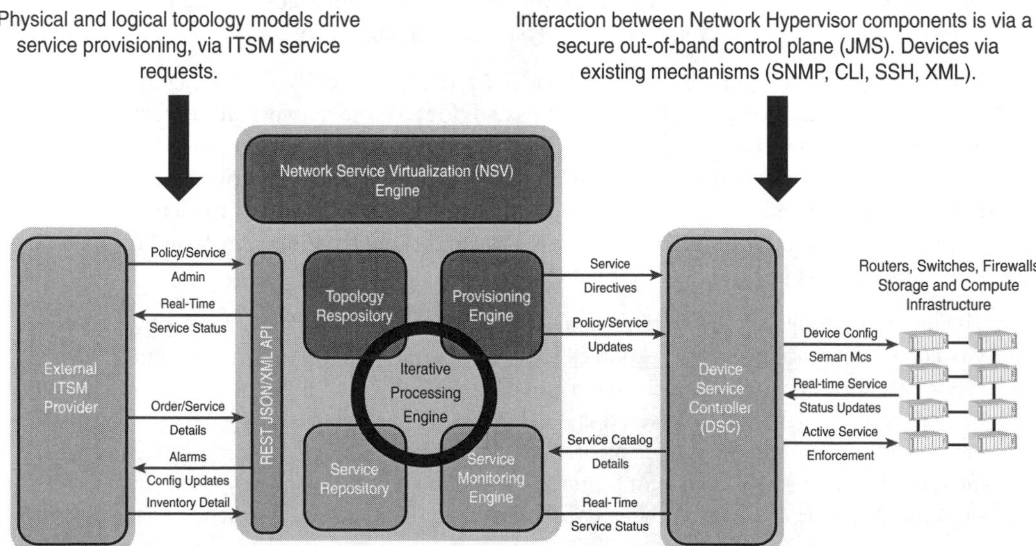

Figure 5-6 *Cisco Network Hypervisor – A Metamodel-Driven Architecture*

Thus, Network Hypervisor invents and defines network services virtualization as a model-based definition of a network addressing space, the physical and virtual (VM) resources in that space, and the managed services, capabilities, and relationships between those network resources, that is, the deployed network and service infrastructure (also known as the network container). In abstracting a logical from a physical network, the model enables dynamic responses to physical network changes. These responses ensure the ongoing operational intent of the logical network services model.

By virtualizing clouds and physical centers, Network Hypervisor provides an infrastructure that is entirely dynamic, controlled by the Network Hypervisor's Network Services Virtualization Engine (NSVE). The NSVE controls the virtualized data center hardware, VM, and cloud environments so that end users are connected to the network resources they need for their particular business responsibilities without requiring someone to reconfigure and reprovision as computing resources change. The result happens quickly, consistently, and predictably. Figure 5-7 provides you with some more detail on the capabilities of the functional components of Network Hypervisor.

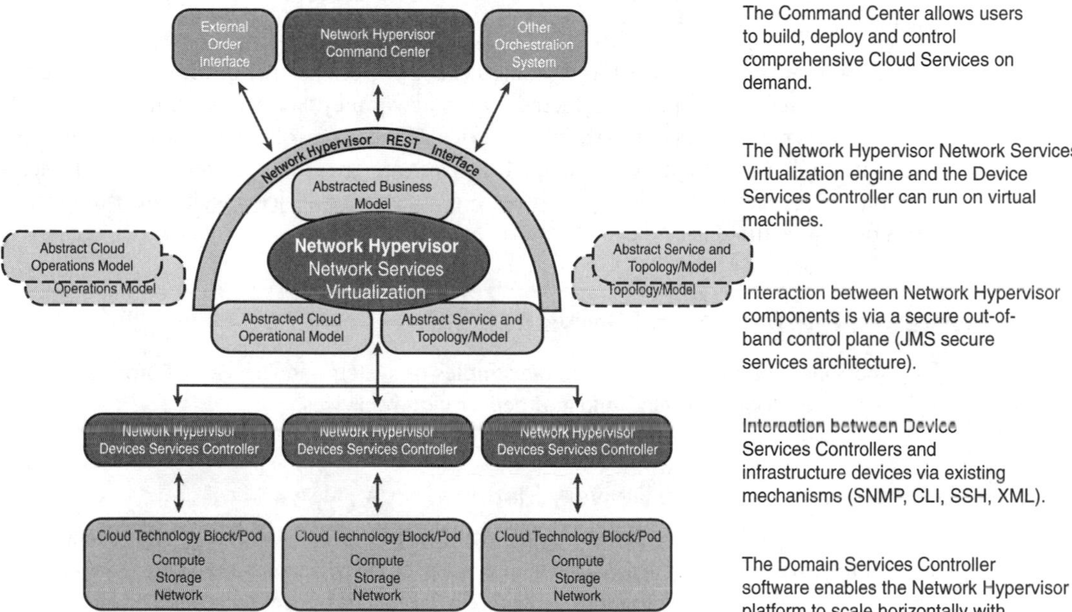

Figure 5-7 *Cisco Network Hypervisor Architecture*

This orchestration is based on business semantics. It is a top-down approach to managing a network instead of a bottom-up approach that concentrates on routers, switches, and other network hardware.

To support this business policy emphasis, Network Hypervisor automates device-level configurations, thereby automating network service delivery and network management. The NSVE interprets the policy, identifies the devices and services that need to be modified to satisfy it, and dynamically pushes configuration updates to the selected devices. In brief, the Network Hypervisor

- Creates all configuration updates for appropriate devices
- Negotiates required services among selected devices
- Initiates multiple services in parallel and in concert
- Provides real-time feedback as services are initiated across the network

In other words, Network Hypervisor provides the services and configurations that each business policy needs.

A key component of the NSVE is a process called the provisioner or provisioning engine. This determines which sites are affected by the new policy. For each one, it constructs a set of abstract directives to tell the site's device service controller (DSC) which policies it needs to implement. Depending on which services are enabled at the sites, when the service controller receives the directives, it converts them into device-specific instructions and configures the devices accordingly.

Systems, Platforms, and Services

The sections that follow look at some examples of systems and service platforms that Cisco has developed to help build and deliver cloud services.

The Cisco Unified Service Delivery Platform

The Cisco Unified Service Delivery Platform (CUSDP) is a conceptual goal of a single horizontal infrastructure that spans a provider's (service provider or a large enterprise) entire service portfolio, bringing together best-in-class data center technologies as well as IP WAN technologies. Doing this provides three main advantages to the business in general:

- Increases service and feature velocity
- Optimally utilizes capital and operating assets
- Ensures and secures the user experience

Specific to IaaS offerings, the CUSDP solution enables providers to

- Bring IaaS to market more quickly. Virtualization-aware intelligence is built into the key elements of the Unified Service Delivery solution (for example, Unified Computing and Virtual Network Link).
- Reduce the cost of deploying IaaS and other services. The Unified Service Delivery solution incorporates consolidation and scalability features that are unique to Cisco products.
- Meet customers' service-level and security requirements in IaaS offers. QoS, encryption, and secure partitioning technologies work in concert across the components of the Unified Service Delivery solution.

In addition, the CUSDP can be constructed in a modular fashion with a reference to a baseline architecture that is not tied to any particular service (support the web-shared platform philosophy), providing tremendous flexibility (that leads to greater business agility). Should the market for cloud computing services change, the underpinnings of the IaaS offer based on the CUSDP can be repurposed to support a substantially different service in response to shifting customer requirements.

Similarly, that same baseline infrastructure can be extended to other services beyond IaaS, even while it continues to be used as the foundation of an IaaS service. More traditional hosting or colocation services can be delivered over this infrastructure. Other services, such as hosted collaboration services, can be delivered alongside the IaaS offer but use the same infrastructure. This reduces overall capital costs, increases the utilization of the infrastructure, and simplifies the environment operationally.

This "general purpose" concept, where an organization can utilize the scale-out or even the more traditional scale-up capabilities of the underlying infrastructure, provides maximum flexibility in regard to IT infrastructure supporting the agile business. *Integrated Compute Stacks* (also known as infrastructure packages) provide the modular building blocks of the Unified Service Delivery platform. Productized examples of ICSs would be VCE's Vblock, a product from the Cisco, EMC, VMware, Intel joint venture or, from the Cisco, NetApp alliance, the FlexPod building block. Figure 5-8 depicts an abstracted view of CUSDP in relation to NIST's taxonomy on cloud service models in addition to some of the infrastructure building blocks for CUSDP.

Cisco Virtual Multi-Tenant Data Center

The Cisco Virtual Multi-Tenant Data Center (VMDC) solution provides reference design and implementation guidance for enterprises planning to deploy private cloud services and service providers building virtual private and public cloud services. The Cisco VMDC solution integrates various Cisco and third-party products (that is, BMC Software's Cloud Life Cycle Manager [CLM]) that are part of the cloud-computing ecosystem.

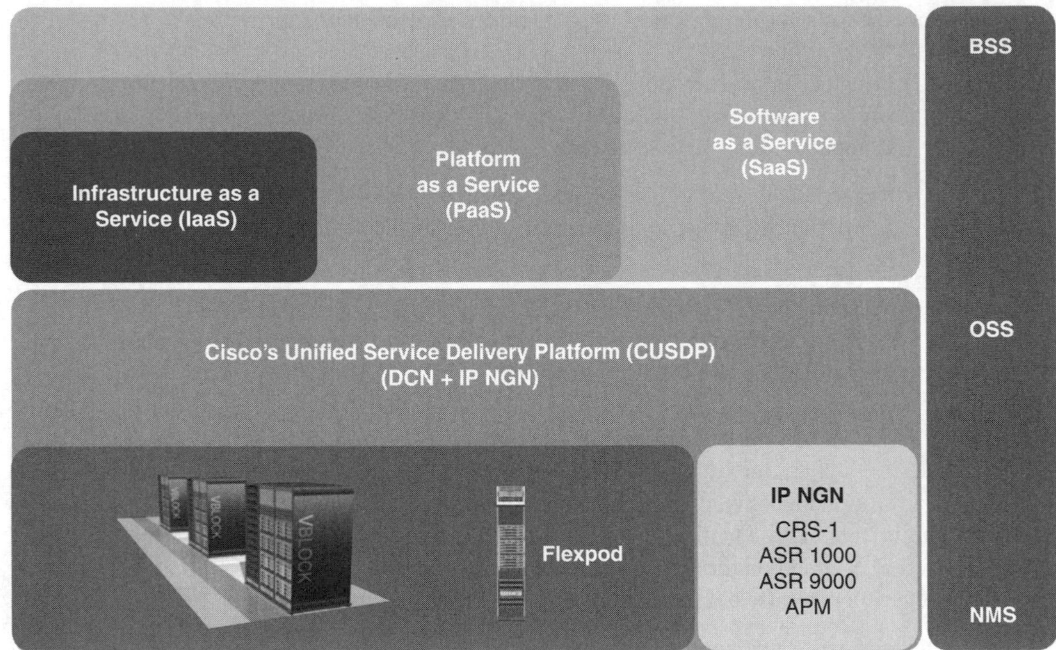

Figure 5-8 *Cisco Unified Service Delivery Platform*

Cisco VMDC delivers a validated architecture that delivers a highly available, secure, flexible, and efficient data center infrastructure. It provides the following benefits:

- **Reduced time to deployment:** Provides a fully tested and validated architecture that accelerates technology adoption and rapid deployment
- **Reduced risk:** Enables enterprises and service providers to deploy new architectures and technologies with confidence
- **Increased flexibility:** Enables rapid, on-demand workload deployment in a multitenant environment because of a comprehensive automation framework with portal-based resource provisioning and management capabilities
- **Improved operational efficiency:** Integrates automation with a multitenant resource pool (compute, network, and storage), improves asset use, reduces operational overhead, and mitigates operational configuration errors

Cisco VMDC 2.0 provides a scalable solution that can address the needs of smaller, as well as larger, enterprise and service provider data centers. This architectural consistency enables providers to select the design that best suits their immediate needs, while providing a solution that can scale to meet future needs without retooling or retraining staff.

This scalability with a hierarchical design is based on two modular building blocks: point of delivery (POD) and Integrated Compute Stack (ICS).

An ICS is a predesigned and sometimes prebuilt/integrated finite set of compute, storage, and networking infrastructure components. Commercialized examples of an ICS include Vblock (from www.vce.com) and FlexPod (see www.imaginevirtuallyanything.com). An ICS would form part or all of a PoD infrastructure block. An ICS forming a subcomponent of a POD is shown in Figure 5-9 within the context of the VMDC 2.0 reference design. The VMDC reference design is constantly being updated. For example, in VMDC 2.5, the ASR 9000 router has been certified for the provider edge role in a large PoD implementation.

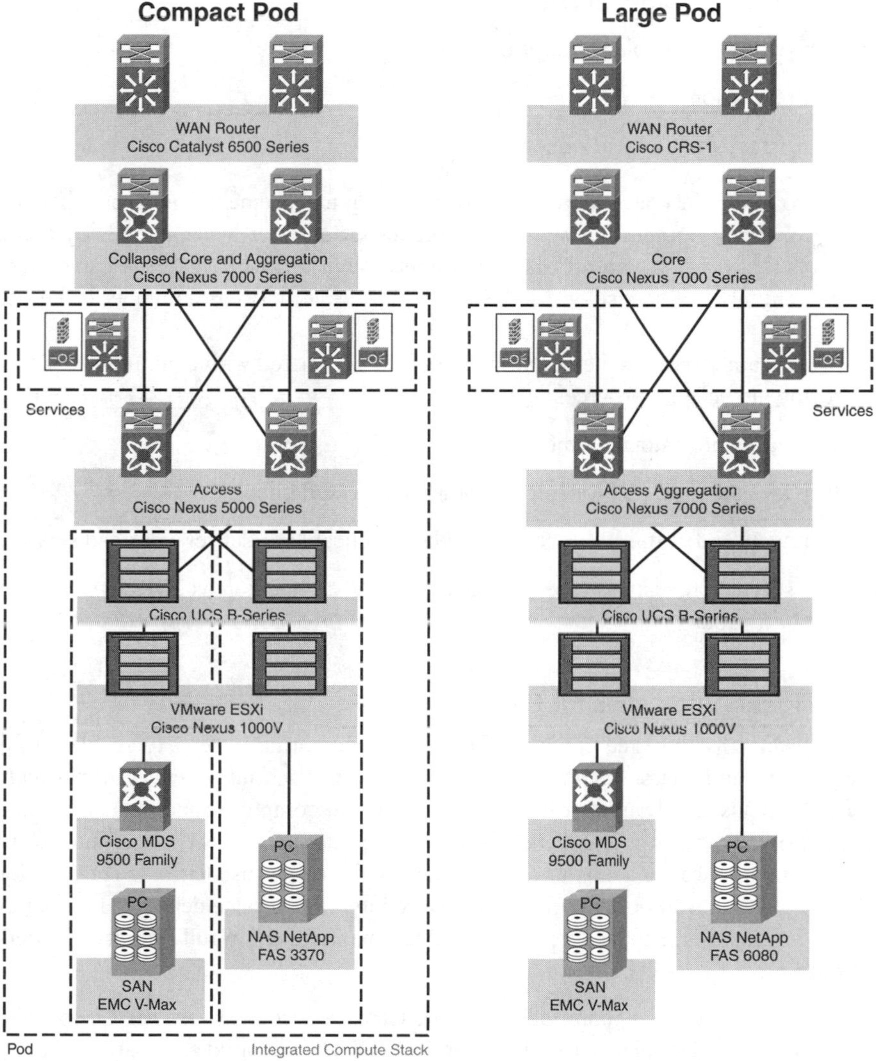

Figure 5-9 *VMDC 2.0 PoD Designs Showing ICS as a Key Subcomponent Building Block*

The modular design starts with a basic infrastructure module called a PoD. A PoD allows providers to add network, compute, storage, and service resources incrementally that provide all the infrastructure components to suffice the service use cases that are offered within the service catalogue. As an example, the Cisco VMDC 2.0 architecture specifies two PoD designs: compact and large. Essentially the difference between the PoDs is mainly around capacity provided rather than capability.

The PoD concept offers a number of benefits:

- Predefined logical units (LUN)
- Simplified capacity planning
- Ease of new technology adoption
- Fault isolation
- Consistent and efficient operation

The Cisco VMDC 2.0 architecture includes an open management framework that enables provisioning of resources through service orchestration. A provider can deploy orchestration tools that provide a portal-based configuration model where a tenant can select from a defined number of service options. Service orchestration offers a number of benefits:

- Significantly reduces the operating expenses associated with administering and monitoring virtualized resources
- Decreases provisioning time
- Provides an audit trail for fulfillment assurance and billing
- Connects and automates workflows when applicable to deliver a defined service
- The service orchestrator used in the VMDC 2.0 architecture is BMC Atrium Orchestrator.

Cisco Intelligent Automation for Cloud

Cisco Systems has invested in best-of-breed cloud operating systems to enable it to provide partners and customers with a full IaaS solution. Cisco Intelligent Automation for Cloud (CIAC) is an advanced software stack for cloud computing and data center automation. It works with both virtual and physical infrastructure across the compute, network, storage, and application domains and supports multivendor installations. The solution provides a web-based portal with a self-service interface, service delivery and operational process automation, and resource and life cycle management in full support of cloud computing.

Figure 5-10 shows the subcomponents of the CIAC solution, namely, the Cisco Cloud Portal (CCP), the Tidal Enterprise Orchestrator (TEO) with cloud automation packs (predefined best-practice workflow), and the Tidal Server Provisioner (TSP) for server OS image boot management.

CIAC forms the "backbone" of service automation capabilities required for an IaaS platform. Added to this backbone would be back office capabilities (for example, service desk, change management, and CMDB) as well as service assurance tools (for example, Zenoss).

Cisco Systems plans to qualify CIAC with its VMDC infrastructure best-practice reference design, with a focus on private cloud installations.

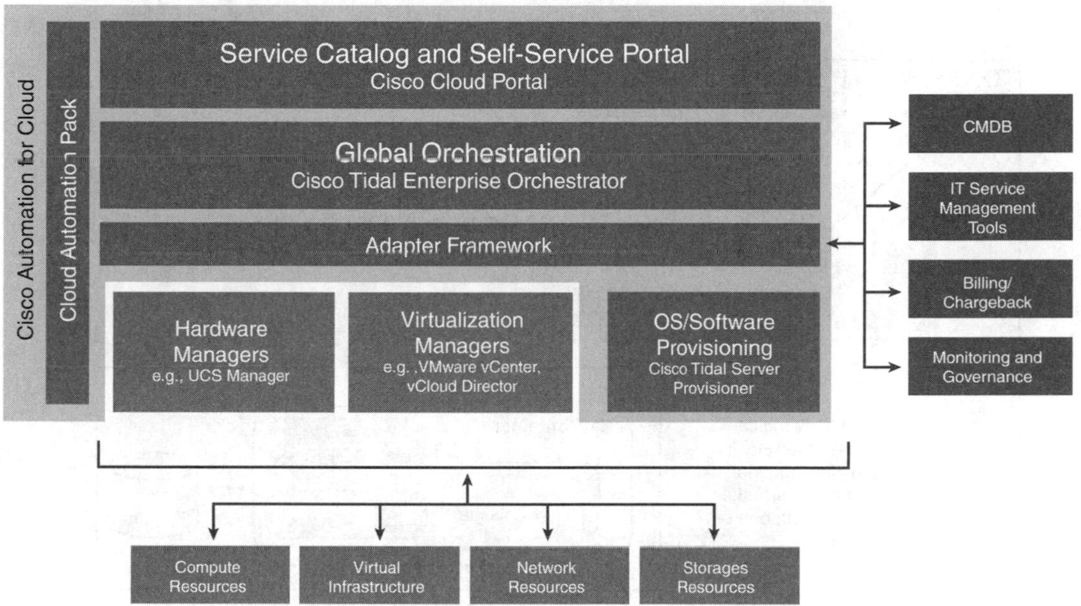

Figure 5-10 *Cisco Intelligent Automation for Cloud "Stack"*

Open Source Projects

OpenStack (www.openstack.org) is an open source community effort initiated by NASA and Rackspace Hosting to build operational management tools for a the cloud (IaaS) platform. Today, the OpenStack software stack consists of three core "projects": Compute (code name Nova), Storage (Swift), and Image Management (Glance). At the time of this writing, many other adjacent projects are being undertaken within the OpenStack governance model.

At the OpenStack Design Summit that took place in April 2011 in Santa Clara, California, Cisco joined the OpenStack community in shaping new technologies for next-generation cloud computing.

Cisco recognizes that any one company on its own cannot shape the future of cloud-computing architectures. Innovating in collaboration with others is essential. The Cisco strength in networking technologies and Unified Service Delivery puts it in a knowledgeable position to help form how the network is utilized in cloud-computing services.

Prior to the aforementioned summit, Cisco submitted a blueprint (one of four in total submitted by various contributors) that focused on network and network services provisioning. This was called Network as a Service, or NaaS. Figure 5-11 illustrates the NaaS concept and the network container service fulfillment operational methodology.

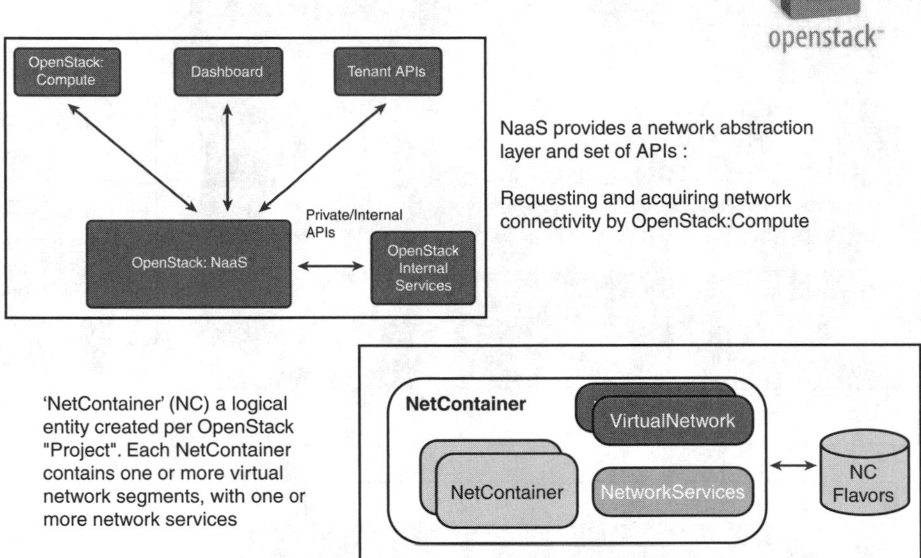
openstack
OpenStack: Compute
Dashboard
Tenant APIs
Private/Internal APIs
OpenStack: NaaS
OpenStack Internal Services
NaaS provides a network abstraction layer and set of APIs :
Requesting and acquiring network connectivity by OpenStack:Compute
'NetContainer' (NC) a logical entity created per OpenStack "Project". Each NetContainer contains one or more virtual network segments, with one or more network services
NetContainer
VirtualNetwork
NetContainer
NetworkServices
NC Flavors

Figure 5-11 *Cisco NaaS Proposal to OpenStack*

The NaaS blueprint introduces the concept of network containers as a deployment methodology to be added to OpenStack capabilities. This is similar to what Cisco, along with its partner BMC Software, has utilized in the Cisco VMDC solution, as discussed previously in this chapter.

The OpenStack NaaS entity provides policy abstraction through APIs for network resources grouping/management that can be used by OpenStack projects. The NaaS capability fills a gap in the capability to allow IT administrators to build a service chain that includes not only compute and storage but also network services (for example, VLANs, QoS, ACLs, stats, and so on). Cisco Systems has contributed code for the NaaS API (specifically code for a plug-in framework as well as plug-ins for Nexus switches. These are part of the OpenStack "Diablo" release under the OpenStack project name Quantum (http://wiki.openstack.org/Quantum). Note that Quantum initially only supports basic Layer 2 connectivity, that is, vNIC-to-vNIC (vNIC = virtual network interface card). The 'container' operational methodology is planned for the Donabe (an OpenStack 'incubator' project) that may be part of the main 'Essex' release planned for first quarter of 2012.

Cisco Systems is now a full member of the OpenStack community that is quickly becoming the central industry community for service provider–scale cloud operating system software. As such, Cisco Systems is sponsoring and playing a primary role within the OpenStack community.

Infrastructure Evolution to Support Cloud Services

Cloud computing is still very much in its adolescence; the lack of standards does inhibit the adoption of services. We also have to take a careful look at how currently available technology has evolved and more importantly its suitability in the new cloud operational and consumption model. This will inevitably lead to new standards, both technological- and operational-based capabilities being developed. In short, how can the network optimize applications (workloads) and vice versa in a real-time consumption model? Figure 5-12 illustrates a highly abstracted representation of this concept.

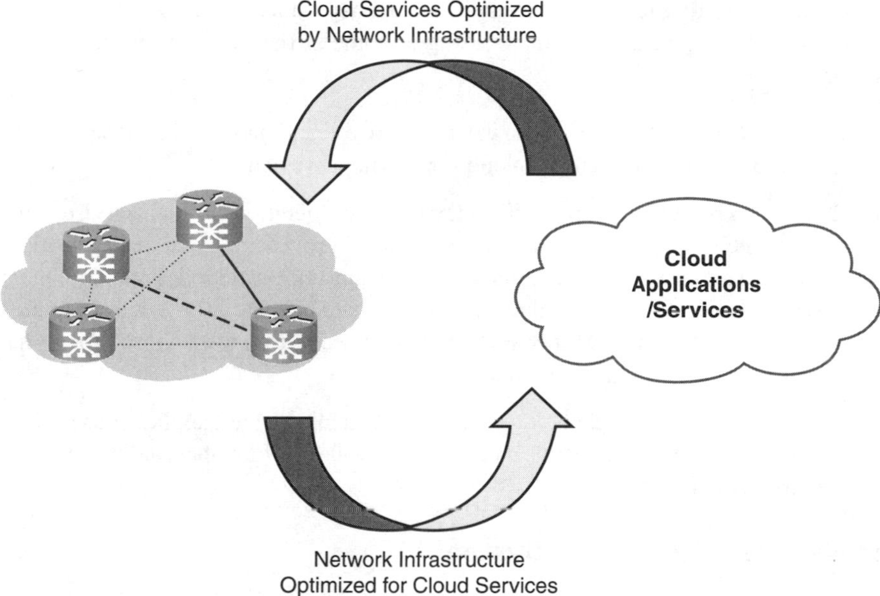

Figure 5-12 *Intelligent Cloud Platform: Infrastructure as the Service Enabler*

Take, for example, the ability to spin up a workload in a geographic location that is compliant in regard to legal, taxation, and regulatory demands. We need mechanisms and information/metadata that allows automatic geoplacement of workloads. Where better to derive such information than the network?

How about making it easier to manage infrastructure through programmatic modeling (abstraction) of the underlying infrastructure resources to deliver the required service chain?

How about linking the WAN with the services running within the data center? That is, the WAN becomes "service aware" and provides end-to-end visibility and control, that is, vNIC to vNIC (a vNIC being a virtual machine interface).

How do we make it easy to signal between different autonomous domains or clouds like we do today at scale with IP services using well-established protocols like BGP?

This is just a few of the use cases or examples that are being asked by end users, architects, and engineers alike.

Intelligent Cloud Platform

Cisco has started an internal cross-platform effort—let's call it Intelligent Cloud Platform (ICP)—to enable Cisco products and systems to deliver greater value to the end customer or partner by making it easier to consume and manage cloud services, including the underlying physical infrastructure, focusing on some of the use cases we have already discussed:

- The ICP concept focuses on the value of network and network-based services that adapt to dynamic, virtualized cloud-computing environments.
- It seeks to bring operational efficiency in cloud operation through service automation of the networking infrastructure. Network provisioning and management are repetitive and time-consuming tasks that are a major bottleneck in deploying network services to cloud-based tenant Virtual Data Centers (VDC). ICP goals are to automate the tenant VDC network provisioning and management into the dynamic service provider cloud infrastructure.
- ICP seeks to develop technology/interfaces that allow cloud applications to utilize network intelligence to enable a new level of scale, performance, agility, elasticity, security, and reliability.

Cisco Network Positioning System

One of the core capabilities of the ICP is Network Positioning System (NPS) (also known as *proximity* or *locality*). NPS is a set of technologies that compute the location of and distance between endpoints. Examples include an application client willing to locate the closest instance of a movie, a peer-to-peer client willing to find the closest set of peers sharing the requested piece of content, or a voice/videoconferencing service willing to locate the closest bridge for a given user.

The Cisco NPS is a prestandard implementation of the IETF's ALTO (Application-Layer Traffic Optimization) proposed standard. (Refer to http://tools.ietf.org/html/ietf-alto-protocol-07 for details.)

In today's applications, caching and replication are vital mechanisms that provide redundancy, availability, and efficiency in content and services delivery.

Locating objects and services (files, movies, VoIP gateways/bridges, peers, servers, and so on) is a critical aspect of content/service delivery, and different methods and technologies have been proposed thus far but with limited efficiency.

The idea is that the service provider delivers the NPS service as a generic service to the Content Delivery Network (CDN) /application overlay. The service provider leverages its routing layer information to deliver intelligence to the application layer in terms of location and preference/ranking based on distance.

In its generic form, the NPS service is implemented in a server accessible to applications and invoked through a request in the form of "Which of several candidate nodes are closest to some point of interest?"

The NPS server leverages different information sources to accurately compute the distance between endpoints. Sources can be

- Routing layer (that is, routing protocols such as Intermediate System–to–Intermediate System [IS-IS], Open Shortest Path First [OSPF], and BGP)
- Policy database (to represent network policies as deployed by the service provider)
- Network Management Servers (NMS) for state and performance information
- Application-specific information (for example, Distributed Hash Table [DHT] state)

The NPS service is a ranking service allowing any client to obtain a ranked list of addresses. The NPS client submits a request to the NPS server with a list of addresses to be ranked.

The NPS server has precomputed a set of algorithms and maintains a topology database that allows ranking the list of addresses received in the request. It then generates a reply with the ranked list and sends it to the requester.

NPS is a "win, win" for both the end user and the service provider, providing better Quality of Experience (QoE) to the customer and minimizing transportation costs for the service provider.

Evolution Toward Hybrid and Community Clouds

The logical evolution to community clouds requires the development of an e-marketplace for intercloud services.

To build a dynamic reference marketplace for a particular sector by grouping together those who have commercial interests in a particular field (for example, construction, mining, and medical) requires standardization of effective and efficient homogeneous procedures and processes (that is, common governance and operational model) able to sustain all the actors in the sector, whether they are service component producers or consumers.

Much or the time we think about technology alignment and capability (for example, "live" migration of VMs) and not about the business alignment (for example, common service descriptions, units of exchange, business processes) between trading parties. A common services framework would allow the creation of service aggregators by helping define and shape an e-marketplace and enable what Gartner describes as cloud service resellers.

One of the fundamental aspects of a marketplace is its neutrality, an indispensable condition for a marketplace's success. Neutrality in this context means respect for the rules of the market with no interference into the way the actors do their business. They can act with complete autonomy and with no intrusion into the affairs of their own activities. In today's networked world, these actors need to be securely connected through the Internet or private exchange points to the marketplace.

What is required is a service framework that provides a Service Definition Language (SDL) that enables the creation of service widgets that express offered technical service components (hardware, software applications) as attributes and variables of the service.

We can also create a service product similar to a service widget for the nontechnical business attributes of the service. Such a service framework would need to include a built-in process engine for business process management as well as the ability to dynamically and securely create communities of interest (that is, community clouds) with minimum threshold-based cryptographic VPNs (based on the old idea of a minimum set of keys with different owners are needed to open a door, for example).

In summary, a service product captures the business aspects and a service widget captures the technical aspects. These capabilities within a common service framework are the baseline requirements to building a marketplace and ensuring fulfillment of service.

Summary

This chapter discussed many of the drivers (megatrends) that are forcing business to rethink how they architect and manage their information services portfolio. We have seen a huge rise in unstructured data sets for various regulatory and commercial reasons in addition to the mobility of data and information access and the "consumerization" of IT devices used by employees.

As a result, new models of consuming information services are resulting in the use of innovative technologies and service platforms that not only allow corporations to reduce the cost of delivery but also to maintain a level of risk exposure that is acceptable to the business while tapping into the economic benefits of consumerization on IT endpoints and the mobility of its workforce.

Cisco Systems is continuing to develop and deliver technology, systems, service platforms, and programs that adhere to the needs of its customers and partners, making it easier for them to focus on their own core business.

Chapter 6

Cloud Management Reference Architecture

Upon completing this chapter, you would be able to understand the following:

- Tele-Management Forum (TMF) eTOM (enhanced Telecom Operations Map) standard
- Information Technology Infrastructure Library (ITIL) standard
- International Telecommunications Union - Telecommunication Standardization Sector (ITU-T) Telecommunication Management Network (TMN) standard
- Cloud management reference architecture process/functions
- Cloud framework and management framework
- Integration of management systems

Standards

Standards play an important role in the realization of cloud services. For all management systems, such as customer care systems, service provisioning/configuration systems, service assurance systems, and billing/charging systems, to work together in a seamless way from end-to-end in a multivendor environment, standards need to be in place to quickly integrate many of these systems.

Why do we need standards in cloud computing? If you want to have some capabilities reside in your own private cloud and want to rely on some capabilities from other clouds, for example, interoperability between the systems in your cloud and other clouds is required. Furthermore, to have interoperability between systems, open interfaces are required. Otherwise, custom interfaces have to be developed every time (which is very expensive), and after that is done, it is difficult to change the vendor systems (vendor lock-in). In other words, custom interfaces add additional integration tax and inhibit wide adoption of cloud computing.

Small companies are more interested in open standards for cloud computing because it will provide many opportunities for them. The large cloud service leaders, such as Amazon, Google, and others, might have little interest to develop open standards for fear of losing their lock on many of their existing customers.

Some of the standards organizations and standards-related forums are as follows:

- **TM Forum (TMF):** Provides an open forum to discuss and develop standards that can benefit the industry overall.
- **International Telecommunication Union-Telecommunication Standardization Sector (ITU-T):** This organization has a focus group that provides a forum that is developing functional reference architecture, cloud security requirements, and other cloud activities.
- **ITIL V3:** This organization provides many of the best practices for the IT industry.

Other standards bodies are also discussing the cloud standards, but we will limit our discussion to the three standards bodies mentioned in the preceding list. The following sections will discuss TMF, ITU-T, and ITIL standards in more detail.

TMF eTOM

The Telecommunications Operations Map (TOM) and more recent enhancements to the model (eTOM) are sponsored under the TMF. eTOM is a business process framework targeted at the development of business and operations support systems that exist within network service providers, network operators, and their suppliers. TOM and eTOM processes are developed by the TM Forum participants and are widely supported throughout the telecommunications industry.

The enhanced Telecom Operations Map (eTOM) business process is an enterprise process framework for service providers and provides direction for the development and integration of Operations Support Systems/Business Support Systems (OSS/BSS). For service providers, it provides a neutral reference point as they consider internal process needs, partnerships and alliances, and general agreement with other service providers. As cloud computing becomes more pervasive, the interoperability needs become more important between clouds, and TMF standards could help ease the interoperability pain among the cloud service providers. The following sections provide a high-level view of eTOM business processes.

Note You can find more details on all TMF activities, including ongoing work on cloud-related activities, at the TMF website (http://tmforum.org).

The purpose of eTOM is to set and implement a common set of business-driven processes for managing an enterprise. This includes integration of enterprise support systems concerning service delivery and ongoing support. eTOM focus is on common processes used by service providers (SP) for process integration, for interface standardization, and for common information from the customer, service, resource, supplier, or partner. The high-level objectives of eTOM are as follows:

- Establish an "industry" common business process framework.
- Establish common definitions to describe service provider processes.
- Establish agreement on basic information required in these processes.
- Identify the processes, interfaces, integration, and automation requirements.

The eTOM model consists of Level-0, Level-1, and Level-2 processes. Each level drills into further details and provides more specific processes. Level-0 is at the highest level, Level-1 provides more details on Level-0, and Level-2 provides more details on Level-1. This section focuses on Levels 0/1. You can find more details on Levels 0/1/2 from the TMF website (http://tmf.org). The graphic representation of the eTOM model has vertical columns and horizontal layers called *swim lanes*, and the intersection of horizontal layers and vertical columns provides specific eTOM processes.

Figure 6-1 shows highest-level (Level-0) conceptual view of the TMF Business Process Framework (eTOM).[1] It describes and analyzes different levels of enterprise processes according to their significance and priority for the business. The framework is defined as generically as possible so that it remains organization-, technology-, and service-independent.

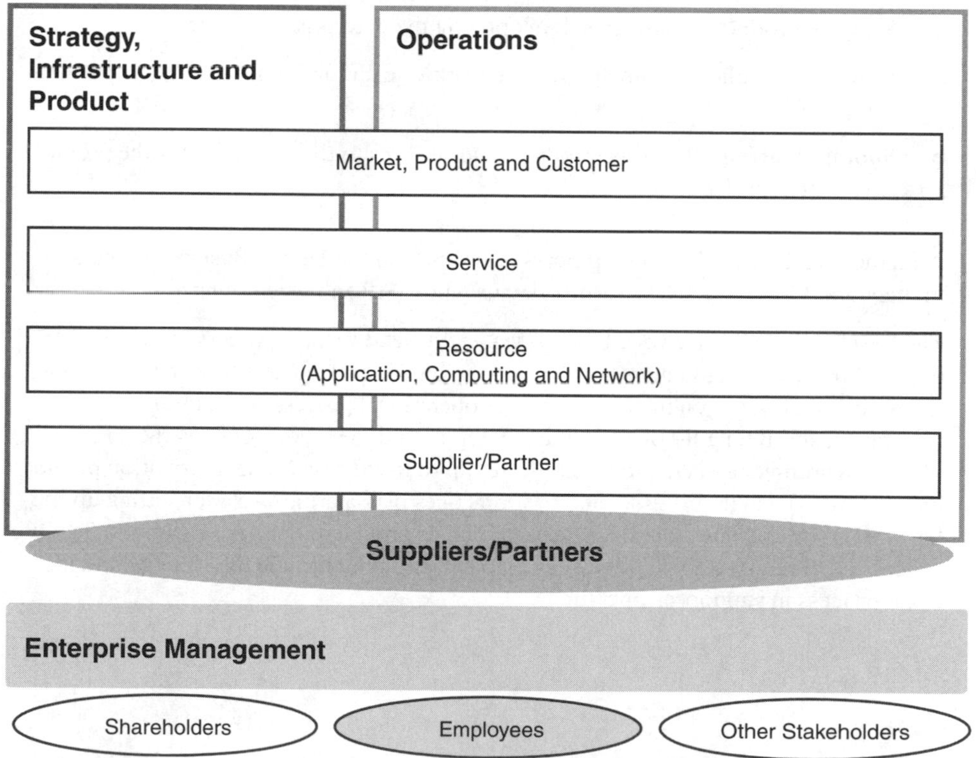

Figure 6-1 *eTOM Level-0 Model (Business Process Framework)*

For service providers, the Business Process Framework serves as the blueprint for process direction and provides a neutral reference point for internal processes, reengineering needs, partnerships, alliances, and general working agreements with other companies. For suppliers, the Business Process Framework outlines potential boundaries of software components that should align with their customers' needs, as well as highlights the required functions, inputs, and outputs that must be supported by their products. At the overall conceptual level, the Business Process Framework can be viewed as having the following three major process areas:

- Strategy, Infrastructure, and Product (SIP) covering strategy and life cycle management process in support of operations
- Operations covering day-to-day operational management
- Enterprise management covering corporate or business support management

As previously mentioned, Figure 6-1 shows two vertical layers (SIP and Operations) and several horizontal layers (called swim lanes) that cut across the two vertical layers. The horizontal functional areas cover the following:

- **Market, product, and customer:** Showing a high-level view of the market and the enterprise's offerings
- **Service:** Product components developed by the enterprise
- **Resource:** Application, computing, network, and storage consumed in the production of the service
- **Supplier/partner:** Providing products and services to the enterprise for the production of the service

A further breakdown of Level-0 processes is shown in the Level-1 Business Process Framework. Figure 6-2 shows further details on the SIP and Operations.[2]

The Level-2 eTOM framework shows seven end-to-end vertical process groupings required to support customers and manage the business. Among these vertical groupings, the focus of eTOM is on the core customer operational processes of Fulfillment, Assurance, and Billing (FAB). Operations Support and Readiness (OSR) is the "back-office" environment where processes are set up to use the real-time information provided by the FAB. The ITIL processes and best practices play a critical role for setting up the back-office operations processes. More on ITIL is provided in the next section. The SIP processes do not directly support the customer, and they include the strategy and life cycle process in support of operations.

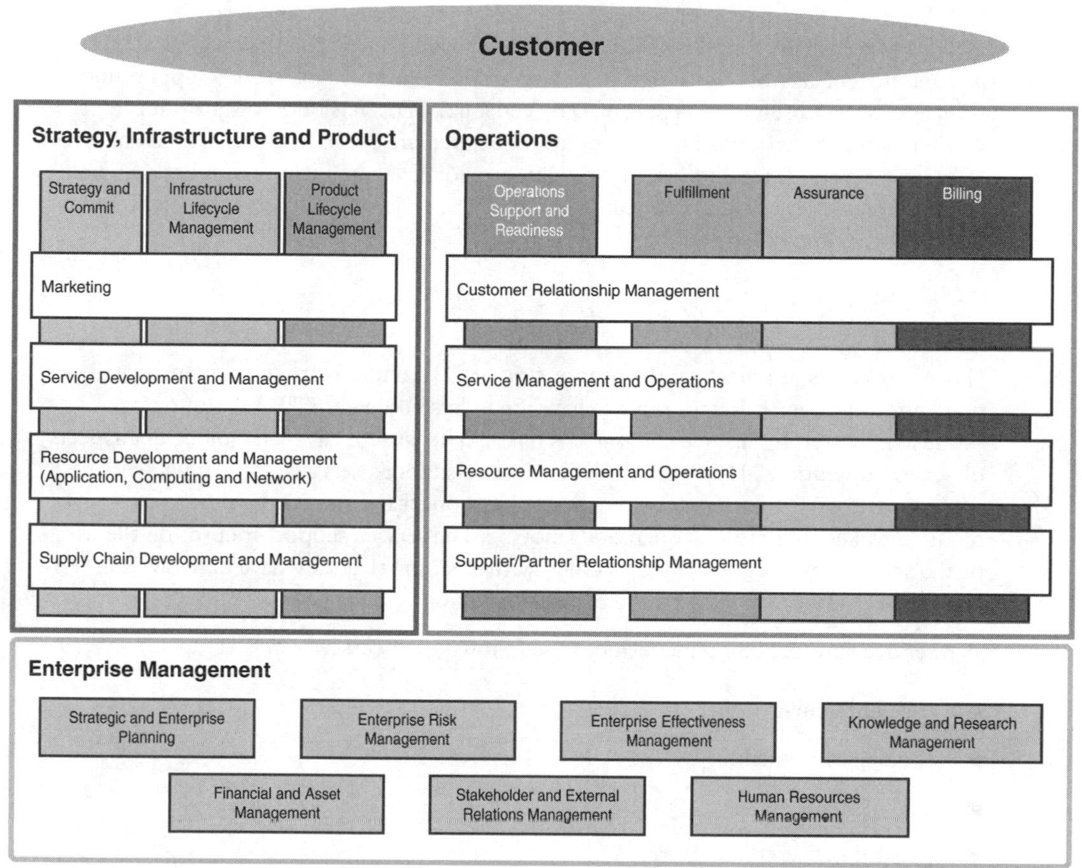

Figure 6-2 *eTOM Level-2 Processes (Business Process Framework)*

Information Technology Infrastructure Library

Information Technology Infrastructure Library (ITIL) provides a framework of best-practice guidance for IT service management and has grown to become the most widely accepted IT service management in the world. Some of the benefits that can be achieved using ITIL are as follows:

- Increased user and customer satisfaction with IT services
- Increased availability leading to business benefits and increased revenue
- Financial savings from reduced rework, lost time, and improved resource usage
- Improved time to market for new products and services
- Improved decision making

ITIL Version 1 was developed by the Office of Government of Commerce (OGC) in the 1980s and was mainly used by the government agencies. From 2001 through 2006, ITIL became the cornerstone of IT service management by introducing service support and service delivery disciplines as part of ITIL Version 2. ITIL Version 3 was introduced in 2007, as a natural progression to introduce IT service life cycle. Its focus is much more on IT being a service, an entity in its own right, providing value to its users rather than being considered as a series of components, the entire IT service considered being greater than the sum of its individual parts.

ITIL Version 2

ITIL Version 2 is important in the progression of ITIL, and it is still used in many enterprise organizations. It is important to have an understanding of ITIL V2, not only because it is used by many organizations but also because it has many important aspects of service operations. ITIL V2 introduced service support, service delivery, and service desk as part of IT service management. Service support focuses on the processes required to keep day-to-day operations moving. The service support focuses on the users of the services and is primarily concerned with ensuring that they have access to the appropriate services to support the business functions.

The service support discipline includes the following processes:

- Incident management
- Problem management
- Change management
- Release management
- Configuration management

The service desks own the incident management and provide foundations for users' issues by coordinating with various management functions and resolve issues on time. Figure 6-3 shows how the service desk (function) interfaces with various processes to support the end user/customer. The service desk functions as the single point of contact (SPOC) for end users' incidents. Its first function is always to "create" an incident ticket. If there is a direct solution, it attempts to resolve the incident at the first level. If the service desk cannot resolve the incident, it is passed to a second/third level group within the incident management system. Incidents can initiate a chain of processes described previously (incident management, problem management, and so on). This chain of processes is tracked using the Configuration Management Database (CMDB), which records each process and creates output documents for traceability.

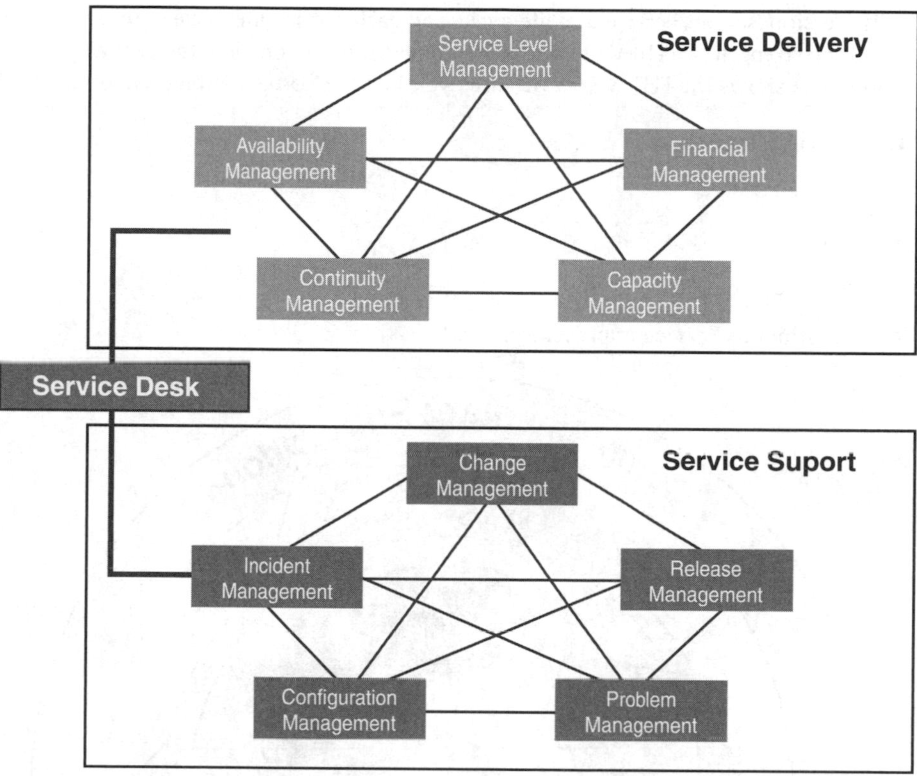

Figure 6-3 *Service Desk Interface to Service Support and Service Delivery*

The service delivery discipline concentrates on the proactive services that must be delivered to provide adequate support to business users. It focuses on the business as the customer of the Information and Communication Technologies (ICT) services. This discipline consists of the following processes:

- Service-level management
- Capacity management
- IT service continuity management
- Availability management
- Financial management

ITIL Version 3

ITIL Version 2 was useful for defining the fundamental business processes and coming up with the best practices for all the ITIL management processes detailed in the previous section. It is becoming more apparent that IT departments are there not just to support some products, but to provide services to its end users. Hence, ITIL Version 3 was born.

ITIL Version 3 treats service as a life cycle, and each service life cycle core process recognizes the strength of ITIL V2 and uses it as a platform to complete the entire life cycle. Figure 6-4 shows the ITIL V3 service life cycle and the corresponding five processes:[3]

- Service strategy
- Service design
- Service transition
- Service operate
- Continuous Service Improvement (CSI)

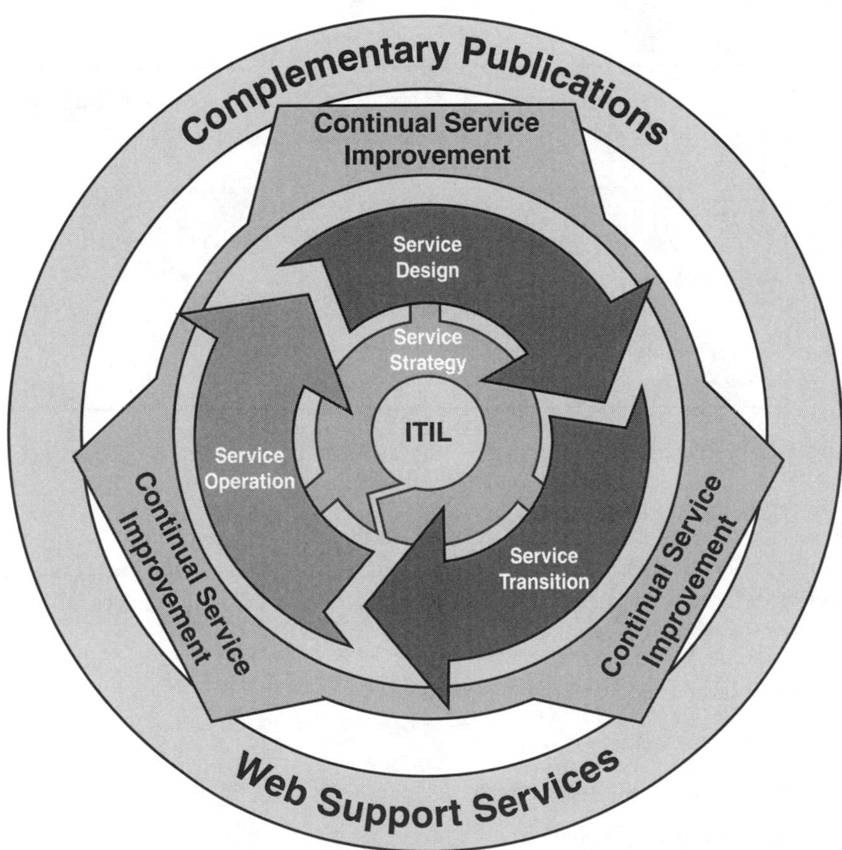

Figure 6-4 *ITIL V3 Life Cycle*

These five processes are further explained in the sections that follow.

Service Strategy

At the center of the ITIL service life cycle, service strategy provides guidance and prioritization of service provider investments in services. Service strategy relies on a market-driven approach and introduces new concepts such as value creation, business case analysis, and market analysis, with the ultimate aim of increasing economic life of the services. It specifically covers the following processes:

- Service portfolio management
- Demand management
- IT financial management

Service Design

Service design provides guidance on the design of IT services, processes, and other aspects of the service management effort. Service design assures that new services and changes or modifications to services are designed effectively to meet customer expectations. It focuses on technology relevant to service delivery and customer usage, rather than focusing solely on the design of the technology itself. The processes required to manage service is also part of service design. Additionally, management systems and tools required to monitor the service must be considered as well as mechanisms for measuring service levels, technology, and process efficiency. It specifically covers the following processes:

- Service catalogue management
- Service-level management
- Risk management
- Capacity management
- Availability management
- IT service continuity management
- Information security management
- Compliance management
- IT architecture management
- Supplier management

Service Transition

Through the service transition phase, the design that is built in the service design phase is built, tested, and put into production to assure that business value can be achieved by the customer. This phase addresses managing changes, controlling assets, configuring items (hardware and software), validating services, testing, and transitioning services to ensure that the service provider people, process, and systems can deliver the services to the end user meeting the service-level agreements. The service transition phase specifically covers the following processes:

- Service asset and configuration management
- Service validation and testing
- Evaluation
- Release management
- Change management
- Knowledge management

Service Operation

In the service operation phase of the life cycle, the requested services and value are directly delivered to the customer. Also, it includes monitoring and rapid restoration of incidents, determining the root cause of problems, and determining the trends associated with recurring events, executing daily provisioning requests to meet the service demands and managing service access. The service operation phase specifically covers the following processes:

- Event management
- Incident management
- Problem management
- Request fulfillment
- Access management

Continuous Service Improvement

The Continuous Service Improvement (CSI) phase is about aligning and realigning for IT services to changing business needs, by implementing improvements to the IT service that support the business processes. CSI envelops the entire life cycle and offers a mechanism for measuring service and making improvements by adjusting/fine-tuning systems and processes in the entire management life cycle. Specifically, the CSI phase supports the following processes:

- Service-level management (SLM)
- Service measurement and reporting
- Continual service improvement

Comparison of ITIL and TMF eTOM

The ITIL processes from ITIL V2 laid the foundation for service support and service delivery for service management, which was later developed into a service management life cycle with the changing times by ITIL V3. However, ITIL does not address enterprise business architecture the way that TMF eTOM does. Some of the flaws of ITIL do not stem from the flaws in the design and implementation of the service management to meet business needs, but are due to a lack of addressing the enterprise business architecture.

Surprisingly, there are more similarities between eTOM and ITIL, and Table 6-1 shows the similarities and differences between eTOM and ITIL taken from the reference and provided here for convenience.[4]

Table 6-1 *eTOM and ITIL Comparison*

	TMF eTOM	ITIL
Context	eTOM is a prescriptive catalogue of process element categories and a total enterprise process framework for the ICT industry.	ITIL is a set of nonprescriptive guidelines for IT/ICT service management.
Objectives	Provides a business process blueprint for service providers to streamline their end-to-end processes. Enables effective communication and common vocabularies within the enterprise as well as with customers and suppliers.	Aligns IT services with the current and future needs of the business and its customers. Enables standard terminology across business and IT. Improves the quality of the IT services delivered. Reduces the long-term cost of service provision.
Scope	Provides a top-down hierarchical view of business processes across the entire enterprise and does not itself address how these processes are supported—by automated or human action (this is, however, addressed in the wider NGOSS program of the TMF). Processes are developed through iterative decomposition. It focuses on identifying the commonality of enterprise processes required among similar services, such as telephony, data, Internet, mobiles, and so on, for delivering high-quality, end-to-end service management. eTOM focuses on service delivery to external customers.	The ITIL processes represent flows in a number of key operational areas, with a strong orientation toward how these processes will map onto IT support environments. Processes are developed through flows. It is primarily nonprescriptive, offering advice and guidance on the implementation and continued delivery of service management, including planning common processes, roles, and activities with appropriate reference to each other and how the communication lines should exist between them. ITIL is primarily focusing on serving internal IT customers.
Adoption	eTOM has been adopted as ITU international standards for the telecom sector and is primarily used by service providers in the ICT industry. eTOM is advanced by the TM Forum: www.tmforum.org.	ITIL is a set of best practices used by tens of thousands of companies worldwide, and it continues to be advanced by itSMF local chapters: www.itsmf.com.

Table 6-1 *eTOM and ITIL Comparison*

	TMF eTOM	ITIL
Implementation	eTOM is a framework; therefore, the implementation will be different from company to company. The implementation of eTOM is supported by other TMF/NGOSS specifications, including the Shared Information/Data (SID) model, NGOSS Lifecycle and Methodology, and other related specifications.	ITIL is a framework; therefore, the implementation will be different from company to company. Until recently, ITIL did not provide guidelines on the implementation order or means to assess the maturity of the service organization. In Version 3, more attention is being paid to implementation guidelines.
Compliance	eTOM compliance is achieved through the TMF/NGOSS Compliance Program; its certification is on tools, not on organizations or processes. The NGOSS compliance program encompasses the conformance tests of other NGOSS specifications that further define the business objects and operations framework required for effective eTOM implementation.	ITIL is not a standard, nor is it a set of regulations, and therefore, neither tools, processes, or people can be deemed "ITIL compliant." Processes and organizations can be assessed against ISO 20000, the IT service management standard based on ITIL. However, neither tools nor individuals can be certified against ISO 20000.

The terminology between eTOM and ITIL is not always consistent and creates confusion among many engineers. eTOM and ITIL have been working together as a part of a harmonization process and have been mapping the terminology. Table 6-2 illustrates how some of the common terms are used between eTOM and ITIL.

Table 6-2 *Common Terminology Between eTOM and ITIL*

eTOM	ITIL
Resource	Asset
Fault	Incident: An event that is not part of standard operation that causes or can cause an interruption to service or a reduction in the quality of service
Fault: Inability of an item to perform the required function Trouble: Perception of a fault or degradation of service that requires maintenance Failure: Termination of the ability to perform the required function	Problem: An unknown underlying cause of one or more incidents

Table 6-2 *Common Terminology Between eTOM and ITIL*

eTOM	ITIL
Service: Developed by a service provider for sale	Service: One or more IT systems that enable a business process
User: Subscriber who uses the service	User: The person who uses the service on a day-to-day basis
Customer contact point	Service desk

ITU-T TMN

ITU, the international organization for standardization in the telecom world, and ISO, the international standardization organization, have jointly defined a concept for standardization of protocols for monitoring and management of the Telecommunications Management Network (TMN). The TMN concept deals with issues related to management systems that support planning, provisioning, installing, maintaining, and administering the network. The TMN model is often referred as the FCAPS (Fault, Configuration, Accounting, Performance, and Security) model.

TMN and eTOM are the global de facto Business Process Frameworks at the enterprise level for the telecommunications Industry. The TMN model is a way to think logically about how the business of a service provider is managed, whereas eTOM is a Business Process Framework targeted at the development of business and operations support systems that exist within network service providers.

The Open Systems Interconnect (OSI) group has defined management functionality in network operations, as shown in the five categories listed in Table 6-3. This same model has also been adopted and supported by the standards body ITU-T. This categorization is a functional view and does not attempt to describe business-related roles within a telecom or data network.

The FCAPS subfunctions within each of the five major groups are typically performed at differing levels within the TMN model. For example, fault management at the element management level in TMN is detailed logging of all discrete alarms or other events. The element management level then filters and forwards alarms/events to the network management level, where alarm correlation, corrective action, and other actions take place.

The communications industry has embraced the Telecommunications Management Network (TMN) model as a way to think logically about how the business of a service provider is managed. The TMN architecture model is designed for hierarchical telecommunications management. Sponsored by the International Telecommunications Union (ITU) and its standards body (ITU-T), this model was initially created in 1988.

Table 6-3 *FCAPS Management Functions*

Fault Management	Configuration Management	Accounting Management	Performance Management	Security Management
Alarm handling	System turn-up	Usage tracking	Baseline definition	Access control
Trouble detection and logging	Provisioning	Billing	Capacity planning	Security administration
Diagnosis	Autodiscovery	Asset tracking	Performance analysis	System audit
Trouble correction	Backup and restore	Service-level management	Monitoring	Alert monitoring
Test and acceptance	Database handling	Vendor management	Reporting	Encryption
Network recovery	Change/inventory management			Policy management
Fault reporting	Certifications			

Figure 6-5 shows the TMN logical layers. The TMN model consists of five layers, usually arranged in a triangle or pyramid. Business management is at the apex, service management is the second layer, network management is the third layer, element management the fourth layer, and the fifth or bottom layer is the network element or device layer that is being managed. The concept is that management decisions at each layer are different but interrelated. For example, detailed information is needed to keep a switch operating (at the element management layer), but only a subset of that information is needed at higher TMN layers to keep the network operating. Working from the top down, each layer imposes requirements on the layer below. Working from the bottom up, each layer provides capabilities to the layer above.

For network management, this model is particularly relevant and understood by the telecommunications carriers and management tools used in this space. The management functions in each of the TMN layers are as follows:

- **Business Management Layer (BML)**
  - Manage the overall business (strategic planning)
  - Achieve ROI (revenue assurance)
  - Business process engineering

- **Service Management Layer (SML)**
    - Manage the services offered to clients
    - Meet SLAs and service quality (service assurance as defined in this model)
    - Meet cost, delivery, and time to market
- **Network Management Layer (NML)**
    - Manage network end-to-end performance (network assurance as defined in this model)
    - Manage network capacity, diversity, congestion, and so on
- **Element Management Layer (EML)**
    - Manage specific elements in the network
    - Configure devices
    - Load software into the devices
- **Network Element Layer (NEL)**
    - Compute resources (servers)
    - Storage resources
    - Network resources (switches, routers, firewalls, load balancers, and so on)

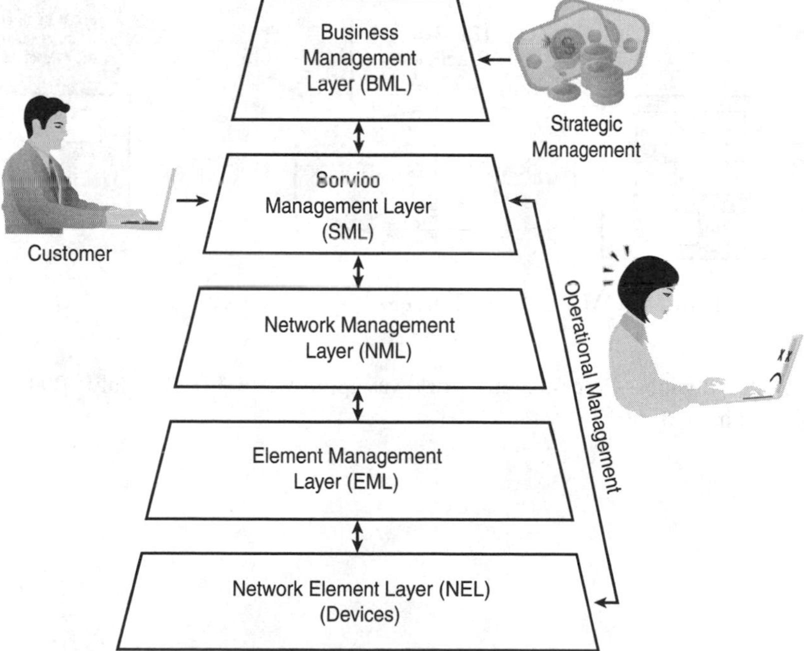

Figure 6-5 *ITU-T TMN Logical Layers*

The main differentiator between eTOM and TMN is that the TMN approach was built on the requirements to manage network equipment and networks (bottom up), while eTOM was built on the need to support business processes of the entire service provider enterprise (top down).

In June 2004, a joint eTOM-ITIL team was created to explore the interworking of the two frameworks. The team's findings are published in the GB921V and TR143 documents, part of the eTOM specification. GB921V shows how the two frameworks can work together by integrating ITIL processes into eTOM process flows. TR143 presents a strategy for further converging the two frameworks, as shown in Figure 6-6.

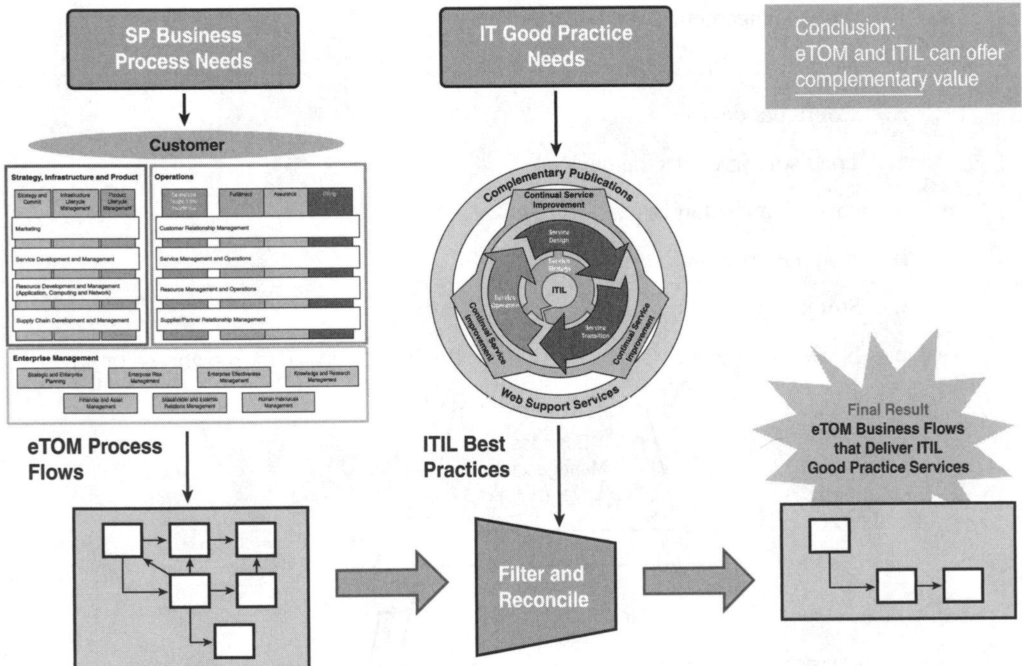

Figure 6-6 *ITIL and eTOM Working Together*

The eTOM Business Process Framework was approved by ITU-T in July 2004 and was published in M 3050.[5]

Building Cloud Models Using Standards

The following sections will describe several enterprise architecture reference models using the standards such as eTOM, ITIL, and TMN described in the previous sections. The term *enterprise* refers to entities such as a public or private sector organization, an entire business, a corporation, or part of a larger corporation such as a business unit. An enterprise architecture framework has items such as

- Processes and functions considered in ITIL V2
- Life cycle phases used in ITIL Phase 3
- Business process models of various functions and how they interact at each of the layers such as resource management and service management as in eTOM

An enterprise architecture framework also includes operations readiness using various teams in an enterprise to deliver services. It is very difficult and cumbersome to depict all of these on one enterprise architecture diagram. So, it is advisable to break it down into a few practical reference architectures such as process architecture, functional architecture, and services architecture. These models are described further in the following sections. Specifically, the following enterprise reference architectures are discussed:

- Cloud process model using ITIL V3
- Cloud framework and management model using eTOM/ITIL/TMN

Cloud Reference Architecture: Process Model

Figure 6-7 shows a traditional reference architecture that might be used in any IT organization.[6] The service desk handles incidents and problems and provides an interface for other activities such as change requests, maintenance contracts, software licenses, service-level management, configuration management, availability management, financial management, and IT services continuity management.

Incident and *problem management* are ITIL terms and not used in TMN or eTOM; however, they are equivalent to *fault management* in TMN. ITIL distinguishes between incident and problem management. An *incident* is any event that is not part of the standard operation of the service and which causes, or can cause, an interruption or a reduction of the quality of the service. *Incident management* aims to restore normal service operation as quickly as possible and minimize the adverse effect on business operations, thus ensuring that the best possible levels of service quality and availability are maintained. *Normal service operation* is defined here as service operation within service-level agreement (SLA) limits. A *problem* is a condition often identified as a result of multiple incidents that exhibit common symptoms. Problems can also be identified from a single significant incident, indicative of a single error for which the cause is unknown, but for which the impact is significant. ITIL treats problem management differently than incident management. The purpose of problem management is to find and resolve the root cause of a problem and prevent any further incidents, whereas the purpose of incident management is to return the service to a normal level as soon as possible, with the smallest possible business impact.

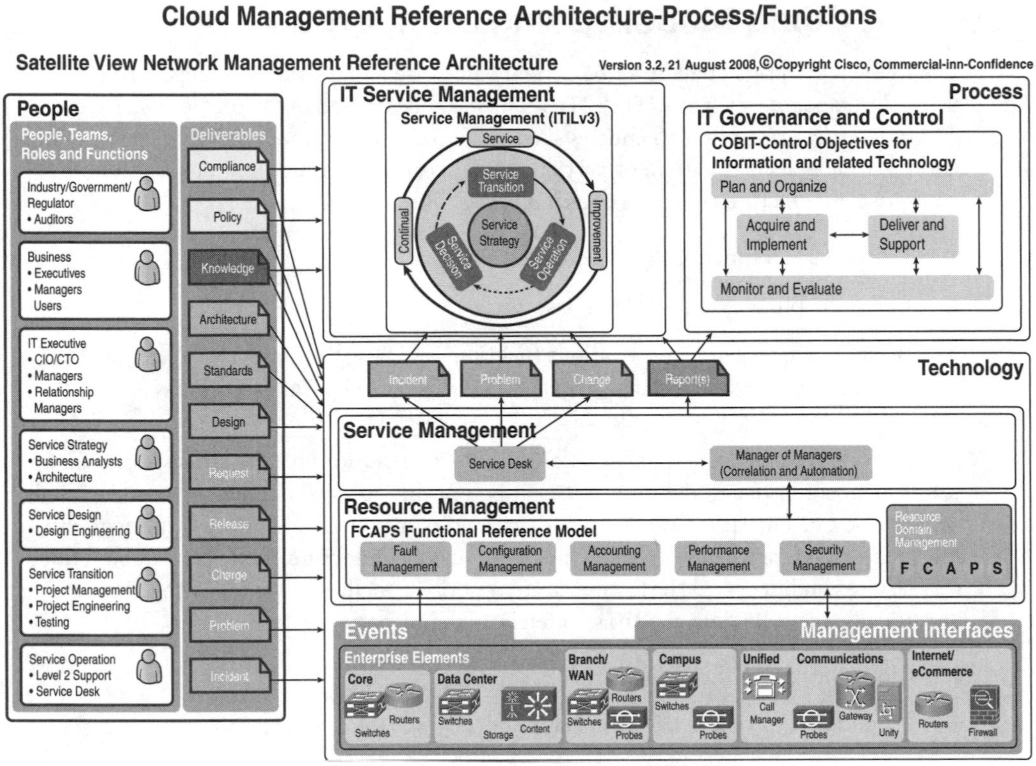

Figure 6-7 *Cloud Management Reference Architecture - Process/Functions*

The service desk function, as explained in the previous section (refer to Figure 6-3), is the single point of contact (SPOC) to meet communications needs. It coordinates with service support and service delivery processes and also all the people such as industry/government regulators, business IT executives, and IT processes such as service strategy, service design, service transition, and service operation. The service desk also interfaces with various tools, such as Manager of Managers (MOM), that correlate events and alarm messages received either directly from the infrastructure devices or through domain managers.

Cloud Framework and Management Model

Figure 6-7 illustrates a traditional reference architecture for management, given the dynamic nature of cloud it is important enhance the resource management and technical orchestration capabilities of this model.. Not every customer might be offering all the services that are possible through the cloud. The cloud framework and management functions provided here are generic, and a subset of functions from the infrastructure and management might be adequate for many customers. Typically, the infrastructure and the management of the infrastructures are determined as part of the assessment service done in the ITIL V3 strategy phase.

An enhanced cloud framework has four horizontal layers, as shown on the left side of Figure 6-8:[7]

- Application/service layer
- Resource control layer
- Resource-abstracted virtualization layer
- Physical resource layer

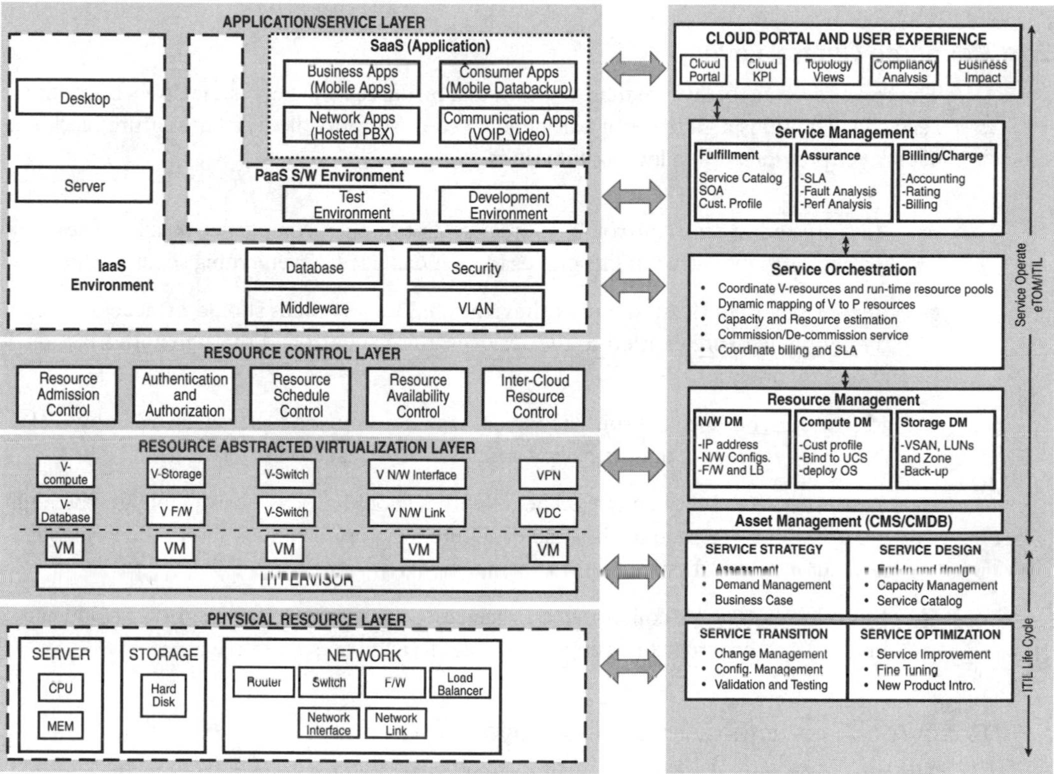

Figure 6-8 *Cloud Reference Architecture (Infrastructure and Management)*

The sections that follow describe the layers of the cloud framework in greater detail.

Application/Service Layer

The application/service layer contains the SaaS applications, PaaS environment, and IaaS environment with the following attributes:

- Server, desktop, database, and VLAN for IaaS
- Development environment and test environment for PaaS
- Business, consumer, network, and communication applications

Resource Control Layer

The resource control layer manages the virtual resources and serves the application and service layer and is area that is greatly enhanced to support the dynamic nature of cloud. This layer provides the following functions:

- **Resource admission control:** It enforces security policy compliance on all devices seeking access to infrastructure resources to limit damage from emerging security threats.
- **Resource authentication and authorization:** The resources should be accessed only by people who are entitled to the services; this is controlled through authorization and authentication.
- **Resource schedule control:** The virtual resources must be accessed from physical resources for maximum efficiency and allotment based on prioritization.
- **Resource availability control:** The resources should always be available for the highest possible SLAs, and in the case of failure, backup resources should be available. It also should have disaster recovery capability.
- **Intercloud resource control:** In this scenario, the resources from another cloud can be used and controlled to support services to end users.

Resource-Abstracted Virtualization Layer

The resources from the physical layer are abstracted using a collection of technological capabilities to hide physical characteristics, and made available to users so that they can be used at scale and in a multitenant environment. It has the following characteristics:

- Allocated to customers on demand and at scale
- Capabilities of physical devices but in a virtual mode (PtoV)
- Migration of one VM to another VM on another server seamlessly
- Presenting physical devices as multiple logical devices (VDC)

Physical Resource Layer

The physical resources at the lowest layer contain the physical devices for network, compute, and storage. These resources are not visible to the user, and they are abstracted and provide to the user through the cloud portal as cloud services. The physical layer has

- Compute resources (servers with CPU and memory)
- Storage resources with disk space
- Networks with routers, switches, load balancers, firewalls, network links, and network interfaces

Management Reference Architecture

The management of the four horizontal layers of the cloud framework shown on the left side in Figure 6-8 is done through the management architecture on the right side of the figure. The right side has several layers as well, and the number of management layers varies from standard to standard. In the case of ITU-TMN, they are managed through

- Business management and presentation layers
- Service management and orchestration layers
- Resource and asset management layers
- Operational management layer

The Business, Service and Resource layers roughly correspond to the management layers in the TMF eTOM and TMN, which are as follows:

- Customer relationship management
- Service management and operations
- Resource management and operations

The operational management layer aligns to ITIL V3, which treats management as a life cycle with the following phases:

- Service strategy
- Service design
- Service transition (implementation)
- Service operate
- Continuous service improvement (optimization)

All the listed standards (TMN, eTOM, and ITIL V3) have merits and are required to be considered to build management architecture for cloud management. The TMN approach was built on the requirements to manage infrastructure equipment from the bottom up, while eTOM was built on the need to support processes of the entire service provider enterprise from the top down.

The right side of Figure 6-8 illustrates the hybrid reference management architecture using the various standards discussed, with the recommended tasks that need to be performed for managing clouds. More details on functions that are shown on the right side of Figure 6-8 are covered throughout this book.

Integration of Management Systems/Functions

The service providers face many challenges with the legacy systems they have and the new systems to be added to manage advanced technologies such as cloud-based services. Many of the best practices in systems and processes developed as part of ITIL V3, eTOM, and TMN should be used to build a sustainable architecture with long-term business requirements in mind. The following sections provide some of the service provider challenges, Service-Oriented Architecture (SOA), and integration recommendations to build and manage a cloud infrastructure and provide cloud services (IaaS, PaaS, and SaaS).

Cloud Provider Challenges

The cloud provider environment is rapidly changing. The IT architects who are planning both private and public cloud services are faced with some key challenges:

- **Reduction of OPEX:** Doing more with less is a reality, and automating the repetitive tasks, reducing the labor, and reducing the Operational Expenditure (OPEX) without sacrificing customer service is required.
- **Reduction of integration tax:** Diverse systems bring many integration challenges, and the effort to integrate and maintain the systems could be very expensive. This problem should be dealt with by selecting the systems that are fit for purpose and fit for use, and with the right APIs in order to be able to integrate with other systems with ease.
- **Best-of-breed systems:** No one vendor can provide all the functionalities and expertise needed to provide end-to-end functionality; also, service providers do not want to be locked in to one vendor.
- **Shift from product-based to solution focus:** Though products from many vendors are used, all the systems need to work together and act as if it is one end-to-end system.
- **Order to cash (OTC):** Refers to the business process for receiving and processing customer sales. To provide OTC, automation/orchestration of service orders is required, and appropriate integration to assurance systems and billing systems is required.

- **Quick problem identification and remediation:** To maintain appropriate SLAs and differentiated service and quick identification of events/faults, correlation of events and remediation of the faults are required, before the service is affected.
- **Open APIs:** The open APIs is essential for many cloud providers to interconnect many diverse systems in the organization.

Service-Oriented Architecture

Service-Oriented Architecture (SOA) is the most important technology initiative for businesses today but one of the most difficult to implement. SOA is an architectural style that views IT solutions essentially as a collection of services. These services communicate with each other in support of the business. The communication can involve either simple data passing, or it could involve two or more services coordinating some activity. SOA represents a dramatic change in the relationship between business and IT. SOA is the principle behind the layered architecture, where each layer is providing services corresponding to that layer and providing the services to the upper layers. Service orchestration is a very important aspect of SOA and is important in the integration of layers to connect all the management functions/systems to interwork seamlessly so that the abstracted cloud services can be provided to the customers without dealing with any of the complexities of the physical layer. To enable the ecosystem of suppliers, the following principles should be followed:

- **Consistent interfaces so that the data should be mappable through parameter translations:** TMF provides guidance in this area, and offers OSS/J (OSS through Java) SOA enablement APIs. This set of APIs is most suitable for the implementation and deployment of OSS solutions that require the use of several APIs in accordance with SOA. The APIs offer three programmatic or message-driven integration profiles: tight coupling with Java/RMI (Remote Method Invocation)/IIOP (Internet Inter-ORB Protocol), loose coupling with XML/JMS, and cross boundaries with Web Services.[8]
- **Consistent data modeling:** Data modeling between layers should be done in a consistent manner. There should be unambiguous mappings between different data sets, and the TMF SID (Shared Information Data) model offers guidance in this area.

Integration Enablers

The integration between various SOA layers can be done using integration enablers. Figure 6-9 shows the SOA layered architecture and interfaces between the layers.[9]

The standard APIs provide the best approach for integrating the interfacing systems. This enables the systems to be plug and play. The integration technology provides the true runtime environment for managing the infrastructure. The integration technologies include J2EE, Enterprise Java Beans (EJB), Web Services, and the Enterprise Application Integration (EAI) message-based integration framework.

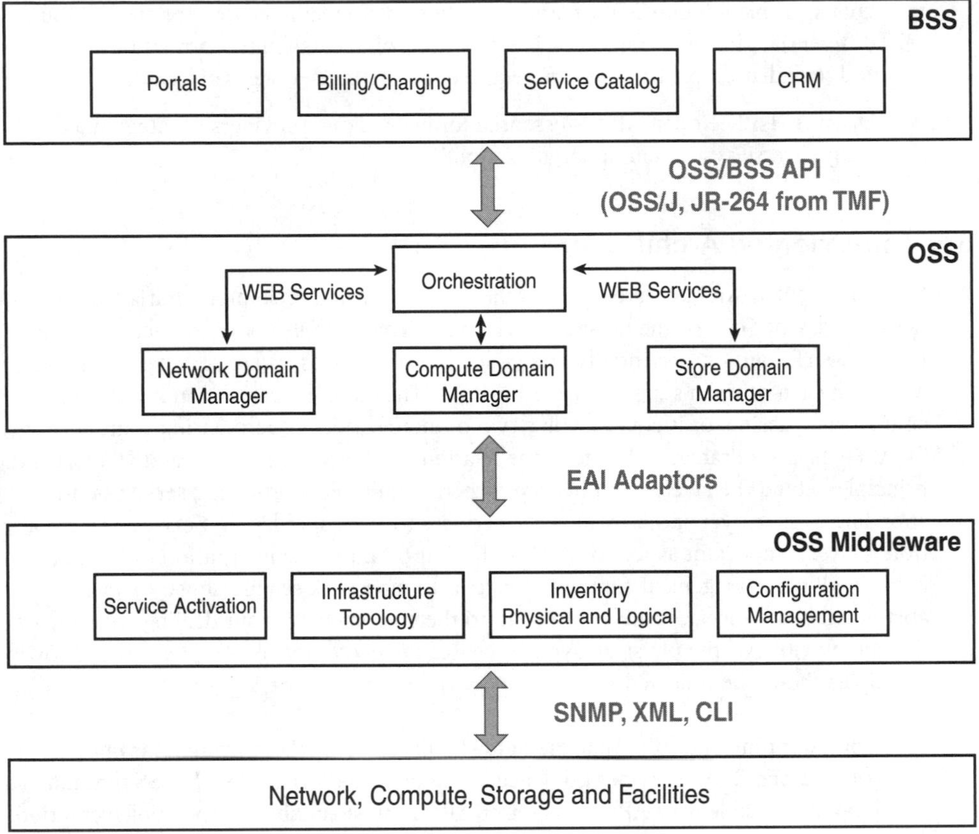

Figure 6-9 *OSS/BSS Integration Enablers*

The following list describes some of the integration enablers:

- The integration between the BSS layer and OSS layer is through OSS/J when standard interfaces exist. The OSS/J is implemented using EJB.
- If the interfaces are not standard, custom API tool kits become necessary (for example, EAI tool kits).
- Use web services between orchestration and domain managers.
- Use standard middleware (EAI adapters) for applications such as service activation, topology, and inventory and configuration management.
- The data collection from the devices is mainly through Simple Network Management Protocol (SNMP), XML, and the command-line interface (CLI).

The middleware shown in Figure 6-9 sits between network and OSS and provides some of the standard OSS middleware service components:

- **Topology service:** Infrastructure topology comprising network, compute, and storage
- **Fault management service:** Components for fault management by receiving events from the devices
- **Network abstraction service:** Abstraction service using specific service components
- **Inventory service:** Network and service inventories

The preceding list is not exhaustive, but it gives you the general idea of the type of middleware service components.

Summary

This chapter provided information on three key standards used in IT organizations for designing and managing data centers and clouds. The TMF eTOM is a prescriptive catalog of processes for the service provider from the top down, and ITU-T TMN was built on the requirements to manage infrastructure equipment from the bottom up. ITIL is not a prescriptive standard like eTOM and TMN, but it provides best practices for IT management and is widely used by many IT organizations. Using these three standards and best practice approaches, two reference architectures are described. Also, integration of management systems methodology and recommendations are provided in order for the management systems from various vendors to work together seamlessly.

References

[1] enhanced Telecom Operations Map (eTOM) Level-0, at www.tmforum.org/sdata/browsable/etom/dI121.htm.

[2] enhanced Telecom Operations Map (eTOM) Level-1, at www.tmforum.org/BusinessProcessFramework/6775/home.html.

[3] ITIL V3 process flows, at http://tinyurl.com/3phkuvd.

[4] TOM and ITIL comparison, at www.bptrends.com/publicationfiles/01-05%20eTOM%20and%20ITIL%20-%20Huang.pdf.

[5] ITU-T Recommendation, Introduction of eTOM, at www.billingcollege.com/upload/M.3050.0.pdf.

[6] Keith Sinclair, "Network Management Reference Architecture," at www.cisco.com/en/US/technologies/collateral/tk869/tk769/white_paper_c11-453503.html.

[7] Cloud Reference Framework, IETF, draft, December 2010, at http://tools.ietf.org/html/draft-khasnabish-cloud-reference-framework-00.

[8] TMF Forum SID, at www.tmforum.org/SOAEnablementView/4492/home.html.

[9] OSS/BSS Architecture and Its Implementation Scenario for Fulfillment; white paper from Nokia and TietoEnator, at www.nokia.com/NOKIA_COM_1/About_Nokia/Press/White_Papers/pdf_files/nokia_tietoenator_0605_net.pdf.

Chapter 7

Service Fulfillment

Upon completing this chapter, you should be able to understand the following:

- Cloud service fulfillment (cloud service provisioning) using ITIL processes
- Steps involved in cloud service provisioning on an end-to-end basis
- Service orchestration/service automation
- Cloud functional reference architecture

This chapter describes the details of cloud service fulfillment, also referred to as cloud service provisioning. Service fulfillment is responsible for delivering products and services to the customer. This includes order handling, service configuration and activation, and resource provisioning. In Chapter 6, "Cloud Management Reference Architecture," two cloud reference architectures are covered from a management perspective. This chapter will provide details on cloud service fulfillment and an end-to-end logical functional architecture for managing clouds. The end-to-end logical functional architecture is built based on the Tele-Management Forum (TMF) eTOM (enhanced Telecom Operations Map)[1] and the Information Technology Infrastructure Library (ITIL) V3 life cycle.[2]

Cloud Fulfillment Using ITILV3

ITIL V3 provided the IT life cycle processes: service strategy, service design, service transition, service operate, and Continuous Service Improvement (CSI). Applying these processes is a good way to establish service provision processes for data center/virtualization (DC/V) and cloud provisioning. Figure 7-1 shows cloud service provisioning flow based on ITIL Version 3.

Building data centers that are capable of providing service on demand, at scale, and with multitenancy requires principles of cloud computing and transformation from the current operational environment (current operational state) to the cloud environment (target operational state). Cloud management should be seen as a life cycle rather than an IT providing product support. These principles are well articulated in ITIL V3. Figure 7-1 shows the five phases of the cloud ITIL V3 service life cycle:

1. Service strategy
2. Service design
3. Service transition
4. Service operate
5. Continuous Service Improvement (CSI)

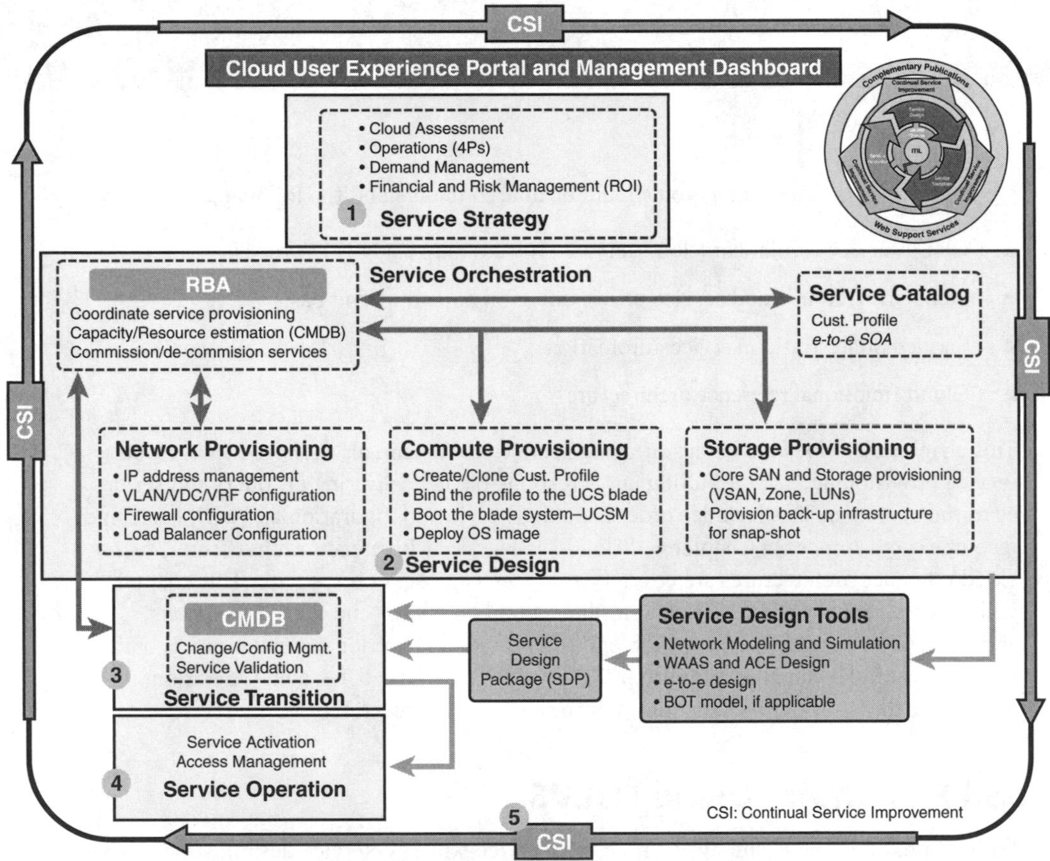

Figure 7-1 *Cloud Service Provisioning Flow Based on ITIL V3*

Figure 7-1 also shows some of the items that need to be considered in each of the five phases of the cloud service life cycle to provision a cloud. More details are provided in the following sections describing the ITIL V3 phases.

Service Strategy Phase

Data center/virtualization (DC/V) and cloud-computing technologies can have a significant impact on IT service delivery, cost, and continuity of services, but as with any transformative technology, the adoption is greatly influenced by the up-front preparedness and strategy.

In a dramatic change from just a few years ago, the role of CIO has changed from keeping the lights on to becoming a strategic thinker and transforming the IT department from a cost center or a commodity center to a strategic value provider. The CIOs are being invited into board rooms for strategic planning, and with the increased visibility comes increased responsibility to bring both top-line and bottom-line business value. When CIOs lack voice in the boardroom, their job becomes more of a keep-the-lights-on position and eventually becomes victim to budget cuts and outsourcing many of the IT functions. IT governance can help the CIOs to become the agent of change and be an active partner in laying out the company's strategy. The IT organization's success factors include the following:

- Technology decisions driven by a business strategy (not the other way around)
- Sustaining the IT activities as efficiently as possible
- Speed to market
- Technology architecture aligning with the business initiatives, and technology is at the heart of value proposition

With the preceding principles in mind, we will develop high-level tasks that are needed in each of the five areas of ITIL V3. During the service strategy phase, the following items should be considered at a minimum to be successful in cloud services:

- Cloud architecture assessment
- Operations (people, processes, products, and partners [the 4Ps])
- Demand management
- Financial management or value creation (ROI)
- Risk management

These items are discussed further in the sections that follow.

Cloud Architecture Assessment

Enterprises today are facing challenges to meet increasing demand for automating the services and how best to meet the demand as the business evolves. The cloud architecture assessment looks into current architecture and technology choices (with a focus on the future) to determine the most appropriate cloud strategy, architecture, and operations management. The architecture assessment analyzes current tools and new tools required for automation, current operating practices with an eye for improving the operations of cloud management, demand management, financial management, and risk management. This architecture assessment helps make sure that the customer's updated infrastructure meets reliability and capacity goals and can scale to meet future requirements. The salient points of cloud architecture assessment are as follows:

- **Current tools and architecture:** This depends on whether the customer is planning to move to clouds from a greenfield or a brownfield. If it is a greenfield, it would be easier from a product vendor perspective because the product vendors do not have to deal with the legacy equipment and all the integration issues with the legacy equipment. For a brownfield, more work is involved. It is possible that the customer infrastructure might have only parts of the network (compute and storage) or all the parts, and it is important to see how the customer is operating various parts of the infrastructure. Operating the infrastructure as silos using disparate systems is not only inefficient technically, but also operationally. So, it is possible that sufficient savings can be achieved in Operational Expenditure (OPEX) with changes in the management and operations architecture. Also, operating the infrastructure as silos is very inefficient because it would require so much coordination between the siloed operations centers that it would take much longer to isolate faults in the network, compute, and storage, all of which affect the service-level agreements (SLA) offered to the customer. These SLAs are always based on service and not individual parts of the cloud infrastructure.
- **Cloud-provisioning tools:** The provisioning assessment of tools should include, at a minimum, service portal, service catalog, Configuration Management System/Configuration Management Database(CMS/CMDB), service automation, and domain configuration tools. Depending on the size of the company and the type of the company (enterprise or service provider), investigate whether tools should be purchased or leased. Also, consider whether to host in the enterprise data center, in the enterprise private cloud, in the service provider cloud, or in Software as a Service (SaaS) provider clouds.
- **Replacement of tools:** This should be done carefully and can be achieved only by cooperatively working with the operations personnel. Operations personnel are used to legacy systems and would resist changes because they require learning and changes in operations. So, care should be taken to recommend replacement only if it is necessary.
- **Addition of new tools:** The need to add new tools to address gaps in the current architecture and new cloud services should be addressed. The new systems selection should be based on several factors, including ease of integration with the existing systems, open APIs, implementation costs, license costs, integration costs, and support from the vendor after it is implemented.
- **Security:** Security is a big concern for enterprises and service providers who want to move to the cloud. The business requirements are very important here during the assessment phase. Identity management (IDM) in cloud computing is a nebulous application for most enterprises. Although cloud efforts promote cost savings and management efficiencies, it all boils down to trust. Federating identity management

might make sense in a cloud environment where users might be logging in to applications within and outside of firewalls. Authenticating every user will come at a cost, because it would involve constant password resetting and more calls to the help desk. Security is more than identity management and is discussed in detail in Chapter 4, "IT Services," and Chapter 5, "The Cisco Cloud Strategy."

- **Identity management (IAM):** Some SaaS applications might be more cost effective for identity management because they are designed for efficiency, rapid time to value, and minimal disruption, and they can be rightsized. Also, a full-blown suite might not be necessary when all you need is a small subset of functions. This would keep client costs down from the perspective of both monthly services and professional services. For example, having an in-house IAM product could cost a total of $700,000 to $1 million (acquisition + license and connectors + implementation costs + administrator costs + infrastructure [servers and so on]).

All the preceding items should be documented in Current State Architecture (CSA) and Target State Architecture (TSA) documents. The CSA and TSA documents that document a customer's architecture become a blueprint of the customer architecture, as they provide documentation for all the changes and the rationale for making those changes.

Operations People, Processes, Products, and Partners (4Ps)

The move to cloud computing is well under way, and companies are investing for rolling out cloud services. The basic value proposition for cloud computing is straightforward: Users can leverage a wide range of computing resources without the capital investment or maintenance infrastructure necessary to build and maintain these services internally. However, companies considering a move to the cloud must understand whether and how cloud services might fit into their IT strategy and operations. IT operations is responsible for delivering the agreed-upon level of IT services to the business and to maintain the SLAs, even if the infrastructure is in an external cloud. Although not owning infrastructure provides Capital Expenditure (CapEx) benefits which is one off-benefit in CapEx, making operations more efficient improves the Operational Expenditure (OPEX), which is a benefit enjoyed year over year. As a part of a strategy, service providers should look into IT operations and make changes in operations to support cloud-based services. The following list provides some insight into operations with an eye toward cloud management:

- Current operations processes and products might need improvement based on new services and support. Many of the customer's organizations are established in silos. Operations processes need to be improved so that the organizations are more agile and inter-connected to operate new cloud-based services. Speed to market and speed to react are essential for service delivery and service support.

- Current methods and procedures should be checked and improvements/adjustments made to provide service delivery and service support for cloud services. Figure 7-2 shows the transformation to a virtualized infrastructure management. Today, some of the IT organizations might be organized in silos to support network, compute, and storage services. ITIL V3 teaches us that products and services should be not only fit for purpose (utility) but also fit for use (warranty). In the cloud context, many organizations might be providing services "fit for purpose" for network, compute, and storage silos, as shown on the left side of Figure 7-2. For cloud management, it is essential to operate in a holistic way with the overall business in mind, as shown on the right side of Figure 7-2. Cisco's operations assessment service reviews current operations, and provides recommendations and roadmap for transforming the current operation into future-state operations required for managing cloud based services.

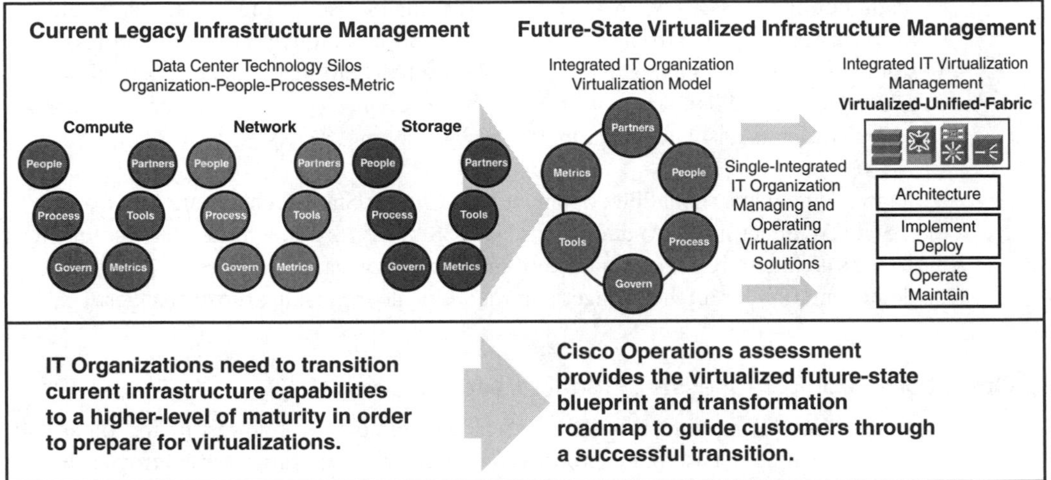

Figure 7-2 *Transformation to Virtualized Infrastructure Management*

- Figure 7-3 shows how the functional areas of the enterprise (people, processes, organization, and governance metrics) might be addressing products/services in a siloed and nonvirtualized manner. The Cisco operations assessment reviews these enterprise functional areas and provides recommendations to transform from a non-virtualized to a virtualized environment.
- A partner's capability should be checked for its capability to manage the new services, and any gaps should be addressed through training, or replace the current partner with a new partner that has the required capabilities. The SLAs offered depend not only on contracts with the internal organization, but also with the external partners.

Functional Areas	Non-Virtualized		Virtualized
People: • Skills • Roles • Responsibilities •Training	• Technology Specific Silos • Deep Domain Expertise • Point Technology Staffed • Silo Career Path Training • Limited Cross-Technology Collaboration	Transform To	• E2E Services Focused • Consolidated I/O–FCoE • Compute-Network-Storage Skills • New Role–Virtualization Architects • New Role–Virtualization Engineers
Process: • Operation Management • Availability Management • Performance Management • Testing and Deployment • Architecture Planning	• Box Based Provisioning • Poor Process Integration • Silo Point Technology Driven • Not Well Documented–Understood • Throw-Over Wall Approach • Point Technology Defines Tools	Transform To	• Intelligent Software Based • Well Orchestrated Procedures • Integrated SLA and OLA • IP Management (Repository) • Shared Services Driven • Integrated Fabric Tool-Suite
Organizations: • Structures • Departments • Charters • Reporting • Culture	• Hierarchical • Department Technology Specific • Technology Funded–Silo • Technology MBOs–Metrics • Poor External Communication	Transform To	• Services Centric • Shared MBOs • Shared Services • Cross-Functional • Highly Collaborative
Governance–Metrics: • Architecture Standards • Virtualization Patterns • Security Policies • Financial Management • Metrics Monitoring	• Ad-Hoc • Limited Documentation • Silo-Not Shared • Limited Compliance • Not Measured/Monitored	Transform To	• Virtualization Standards • Consolidated I/O Guidelines • Cross-Functional Managed • Well Define Metrics • Architecture Review Board

Figure 7-3 *Transformation of Functional Areas: Nonvirtualized to Virtualized Environment*

Demand Management

Service management is faced with the task of finding a continual balance between consumption and delivery of resources. Demand management calculates this demand for service capacity and controls the necessary capacity with the expected flexibility. Demand management is a critical aspect of service management. Unlike goods, services cannot be manufactured, stored, and sold at a later time. Poorly managed demand is a source of risk for service providers because of the uncertainty in demand. Excess capacity generates cost without creating value, and customers do not like to pay for idle capacity unless it has value for them. Demand management includes the following important aspects:

- At a strategic level, cloud demand management involves determining Patterns of Business Activity (PBA). A PBA is a workload profile of one or more business activities, and it helps the service provider to understand and plan for the different levels of business activity. Understanding the customer's PBA, such as when he watches cable TV and when he accesses the Internet, would be important activities of the demand management process.
- At a tactical level, cloud management can involve different charging mechanisms based on service levels, and also encourage users to use service at less-busy times and provide incentives for using it. This is similar to how the telephone companies charge for telephone calls, often charging lower rates during off-peak hours on weekdays and weekends and charging more during business hours on weekdays. The charging

methods vary between private and public clouds, and Chapter 9, "Billing and Chargeback," provides more details on billing and chargeback for public and private clouds.

Financial Management and Business Impact

Before embarking on cloud services, one of the key steps is performing service value creation, service investment analysis, and service business impact analysis. The following steps will help in the financial management and value creation:

- **Service valuation:** This determines whether the service differentiation results in higher profits or revenue, lower costs, or better adoption of the services.
- **Service investment analysis:** This provides investment analysis for the stakeholders. Some SaaS applications might be more cost-effective because they are designed for efficiency, rapid time to value, and minimal disruption, and they can be rightsized. Consequently, companies face the challenge of determining between the two options: in-house development (packaged software deployed internally) versus the SaaS model (deployed and sourced by an external vendor).
- **Business impact analysis:** The cloud model introduces some pro and con business impacts, and that should be considered as well.
- **Some pro-business impacts include the following:**
  - Access to subject matter experts that are not available in-house
  - Automated upgrades
  - Ability to move service complexity off-site
  - Dynamically source and consume IT services
- **Some con-business impacts include the following:**
  - The boundary of service has moved from internal to external, which might result in support issues not being addressed properly and might affect customer support SLAs.
  - Cloud services can contribute to performance issues because of elasticity changes with demand fluctuations.
  - The capability of cloud providers to provide the same level of SLAs as the enterprise to which customers have become accustomed and expect.

Risk Management

The *risk* is defined as an uncertainty of outcome, whether a positive opportunity or a negative threat. A risk is measured by the probability of the threat happening. Risks can come from uncertainty in financial markets, project failures, accidents, natural causes, and disasters, as well as from deliberate attacks from an adversary. The strategies to manage risk include avoiding the risk, reducing the negative effect of the risk, and accepting some of or all the consequences of a particular risk. Unfortunately, risks cannot be totally avoided. The main areas of risk in the cloud include security threats, failure of equipment, and the inability to provide services to customers. The security threats can be avoided by having security all over, and failure of equipment and, in return, failure of service can be avoided by having a strategy for business continuity through disaster recovery (BCP/DR). Risk management covers a wide range of topics, including

- Business continuity process (BCP) and disaster recovery (DR)
- Security
- Program/project risk management
- Operational service management

These topics need to be supported by a risk management framework that is well documented and communicated throughout the organization.

Service Design Phase

The service design provides guidance on the design and development of cloud services and for converting strategic objectives into a portfolio of services and service assets. It includes changes and improvements necessary to increase and maintain value to the customer over the entire life cycle.

During the service design phase, the following items should be considered, at a minimum, taking input from the service strategy phase:

- Service catalog management
- Orchestration
- Security design
- Network configuration and change management (NCCM)
- Service-level agreements (SLA)
- Billing and chargeback

The following sections describe these considerations for a cloud design in greater detail.

Service Catalog Management

Service catalogs have been around for decades, and ITIL books had them for many years. However, service catalogs have been used only by the service providers so that they can be paid for the services rendered to their customers. With the advent of cloud computing, any cloud provider has instantly become a service provider and hence needs a service catalog. Amazon EC2 provides a service catalog to order virtual machines (VM) that can be provisioned in a matter of minutes. This saves lots of money in provisioning time. A good cloud service catalog should consider the following:

- **Elastic:** It allows increasing or decreasing the required capacity through a self-service portal and it is provisioned in minutes, not hours and days. One can order one instance, hundreds, and even thousands of server instances in minutes, all done at the click of button on a portal.
- **Self-controlled:** The user should have complete control and interact with the service catalog remotely using self-service portals (Web Services API).
- **Flexible:** It allows the user to select memory, CPU, and instance storage space. The operating system choice should include Linux, Microsoft Windows, and Solaris.
- **Reliable:** The service runs with proven network infrastructure and data centers and should offer a highly reliable environment where replacement instances can be rapidly and predictably commissioned.
- **Secure:** It offers an interface to configure firewall settings that control network access to and between groups of instances.

All the aforementioned features are offered today by Amazon EC2 cloud services. In addition, many service providers might require additional customizations in the service catalog and might need the following:

- **Firewall service options:** Some cloud providers might want to offer additional firewall services that can provide Low (L), Medium (M), and High (H) security options with various pricing options for users. In addition, some end customers might choose to configure the firewalls themselves, and cloud providers might want to provide that option in addition to the L/M/H security options. Note that a customer can choose Gold, Silver, and Bronze service levels, as mentioned in other parts of this book, and still be able to select L/M/H security options in the service catalog for each of the Gold/Silver/Bronze service levels.
- **Load balancing:** A cloud-based load-balancing service that allows the cloud provider to manage the content based on service delivery policies based on real-time conditions and user targets. This empowers the service provider to react to market-specific conditions without compromising availability, performance, and operational efficiency. The traffic management could be done dynamically so that the traffic can be moved based on the user requirements. For example, all traffic generated in the United States could go to servers in the United States, and all other traffic could go to servers in Europe and Asia.

Orchestration

Orchestration is important in service activation and interfaces to service catalog, CMS/CMDB, and the respective domain managers to activate a service. Many vendors, including Cisco, offer orchestration systems, and most of them allow making changes in the workflow to meet the customer's requirements. Orchestration need to ensure that the workflow is seamless and interfaces to all the required parts of the organization (tools, processes, and so on). More on orchestration is described later in this chapter.

Security

Security should be designed both in the network (firewall locations, access control lists, and port security) compute, storage, and access. Basically everywhere. The authentication and authorization should be designed as part of all service offerings so that the applications can only be accessed by the users that are authorized and entitled to access the services. Security is one of the most important areas in the cloud and is discussed extensively in Chapters 3, 4, and 5.

Network Configuration and Change Management

Network Configuration and Change Management (NCCM) plays a key role in the overall management. With DC/V and cloud, the role of NCCM has expanded to not only network devices but also to compute devices, storage devices, and applications. The NCCM systems should pay attention to some of the following areas:

- Configuration management plays a critical role in change management because detailed maps of the infrastructure devices and the configuration of each device and the connectivity between them are required.
- The topology views of the infrastructure are kept in Configuration Management Databases (CMDB) that contain detailed recordings of the configuration of each component and all updates or changes that have been made along the way.
- It would be ideal to have the CMDB updated automatically whenever changes are made to the infrastructure through audits or periodic polling. If this is not available, the operation would have to manually update the CMDB whenever a change is made.
- Compliance analysis is an important part of NCCM, and many of the tools available provide HIPAA (Health Information Portability and Accountability Act), PSIRT (Product Security Incident Response Team), and other audits and provide alerts whenever the configuration of the devices does not meet these standards. In addition, the device vendors provide field notices and configuration best practices that can be checked against the device configuration, and remediate whenever there is a discrepancy. Cisco SMART services audit and automate the changes without manual intervention.
- In addition to tools providing configuration and changes, the organization should be cognizant of the changes and should have a CAB (Change Advisory Board) and ECAB (Emergency Change Advisory Board) in place to address changes and compliance reports.

SLA

Service-level agreements (SLA) guarantee most aspects of service delivery, both technology and service aspects. Technology guarantees are concerned with system response time, system uptime guarantees, and error resolution time. The customer service guarantees are concerned with availability, support staff availability, and response time. The SLA should be designed through a collaborative effort between the marketing and technology groups. If it is only marketing, the technology and support staff might not deliver the SLAs offered, and if it is only technology, it will be filled so many loopholes and "it depends" that it would not be appealing to customers. Typically, service providers offer five 9s, or a 99.999 percent uptime guarantee. 99.9 percent uptime equals 8 hours, 45 minutes, and 57 seconds of downtime per year, while 99.999 percent uptime equals 5 minutes and 42 seconds of downtime per year. You should make sure that the uptime guarantees include only what the provider and the partner can cover and not what the customer can bring down. As long as you clearly define what you include in your guarantee, you can make aggressive uptime claims like 99.999 percent. However, it is important to make only promises that can kept and avoid making promises that are not in anyone's best interest.

Billing and Chargeback

Billing and chargeback are an important part of providing cloud services; Chapter 9 is dedicated to billing and chargeback. The following are some of the billing and chargeback considerations that should be kept in mind:

- Design of services in the service catalogue should pay attention to billing and charging capability. They should go hand in hand. There is no use in offering sophisticated services if the billing and charging systems cannot accommodate the new way of charging for the services.
- Ensure that proper data collection, metering, and charging systems are in place.
- The cloud providers typically break down their charges into various items such as servers in the cloud, storage in the cloud, applications in the cloud, bandwidth, space, heating, and cooling.
- The cloud pricing structure is based on many other factors as well, including service support, duration of the contract, security load balancing, disaster recovery, and additional charges hidden deep within the SLAs.

Service Transition Phase

The service transition phase implements the service design that was built in the design phase into production at the service provider location. Cloud computing is no shortcut to process maturity. It would require the same processes that are in existence today, but needs to make changes to adopt to cloud computing to deliver cloud services. The service providers must understand their goals and objectives, and without a clear understanding of the business processes and supporting IT processes they have in practice today, and determining and adjusting what is needed for the future, success will be difficult to achieve. You need to know what to expect and where you hope to gain efficiencies and savings before you dive into the deep end. The following items are considered in the service transition phase:

- **Change management:** This process ensures that changes are recorded and then evaluated, authorized, prioritized, planned, tested, implemented, documented, and reviewed in a controlled manner. The objective of change management is to support the business and IT when it comes to outages and changes. A cloud service provider must ensure that all exceptions to normal operations are resolved as quickly as possible while capturing the required details for the actions that were taken. In a cloud-computing environment, network, compute, storage, applications, and middleware are all connected, and any changes can have an unintended consequence. CMDB is important here, because it provides the interrelationships among all the infrastructure resource configuration items (CI). Knowledge of CI relationships allows changes to be made with authority. This provides more visibility into the cloud environment for the change managers, allowing them to make more informed decisions, not only when preparing for a change but also when diagnosing incidents and problems.
- **Service asset and configuration management:** This process ensures that accurate configuration information of the current, planned, and historical services and infrastructure is available. Because IT organizations are accountable for the quality and SLA of the services offered to the end users, accurate information on the services contracts (SLAs, Operational Level Agreements [OLA], and Underpinning Contracts [UC]) is required and should be maintained.
- **Orchestration and integration:** The design and implementation of orchestration flows and integration into any legacy systems are important, if a provider is moving to cloud computing to offer cloud services. Many orchestration tools allow building process flows and should be built to meet the customer business flows.
- **Migration:** The operations should move from current state to target state (people, processes, products, and partners) to manage the cloud based services.
- **Staging and validation:** The systems and software are validated, and required testing should be completed to transition the systems/software to the provider organization.

Service Operate Phase

The service operate phase is where the service provider takes possession of the management of the cloud operations from the equipment vendors, system integrators, and partners, and will be taking service orders from its end customers. All ITIL V3 phases are important, but the service operate phase draws the most attention because 60–70 percent of the IT budget is spent in dealing with day-to-day operations. To reduce OPEX, it is important that attention is paid in the planning, design, and CSI phases. In the service operate phase, the service provider not only takes the service orders for service fulfillment but also monitors and audits the service using the monitoring systems to ensure that the SLAs are met. The monitoring portion of operations is discussed separately in the next chapter under "Service Assurance." The following items are considered in the service operate phase:

- Service desk
- Incident management
- Problem management
- Service fulfillment
- Event management
- Access management

Service Desk (Function)

The service desk is an important function in the overall operations because it provides the first point of contact for the customer into the service provider organization. Figure 7-4 shows the service desk functions.

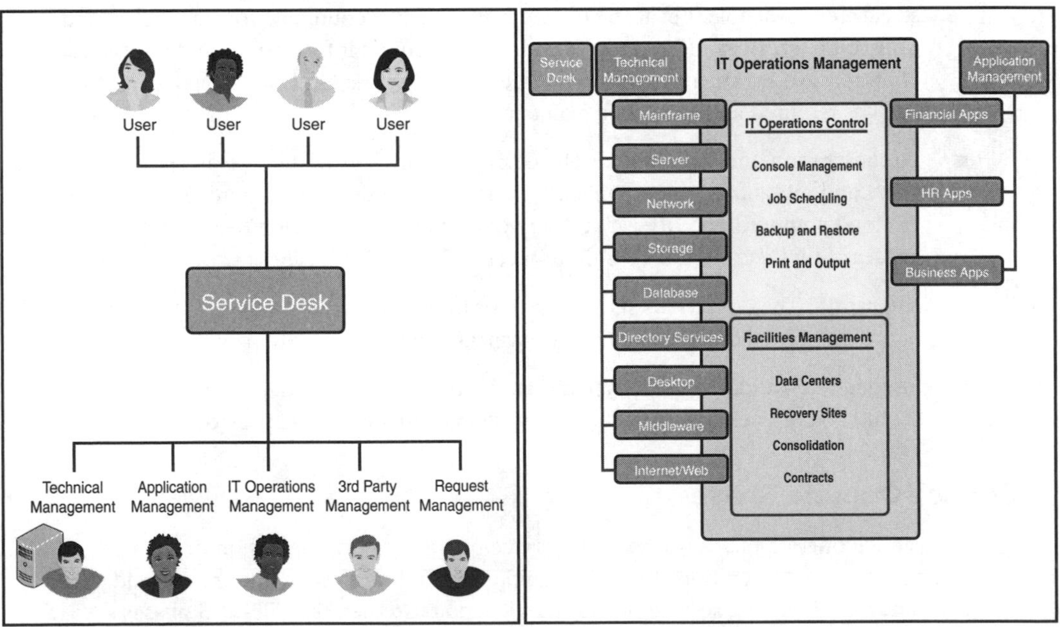

Figure 7-4 *Service Desk Functions*

Depending on the size of the company, service desk functions can be as follows: a local service desk for small organizations to meet local business needs, a centralized service desk for organizations having multiple locations, and a virtual service desk for organizations having multicountry locations. As shown in Figure 7-4, the service desk handles technical management, IT operations management, and applications management that are described in the following list:

- **Technical management:** Provides detailed technical skills and resources needed for the day-to-day operations of the IT infrastructure. The objective of technical management is to help plan, implement, and maintain a stable technical infrastructure to support an organization's business process.
- **IT operations management:** Provides day-to-day operational activities needed to maintain the IT infrastructure and provides service to meet the performance standards designed in the service design phase. Two key areas within the operations function are important:
  - IT operations control is responsible for console management, job scheduling, backup and restore, and reports.
  - The facilities management is responsible for data centers, backup sites, and contracts.
- **Applications management:** This supports and maintains operational applications and plays an important role in the design, testing, and improvement of IT applications that form part of IT services. The object of application management is to support the organization's business processes by helping identify functional and management requirements for applications software and to assist in the design and deployment of those applications and ongoing support and improvement of those applications.

Incident Management

An *incident* is any event that is not part of the standard operation of the service and which causes, or might cause, an interruption or a reduction of the quality of the service. The objective of incident management is to restore normal operations as quickly as possible with the least possible impact on either the business or the user, at a cost-effective price. When an incident happens, the service desk function (operator) follows the incident management process to resolve the incident. Incident management has three aspects to it:

- **Impact:** This gives an indication of the effect of the incident, whether it needs escalation, and whether it would have any effect on the SLA, time, and cost of resolving the incident.
- **Urgency:** This provides an indication of how long until an incident, problem, or change has a significant impact on the business. A high priority might not be urgent if it does not have a financial impact on the business.
- **Priority:** This indicates the relative importance of an incident, problem, or change on the business. Table 7-1 shows the relationship among priority, impact, and urgency.

The numbers 1 though 5 in Table 7-1 represent priority, as follows:

- 1: Critical
- 2: High
- 3: Medium
- 4: Low
- 5: Planning

Table 7-1 *Priority, Impact, and Urgency Relationship*

		Impact		
		High	**Medium**	**Low**
Urgency	High	1	2	3
	Medium	2	3	4
	Low	3	4	5

A high-impact item could have a low urgency (say 3) and a medium-impact item could have a higher urgency (say 2). The resolution of the impact should be based on the urgency of the impact. Some high-impact items might not need to be attended to if they do not immediately impact the business.

Problem Management

A problem is a condition often identified as a result of multiple incidents that exhibit common symptoms. Problems can also be identified from a single significant incident, indicative of a single error for which the cause is unknown, but for which the impact is significant. The primary focus of Problem Management (PM) is to identify causes of service issues and commission corrective work to prevent recurrences. PM processes are reactive and proactive—reactive in solving problems in response to incidents and proactive in identifying and solving potential incidents before they occur. Problem management activities include

- Recording, managing, and escalating service problems as appropriate
- Analyzing historical data to identify and eliminate potential incidents before they occur
- Identifying the underlying causes of incidents and preventing recurrences

- Developing workarounds or other solutions to incidents
- Submitting change requests to change management as required to eliminate known problems

Service Fulfillment (Service Provisioning)

This process deals with taking orders from users/customers through service requests. A service request is generated by the user and might be asking for information, a standard change, or a service. The request can come through email, a telephone call, or a web interface. The service requests are handled by the service desk. In a cloud environment, most of the service orders come through web interfaces (self-service portals), and the service requests are provisioned seamlessly using many systems. The detailed step-by-step end-to-end service fulfillment/service provisioning for a cloud is discussed in the next section.

Event Management

An event is a change of state of a configuration item (CI) or an IT service, or an alert created by a CI, IT service, or a monitoring system, and can require operations people to take action. Events could be notifications that indicate a regular operation (such as scheduled workload uploaded, a user logged on to an application, and so on) or an unusual activity (such as a user attempting to log on to an application without the correct password). The event management process collects events from the infrastructure devices, makes sense of them, and determines appropriate action. More on this is discussed in the next chapter.

Access Management

This process allows authorized users the right to use the service while blocking unauthorized users and making sure that the policies and actions defined in security management and availability management are executed properly. The access methods that are applicable for cloud services include the following:

- **Identity management:** The identity of a user is unique to that user and is managed through identity management systems, such as Lightweight Directory Access Protocol (LDAP), LDAP over Secure Sockets Layer (SSL), and TACACS.
- **Access:** The level and extent of service functionality or data that a user is entitled to use.
- **Rights:** Also known as privileges, rights refer to the actual settings where a user is provided access to a service or group of services (for example, read/right/change/delete privileges).

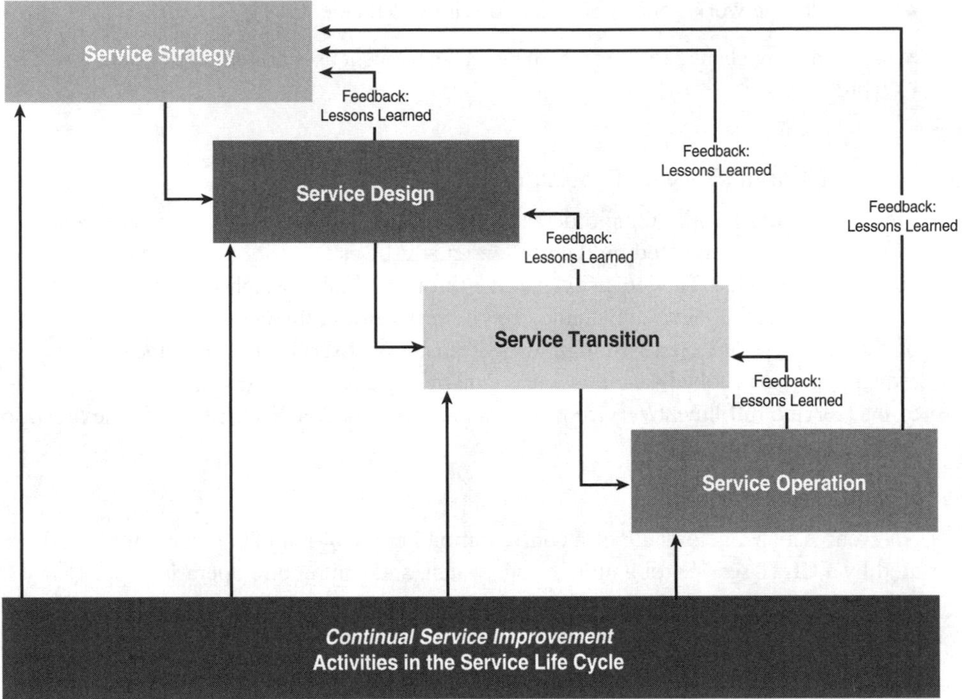

Figure 7-5 *Role of Continuous Service Improvement*

Cloud CSI (Optimization) Phase

The Continuous Service Improvement (CSI) phase is, as its name implies, an ongoing practice to improve the IT organization activities using best practices, as opposed to a reactive response to a specific situation or a temporary crisis. The CSI phase plays a role in all phases of the ITIL life cycle to provide improvements, as shown in Figure 7-5.

Figure 7-5 shows how CSI interacts with service strategy, service design, service transition, and service operation to help improve each of the phases through feedback loops with the lessons learned from each phase. Specifically, the following objectives are met through CSI:

- Review, analyze, and make recommendations on improvement opportunities in each life cycle phase: service strategy, service design, service transition, and service operations.
- Review and analyze service-level achievements.
- Review and improve effectiveness of IT delivery.

- Identify and incorporate best practices/good practices to improve IT service quality and improve the efficiency and effectiveness of enabling ITSM (IT Service Management) processes.
- Ensure that applicable quality management methods support continual improvement activities.

Some of the CSI/optimization-specific activities that can be related to DC/V and the cloud that can be quickly adopted include

- Audit the configurations in all the infrastructure devices in the network, compute, and storage areas (this includes core and access aggregation layers). There could be hundreds—even thousands—of devices, depending on the size of the network. The inventory and collection of data from all devices must be done to ensure the manageability of the cloud infrastructure.
- Compare the configurations against the best-practice configuration and make changes as appropriate to ensure that the infrastructure is up to date.
- The infrastructure devices should be compared with end of life (EOL), end of service (EOS), and field notices and make recommended changes to the infrastructure. Many times, business impact analysis is done to show the importance for the need to make the recommended changes.
- Fine-tune the management tools and processes based on best practices.
- Adding new products and services requires assessment to ensure that the new services can be incorporated into the current operating environment without sacrificing the quality of service to customers.

Cloud End-to-End Service Provisioning Flow

The previous sections discussed all ITIL V3 life cycle processes (service strategy, service design, service transition, service operate, and CSI) for service provisioning (also referred as fulfillment in TMF eTOM). This section will provide end-to-end service provisioning flow. Figure 7-6 shows end-to-end provisioning steps for a customer reaching the service provider through a self-service portal and ordering a web service, and then getting a confirmation from the service provider that the service is ready for use.

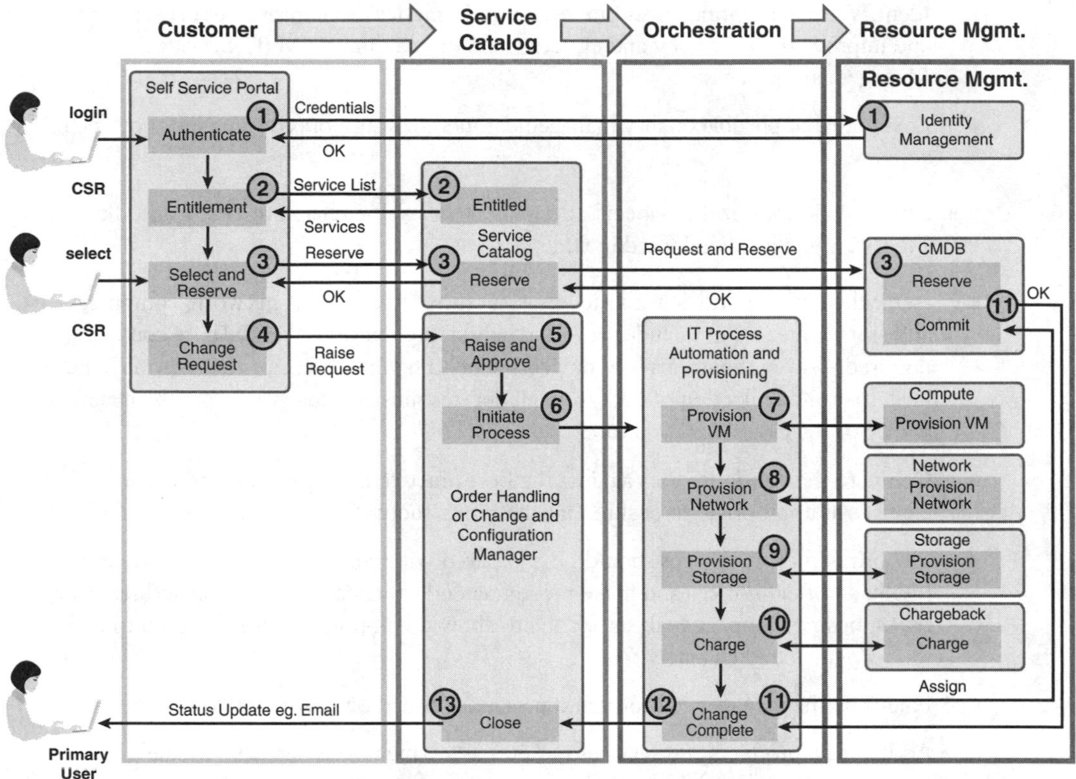

Figure 7-6 *Cloud Service Provisioning Flow Steps (End-to-End)*

The steps illustrated in Figure 7-6 are explained as follows:

Step 1. The user logs on to the self-service portal and is authenticated by the identity management.

Step 2. Based on the user's role and entitlement, the self-service portal extracts a subset of services that the user can order from the service catalog.

Step 3. The user selects a service to provision—perhaps a nonvirtualized web server, for example. Associated to this service is a set of technical requirements, such as RAM, processor, and so on, along with business requirements such as high availability or service-level requirements.

- **a.** The self-service portal will query the Capacity Management System or CMS/CMDB to see whether these technical requirements can be met by existing resources. For a virtual resource, it's likely that more emphasis will be placed on capacity requirements—for example, can my ESX host support another virtual machine?—whereas physical servers will be more inventory based.
- **b.** The resource details are passed back to self-service portal, which displays these resources to the user who selects one, which is then reserved in the Capacity Management System or CMDB.

Step 4. The self-service portal now raises a service request with the service desk which, when approved, will create a service instance in the service catalog and notify the self-service portal. It is assumed that the approval process is automatic and happens quickly; otherwise, the notification step might be skipped. The service request state is maintained in the service desk and can be queried by the user through the self-service portal.

Step 5. The service desk will now raise a request with the IT process automation tool to fulfill the service. The orchestration tool extracts the technical service information from the service catalog and decomposes the service into individual parts such as compute resource configuration, network configuration, and so on.

Step 6. In the case of our "nonvirtualized web server" running on UCS (Unified Computing System), we have three service parts: the server part, the network part, and the infrastructure part. The provisioning process is initiated.

Step 7. The virtual machine running on the blade or server is provisioned using the server/compute domain manager. (There are several domain managers available in this area from Cisco, EMC, BMC, CA, HP, IBM, and other vendors.) The following steps provide information on how to provision a VM for a customer:

a. Create or clone a customer profile with the applicable parameters (UUID, MAC address, IP/subnet, WAN, VLAN, VSAN, adapter properties, and boot policy).

b. Select the blade from the available pool and bind the profile to the blade.

c. Boot the server (done by the Cisco UCS Manager).

d. Deploy the OS image using standard tools.

Step 8. The network, including firewalls and load balancers, is provisioned using the network domain managers. (There are several domain managers available in this area from Cisco, EMC, BMC, CA, HP, IBM, and other vendors.) The following steps provide information on configuring the network and network services, such as firewalls and load balancers:

a. IP address assignment and management

b. VLAN/VDC/VRF configuration

c. Firewall configuration for ACL, ports, and IP

d. Load balancer configuration to map servers to the VIP

e. Wide Area Application Service (WAAS) configuration, if required

Step 9. The storage is provisioned using the storage domain manager. (There are several domain managers available in this area from EMC, NetApp, and other vendors.) The following steps provide information on storage provisioning:

a. Provision VSANs, zones, and Logical Unit Numbers (LUN).

b. Provision backup infrastructure for snapshot.

Step 10. The change process for billing or chargeback is initiated.

Step 11. The service is committed by the cloud provider by committing the resources in the CMDB, and the resources are locked for this customer.

Step 12. The change process is completed.

Step 13. The customer is informed through email or other electronic medium.

Service Orchestration

Although service orchestration is not a separate phase in ITIL V3, it is described here separately because of its key role in the overall service management process and the benefits it provides in automating many tasks in cloud service provisioning.

As shown in the previous section, Steps 6 through 12 are automated through service orchestration. Service orchestration refers to coordinated provisioning of virtualized resources, as well as the runtime coordination of resource pools and virtual instances. Service orchestration also includes the static and dynamic mapping of virtual resources to physical resources, and overall management capabilities such as capacity, analytics, billing, and SLA.

Figure 7-7 illustrates some of the provisioning realities for cloud provisioning. The very essence of cloud computing is being able to provide services to customers on demand and at scale in the most efficient way possible using less human resources and more automation. In most of the IT organizations, 70 percent of the IT budget is being used in maintenance activities, with the remaining going toward strategic activities. For IT organizations and CIOs to be relevant, they need to be more strategic thinkers and make IT organizations more nimble. To this end, orchestration and automation can help in automating the repetitive tasks and using the IT staff for doing more strategic activities.

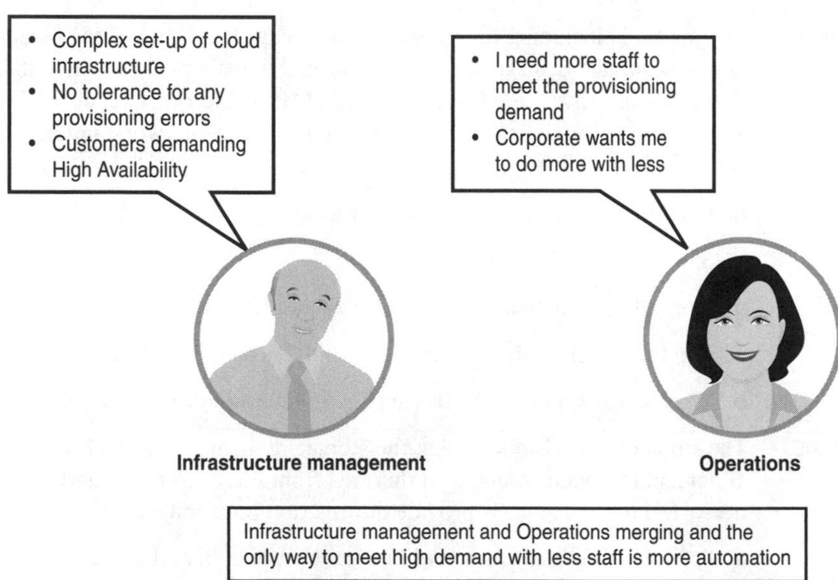

Figure 7-7 *Cloud Provisioning Realities*

The EMA (Enterprise Management Associates) showed from its research that there is clear evidence that virtualization delivers savings, and over 70 percent of the organizations queried reported that virtualization provided "real, measurable cost savings" in CapEx. However, the CapEx reduction is a one-off capital budget, but the Operational Expenditure (OPEX) benefit is year over year. The EMA research further concludes the following OPEX benefits because of automation:[3]

- **Reduction of service failures:** Fixing problems up to 24 times faster, eliminating up to 43 hours of downtime, and increasing the uptime to 99.999 percent.
- **Improved staff efficiency:** Automation improved the staff efficiency as much as 10 percent, reducing annual management costs as much as $1000/server, and each administrator was able to manage up to 1800 servers.
- **Faster service deployment:** Allowed new systems to be deployed 24 times faster and applications 96 times faster, saving almost $2000 per deployment while reducing downtime and improving time to market new products and services.

Service orchestration/automation is important for cloud provisioning because it automates some of the repetitive tasks and reduces the time it takes to provision a service. However, there is no gain to using automation when the task is not repetitive or requires human intelligence to perform. For example, if the customer has only ten servers, there are not many manual tasks involved and automation might not make sense; however, most medium to large service providers have thousands and even hundreds of thousands of servers, network elements, and storage device pools. Figure 7-8 shows the ROI factors for orchestration.[4] As service requests increase, the staff demands increase to fulfill those service requests that require many manual tasks. If the staff level remains the same or goes down, as is the case many times, the manual tasks take much longer to complete. This results in longer provisioning intervals and customer satisfaction going down, and ultimately the customer will switch to another service provider.

As shown in Figure 7-8, the orchestration value is medium when the staff demand is low and staff level is high, and as the staff level remains the same or goes down and the staff demand goes up with an increase in service requests, the need for orchestration increases. After a threshold point (see the dotted line), orchestration/automation is mandatory and the return on investment (ROI) for orchestration is high. After the threshold point, the demand for the labor increases exponentially, and automation/orchestration is not something nice to have, but it is mandatory. A lot of manual tasks that are done by talented staff need to be automated, and the talented staff can be used for doing other intelligent tasks. Another point for quality/consistency is that the errors are reduced, improving the quality, because machines tend to make less errors in the repetitive tasks.

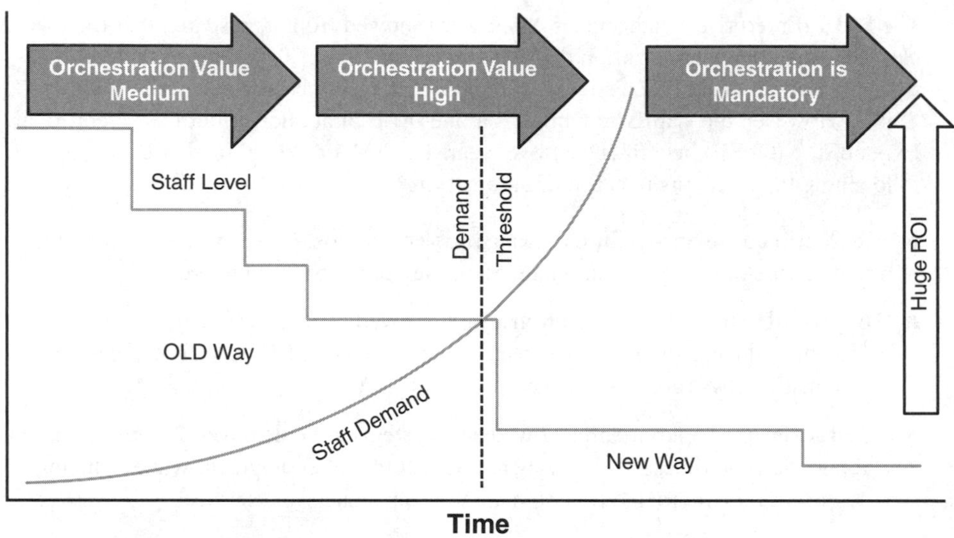

Figure 7-8 *ROI Factors for Orchestration*

Cloud End-to-End Architecture Model

To deal with complexity, end-to end cloud management is presented in a logically layered architecture (LLA) for showing all the functional blocks. The LLA is a concept for the structuring of management functionality that organizes the functions into a grouping called "logical layers" and describes the relationship between layers. A logical layer reflects particular aspects of management and implies the clustering of management information supporting that aspect. The grouping of management functionality implies grouping certain functions into layers. For cloud management, a hybrid approach is used with TMF eTOM and ITIL V3. This hybrid approach will allow grouping of all the cloud management required functions into a user experience that includes user experience functions, service and resource management functional groupings (from eTOM), and services life cycle from ITIL V3. In addition, we added the collection layer that can be used for discovery, collection of events, alerts, and so on, and an infrastructure layer that has all network, compute, and storage devices. Figure 7-9 shows this end-to-end logical architecture for cloud management.

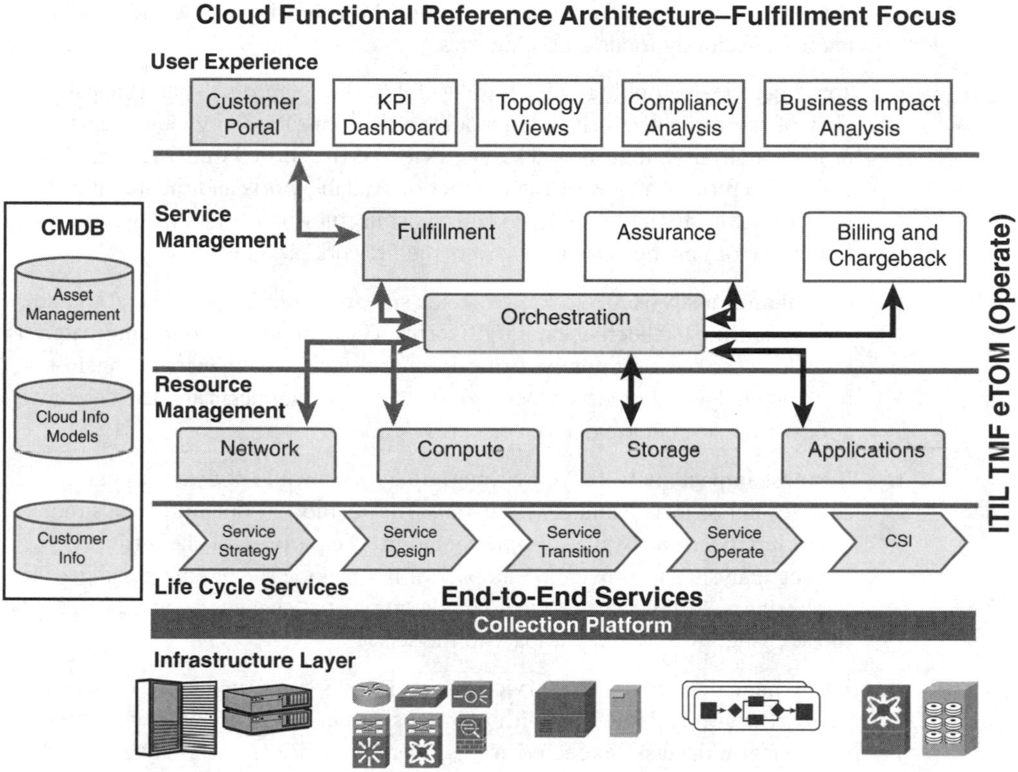

Figure 7-9 *End-to-End Cloud Management Architecture - Functional*

The functional groupings contained in each layer in Figure 7-9 are further explained here:

- **User experience layer:** The user experience function group contains the following:
  - **Customer portal:** Also referred as the customer or user self-service portal. This is where the customer/user orders services by selecting from the user interface screen. For cloud Infrastructure as a Service (IaaS), the customer could be selecting, for example, Gold, Silver, or Bronze service on the portal from the available services in the service catalog. In addition, the customer can select CPU, memory, and storage space based on the pricing options provided on the portal.
  - **KPI dashboard:** Key performance indicators (KPI) are the building blocks of many dashboard visualizations because they are the most effective means of alerting users as to where they are in relationship to their objectives. Chapter 8, "Service Assurance," provides some key KPIs for availability, capacity management, service-level management, and a relationship between KPI, KQI, and SLA is discussed. A KPI is simply a metric that is tied to a target, and often a KPI represents how far a metric is above or below a predetermined target. KPI dashboards usually show as a ratio of actual to target and are designed to instantly

show a business user whether he is on or off his plan without the end user having to consciously focus on the metrics.

- **Topology views:** Topology views are useful for IT operators to get a snapshot view of the entire network and in trouble resolution. Topology views generally provide a physical, logical, and services view of the entire infrastructure. They could also provide a view of the number of available ports and the number of hops to the host. The topology view is most useful when combined with the traceroute option, because it discovers the network path to a host.
- **Compliance analysis:** Cisco has created a suite of applications and methodologies to capture intellectual capital (IC). This IC can be leveraged to automate this knowledge so that vast numbers of customer devices can be matched against this knowledge and reports generated to inform the engineers and the customer about issues seen in the devices or network.
- **Business impact analysis:** Many times, operations would not want to make changes unless it is absolutely necessary. This method of operation leads to operating the network in a suboptimal mode. The purpose of the business impact analysis is to provide the impact of not making the required changes on the business. Cisco smart services can determine the changes required and apply those changes without any impact to the service.

- **Service management layer:** The service management is concerned with services offered to customer and interacts with functions within the same layers and other layers to perform the tasks expected at this layer. The services in this layers include the following:
  - **Fulfillment:** Fulfillment is responsible for delivering products and services to the customer. This includes order handling, service configuration and activation, and resource provisioning. A detailed explanation of this was provided in the section, "Cloud End-to-End Service Provisioning Flow."
  - **Assurance:** Assurance includes proactive and reactive maintenance activities, service monitoring (SLA or QoS), resource status and performance monitoring, and troubleshooting. This includes continuous resource status and performance monitoring to proactively detect possible failures, and the collection of performance data and analysis to identify and resolve potential or real problems. Service assurance is discussed in Chapter 8.
  - **Billing and chargeback:** These activities require the collection of usage data records, various rating functions for billing customers in the case of service providers, and chargeback/showback to the business units for enterprises. Chapter 9 covers this in detail.
  - **Orchestration:** Service orchestration/automation is important for cloud provisioning because it automates some of the repetitive tasks and reduces the time it takes to provision a service. Orchestration and the value of it to cloud provisioning was discussed earlier in the chapter.

- **Resource management layer:** The resource management grouping functions include management systems to manage network, compute, storage, and applications. The resource management layer should know what resources are available, how these resources are interrelated, and how these resources should be allocated based on the instructions received from the higher layer (for example, a self-service portal). Furthermore, this layer is responsible for the technical performance of the actual infrastructure and will control the available infrastructure capabilities and capacity to give the appropriate accessibility and quality of service.
- **Life cycle services:** The complete life cycle services is described as part of ITILV3, and the cloud tasks for all ITILV3 phases (service strategy, service design, service transition, service operate, and CSI) were described earlier in this chapter. The life cycle services layer ensures that the entire business service, along with its underlying components, cohesively assures that we are considering every aspect of a service (and not just the individual technology silos) to assure that we are delivering the required functionality and service levels (delivered within a certain time frame, properly secured, and available when necessary) to the business customer.
- **Collection platform/layer:** The collection layer enables device discovery and collection of data for postprocessing and display of data for the user experience, including the KPI dashboard, topology views, compliance analysis, and business impact analysis. The data collection schemes will include domains where a network device pushes the data to the Data Collection Service (DCS) or where the DCS will pull data from these network devices at a periodic interval. An example of a periodic pull model is where DCS will use Simple Network Management Protocol (SNMP) to pull data from the device at periodic intervals. The push model is used when the device pushes the data on a periodic interval to the DCS, for example, RADIUS (Remote Authentication Dial-In User Service) call detail records (CDR) and NetFlow records being sent by the network devices. In this push model, DCS waits for the data to arrive. The discovery of infrastructure includes the periodic collection of devices to ensure that infrastructure changes are captured and reconciled with the CMS/CMDB.
- **CMDB:** The Configuration Management Database (CMDB) is not shown in any layer and is shown separately. The CMDB is a critical part of running the traditional enterprise and touches many layers of the reference architecture. The CMDB contains

  - All the configuration items (CI)
  - A relationship model between the CIs
  - How the CIs are connected

  CMDB includes the services for the enterprise business and provides the links across ITIL V3 processes to tie it to the services. CMDB contains physical, logical, and conceptual data that are important and relevant to your business. Many of the ITIL processes require the data from CMDB to enrich the data that is collected from the devices. Also, it is important to keep the data up to date through autodiscovery and audit processes. CMDB also provides the interrelationships among all the infrastructure resource CIs. Knowledge of CI relationships enables changes to be made with authority because it provides more visibility into the cloud environment for the change managers, allowing them to make more informed decisions, not only when preparing for a change but also when diagnosing incidents and problems.

For scaling purposes, it is expected that CMDB should be able to hold about 1 million CIs, and that number appears to be an industry standard. For cloud services, it is essential to build the relationship models for network, compute, and storage and place them in the CMDB so that the entire infrastructure CIs are used when determining the relationships.

A further discussion of the relevance of the CMDC/CMS and service inventory in cloud can be found in Chapter 10 "Technical Building Blocks of IaaS"

- **Infrastructure layer:** The infrastructure layer is the foundation of the cloud pyramid and is what cloud platforms and applications are built on. Cloud infrastructure providers such as Cisco provide network, compute, and storage devices and also assist in putting together all the facilities, cabling, and so on. Cloud vendors provide network devices (access, aggregation and core devices, plus firewalls and load balancers for services), compute devices (servers such as Cisco UCS, MS Windows, or Linux servers), and storage devices (online storage to store virtually unlimited amounts of data). In a cloud environment, the infrastructure layer (consisting of network, compute, and storage devices) is virtualized and offered to customers on demand and at scale through service portals. The virtualized resources are provisioned dynamically, and billing for the services is typically done on a usage basis and by the quality of service offered.

Summary

This chapter covered cloud service fulfillment (service provisioning) using ITIL V3 phases (service strategy, service design, service transition, service operate, and CSI) as a guide and detailed cloud service provisioning steps for provisioning network, compute, and storage. The chapter also presented the rationale for orchestration/automation for automating cloud-provisioning activities. In addition, you learned about the cloud functional reference architecture using eTOM and ITIL standards for a complete cloud life cycle.

References

[1] TMF document "Guide to Applying Business Process Framework (eTOM)," GB 921 Addendum G, version 0.10, March 2010, at www.tmforum.org/Guidebooks/GB921BusinessProcess/43162/article.html.

[2] IT Service Management - IT Infrastructure Library (ITIL) - ITIL V3, at www.best-management-practice.com/officialsite.asp?FO=1253138&ProductID=9780113310500&Action=Book.

[3] "Reducing Operational Expense (OPEX) with Virtualization and Virtualization Systems Management," an Enterprise Management Associates (EMA) white paper prepared for VMware, November 2009.

[4] Forrester presentation to Cisco on orchestration.

Chapter 8

Service Assurance

Upon completing this chapter, you should be able to understand the following:

- Cloud service assurance tasks using Information Technology Infrastructure Library (ITIL) processes
- Cloud assurance (fault and performance) architecture and solutions
- Key performance indicators (KPI) and the relationship between KPIs, key quality indicators (KQI), and service-level agreements (SLA)
- Use cases for fault and performance management

Chapter 7, "Service Fulfillment," covered cloud service fulfillment using ITIL V3 phases, and this chapter will provide details on cloud service assurance using ITIL V3, addressing some key areas such as availability management, demand/capacity management, KPIs, and service-level management. This chapter also presents several use cases with cloud end-to-end monitoring flow and service assurance architecture (fault and performance).

Cloud Assurance Flow Using the ITIL Process

ITIL V3 provided the IT life cycle processes: service strategy, service design, service transition, service operate, and Continuous Service Improvement (CSI). Applying these processes is a good way to establish service assurance processes for Data Center/Virtualization (DC/V) and the cloud (although the dynamic aspect of cloud will present some challenges to ITIL). Chapter 7 dealt with the cloud service provisioning process using ITIL V3, and this chapter details the cloud assurance process (fault and performance management). Cloud assurance solutions, like cloud provisioning, should be seen as life cycle rather than a one-time event. Figure 8-1 shows the cloud assurance life cycle showing all the ITIL V3 phases.

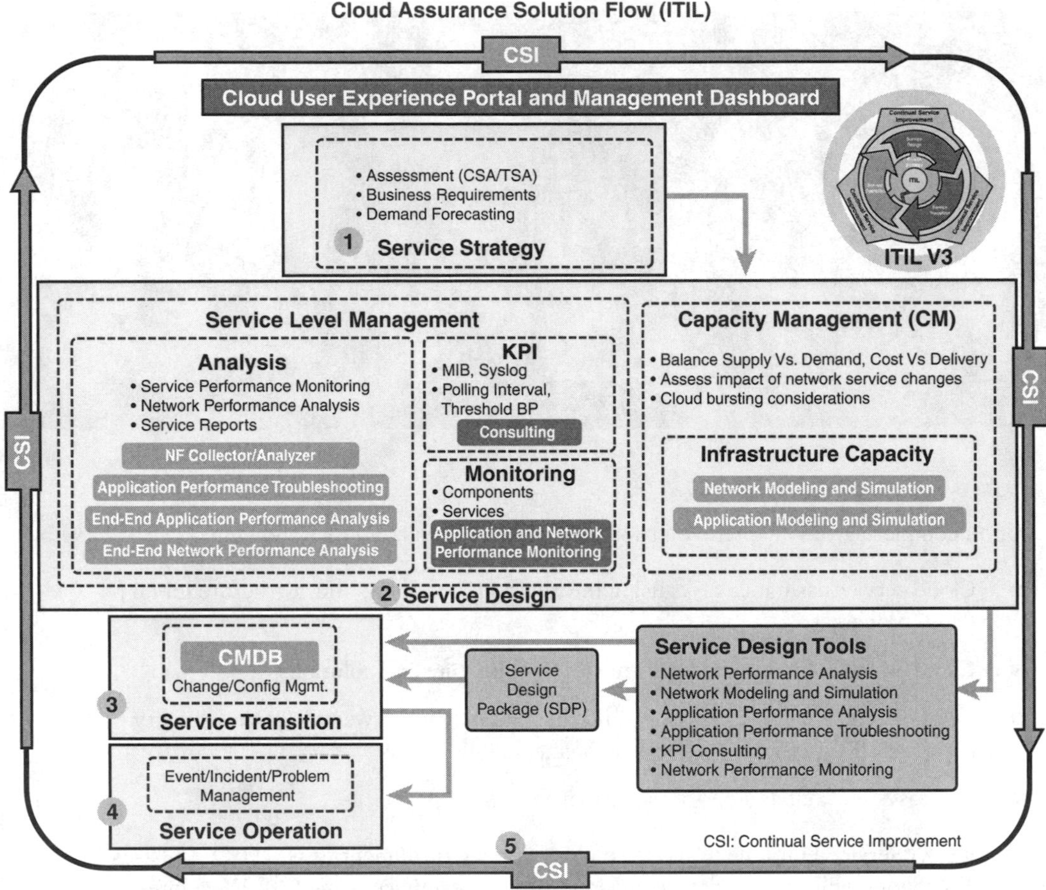

Figure 8-1 *Cloud Service Assurance Flow Based on ITIL V3*

Figure 8-1 shows the five phases of cloud ITIL V3 service life cycle for cloud assurance:

1. Service strategy
2. Service design
3. Service transition
4. Service operate
5. Continuous Service Improvement (CSI)

Figure 8-1 also shows some of the items that need to be considered in each of the five phases of the cloud service life cycle for cloud assurance. More details are provided in the following sections along the lines of ITIL V3 phases.

Service Strategy Phase

The strategy phase for cloud assurance considers the following topics:

- Architecture assessment
- Business requirements
- Demand management

Architecture Assessment

The architecture assessment is typically performed by consultants from vendor companies, system integrators, and solution providers by interviewing various people in the client's organization. The client's organization makes its engineers and marketing, support, testing/development, and other organizations available to these consultants. Typically, assessments could take 2–6 weeks, depending on the size of the client's organization, the number of services offered, and the extent of changes required to change from current-state architecture to target-state architecture.

One proven way to perform architecture assessment is to do the following:

- Analyze current capabilities and identify gaps in the current environment.
- Identify gaps due to new services that will be offered in the near future.
- Align IT objectives with the business objectives, and prioritize the IT objectives based on the customer demand and business requirements.
- Document the current tools that are used to monitor network, compute, storage, and applications in a current-state architecture (CSA) document.
- Document a target-state or future-state architecture (TSA/FSA) based on customer business and technical requirements to manage cloud based services.

Figure 8-2 shows a methodology using enhanced Telecom Operations Map (eTOM) and other standards to perform the assessment. In the assessment document, people who are performing the assessment, document the current client environment, compare it with the best practices (also referred to as *leading practices*), and document the gaps. The identified gaps should be addressed by working with the customer to determine how the current-state environment can be moved to the target-state environment. Also, determine the need for replacement of existing monitoring tools to improve monitoring for the cloud services. Some legacy products are hard to replace because IT personnel are used to these systems, and they might have been developed to meet company-specific requirements. In these situations, it can be expensive to change the internal processes and retrain personnel, and any new systems must integrate with the legacy systems. Integration with legacy systems requires customization that might be worthwhile to do instead of completely replacing the existing systems and going through several years of personnel training.

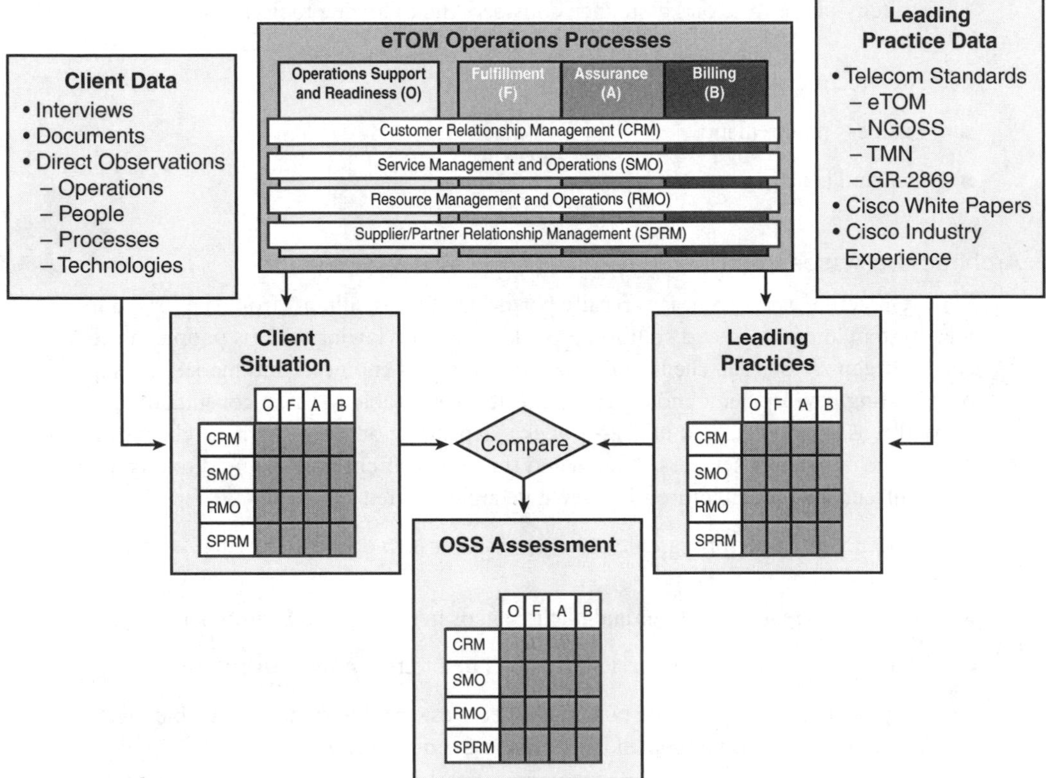

Figure 8-2 *Assessing the Customer Environment Using Best Practices*

Business Requirements

The growing adoption of standards has been driven by the business requirement that IT organizations do a better job of managing the quality and reliability of IT services because of the growing number of regulatory and contractual requirements. Some of the business requirements that most IT organizations need to pay attention to include the following:

- IT should not be a cost center and should provide business value in line with the IT investments.
- Regulatory requirements, such as the U.S. Sarbanes-Oxley Act (SOX) for privacy and financial reporting, Health Insurance Portability and Accountability Act (HIPAA)

regarding the protection of individual health information, and other regulator compliances in specific sectors, such as finance, pharmaceutical, and healthcare.

- Service-level agreements (SLA) should have the capability to offer and monitor and the means to give credits when the SLAs are violated. SLAs are important in any service offering and are described in the "Service Design Phase" section.
- IT governance initiatives such as the adoption of standards and best practices in lieu of locally developed methodologies to reduce cost and improve effectiveness. Also, the adoption of best practices to help monitor and improve critical IT activities to increase business value and reduce business risk.

Demand Management

In cloud applications, ITIL service management has the task of providing resources on demand and at scale to customers. To provide these resources on demand to customers, IT organizations within service providers require the availability of resources. No service provider has infinite resources and has to manage the resources based on the consumption, and service management is faced with the balancing act between consumption and delivery. Demand management deals with activities that understand and influence customer demand for services and provisioning the services to meet the demand. At a strategic level, it involves an analysis of Patterns of Business Activity (PBA), and at a tactical level, it can involve a differentiated level of charges to encourage users to consume the services at less-busy time. The following salient points should be kept in mind when forecasting the demand for cloud resources:

- Insufficient capacity could lead to users being turned away without services, and provisioning more customers with fewer resources could lead to poor quality of service (QoS) and violation of SLAs. Providing services that do not meet SLAs could result in not only giving credits and paybacks but also more importantly having dissatisfied customers and losing the trust of the customer.
- Poorly managed demand is a risk for the service provider, with potential impacts being felt by the IT organization and by the customers. If the demand is not predicted accurately, there will be idle capacity, and this will result in wasted resources without generating any value.
- Demand management during the service strategy phase plays a critical role in determining and designing capacity management in the service design phase, although as discussed in Chapter 12, "Cloud Capacity Management," demand management tends to be an art and not a science..

Service Design Phase

IT operations must manage a large number of moving parts to produce the desired outcome. Historically, IT organizations have operated in siloed organizations and more or less cost centers. In today's world, IT organizations cannot afford to operate in silos and must think in terms of a holistic organization serving their customers. IT operations have many components including the technologies (network, computer systems, applications, and databases) as well as the related IT staff that supports services to end users. For IT operations, the desired outcomes are to maintain the quality and availability of IT-based business services according to SLAs, Operational Level Agreements (OLA), and end-user expectations. ITIL promotes a method for managing IT according to the services delivered to end users and emphasizes the coordination of processes and mutually reliant IT roles and disciplines.

Service design takes input from the service strategy and specifically performs the following functions:

- Service catalog management
- Availability management
- Capacity management
- Service-level management
- Supplier management
- Information security management
- Service continuity management

For cloud service assurance, we will discuss service-level management (including SLAs, OLAs, and Underpinning Contracts [UC]), availability management, capacity management, supplier management, and service continuity management in this chapter. Service catalog management is discussed in Chapter 7. Security management for clouds is a major topic and is discussed in Chapters 3, 4, and 5.

Availability Management

The objective of availability management is to ensure that availability of the services delivered to the customer meets or exceeds the committed needs of the customer. Availability is determined by reliability, maintainability, serviceability, performance, and security. The following availability calculation is often based on the agreed service time and downtime, which ITIL defines as

Availability = [(Agreed Service Time – Downtime) / Agreed Service Time] * 100

For cloud computing, the availability considerations should include network, compute, and storage infrastructure in the cloud and applications. Some service providers offer other services such as account management, identity and authentication services, billing services, and monitoring services. Hence, availability management should take into consideration all the services that you depend on for your IT and business needs. Availability depends on the following factors:

- The cloud infrastructure that includes network, compute, storage, applications, firewalls, and load balancers.
- The reliability of network connectivity between the customer and the cloud service provider as well as the reliability of authentication systems.

- The Business Continuity Process and Disaster Recovery (BCP/DR) established by the cloud vendor.
- The availability of storage required by the end users and virtual machines for storage service. For example, Amazon recently started offering a service to end users where they can store music and play from their end devices such as iPods, laptops, and so on. The storage needs include the following:
  - **Asynchronous:** Examples include end users wanting to store the data (such as music and videos).
  - **Synchronous:** These storage needs include virtual machines accessing the storage data for video-streaming applications.
- Monitoring of the cloud infrastructure and proactively resolving issues.

Table 8-1 lists the key performance indicators (KPI) for availability.[1]

Table 8-1 *Key KPIs for Availability Management*

Availability KPI	Definition
Service availability	Availability of the services at the agreed SLAs
Number of service interruptions	Number of service interruptions reported and measured
Duration of service interruptions	Average duration of time the service is not available
Availability monitoring	Number of services and infrastructure components under availability monitoring
Availability measures	Number of implemented measures with the objective of increasing availability

Capacity Management

Chapter 12 will explore this subject more thoroughly in the context of cloud, but the goal of capacity management for traditional IT is that cost-justifiable IT resources in all areas exist and are matched to the current and future business needs of customers in a timely manner. Cloud capacity management on the other hand needs to provide the required capacity on demand and at scale. The following items are important for capacity management:

- **Capacity:** Think resources and units of growth (network bandwidth, VMs, storage, applications)
- **On demand:** Think automation (service activation in minutes)
- **Scale:** Think cloud bursting (demand going up and down, peaks and valleys)
- **Current:** Think monitoring (user experience, SLAs, incident/problem management)

- **Future:** Think new technology
- **Cost:** Think financial management

Capacity management ensures that demand for and supply of capacity are balanced. If supply and demand are out of balance, it impacts the cost of service delivery for application infrastructures. Capacity management is essentially a balancing act of cost against capacity, and supply against demand. The purpose of capacity management is to provide a point of focus and management for all capacity- and performance-related issues, relating to both services and resources, and to match the capacity of IT to the agreed business demands. ITIL V3 capacity management includes business, service, and component capacity management across the service life cycle. Figure8-3 shows the implications of ITIL V3 subprocesses: business management, service capacity management, and component capacity management on the cloud services models: Infrastructure as a Service (IaaS), Platform as a Service (PaaS), and Software as a Service (SaaS).

ITIL Capacity Management Subprocesses	IaaS (Amazon)	PaaS (Azure, Google)	SaaS (Sales Force)
Business Management (Trend, forecast, model, prototype, size and document future business requirements)			
Service Management (Monitor, analyze, tune and report on service performance, establish baselines and profiles of use of services, manage demand for services)			
Component Management (Monitor, analyze, run and report on the utilization of components, establish baselines and profiles of use of components)			

Figure 8-3 *ITIL V3 Implications on the Cloud*[2]

As a forward-looking process, ITIL capacity management, if properly carried out, can forecast business impacts before they happen. In addition, information is provided regarding current and planned resource utilization of individual components, assisting in determining which components to upgrade and when, together with how much the upgrade will cost. Capacity management activities include the following:

- Implementing the right resources at the right time (just-in-time approach). This would require monitoring, analyzing, tuning, and using the appropriate resources.

- Infrastructure discovery, application discovery, and dependency mapping and virtualization analysis to help in determining the demand.
- Modeling to simulate infrastructure performance and understand future resource needs.
- Infrastructure sizing (network, compute, storage, and applications) to meet required service levels.
- Configuration Management Database/Configuration Management System (CMDB/CMS): Strong insights into interdependencies need to be leveraged in a more systemic approach. Cloud computing is also pushing CMDB design toward more versatile, federated, and real-time design points.
- Producing a capacity plan document showing current utilization and forecasted requirements, as well as support costs for new applications or releases.
- Input from demand forecasting is used to establish capacity requirements.
- Monitoring user experience and determining end-user response time, and sending alerts for incidents to pinpoint which part of the infrastructure was causing the fault.
- Capability to increase capacity with demand and shut down the virtual machines automatically when the capacity decreases will save the IT organization not only in energy savings but also in valuable people resources as well. Table 8-2 lists the key KPIs for capacity management.[1]

Table 8-2 *Key KPIs for Capacity Management*

Capacity Management KPI	Definition
Incidents due to capacity shortages	Number of incidents because of short supply of services and components
Capacity adjustments	Number of adjustments because of short supply of services and components
Exactness of service forecast	Deviation of the predicted capacity development from the actual course
Unplanned capacity adjustments	Number of unplanned increases to service or component capacity as result of capacity bottlenecks
Resolution time of capacity shortage	Resolution time for identified capacity bottlenecks
Capacity reserves	Percentage of capacity reserves at times of normal and maximum demand
Percentage of capacity monitoring	Percentage of services and infrastructure components under capacity monitoring

Service-Level Management

Cloud service-level management defines the level of service needed to support cloud customers. After a service provider defines this service level for an application, it needs to monitor that application to ensure that service delivery objectives are met. The formal definition of a service level can be documented in an SLA and used to manage all vendors participating in the service delivery process.

Figure 8-4 shows service-level management with interrelationships between SLAs, OLAs, and UCs. The SLAs are the service-level agreements made between the IT service department/organization and the customers. The OLAs are the agreements between internal organizations and the IT organization. The UCs are the agreements between the suppliers and the IT organization. The SLAs have certain KPIs that should be measured and regularly reported. As an example, if the provider offers an SLA that states 8 hours, the provider might have an OLA with internal organizations of 6 hours and with suppliers a UC of 2 hours. This framework of agreements should make sure that the levels of service agreed within the SLA (in this case, 8 hours) are not breached.

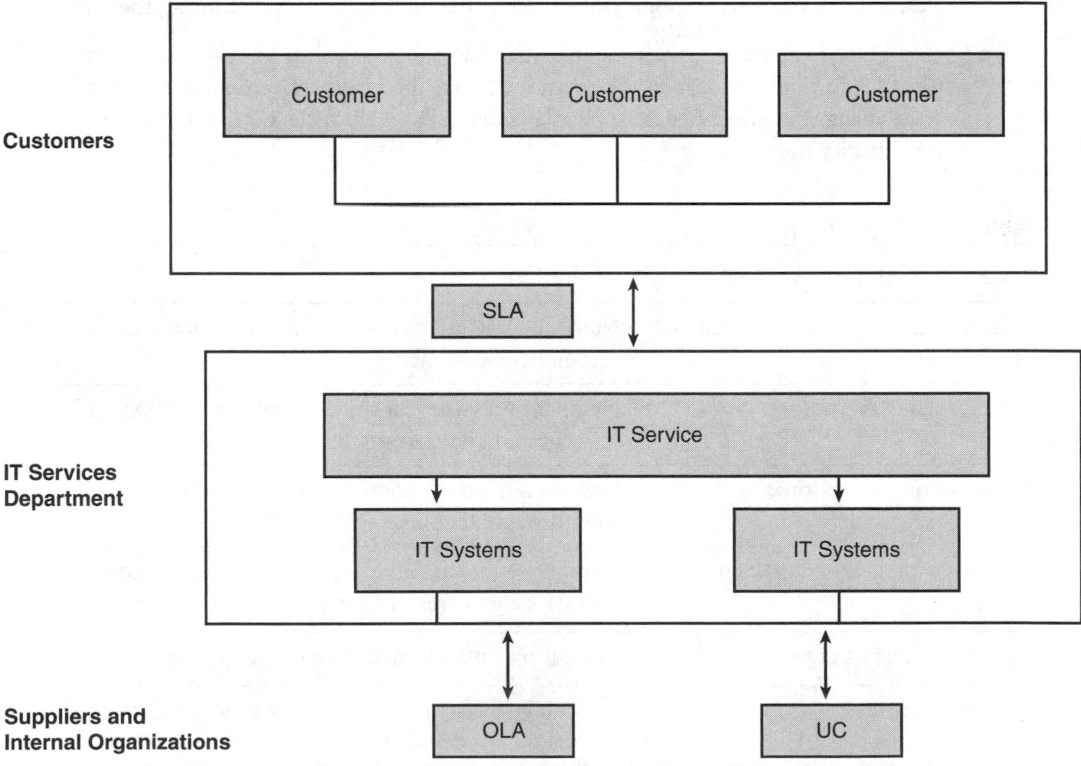

Figure 8-4 *Service-Level Management*

SLAs guarantee most aspects of service delivery, both technology and service aspects. Technology guarantees are concerned with system response time, system uptime guarantees, and error resolution time. The customer service guarantees are concerned with availability, support staff availability, and response time. The SLA should be designed to work with marketing and technology groups (OLAs) and the suppliers (UCs). Table 8-3 lists the key KPIs for service levels.[1]

Table 8-3 *Key KPIs for Service Levels*

Service-Level KPI	Definition
Services covered by SLAs	Number of services covered by SLAs
Monitored SLAs	Number of services monitored that have SLAs
SLAs under review	Number of services/SLAs that are reviewed on a regular basis
Fulfillment of service levels	Number of services/SLAs where the service levels are met
Number of service issues	Number of issues in the services that are identified and addressed in an improvement plan

There is always difficulty in negotiating SLAs. The main contention is how it is defined, measured, and applied/credited. Many times, it is difficult to read the SLAs offered because they are filled with all kinds of clauses and legal jargon. Tele-Management Forum (TMF) has an SLA handbook that explains how to specify SLAs and the interrelationships among KPIs, key quality indicators (KQI), and SLAs. Here, we briefly cover these relationships; for detailed calculations, refer to the SLA handbook.[3]

The perception of quality or quality of experience (QoE) is something experienced by the end user, and many times it is subjective. As such, QoE and the SLA are related in that if the perception of the service or product is poor and yet the service parameters fall within the limits defined by the SLA, the SLA must be redressed. KQIs, being subjective, can be hard to specify in contracts; however, a number of KQIs relate to the QoE that should be included in the SLA. To obtain a KQI, some KPIs must be defined as well and agreed in the SLA. KQIs are typically a combination of several KPIs that can indicate to operators about the end-user experience. In a world with an increasingly complex mix of services, an operator can combine KPIs into KQIs to provide not only a true picture of customer satisfaction but also a picture of how this satisfaction can be related to the network itself. An operator can use this knowledge to preempt problems, quickly resolve issues before they impact the end-user experience, and document performance as seen from the customer point of view.

Figure 8-5 shows a relationship among KPI, KQI, and SLA. The concept here is to define and agree on KPIs for products and services and map them to create KQIs. The SLAs are derived from KPIs and KQIs. The KPIs exist at each level of hierarchy of the network, and the higher level of hierarchy KPIs will have a dependency on the lower level of KPIs. The KPIs are then combined by some empirical or experimental relationship to form a KQI. The relationship between KPI and KQI is an important concept for SLA negotiation. The KPIs and KQIs are measured by setting thresholds.

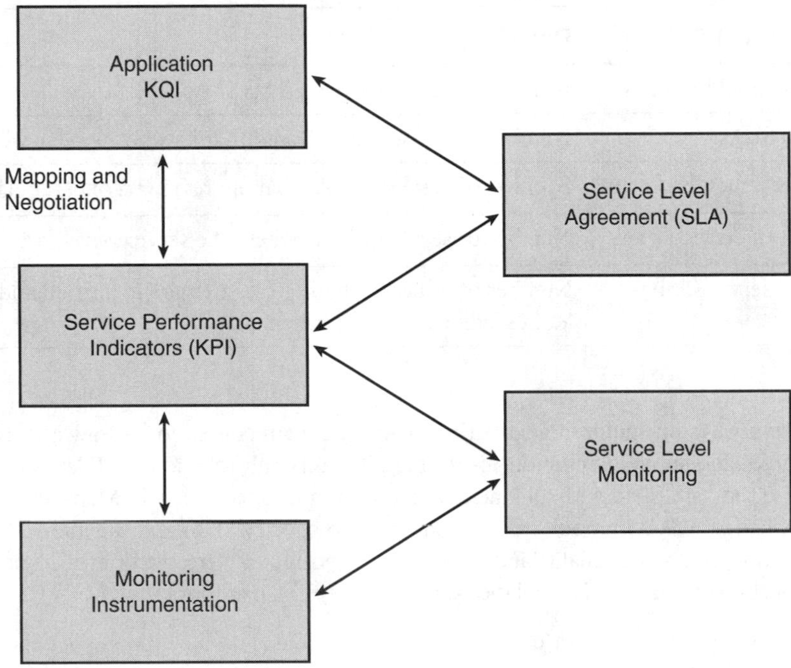

Figure 8-5 *KPI, KQI, and SLA Relationships*

Table 8-4 provides three examples of how SLAs are delivered by cloud providers today.[4]

As you can see from Table 8-4, many cloud providers are not really measuring the KPIs, KQIs, and SLAs because of the complexity of the relationship. They are basically taking a simplistic approach by offering some credits when the customer reports a problem regarding his service. More work is needed in measuring KPIs, KQIs, and SLAs and linking them together.

Table 8-4 *Key KPIs for Service Level*

	AWS EC2	RackSpace	3Tera
SLA offered	99.95% based on the previous 365 days. If it is less than 365, AWS claims 100%.	99.95% (RackSpace claims 100% availability because it will give 5% credit for 1–30 min. downtime.)	99.999%
Credits	Customer has to capture, document, and send a request to Amazon to prove the outage to get credit.	Supposedly tell the rep there is an outage, and the provider will give credit. The credit is a percentage off monthly fees equal to the portion of the monthly outage.	3Tera automates the process, and the customer does not have to report. The extent of automation is related to fault management.
Duration	No monitoring; customer must to monitor and report the duration of outage and supporting evidence.	No monitoring; customer has to monitor and report the duration of the outage.	The AppLogic Cloud Computing Platform constantly monitors and reports the availability, and the customer does not have to report the outage.

Supplier Management

Supplier management is part of the service design in ITIL V3, and it involves managing suppliers, typically external vendors/suppliers, although it can involve internal company departments/organizations. The goal of supplier management is to ensure quality, consistency, and value for money:

Supplier Management = Manage Supplier Relationships and Performance

In the case of using external vendors/suppliers, it is important to have a formal contract. Steps to formalizing and creating contracts include

- **Identify business requirements:** Provide agreement by documenting a strategy and policy, and finally develop a business case, as needed.
- **Evaluate and select new suppliers:** Points to consider are obtaining references from the past engagements and also the financial position of the vendor.
- **Introduce new suppliers and contracts:** Use the change management process to introduce new suppliers/vendors into the Suppliers and Contract Database (SCD).

- **Manage performance of suppliers and contracts:** Evaluate the performance of the supplier and take appropriate action for nonperforming suppliers based on the contract.
- **Renew or end a contract:** Based on the business needs, the contracts need to be reviewed and renewed or terminated.

Table 8-5 lists key supplier management KPIs.[1]

Table 8-5 *Key KPIs for Service Level*

Service Level KPI	Definition
Number of agreed UCs	Total number of contracts underpinned by UCs
Number of contract reviews	Total number of contracts reviewed from suppliers
Number of contract breaches	Total number of contract violations by suppliers

Service Continuity Management

IT Service Continuity Management (ITSCM) recovers services in the case of a disaster. ITSCM ensures that the IT service provider can always provide minimum agreed service levels by reducing the risk from disaster events to an acceptable level and planning for the recovery of IT services. ITSCM should be designed to support Business Continuity Process and Disaster Recovery (BCP/DR).

Disaster is something no company wants to go through, but the reality is that every company will to go through it at some point. Therefore, every company needs to have a BCP/DR strategy. The following items are of interest in BCP/DR:

- **Recovery Point Objective (RPO):** This is the point in time that your business data must be restored. For example, if the disaster strikes at 6 p.m., the recovery of data must be restored up to 3 p.m., for a RPO of 3 hours.
- **Recovery Time Objective (RTO):** This is the time it takes to recover certain business functions. The RTOs for a business varies depending on the function.
- **Business Impact Analysis (BIA):** This would provide what the impact of the business would be. The BIA would determine both the RPO and the RTO for the business functions.

Figure 8-6 shows the ITSCM life cycle for BCP/DR. The ITSCM business continuity life cycle is a foundation building block to help assure that the organization's IT service continuity management process is successful.

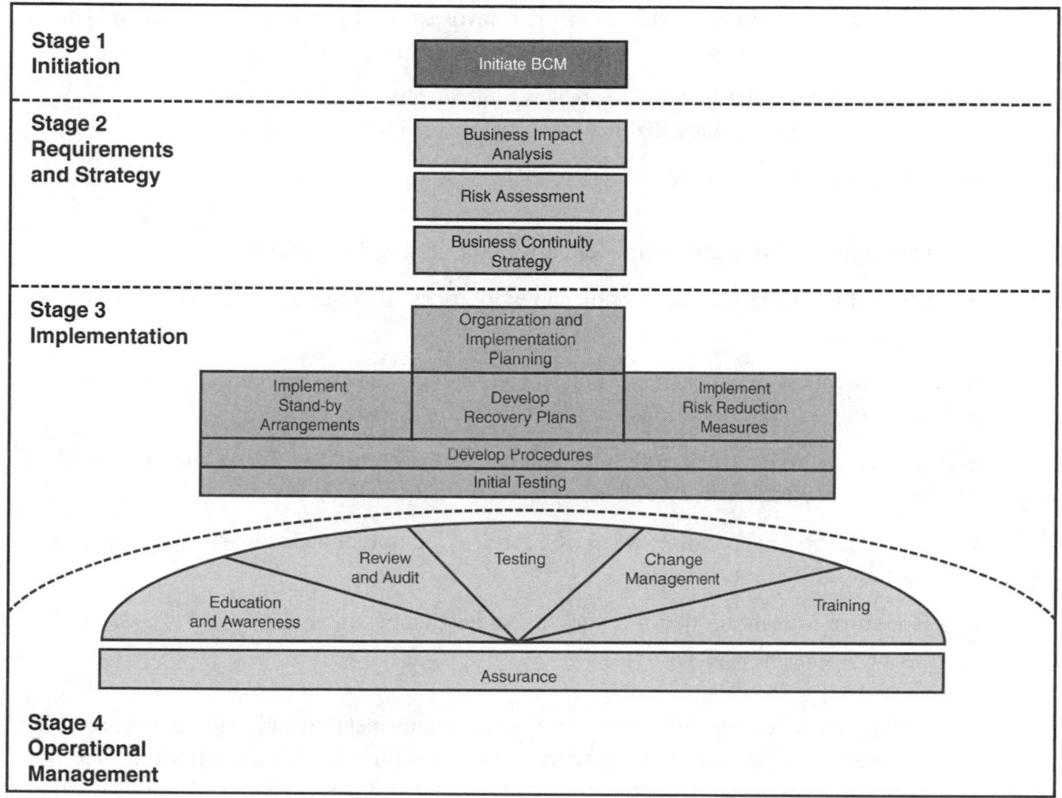

Figure 8-6 *ITSCM Life Cycle*[7]

As shown in Figure 8-6, the ITSCM life cycle for BCP/DR consists of four stages:

Step 1. **Initiation:** This is starting point of the life cycle. The scope is defined here and agreed upon by all the stakeholders.

Step 2. **Requirements and Strategy:** During this stage, the BIA is performed and "what if" scenarios are created to determine what the business impact is because of a certain disaster. Also, recovery procedures are determined based on the business criticality.

Step 3. **Implementation:** In this stage, the recovery plans are detailed. One of the activities conducted in this stage is developing implementation plans, including the emergency response plan, the damage assessment plan, and the salvage plan:

a. **Implementing standby agreements:** The UCs made with external and internal suppliers should be linked to the recovery plan.

b. **Developing procedures:** Develop procedures to detail exactly what each member of the DR team should do, if the plan is invoked.

c. **Undertaking initial tests:** This involves some preliminary tests of the DR procedures.

Step 4. **Operational Management:** This stage involves the maintenance of the life cycle and ensures that maintenance occurs through mock-up trials.

The recovery options for ITSCM include

- **Do nothing:** Few organizations can afford this in this day and age.
- **Manual workaround:** This option can work for some businesses that have few critical IT systems.
- **Reciprocal arrangement:** This option involves agreements made with other companies using similar technology for help during the disaster event.
- **Gradual recovery:** This option is for services that do not have to be restored for 72 hours or so, and recovery will take place gradually.
- **Warm start:** This option is where the services are not immediately required and can wait for 24–72 hours.
- **Hot start:** This means that recovery is required almost immediately and is used for the most critical services.

There will always be some difficulties and costs in implementing and maintaining ITSCM, but the resulting benefits, especially when a disaster is prevented or quickly controlled, outweigh the associated difficulties and costs. Table 8-6 lists some key KPIs for ITSCM.[1]

Table 8-6 *Key KPIs for IT Service Continuity Management*

Service-Level KPI	Definition
Business processes with service continuity agreements	Percentage of the business processes that are covered by explicit service continuity targets such as RPO and RTO
Gaps in DR preparation	Number of identified gaps in the preparation for DR events
Implementation duration for a DR (RTO)	Duration from the identification of a disaster to the implementation of a suitable service recovery mechanism
Number of DR practices	Number of DR practices actually carried out
Number of identified shortcomings during DR practices	Number of identified shortcomings in the preparation of DR that are identified during practices

Transition Phase

The transition phase implements the service design that was built in the design phase into the production phase at the service provider location. The following items are considered in the transition phase:

- Change management
- Configuration and setting up all the assurance systems
- Service asset management in the CMS (CMDB)
- Migration from the current state to the target state (people, processes, products, and partners)
- Staging and validation of all systems and processes for assurance

Refer to Chapter 7 for more details on the cloud transition phase.

Operate Phase

The operate phase is where the service provider takes possession of the management of the cloud operations from the equipment vendors, system integrators, and partners, and will monitor and audit the service using the monitoring systems to ensure that the SLAs are met. The following items are considered in the cloud operation phase:

- Service desk (function)
- Incident management
- Problem management
- Event management
- Other IT day-to-day activities

Refer to Chapter 7 for more details on the cloud operate phase.

CSI (Optimization) Phase

Continuous Service Improvement (also referred to as optimization) for cloud assurance involves improving on the operations by adding best practices to the processes, tools, and configurations. The following list provides some of the tasks that are carried out in the optimization phase:

- Auditing the configurations against best practices and changing the configurations as appropriate.
- Fine-tuning the tools and processes based on best practices.

- Adding new products and services, and performing an assessment to ensure that the new services can be incorporated into the current environment. If not, determine the changes required and go through the cloud life cycle, starting from the cloud strategy.
- Cisco SMARTnet provides optimization services for service improvement that include[5]
  - Global 24-hour access to the Cisco Technical Assistance Center (TAC)
  - Access to an online knowledge base, communities, and tools
  - Hardware replacement options, including 2-hour, 4-hour, and next business day
  - Operating system software updates
  - Smart, proactive diagnostics and real-time alerts on devices enabled with Smart Call Home

Refer to Chapter 7 for more details on the CSI phase.

Cloud End-to-End Monitoring Flow

Service assurance is a combination of fault management and performance management, with probes for collecting information, service management, and trouble ticketing systems to enable operators to proactively manage and correct problems before they impact service.

Cloud assurance requires fault and performance management of the cloud infrastructure that is comprised of network, compute, and storage and also the applications that run on the compute platform, as well as reporting of each incident or problem to the appropriate system for remediation. Also, for assurance management, it is essential that the service provisioning be tied to assurance, because cloud customers might only be using the infrastructure for a defined period of time (for example, customers using the cloud for a test/development environment might only use the service for the period of time when they are developing/testing a service), unlike in the old world where the customers stay on the network for very long periods of time.

Cloud service providers must resolve service-related problems quickly to minimize outages and revenue loss. Cloud service management solutions give you maximum visibility into service performance and cost-effective management of your SLAs, service performance monitoring, and service impact analysis.

Unlike the cloud provisioning cycle, which starts with the customer/user and ends with a provisioning task into the resources, fault and performance events occur in the resources that affect the service and are eventually noticed by the customer in the form of service degradation unless they are fixed proactively before they are perceived by the customer. Figure 8-7 shows end-to-end monitoring of cloud services, the steps for which are described in the list that follows.

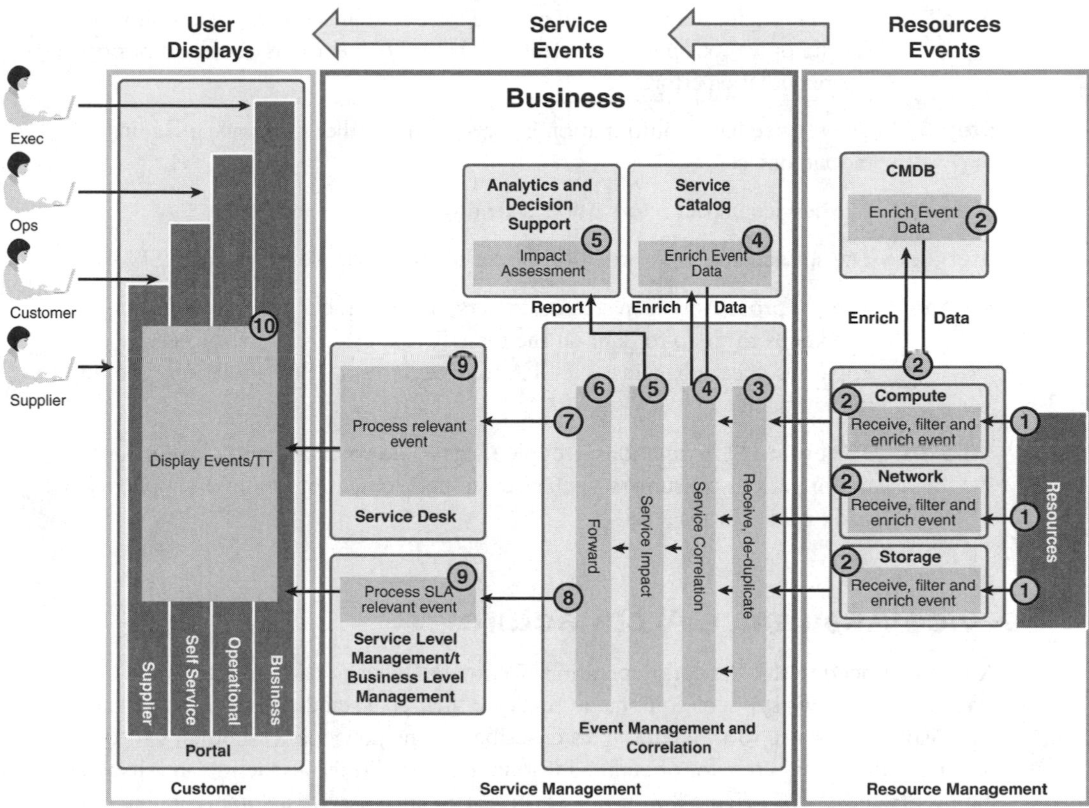

Figure 8-7 *Cloud Assurance Flow - Data Collection and Management Steps*

Step 1. The incident/fault and performance events are sent by the infrastructure devices comprised of network devices, compute/server platforms, storage devices, and applications.

Step 2. The domain managers collect these events from infrastructure devices through the CLI, Simple Network Management Protocol (SNMP) polling, or traps sent by the infrastructure devices. Typically separate domain managers are used for the network, compute, and storage devices.

Step 3. The domain managers receive the messages from the infrastructure devices and deduplicate/filter the events.

Step 4. The device events received by the domain managers have device information only and do not contain any service or customer information. The domain manager will enrich the events by looking into the service catalog. In other words, the events are mapped to the services to determine which services are affected because of the events in the infrastructure. It is also possible to map to customers and determine the customers who are impacted by the events.

Step 5. The service impact is assessed and the information is shown on a dashboard for the operations personnel. This will help the operations people to prioritize the remediation efforts.

Step 6. The service impact information is forwarded to other locations, including mobile devices.

Step 7. The service impact information is sent to the service desk (SD).

Step 8. The service impact information is sent to the service-level manager (SLM).

Step 9. The SD proactively manages customers, informs them of service impacts, and keeps them up to date on the remediation efforts. Also, the service impact is checked against the SLA to determine any SLA violations and business impacts.

Step 10. The events, SLA violations, trouble tickets, and so on are displayed on a portal for various consumers, such as customers, operations people, suppliers, and business managers.

Service Assurance Architecture

A frequent need in the Network Operations Center (NOC) is to capture alarms and events from various types of equipment, translate them to a standardized alarm format, and display the alarm to a web portal, as described in the previous section. This section discusses the architecture for obtaining information from the infrastructure and displaying events and alarms. Figure 8-8 shows a typical customer service assurance architecture. The architecture can be based on the ITU-T Telecommunications Management Network (TMN) layered model or other standards such as TMF eTOM. Based on TMN, the architecture would have an element management layer, a network management layer, and a service management layer. If TMF eTOM is used, the architecture would have resource management and service management layers.

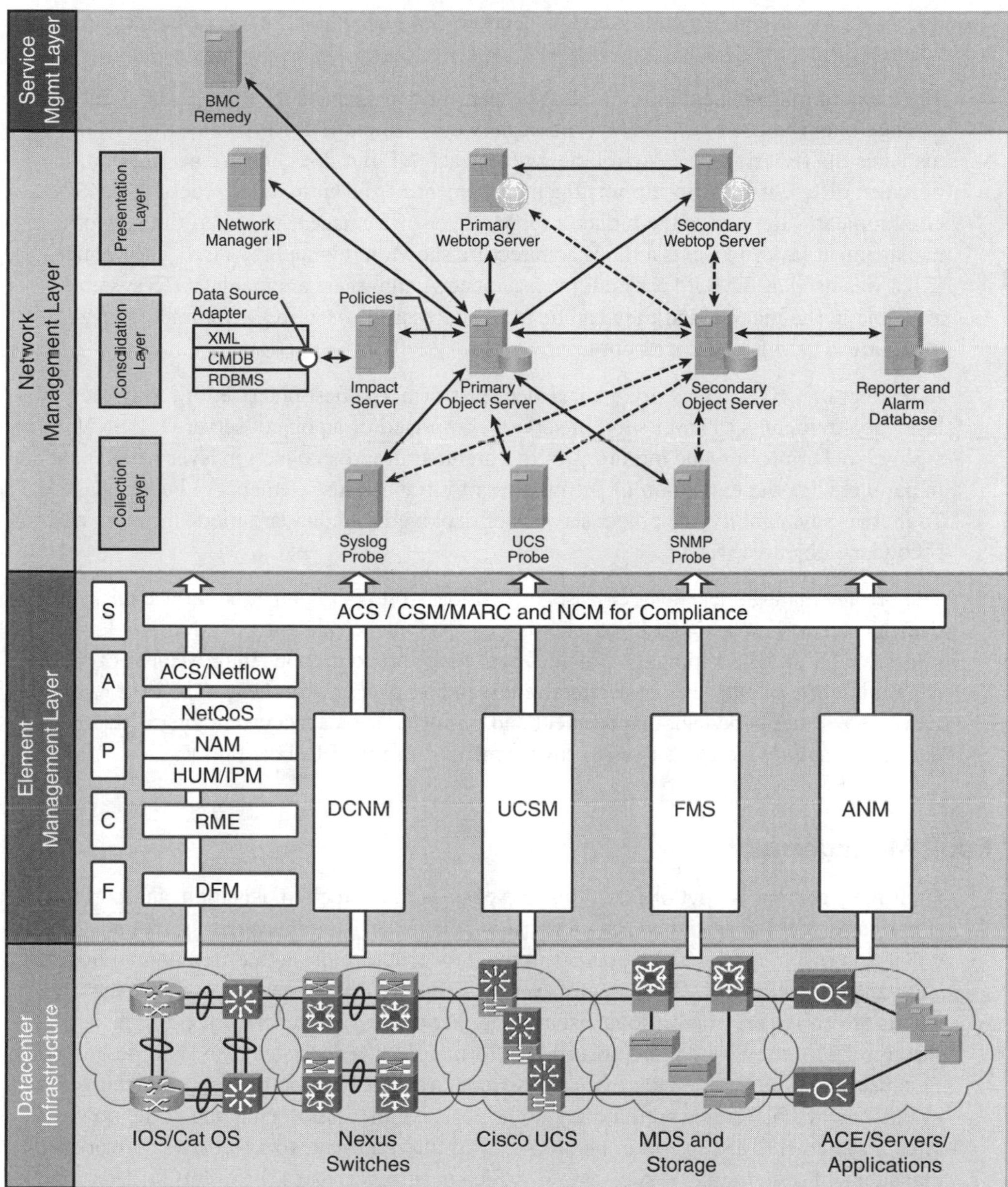

Figure 8-8 *Assurance Architecture for DC/V and Cloud*

Figure 8-8 shows the various element management, network management, and service management systems. These systems are used in a lab validation; however, there are other Commercially-Off-The-Shelf (COTS) systems that might be used in this architecture for service assurance. The service assurance architecture should be determined based on many factors, as detailed in the section, "Service Strategy Phase," of this chapter and in Chapter 7.

The element management layer consists of element management systems (EMS), which manage one or more of a specific type of network element (NE). Typically, the EMS manages the functions and capabilities within each NE but does not manage the traffic between different NEs. To support the management of the entire infrastructure, EMS communicates upward to the higher-level Manager of Manager (MOM) at the network management layer. In the assurance architecture shown in Figure 8-8, Cisco Info Center (CIC) was used as a MOM for fault management. Again, there are many COTS systems available in the market, and they can be used successfully as a MOM for fault management at the network management layer.

In respect of CIC as a network management platform, the best practice for the collection layer deployment is to have "sets" of servers comprised of an object server with SNMP, syslog, socket probes, and monitors. In this architecture, the collection layer will expand in parallel with the expansion of the number of infrastructure elements to be managed. To increase availability, the object servers are deployed in redundant mode (primary and secondary object servers).

The service management layer consists of ITIL-based tools to unify the service desk, incident, problem, change, asset life cycle, service-level management applications, and user interface. This unified approach provides proactive and continuous improvement of service availability, quality, and cost-effectiveness in complex environments. The next two sections will describe fault management and performance management along with some use cases that are executed in a lab environment as Proof of Concept (POC).

Fault Management

Fault management is a set of functions that enables the detection, isolation, and correction of abnormal operation in the infrastructure devices. Fault management requires the collection of faults from the resources in the infrastructure through different methods such as SNMP traps, XML messages, event streams, and syslog messages. After the events are collected from various resources, either directly from network elements or through EMS, they need to be normalized (formatted in a consistent way) and processed. Because the number of events that comes from devices often can be very high, these events need to be filtered so that they do not cause unnecessary clogging in the downstream systems. EMSs shown in Figure 8-8 send filtered events to a top-level network management system (NMS) such as CIC, which in turn correlates the events to determine the root cause of the fault. After the root cause is determined, the faults are displayed on a dashboard or a trouble ticket is created using the remedy system (refer to Figure 8-8) for remediation.

Some key EMSs and NMSs that are shown in Figure 8-8 are described in the sections that follow. You can find a description of other systems in the Cisco white paper "Assurance Management Reference Architecture for Virtualized Datacenters in a Cloud Service Offering."[6]

Cisco Data Center Network Manager

Cisco Data Center Network Manager (DCNM) is a Cisco management solution for Cisco NX-OS operating system–enabled hardware platforms. Cisco NX-OS provides the foundation for the Cisco Nexus product family. Cisco DCNM provides a robust framework and rich feature set that fulfills the routing, switching, and storage administration needs of present and future data centers.

The DCNM server uses the XML management interface of Cisco NX-OS devices to manage and monitor them. The XML management interface is a programmatic method based on the NETCONF protocol that complements the command-line interface (CLI) functionality.

Cisco UCS Manager

Cisco UCS Manager is an embedded device-management software that manages the Cisco Unified Computing System (UCS) as a single, logical, highly available entity from end to end. It provides flexible role- and policy-based management using service profiles and templates, which help to improve IT productivity and business agility. With this approach, infrastructure can be provisioned in minutes instead of days, shifting the IT focus from maintenance to implementing strategic initiatives.

Cisco UCS Manager resides on a pair of Cisco UCS 6X00 Series Fabric Interconnects using a clustered, active-standby configuration for high availability. The manager participates not only in server provisioning but also in device discovery, inventory, configuration, diagnostics, monitoring, fault detection, auditing, and statistics collection.

The software can export the system's configuration information to CMDBs, facilitating processes based on ITIL concepts. Open APIs simplify integration with third-party management software or in-house-developed tools, creating an extensible management architecture. The XML API also facilitates coordination with third-party provisioning tools that can deploy virtual machines as well as install operating systems and application software on servers also configured with Cisco UCS Manager. Cisco UCS provides an XML-formatted event stream for forwarding to a top-layer network management layer, such as the CIC.

Cisco Fabric Manager System

Cisco Fabric Manager System (FMS) manages Cisco MDS NX-OS Release 4.2(1) running on Cisco MDS 9000 family switches. FMS is used for configuring SNMP, Remote Monitoring (RMON), Switch Port Analyzer (SPAN), and the Embedded Event Manager (EEM). Apart from logging every message in the form of syslog messages, it supports most of the Management Information Bases (MIB) for generating SNMP traps and monitors network traffic through a Fibre Channel interface.

Note Cisco recently integrated FMS into DCNM in the newer release; however, the architecture shown in Figure 8-8 is still valid.

Cisco Application Networking Manager

The Cisco Application Networking Manager (ANM) enables centralized configuration, operation, and monitoring of Cisco Application Control Engine (ACE) devices, as well as operations management for the Cisco Content Services Switch (CSS), Cisco Content Switching Module (CSM), Cisco Content Switching Module with SSL (CSM-S), and Cisco ACE Global Site Selector (GSS). ANM also centralizes operation management of virtual IP (VIP) answers and Domain Name System (DNS) rules for GSS devices.

Cisco ANM simplifies Cisco ACE provisioning through forms-based configuration management of Layer 4 through 7 virtualized network devices and services. With Cisco ANM, network managers are able to create, modify, and delete all virtual contexts of the Cisco ACE, as well as control the allocation of resources among the virtual contexts. Within these virtual contexts, Cisco ANM enables the configuration of the content networking and Secure Sockets Layer (SSL) services.

Cisco Info Center

At the network management layer, Cisco Info Center (CIC) is used for overall fault management. The CIC architecture is shown in Figure 8-8. CIC uses various types of probes (syslog, SNMP, and so on) at the collection layer. The object server, in the consolidation layer, is a memory-resident, real-time database that aggregates and deduplicates fault data and correlates it according to user-defined rules. CIC Impact is the analysis and correlation engine for the CIC Object Server. CIC WebTop includes front-end applications that operators see and use and is provided in the presentation layer. CIC Reporter delivers reporting functionality for users who want to view network, compute, and storage event data after it has been cleared from the real-time object servers. The NML layer provides the following:

- Capture of the alarm data through a suitable interface including TCP/IP, SNMP traps, syslog, XML event streams, and so on. It leverages the capability of EMSs in respect to alarm configuration, correlation, and filtering.
- Translation of the alarm data into Cisco CIC standard format, which includes mapping alarm severity, defining appropriate fields for alert groups, and so on.
- Storage of the alarm data for historical purposes. The CIC Reporter stores the alarms in relational database management system (RDBMS), which allows storing virtually unlimited amounts of event information from different sources in a centralized place.
- Correlation of the alarm events to reduce the event storm by aggregating alarms related to the same cause into one single alarm.
- Display of the alarm on the web portal. The final step will be to deliver the alarm to the web portal with role-based access control. CIC WebTop displays the alarms in the form of portlets with customized views and filters. It becomes easy for an operator to create his own private page.

Use Case(s)

Use cases enable engineers, developers, customers, and users to identify how a system should perform and provide value and results. In systems development, use cases serve to demonstrate functional requirements that are defined as conditions that must conform within a system. Use cases are mapped to scenarios to confirm that details of requirements fulfill project or customer expectations. Table 8-7 lists examples of use cases that are used when testing fault management systems.

Table 8-7 *Fault Management Use Case Examples: Collection of Fault Events from Network, Compute, and Storage Devices*

Infrastructure	Description of Use Case
Network	Discover all the network devices.
	Confirm that network device event messages are received by DCNM or directly by CIC from the devices.
	Fault messages are forwarded to CIC by EMS.
	CIC receives traps/syslog/XML messages from the network devices and/or EMS, and event groups are created based on technology and management domain.
	CIC rules file configured to correlate the fault event.
	CIC processes and displays all network events on the WebTop.
Compute	Discover UCS and other compute platforms.
	Confirm that UCS events can be retrieved by CIC through UCSM.
	Identify interested events from the event stream and retrieval of those events.
	Map UCS severity events with existing MOM (CIC).
	Create event groups on the basis of managed objects.
	CIC rules file configured to correlate the fault event.
	CIC processes and displays compute (UCS) events on the WebTop.
Storage	Discover storage devices (MDS).
	Confirm that storage platform (MDS) events can be retrieved by FMS.
	Fault messages are forwarded to CIC by FMS.
	CIC rules file configured to correlate the fault event for storage.
	CIC processes and displays all storage events on the WebTop.

Figure 8-9 shows the cloud infrastructure used in a lab environment to test end-to-end fault management use case (with many subuse cases/examples shown in Table 8-7). The infrastructure is similar to a cloud Infrastructure as a Service (IaaS) and has network, compute, and storage devices. The figure also has all the management systems used. The primary purpose of fault management use cases is to collect all the events/alarms from all the infrastructure devices, correlate the alarms, and display them on a dashboard.

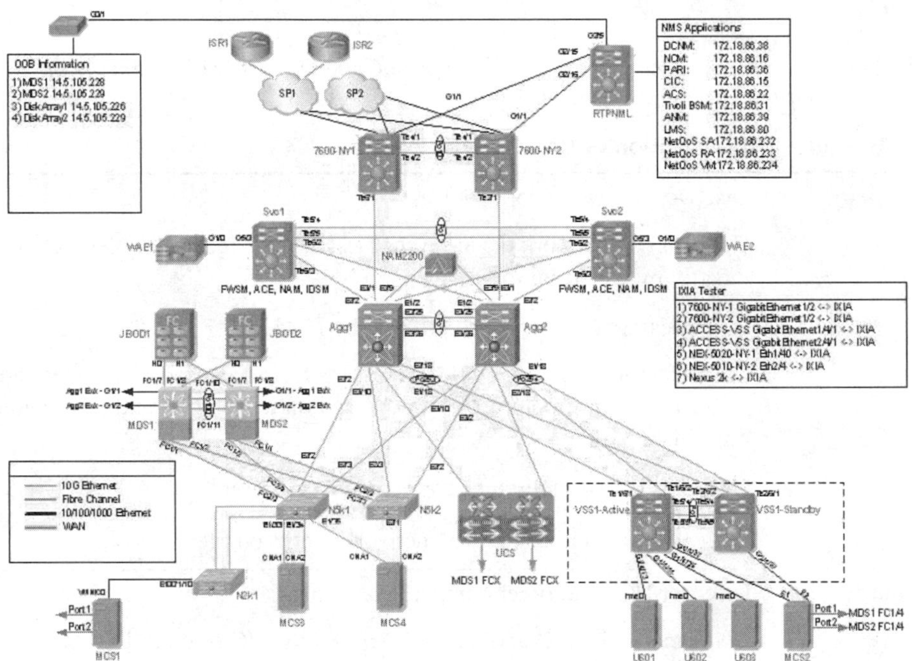

Figure 8-9 *Cloud Infrastructure and Tools Used for Use Cases*

Figure 8-10 shows the results of a fault management use case (Table 8-7) run using the cloud infrastructure shown in Figure 8-9. The consolidated CIC dashboard with alarms from network, compute, and storage are shown in Figure 8-10. The figure is made up of four quadrants. The upper-left quadrant shows a pie chart showing cleared events and indeterminate, warning, minor, major, and critical alarms. The lower-left quadrant shows a summary of all cloud infrastructure events. The same information is also shown in the lower-right quadrant with a more detailed description. The upper-right quadrant shows the infrastructure with all the devices marked, and the rectangular boxes underneath each device show the color-coded alarm condition. By clicking these boxes, the detailed alarm condition can be displayed in the lower-right quadrant.

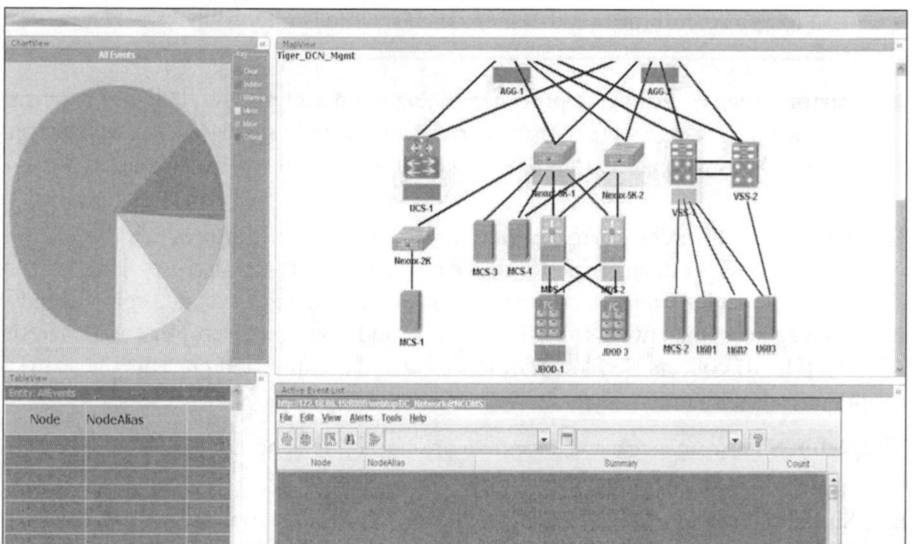

Figure 8-10 *WebTop Display of Network, Compute, and Storage Alarms*

Performance Management

The previous section addressed fault management, and this section addresses cloud performance management. Both fault management and performance management are part of overall cloud assurance. Cloud performance management involves the periodic collection of QoS metrics that characterize the performance of the cloud infrastructure and applications that customers use. One of its goals is to find network congestion and bottlenecks and to minimize them by subsequent action. The following items are important for any IT organization for effective performance management:

- **Utilization and error rates:** It is important to collect errors and set thresholds for appropriate action by operations when the threshold is exceeded. The MIBs in the devices provide tons of indicators on error rate, and it is a matter of collecting this information and making sense of it.
- **Consistent performance level:** The first level of performance is availability, which can be accomplished by periodically polling all the devices in the infrastructure to determine the health and availability of the devices. This will provide the performance of the infrastructure, and this proactive monitoring will prevent any degradation in the service. Additional KPIs that should be monitored are discussed earlier in this chapter.
- **Performance data collection and analysis:** This includes the gathering of data statistics over service intervals. Internal timers from management systems can trigger SNMP polling requests toward the cloud infrastructure devices and retrieve data statistics used for real-time analysis. There are many tools that provide trend analysis

with long-term information that helps the IT administrator to make performance analyses.

- **Performance reporting:** Reports containing trend analysis with long-term information help the IT operators to make performance analyses. In addition, WebTop provides reports with line graphs that are generated from the collected data.

To demonstrate the architecture, keeping the preceding listed features in mind, we chose NetQoS, a COTS product, for performance management. Cisco also uses other partner products in its architecture for performance management and has tested some of those products, such as Solar Winds and InfoVista. In addition, the Cisco Network Analysis Module (NAM) collects NetFlow traffic, analyzes the traffic, and presents the analysis results on a dashboard.

The NetQoS performance management solution has three components:

- **Super Agent (SA):** SA is the end-to-end application performance monitoring and analysis solution that uses spanned traffic (packets) as a data source. The SA has two components: the data collector and an SA console. The data collector captures and stores network traffic captured through a SPAN port in the network. The SA management console acquires data from the data collector and generates end-to-end application performance reports. The NetQoS data collector can be a Cisco NAM or a NetQoS data collector. The SA appliance and/or NAM also manages the virtualized switch—the Cisco Nexus 1000V. The Nexus 1000V switch is a software switch on a VMware ESX server that delivers the Cisco VN-Link services to virtual machines hosted on that server.
- **Route Analytics (RA):** RA is the network traffic analysis solution using NetFlow as a data source. The RA solution uses NetFlow as a data source to monitor and analyze up to one year's worth of network traffic and reports flow traffic on the network. RA identifies the source of network bandwidth–hogging application(s) or host(s) during a specified time frame.
- **NetVoyant (NV):** The NV relies on SNMP polling to manage infrastructure devices and has numerous MIBs precompiled. Any new platform can be supported by adding platform-specific MIBs. NV provides packet loss, latency, jitter, device status, and utilization.

Figure 8-11 shows the performance architecture used in the lab and the NetQoS components: SA, RA, and NetVoyant. To create traffic, an IXIA **company's** traffic generator was used in the lab to demonstrate the performance solution and the NetQoS components. The use cases run in the lab are described in the next section.

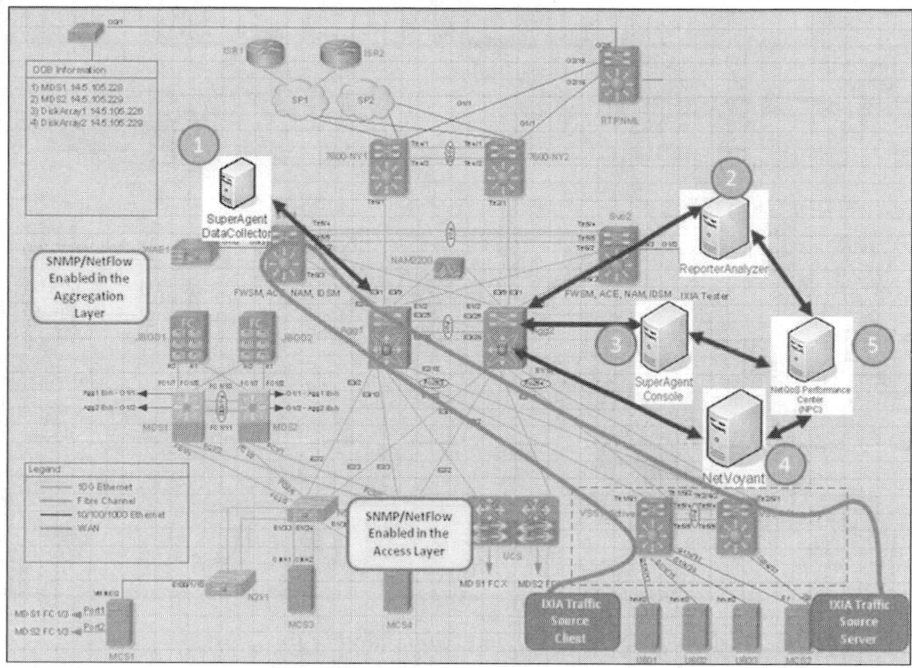

Figure 8-11 *Performance Management Architecture (Lab Simulation)*

Use Case 1: Measure Network Round Trip Time

This test verified that the Super Agent appliance can monitor and measure TCP performance indicators from the cloud infrastructure, as shown in Figure 8-11, by providing the network round trip time between an HTTP client and an HTTP server. Figure 8-12 shows the results of the network round trip time.

The results from Figure 8-12 show the following:

- There were 32 million "observations"—data points collected and analyzed.
- The average network round trip time was 0.12 ms (mean) for the duration of this measurement from Friday, 1/30/2009, through Monday, 2/2/2009.
- The maximum round trip time of 0.25 ms occurred on Sunday, 2/1/2009.

Use Case 2: Validate RA

The purpose of this use case is to test whether RA can receive and process NetFlow data from the Nexus 7000 platforms switches. For this use case, the NetFlow was turned on in the Nexus platform. The NetFlow is available in most IOS platforms and can be turned on in most routers and switches.

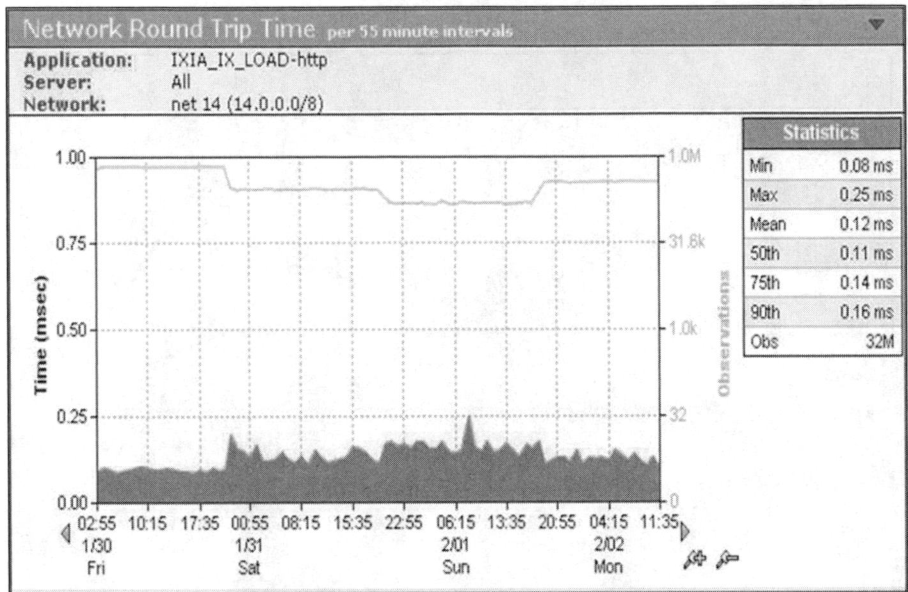

Figure 8-12 *Network Round Trip Time (Simulated in the Lab)*

Figure 8-13 shows the RA results. The RA appliance received and processed exported NetFlow from the Nexus 7000 switches by providing top TCP conversation talkers. The results show that the first three TCP conversations collectively contributed 91.09 percent (49.24 + 21.86 + 19.99 percent) of the total traffic volume during the analysis period.

Conversation Summary - Volume - Total — 15 Feb 2009 13:20:00 - 16 Feb 2009 13:20:00 CST

ACCESS-VSS.cisco.com (14.5.104.250)::Vlan100 — 1.00 Gbps / 1.00 Gbps

Conversation	Volume	Percent
(14.5.104.250) - RTPNML-NETQOS-A (172.18.86.232)	7.55 MBytes	49.24 %
(14.5.104.3) - ALL-ROUTERS.MCAST.NET (224.0.0.2)	3.35 MBytes	21.86 %
(14.5.104.2) - ALL-ROUTERS.MCAST.NET (224.0.0.2)	3.06 MBytes	19.99 %
(14.5.104.250) - rtpnmlz-lms31.cisco.com (172.18.86.80)	1.18 MBytes	7.67 %
(14.5.104.250) - rtpnml-gamma.cisco.com (172.18.86.65)	55.18 KBytes	0.36 %
(14.5.104.250) - rtpnml-v240k.cisco.com (172.18.86.71)	54.87 KBytes	0.36 %
(14.5.104.250) - rtpnmlz-ncm13.cisco.com (172.18.86.16)	40.62 KBytes	0.26 %
(14.5.104.250) - rtpnml-netqos.cisco.com (172.18.86.89)	19.21 KBytes	0.13 %
(14.5.104.250) - rtpnml-dcnm.cisco.com (172.18.86.38)	18.53 KBytes	0.12 %
(14.5.104.250) - rtpnmlv-acs41-p.cisco.com (172.18.86.22)	1.57 KBytes	0.01 %
(14.5.104.250) - rtpnmlz-lms301.cisco.com (172.18.86.19)	252 Bytes	0.00 %
(14.5.104.250) - rtpnml-v240g.cisco.com (172.18.86.84)	252 Bytes	0.00 %
Other	6 Bytes	0.00 %
Total	15.33 MBytes	100.00 %

Figure 8-13 *Top Talkers from RA (Simulated in Cisco Lab)*

Use Case 3: Validate NetVoyant

The purpose of this use case is to ensure that NetVoyant receives SNMP polling data from CAT 6500 VSS switches and processes the SNMP data.

Figure 8-14 shows the NetVoyant output, showing the port channel. The 10-GB interfaces have traffic passing through them, and there are no errors or discards.

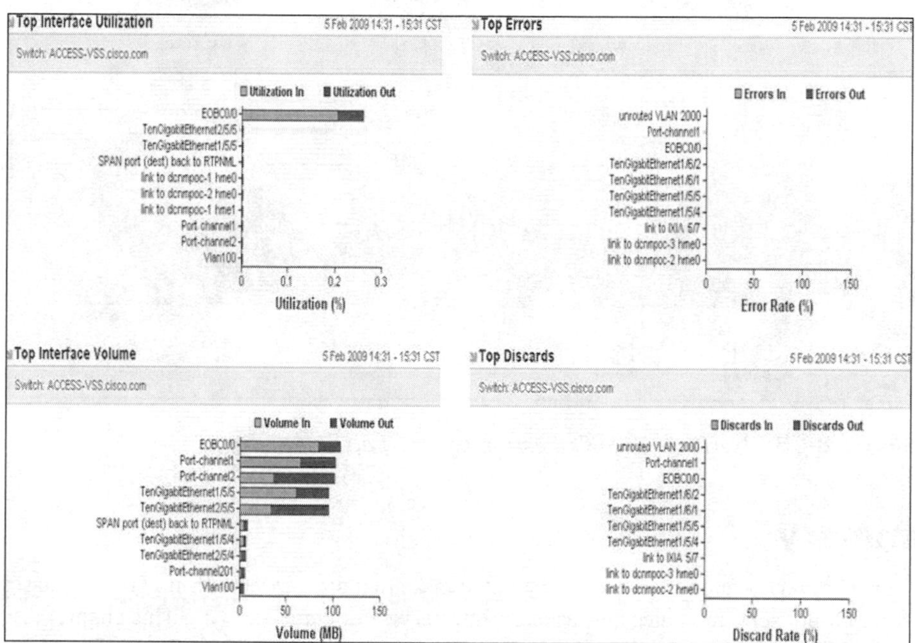

Figure 8-14 *NetVoyant Results (Simulated in Cisco Lab)*

Validate RA for NetFlow Data from Nexus 1000V

The Nexus 1000V switch is a software switch on a VMware ESX server that delivers the Cisco VN-Link services to virtual machines hosted on that server. The NetFlow can be used even on the soft switch. In this use case, the RV is tested to check NetFlow data collection.

Figure 8-15 shows the NetFlow data that is collected and processed by NetQoS- RA. The RA results show outbound network traffic patterns for the Vethernet1 and Vethernet3/1 virtual interfaces. The darker portion on the Vethernet2 interface represents "System Backup" traffic for the VM.

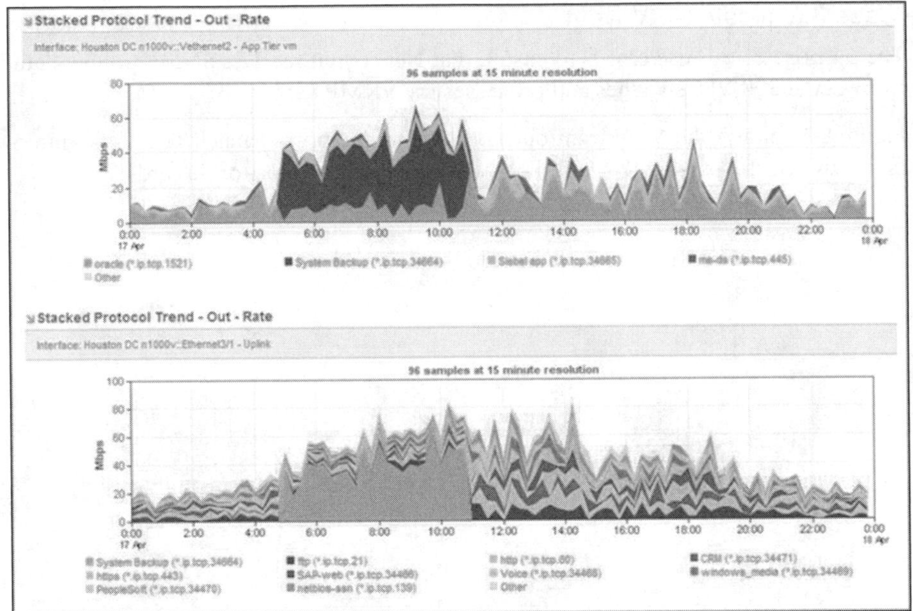

Figure 8-15 *NetFlow Data Collection by RA (Lab Simulation)*

Summary

This chapter covered the service assurance tasks that are carried out in ITIL V3 phases for a cloud: service strategy, service design, service operate, and CSI. This chapter also provided a methodology for conducting an assessment of the service strategy, with several KPIs proposed for availability, capacity management, and service-level management in the service design phase. The chapter also explained the relationship among KPI, KQI, and SLA and presented cloud end-to-end monitoring flow.

In addition, the chapter explored cloud fault management and performance management architectures, and provided an overview of the execution of and end results of several use cases in a lab environment. The cloud assurance use case executed with CIC and NetQoS are examples only, and similar results can be obtained using other COTS software available in the market.

References

[1] http://wiki.en.it-processmaps.com/index.php/ITIL_KPIs_Service_Design.

[2] Molloy, Chris, DE, IBM, "Capacity Management for Cloud Computing," at http://regions.cmg.org/regions/rmcmg/2009Fall/Capacity%20Management%20for%20Cloud%20Computing%20v6%20ext.pdf.

[3] Tele-Management Forum (TMF) GB 917 SLA Management Handbook, at www.tmforum.org/SLAHandbookSolution/2478/home.html.

[4] The Tale of Three Cloud SLAs, at http://itknowledgeexchange.techtarget.com/cloud-computing/the-tale-of-three-cloud-slas-2.

[5] Cisco SMARTnet Service, at www.cisco.com/en/US/products/svcs/ps3034/ps2827/ps2978/serv_group_home.html.

[6] J. Josyula, M. Wakade, P. Lam, and T. Adams, "Assurance Management Reference Architecture for Virtualized Datacenters in a Cloud Service Offering," Cisco white paper, 2010, at www.cisco.com/en/US/technologies/collateral/tk869/tk769/white_paper_c11-575044.html.

[7] ITIL V3 Foundation Training, Pink Elephant.

Chapter 9

Billing and Chargeback

Upon completing this chapter, you should be able to understand the following:

- Billing and chargeback terminology
- Cloud consumers and cloud providers
- Cloud services billing considerations
- Cloud Order-to-Cash process flow
- Billing and chargeback architecture

The cloud service providers will be offering the new cloud services: Infrastructure as a Service (IaaS), Platform as a Service (PaaS), and Software as a Service (SaaS). Also, enterprises will offer cloud services for internal consumption by various departments within the company, such as engineering, payroll, sales, and others. From a service perspective, this new cloud environment creates many important challenges that did not apply in the traditional monopolistic telecommunications environment. One area of concern is applying service-level agreements (SLA) and quality of service (QoS), and associating billing and charging based on the SLAs. This chapter introduces cloud billing/charging terminology; billing considerations for IaaS, PaaS, and SaaS; process flow from Order-to-Cash (OTC); and billing/charging architecture for cloud services.

Billing and Chargeback Terminology

Billing/chargeback is a service offered to external/internal customers for services rendered. The customers would be external in the case of service providers, and they would be billed for services. The customers would be internal in the case of enterprises, and the expenses would be charged back to various departments. In both cases, billing and chargeback have moved from the back office function to a strategic role and are key components in the management of customers, enabling product bundling and allowing fast introduction of new billable/chargeable products and services. More details on billing and chargeback are explained in the following sections.

Billing

Cloud service providers must be creative in creating new services through service portals and tie these services together to creative billing methods to charge for the services rendered.

Cloud service providers need to move away from the traditional monolithic billing systems that slow the introduction of new and exciting cloud services. Managing the cloud customers and the revenue generation are at the core of the cloud business function, and billing and charging systems should consider the following features:

- Customer-centric and offer new services quickly and easily without too much IT intervention
- Flexible subscription models and payment options
- Easy integration into the self-service catalogs, and the provision of assurance systems for offering services and managing credits
- Integration into Customer Relations Manager (CRM)
- Efficient management of customer queries and customer payments
- Reduction of the costs of servicing clients with a built-in, customizable, customer-facing web portal, with online bill payment, presentment, and reporting
- Promotion of customer loyalty by being proactive to customer needs

Chargeback

Chargeback is an IT strategy for enterprise private clouds that assigns the charges to the business units (BU) of a company for the hardware, software, space, power, and services. This differs from the model where a centralized department bears all the costs as IT overhead. Chargeback also differs from the service provider (SP) model where an SP bills the end user(s) for the usage.

Chargeback makes each BU responsible for the usage and charges against the usage. This method of accounting is also sometimes referred to as "responsible accounting" because it would hold each BU or person responsible for the usage and expenses of the IT costs.

The accounting systems that can provide a breakdown of expenses can help the management to clearly see what factors are driving costs and to budget accordingly. Also, these systems provide transparency to the users and management, and identify areas where to cut costs and achieve greater profitability.

Chargeback systems can be simple or complex, and many organizations trade some of the effectiveness of complex systems for simpler systems to reduce the burden, in terms of time and money required for IT chargeback. The simpler systems basically allocate the charges to various BUs based on some usage metrics. In many cases, chargeback systems can simply be used as a pre-cursor to charging or simply to show users what they are spending without actually charging them. This is often referred to as Showback, this has all the same requirements of chargeback minus the charging step.

Rating and Charging

Rating involves converting usage-related data into a monetary-equivalent value. In cloud computing, usage-related data is generated at various resources and can include CPU, server, storage, SLAs, disaster recovery provisions, and others. There might be different rates for each of the resources used. As such, rating information can come from multiple sources, and all that information needs to be stitched together. Rating allows the enrichment of usage data with additional business information necessary for providing multi-service price calculations. It enables comprehensive ratings based on multiple characteristics of complex service schemes and customer accounts.

Charging is a process in which the vendor providing the services establishes charges to be levied against the services rendered and sends an invoice/bill to the customers.

Billing Mediation

Billing mediation (generally used in SP) falls between data collection and charging. Many vendors can provide data collection, data transformation, and data correlation as part of billing mediation as described in the list that follows:

- **Data or event collection:** Collect and decode event information from multiple sources (network, compute, and storage) and from heterogeneous devices. The collection process needs to be streamlined to account for various methods of collection, including real-time, on-demand, and periodic types.
- **Data transformation:** Converts various types of formatted data from multiple sources and from heterogeneous equipment into a single usable format. This can be used for the visualization of data and for tracking purposes.
- **Data correlation:** Provides business rules for grouping events into meaningful entities and forwards the information that can be used for rating and billing/charging.

Pay-Per-Use

Pay-per-use refers to charging customers based on their usage and consumption of a service and has long been a cornerstone of certain businesses, such as utilities, and phone companies. Pay-per-use makes users keenly aware of the cost of doing business and consuming a resource, because the cost comes out of their pockets, or, in the enterprise world, their own budgets. With awareness of the costs comes more efficient and selective usage, thus resulting in less waste and lower costs.

Cloud Consumers and Providers

The previous sections covered billing and chargeback terminology, and the following sections cover cloud consumers, who are charged for the cloud services consumed, and cloud providers, who provide services to consumers and charge for the services rendered.

Cloud Consumers

Because we carry around tablets, laptops, and smartphones and access various forms of data that might be hosted in a cloud somewhere, we are all cloud consumers. It is anticipated that the growth of 4G/5G networks will fuel demand even further as consumers digitize even more data. Most of us have the following basic needs in using the cloud applications:

- Security of the data and personal identity
- Easy access to applications
- Need for storage of information on the web (music, photos, and videos) for later access

Based on these needs, the consumer in this case is an SaaS consumer. Additionally, the other types of consumers are PaaS and IaaS consumers. Figure 9-1 shows these three types of consumers and how they use the cloud for various types of activities.

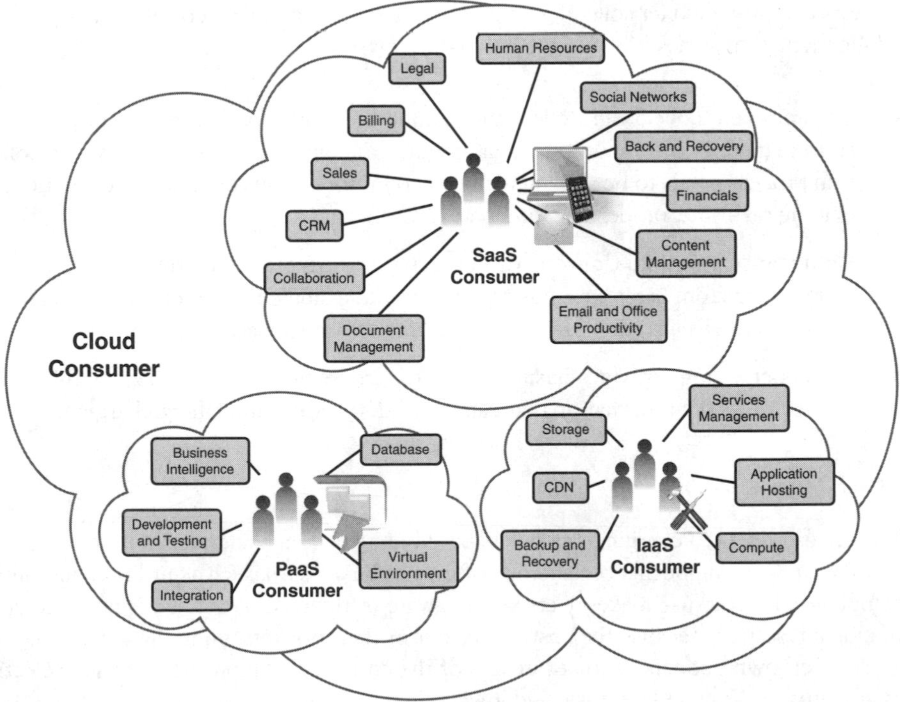

Figure 9-1 *Cloud Consumers (Adopted from NIST)*[1]

Cloud consumers are categorized into three groups based on the services they consume that are provided by the cloud services providers. Table 9-1 lists the key activities performed by the three types of cloud consumers and some example users. The consumers are charged for the consumption of these services, and how they could be charged is the subject of this chapter.

Table 9-1 *Cloud Consumers, Activities, and Examples*

Consumers	Activities	Example Users
SaaS consumers	Use business applications that are hosted in the cloud.	Yahoo! Mail, Hotmail, Google Search, Bing, and MSN Messenger. Another example is the popular Google Docs. In the business world, you might be familiar with SalesForce.com.
PaaS consumers	Develop, test, and deploy business applications. Here, instead of installing software on customer servers, we can install the software on a server owned by PaaS providers and then sell it to consumers in the form of subscriptions.	Software developers, system developers, and IT managers. Examples of PaaS vendors are Microsoft Azure and Amazon Web Services.
IaaS consumers	Create, install, manage, and monitor services for IT infrastructure operations.	IaaS is a provision model in which an organization outsources the equipment used to support operations, including storage, hardware, servers, and networking components. The vendor owns the equipment and is responsible for housing, running, and maintaining it. The client (enterprises or other users) typically pays on a per-use basis.

Cloud Providers

Cloud providers make cloud computing services available through private or public infrastructure (clouds) to consumers, and they have the responsibility to charge and collect revenue for the services provided. Figure 9-2 and Table 9-2 illustrate and summarize typical cloud provider activities as well as cloud-related services and operations.

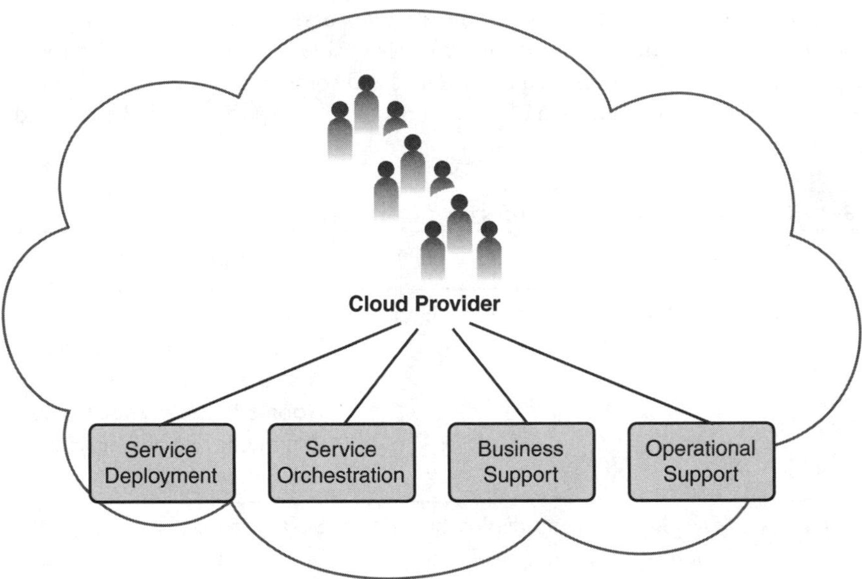

Figure 9-2 *Cloud Provider Typical Activities*

Table 9-2 *Cloud Provider Types*

Provider	Activity
SaaS provider	Install, manage, and maintain the software
PaaS provider	Manage the cloud development resources for the platform or application
IaaS provider	Manage network, compute, and storage infrastructure

The cloud providers also have the responsibility to monitor the service to ensure that the SLAs offered are met. SLAs about uptime and performance are regarded as the most crucial, and they are generally tied to key performance indicators (KPI). Detailed information on KPIs and SLAs and their relationships is provided in Chapter 8.

The cloud provider also has to deal with penalty clauses when SLAs are not met. Many cloud consumers, especially financial enterprises, want to see penalty clauses applied in the event of an SLA breach, with penalties proportional to the business impact of the failure. Amazon offers the customer service credits, regardless of the money lost in the process, and this is regarded as insufficient for SLA violations by financial companies. A financial company, for example, could lose hundreds of millions of dollars if the services are not available during market trading hours, and a few dollars of credit from a cloud service provider would not make a dent in the loss. Therefore, financial companies and mission-critical service companies insist on SLA guarantees and penalties tied to SLAs.

Cloud Services Billing Considerations

Cloud computing is a charge by the usage model where consumers access the resources through the Internet. The user pays by a usage model for the services consumed rather than having resources locally, purchasing licenses, and inflating annual operating expenses. The usage needs to be available on demand and can fluctuate, and the billing/charging systems need to account for the granularity of the business models.

Figure 9-3 shows the areas that are managed by the consumer and the areas that are managed by the vendor for the three cloud services (IaaS, PaaS, and SaaS). The vendor bills for the services provided to the customers. The vendor's responsibility for the SLAs also lies only within the area that is under its control and is not responsible for areas outside its boundary.

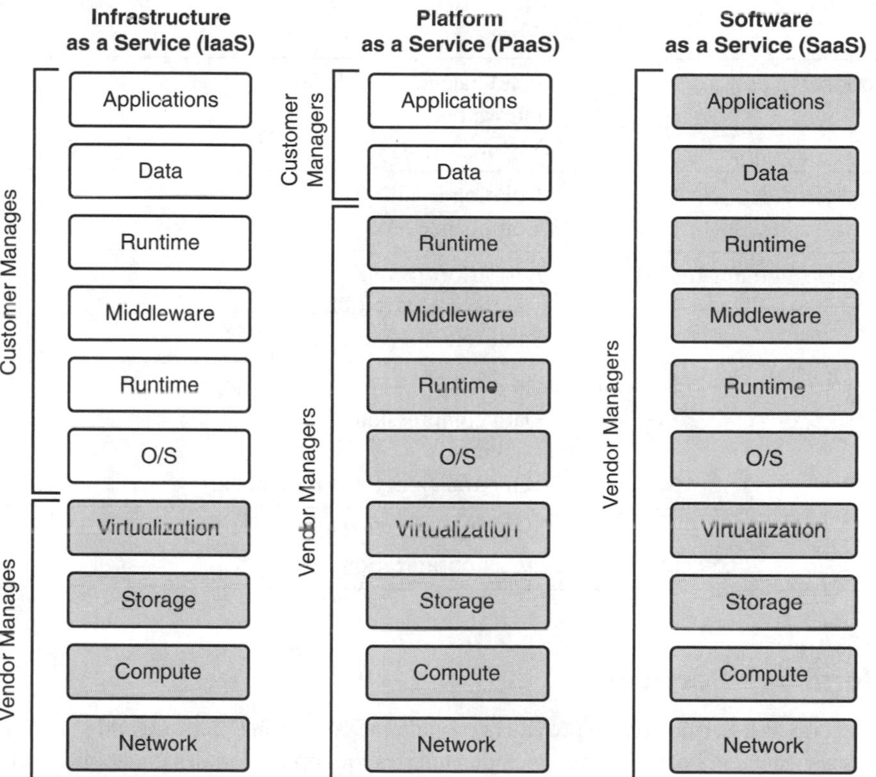

Figure 9-3 *Customer and Vendor Management Domains*

The following sections further describe the billing considerations for the three cloud services.

Infrastructure as a Service

As a part of Infrastructure as a Service (IaaS), a service provider provides many hardware and software resources. These items are available for the customer to choose through a service catalog. Table 9-3 lists some of the resources that can be selected through the service catalog by IaaS customers and would have to be considered in the charging models.[2]

Table 9-3 *Cloud Billing Resources for IaaS*

Billable Resource	Options
Architecture	Multitenancy Scalability Disaster recovery/availability
Server blade	Size Type
Network services	Load balancer Firewall Virtual router
Security services	Isolation level Compliance level
Service-level agreements (SLA)	Best effort (Bronze) High availability (Silver) Fault tolerant (Gold)
Data services	Data encryption Data compression Backups Data availability and redundancy
WAN services	VPN connectivity WAN optimization

Platform as a Service

Platform as a Service (PaaS) providers provide the computing platform and solution stack as a service. PaaS offerings can include facilities for application design; application development, testing, deployment, and hosting; and application services and service integration. With PaaS, developers can build web applications without installing any tools on their computer and then deploy those applications without any specialized system administration skills. Table 9-4 lists some of the additional resources that can be selected through a service catalog by a PaaS customer and would have to be considered in the charging models. The provider has the additional responsibility to manage PaaS services in addition to IaaS services, as shown in Figure 9-3.

Table 9-4 *Cloud Billing Resources for PaaS*

Billable Resource	**Options**
Operating system	Windows Linux Solaris ZenOS
Solution stacks	LAMP MAMP WINS Other
Interfaces for creating Web Services	SOAP REST
Web user interface tools for service creation	HTML, JAVA Applications such a Adobe Flex and Flash

Software as a Service

The Software as a Service (SaaS) delivery model is where software and its associated data are hosted centrally and are accessed by the cloud user using a thin client, normally using a web browser over the Internet. SaaS has become a common delivery model for most business applications, such as accounting, collaboration, Customer Relationship Management (CRM), Enterprise Resource Planning (ERP), and invoicing.

SaaS sales have reached $9 billion in 2010 and are projected to increase to $10.7 billion in 2011 and account for about 10 percent of worldwide software, and estimates are that it will reach 16 percent of worldwide software sales by 2014.[3]

In SaaS, the vendor is responsible for everything, as shown in Figure 9-3. Table 9-5 lists some additional areas to be considered in the charging models.

Table 9-5 *Cloud Billing Resources for SaaS*

Billable Resource	**Options**
Configuration	SaaS applications do not support application customization (for example, change source code, data schema, or GUI) but allow configuration support with a set of parameters that affect their functionality and look and feel.
Accelerated feature delivery	Applications are updated more frequently than traditional software.
Open integration	Applications offer integration through APIs to internal systems and databases.

Cloud Order-to-Cash Process Flow

Many companies can offer services by having applications on top of the cloud infrastructure that is comprised of network, compute, and storage. The users could subscribe to these services because they see value in the applications. The user would have to authenticate using the vendor authentication systems, and the user would be billed for the services rendered.

In this cloud model, the infrastructure (SP, ISP, content provider, and so on) is seen as one entity from the user's perspective. The user connects from his end device (PC, smartphone, iPad, and so on) to the cloud and authenticates for access to the services such as video on demand, voicemail, and so on. These services are not necessarily provided by the ISP and can be provided by the content providers. The cloud can handle the authentication, authorization, and accounting (AAA) services and presents a single bill to the user.

This cloud billing model will typically be implemented by a collection of middleware products that collect the accounting information from the cloud infrastructure, as shown in Figure 9-4.

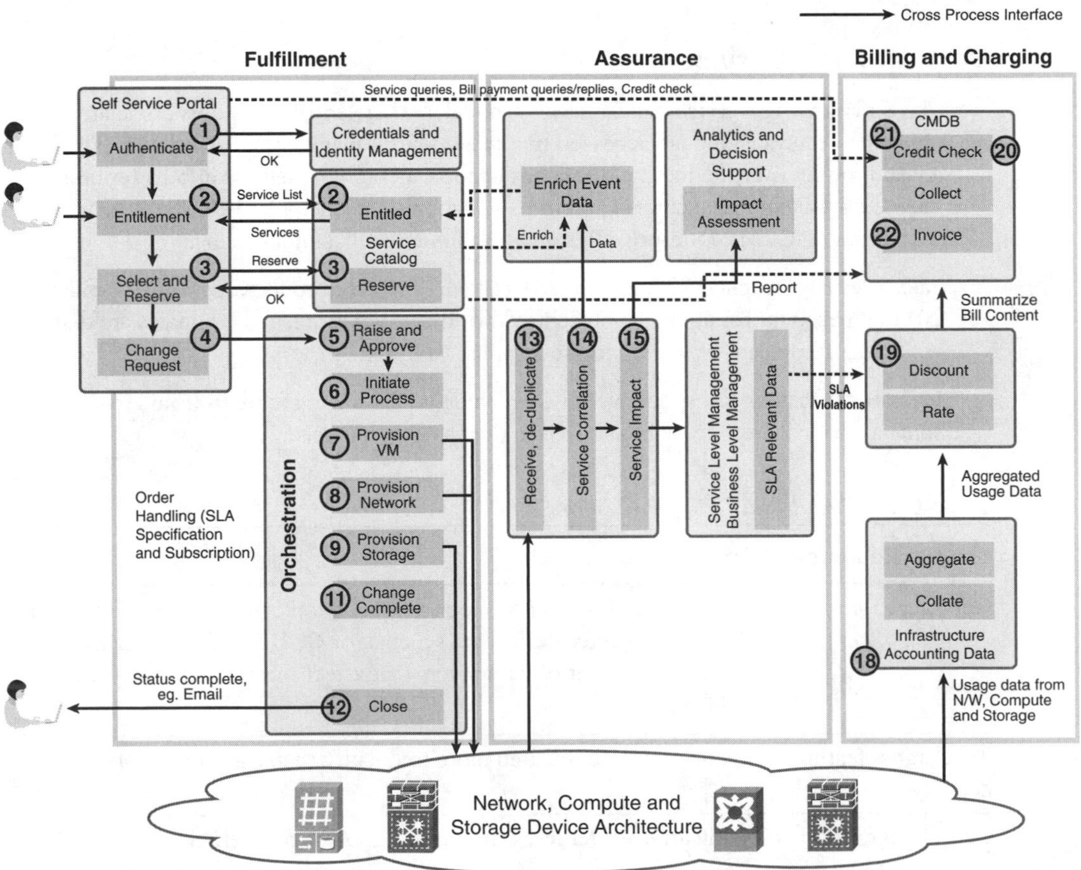

Figure 9-4 *Order-to-Cash Processes*

Figure 9-4 describes the complete Order-to-Cash (OTC) model, showing the processes from the time the order is placed to the point where the bill is rendered for collection. The steps in Figure 9-4 are further described as follows:

- Steps 1–12 are for part of the fulfillment process and are described in Chapter 7, "Service Fulfillment."
- Steps 13–17 are part of the assurance process and are described in Chapter 8, "Service Assurance."
- Step 18 is data collection from the infrastructure devices and is comprised of the following:
  - **Data or event collection:** Collect and decode event information from multiple sources (network, compute, and storage) and from heterogeneous devices. The collection process needs to be streamlined to account for the various methods of collection, including real-time, on-demand, and periodic types.
  - **Data transformation:** Converts various types of formatted data from multiple sources and from heterogeneous equipment into a single usable format. This can be used for the visualization of data and for tracking purposes.
  - **Data correlation:** Provides business rules for grouping events into meaningful entities and forwards the information that can be used for rating and billing.
- Step 19 is where the aggregated usage data is collected and the following activities take place:
  - The rating engine applies customer-specific rates and discounts to the aggregated data from Step 18. The rating application will take into account items such as special offers, cross-product discounts, service discounts, and volume discounts.
  - The SLA violations can be determined from service-level management and business-level management, and this input is used to determine credits and discounts to the customer. As indicated in Chapter 8, many cloud business customers are looking for penalties and credits for business loss, and not just credits for the lost time because of SLA violations. The industry is still in the infancy stage, and many large cloud providers are only proving credits for the lost time. By monitoring the key KPIs and correlating to SLAs, service providers would be able to provide better SLA guarantees to cloud consumers. A detailed explanation of SLAs and KPIs and their relationship is provided in Chapter 8.

- Step 20 involves creating the invoice and collecting the payment. There is no sale until the invoice is created and payment is collected. The following should be kept in mind as part of invoicing and payment collection:
  - Create an invoice with a look and feel that are consistent and include the service provider logo and identity.
  - Facilitate electronic payment through financial institutions, and provide multiple options for payments such as credit card and bank-to-bank transfers.
  - Allow customizable payment terms including the capability to tailor payment terms, discounts, and penalties, depending upon SLAs and customer relationships.
  - Provide real-time invoice and payment history to better manage accounts receivable and cash flow.
- Step 21 involves a credit check to ensure the comprehensive financial risk management. It is important to check the prospective customer's credit status before allowing him to use the services. What good is it for the service provider to provide services and not get paid for the services rendered? The account verification and transaction monitoring are important factors in financial risk management.
- Step 22 involves integrating the service catalog into the billing systems/charging systems so that the new services that are designed and delivered can be billed. What good is it if the new cloud services can be designed and delivered but cannot be billed?

Billing and Charging Architecture

Billing and charging architecture requires that collection of resource usage records be measured, rated, assigned, and communicated among appropriate parties. The billing and charging architecture provides interactions among network devices, compute devices, storage devices, accounting servers, and billing servers. The devices collect resource consumption data in the form of accounting metrics.

In the case of an enterprise, the collected accounting metrics are transferred to an accounting server through an accounting protocol or session records and then for chargeback to the respective business units. The accounting server processes the accounting data received from the network device, and this processing might include summarization of interim accounting information, elimination of duplicate data, or generation of session records.

In the case of service providers, the collection, correlation, and transformation of data into a usable format are accomplished through the billing mediation system. The transformed data passes through rating, charging, and billing systems for invoicing the customers for services rendered by the service provider.

Figure 9-5 shows details on billing and chargeback architecture. For chargeback, we can see that data collection and accounting are potentially simpler as services are normally charged on ownership of physical access, so the data collection and accounting can be decoupled. In an SP environment where there is already a high degree of complexity in the service or infrastructure, the mediation platform provides collection, correlation, and transformation of collected data.

From a chargeback perspective, no charges might be levied. Instead, the business unit might simply receive a summary of its usage, and at least this provides the visibility of IT usage and the understanding of the value of IT. This is often the way that chargeback is introduced: visibility and demonstration of value first followed by charges. In an SP environment, services are always charged, so rating and charging engines will convert IT data to a monetary value and billing systems will apply discounts and generate the bill.

Figure 9-5 shows the logical accounting layers on the left side of the figure—metering, collections, accounting, charging, and billing—each of which is further described in the list that follows.

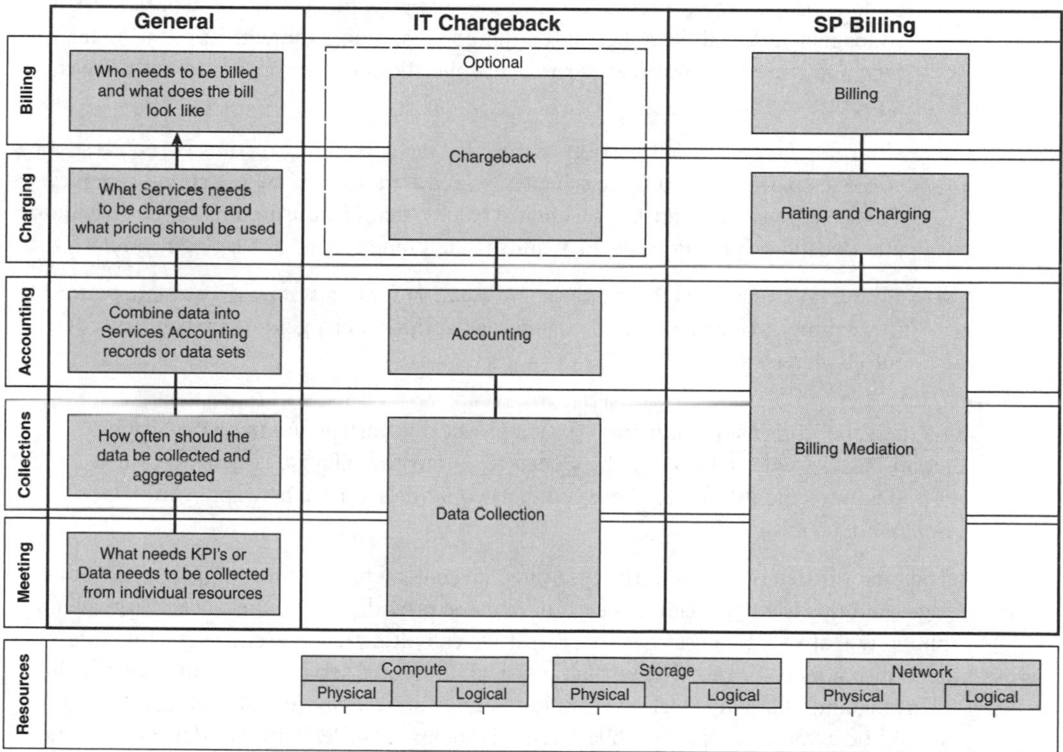

Figure 9-5 *Billing and Chargeback Architecture*

- **Metering layer:** Tracks and records the usage of resources by observing the traffic flows, or usage records, and the metering policy used for configuring the metering layer specifies the attributes that need to be reported. In an IOS device, for example, this might be the configuration of a NetFlow record or template. The metering layer can be part of the resource itself or can be an external entity (such as Cisco Service Control Engine or an application such as Cisco Application Visibility Manager).
- **Collecting layer:** Accesses the data provided by metering entities as well as collects charged-related events and forwards them for further processing to the accounting layer. This layer can collect information from domains such as virtual servers, physical servers, and so on. For this reason, the efforts in standardizing the data exchange format and protocol at this layer will be beneficial. The collection policy will define where to collect the data, the type of data, and the frequency in collecting.
- **Accounting layer:** Consolidates the collected information from the collecting layer, either within the same domain or from other domains, and creates service accounting data sets or records that are passed to the charging layer for the assignment of prices. At this layer, the service dependencies and service definitions need to be understood, so some integration with the service catalogue and/or Configuration Management Database (CMDB) is required as is integration with application mapping and dependency software to understand the actual configuration of the infrastructure in real time.
- **Charging layer:** Derives session charges for the accounting records based on service-specific charging and pricing schemes, which are specified by the charging policy. This layer basically translates technical values (that is, measured resource reservation and consumption) into monetary units using predetermined charging formulas.
- **Billing layer:** Collects the charging information for a customer over a time period (for example, one month) and includes subscription charges and possible discounts into a bill.

As the vendors consider transition from a physical infrastructure to a virtualized or cloud-based services, there will be a need to review the billing/chargeback model. Table 9-6 illustrates the differences between the two models when a new application is deployed.

The major differentiator is in the first three layers—metering, collection, and accounting—and this is where vendors need to focus on providing value, because charging and billing will always be customer specific. If we can ultimately present a set of service accounting records for either virtual, physical, or hybrid services, it means that existing charging and billing applications should integrate seamlessly. In addition, consideration should be given to support mobile standards such as 3GPPP/4GPPP to deliver real-time billing as this is the model that will be most relevant for virtual or cloud-based services.

Table 9-6 *Differences Between Physical and Virtual Models*

Scenario	Physical Model	Virtual Model
Resources	Deploy new hardware; BU or enterprise owns the hardware	Use shared infrastructure; IT owns hardware
Metering	Simple-meter new hardware and application	Complex-meter only the usage of shared infrastructure
Collection	Collect data from the server	Collect data from virtualization manager
Accounting	Process the server data and assign costs to the BU/customer	Look at the aggregate usage of shared infrastructure and assign costs based on usage or occupancy
Charging	Charge for service	
Billing	Bill for service	

Summary

This chapter covered the billing and chargeback for cloud-based services. The billing and chargeback terminology for the cloud and the billing considerations for IaaS, PaaS, and SaaS were covered. In addition, cloud OTC process flow and the billing and charging architecture for the cloud were covered.

References

[1] National Institute of Standards and Technology presentation on "NIST Cloud Computing Reference Architecture," March 28, 2011, at http://collaborate.nist.gov/twiki-cloud-computing/pub/CloudComputing/Meeting12AReferenceArchitecture-March282011/NIST_CCRATWG_029-pdf.

[2] Cisco white papers on "Managing the Real Cost of On-Demand Enterprise Cloud Services with Chargeback Models - A Guide to Cloud Computing Costs, Server Costs, Pricing Plans, and Chargeback Implementation and Systems," at www.cisco.com/en/US/services/ps2961/ps10364/ps10370/ps11104/Cloud_Services_Chargeback_Models_White_Paper.pdf.

[3] SaaS Market Growing by Leaps and Bounds, by Gartner, at http://itmanagement.earthweb.com/entdev/article.php/3895101/SaaS-Market-Growing-by-Leaps-and-Bounds-Gartner.htm.

Chapter 10

Technical Building Blocks of IaaS

Upon completing this chapter, you will be able to understand the following:

- The technical building blocks that make up an IaaS
- How the IaaS is developed and offered
- How the service is provisioned and activated
- How the service data is persisted

This chapter provides an overview of the components that make up a cloud deployment with particular emphasis on the Infrastructure as a Service (IaaS) service model.

IaaS Service Composition

Chapter 2, "Cloud Design Patterns and Use Cases," discussed a number of typical enterprise design patterns. These design patterns were detailed across three application tiers—presentation, application, and data—and consisted of applications such as web, application, and database servers. Also included in the design pattern was the technical capability of load-balancing application requests in a specific manner dependent on the design pattern. With this in mind, you could build a monolithic service that meets these requirements. The problem with this approach is that it meets the requirements of just that one consumer; however, what if the next consumer wants something slightly different or cheaper? This chapter focuses on a more modular approach to building IaaS services to address requirements. Any IaaS offering needs to support a number of technical building blocks:

- Blocks that provide a service topology
- Blocks that provide applications functionality
- Blocks that provide technical capabilities that support applications such as application load balancing and so on

These building blocks need to be delivered in line with the architectural characteristics of a next-generation data center as outlined in Chapter 3, "Data Center Architecture and Technologies," (modularity, flexibility, and so on) and form the basis of any IaaS service offering. Figure 10-1 illustrates some common abstract building blocks.

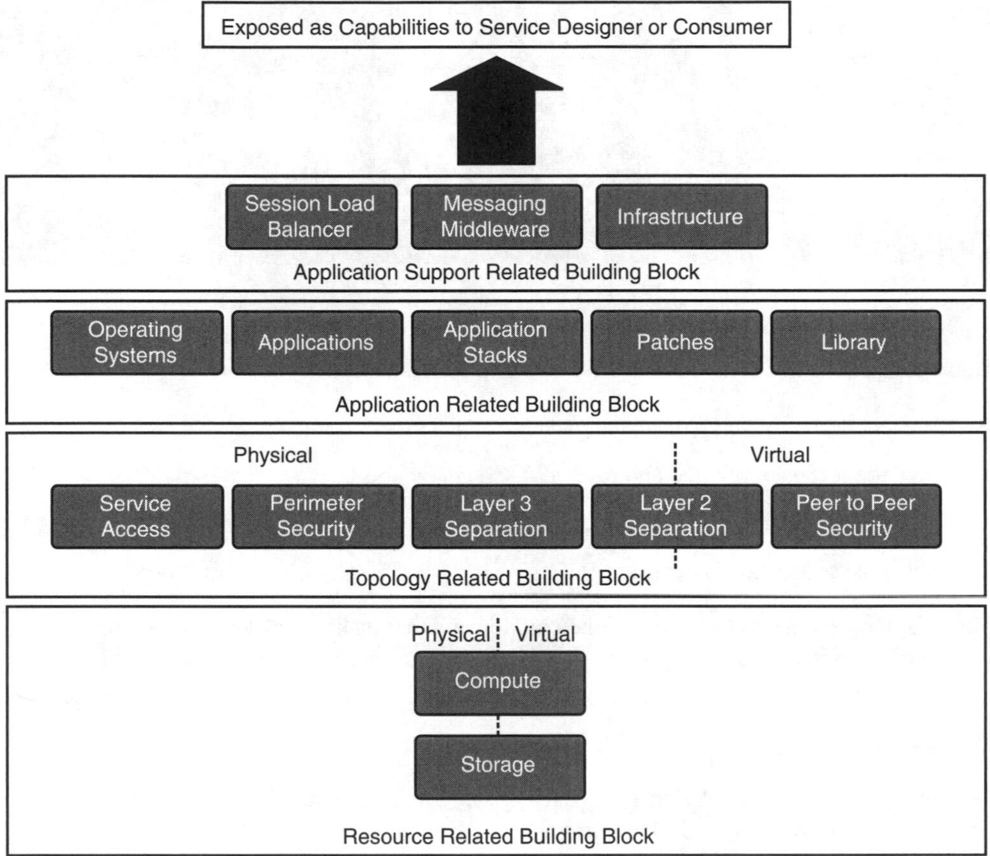

Figure 10-1 *Abstract IaaS Building Blocks*

Table 10-1 describes these abstract building blocks in more detail.

Let's take one of the simple design patterns of a load balancer in a web tier described in Chapter 2. This will be used as the template for the service we want to create in the cloud, and we will call it *website1*, which should be accessible securely through the Internet.

Table 10-1 *Abstract IaaS Building Blocks*

Class	Type	Detail
Resource	Compute	Building blocks of this type will describe a virtual or physical compute instance.
	Storage	Building blocks of this type will describe a virtual or physical storage instance.
Topology	Service access	Building blocks of this type will describe how a service is accessed through the physical network using the Internet, IP VPN, SSL, and so on.
	Perimeter security	Building blocks of this type will describe how access is managed to the service from "outside" the cloud.
	Layer 3 separation	Building blocks of this type will describe how routing is provided within the cloud and optionally how different cloud tenants can be separated at the IP level.
	Layer 2 separation	Building blocks of this type will describe how switching is provided within the cloud and optionally how different cloud tenants can be separated at the MAC level. As we move into the virtual world, this building block might also be provided by a virtualized building block.
	Peer-to-peer Security	Building blocks of this type will describe how access is managed in the service between peer systems/virtual machines.
Application	Operating systems	Building blocks of this type will describe the operating systems available to the service designer or consumer.
	Application	Building blocks of this type will describe the standalone applications available to the service designer or consumer.
	Application stack	Building blocks of this type will describe the application stacks available to the service designer or consumer.
	Patches	Building blocks of this type will describe the application patches available to the service designer or consumer.
	Library	Building blocks of this type will describe the libraries or files available to the service designer or consumer.

Table 10-1 *Abstract IaaS Building Blocks*

Class	Type	Detail
Application Support	Load balancer	Building blocks of this type will describe how application traffic can be balanced between different applications.
	Messaging Middleware	Building blocks of this type will describe how data can be sent between applications in a loosely coupled manner.
	Infrastructure	Building blocks of this type will describe how different infrastructure capabilities such as DNS, testing tools, and so on can be provided.

The cloud provider (the IT department or the telco) has made a technology decision to use Cisco, EMC, and VMware as its cloud infrastructure platform and to support Linux, Apache, MySQL, and PHP as its LAMP (Linux, Apache, MySQL and Perl/PHP) stack with the option to also include Perl. We refer to these as the concrete building blocks, because they are the real things from which the service is built. The service consumer might not care what technology the service is built on, but he will care that his service requirements can be met—and in this case, they can be. So, the website1 service needs to be built around the concrete building block offered by the cloud provider. If the consumer wanted to build the service around a Microsoft IIS web server, the provider would need to create another concrete building block in a stack or as a standalone application to support this. Figure 10-2 illustrates how a simple design pattern is realized as a service instance called website1 using the available concrete building blocks.

The cloud provider might start with a small number of concrete building blocks, but as its solution matures, it will add capabilities to the infrastructure and management tools that will in turn allow it to offer more concrete building blocks. For example, Amazon Web Services (AWS) started with EC2. It has continued to add capabilities and expose them as services; for example, the Elastic Block Store (EBS) and the Simple Queue Service (SQS) capabilities were added to further enhance how application designers can store data and communicate between different components, respectively. Today, AWS can support more advanced design patterns than previously, as it has continued to add more concrete building blocks.

A major facet of a concrete building block is standardization. Standardization allows the provider to deploy consistently, maximize resource usage, simplify support, and bill accurately for the consumer service. Imagine trying to play Tetris with an infinite number of shapes and colors. This would be the cloud provider's challenge in running an IaaS cloud without standardization.

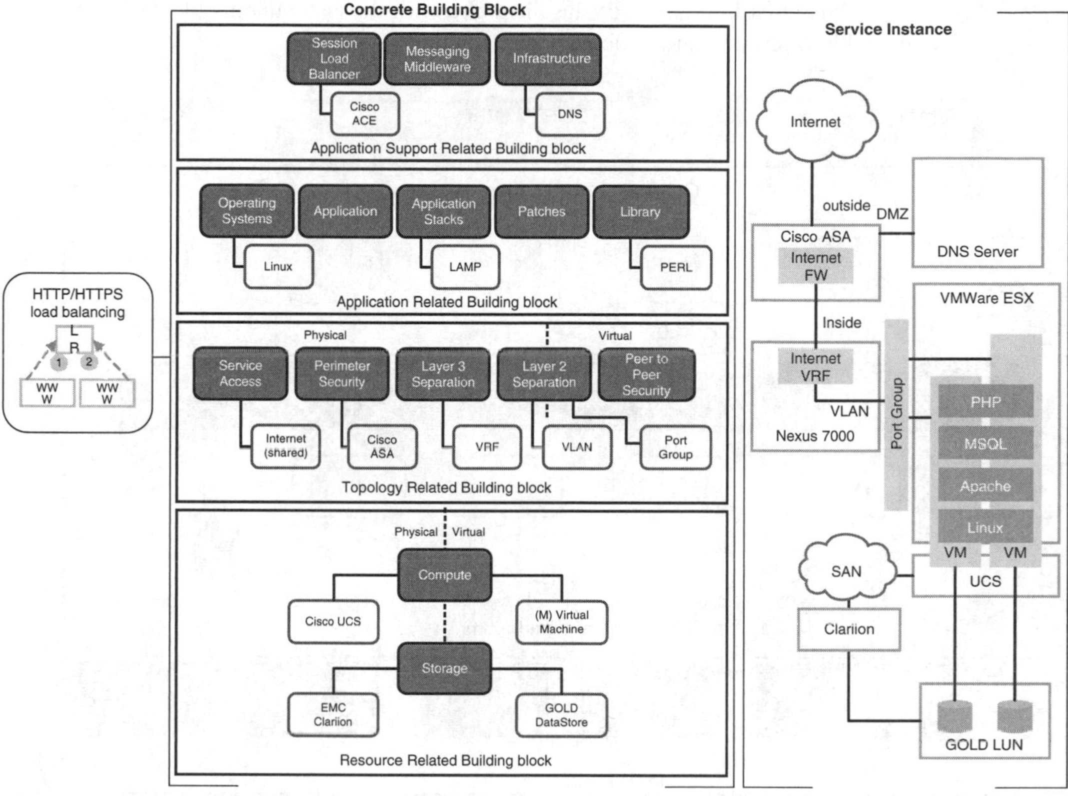

Figure 10-2 *Using Concrete Building Blocks*

This standardization should not come at the cost of choice from the consumer's perspective; however, reality now begins to intrude on the cloud hype. Cloud gives the "illusion" of infinite resources to the consumer; the illusion is constrained by real physical limitations, such as topology. For example, if the provider chooses to deploy VMware vSphere 4.x as its hypervisor technology and offer hypervisor-based virtual machine (VM) fault tolerance, consumers can only utilize this capability if their VM has one vCPU, which could severely limit how the consumer uses this capability, because most large applications support and require multiple processors.

From the perspective of the cloud provider, standardization is achieved by initially defining principles, capabilities, abstract building blocks, and ultimately the platform that will provide the workload execution tier. After the platform is agreed upon, the concrete building blocks that are offered to the consumer are modeled, together with their physical and logical constraints using rules. For example, a load balancer can be modeled as a building block, and if the concrete load balancer building block was provided in the form of a Cisco ACE line card load balancer, a constraint might be that it will support a maximum of only 250 contexts/tenants per line card.

Figure 10-3 illustrates an example of this hierarchy, with the IaaS building blocks being decomposed into physical and logical concrete blocks.

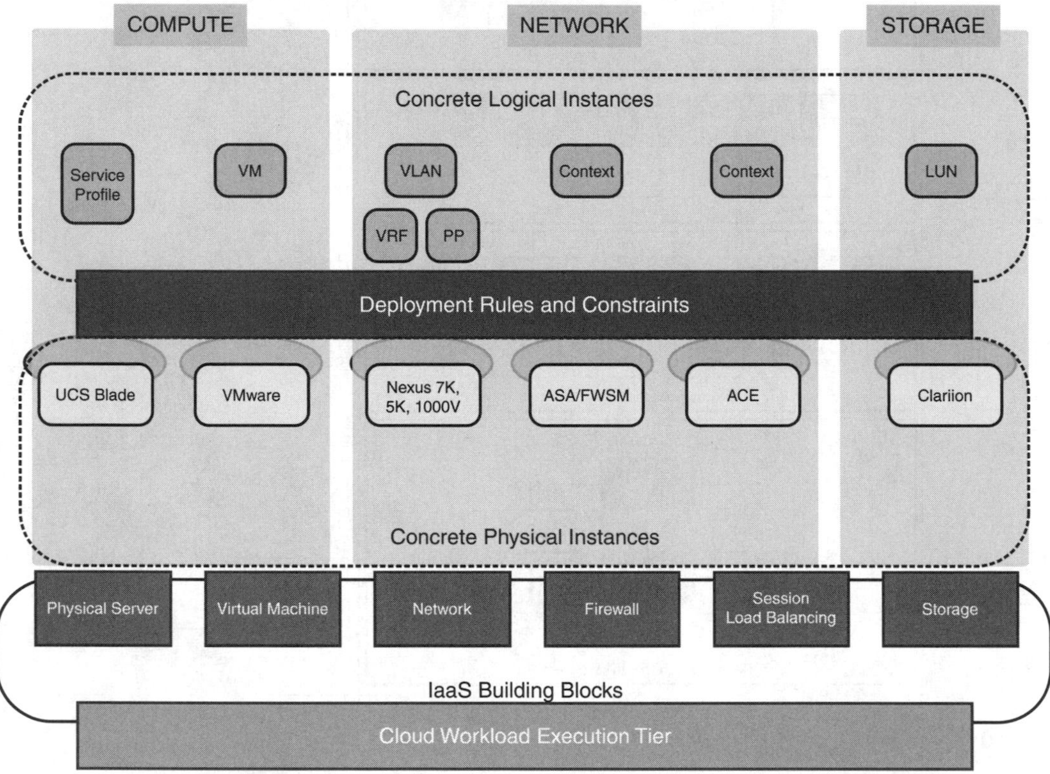

Figure 10-3 *IaaS Components*

As new capabilities are added, these will in turn be standardized into concrete building blocks that are used in consumer services. This provides a much more flexible and agile way of developing services that can flex and grow based on consumer requirements.

Developing and Offering Cloud Products

So far, this chapter has discussed the technical building blocks that are created from the capabilities offered by the cloud platform, and how these building blocks are combined to meet a specific cloud design pattern. Effectively, this is a bottom-up approach, with the platform defining the building blocks. You can call this the *technical service*, and it makes up a part of the overall commercial service or product. The commercial product that a consumer might buy or request from a provider can be seen as a view of the technical service that contains additional commercial data such as price, service level, and so on.

Commercial service data, such as the price of a service, is normally generated from the top down. For example, the consumer will pay a certain price for a compute unit, and that price is typically dictated by whom else in the region or market is offering a similar service. At press time, Amazon currently offers a small Linux compute unit at $0.12 per hour for a Windows instance, so a provider in the same space offering the same product would need to offer something priced at a similar rate or be able to clearly differentiate why it is more expensive—end-to-end QoS or in-country data storage, for example.

Commercial requirements also influence the platform capabilities in most analyst papers today on the cloud; security normally tops the list of the inhibiting factors to cloud adoption. Most product groups within a cloud provider, less so maybe in a private cloud, will require the platform and the building blocks the platform supports to be provided with close adherence to security standards, such as ISO 27001 of Payment Card Industry Data Security Standard (PCI DSS), which look at information security. PCI DSS is an interesting standard because it was originally developed to support the storage of credit card data, but has been adopted by cloud providers as a de-facto standard for cloud data storage.

Another major area is to understand what building blocks will be billed for and how different costs are to be allocated to different contracts or cost centers. A typical way to do this at the product level is to introduce a logical container to put all the cloud services for a given organization or business unit into and associate this container with a contract or cost center. One example of this type of container is a Virtual Data Center (VDC). This concept is found in VMware vCloud Director (VCD) and allows organizational resources to be isolated at a logical level in a multitenant environment.[1] It doesn't exist as a concrete building block; instead, it is used to group resources together. Cisco has a similar concept in a network container in its Virtualized Multitenant Data Center (VMDC) design pattern,[2] but this contains network building blocks and compute building blocks, and other cloud providers have similar containers. Of course, you don't need a container if you are buying a single EC2 instance to run a personal website. However, when you want to support some of the more complex design patterns discussed in Chapter 2 and you want to assure them as a single service, a container makes sense.

The key in developing a cloud product offering, therefore, is to balance the commercial requirements with the platform capabilities and build a set of products that exploit the platform's capabilities and are commercially viable. The service catalogue is the key vehicle for maintaining both the commercial and technical data on the product and providing the different views. A service catalogue can be as simple as a spreadsheet or a standalone application. In many instances, a spreadsheet is a great starting point for capturing the high-level service information, and the following list can be used to model most services from the perspective of the provider:

- **Product descriptions:** A high-level description for all the services in the service catalogue
- **Product attributes:** Descriptions of the service attributes used to define the details of services
- **Delivery model:** Details of how the services will be delivered and to which market segment

- **Product options:** Details of the add-on services that a cloud tenant can request
- **Building block catalogue:** Description of all the available building blocks
- **Product dependency mappings:** Description of the relationship between the products and the platform building blocks
- **Portal-based services:** Details of the functions available to the cloud tenant
- **Professional services:** Details of the professional services that can be offered as part of the cloud portfolio

Figure 10-4 illustrates a service tree that combines building blocks from a technical, commercial, and professional services perspective.

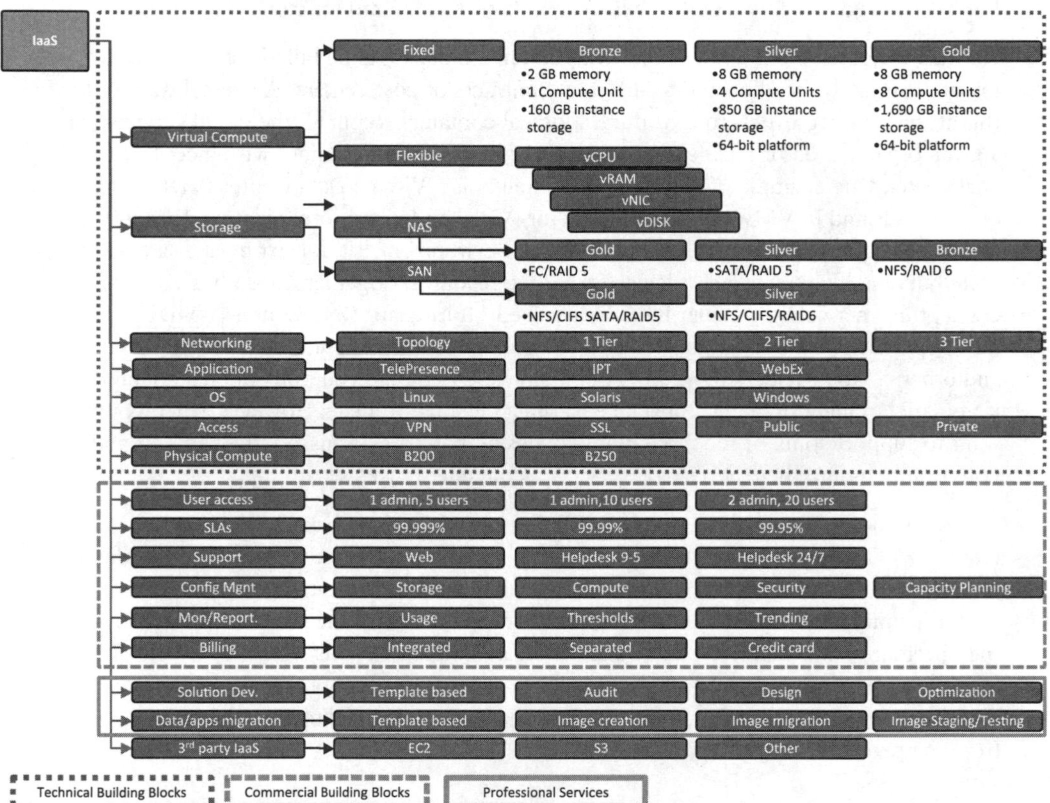

Figure 10-4 *Example Service Catalogue*

Cisco recently acquired Newscale Service Catalogue and Portal technology and has rebranded it as the Cisco Cloud Portal (CCP). The core of this product is a flexible service catalogue that allows service data to be represented in several ways. To represent the catalogue shown in Figure 10-4, you could do it using standards. In CCP, data that is common for all tenants or a group of tenants is represented as a *standard*, so in Figure 10-4, the majority of static categories such as OS, application, and so on (the content of which is controlled by the cloud provider) would be represented as *standards*. These standards are presented to the tenants as drop-down boxes in the web user interface and provide a way to control what is available to that user. In the case of the operating system (OS) category, if the user was entitled to create a virtual machine, he would be presented with three choices of operating system (Linux, Solaris, and Windows). If the provider wanted to add to that, he would simply modify the standard.

Provisioning and Activating Services

At this point, you know what a cloud service could be comprised of and how to create and offer a service from the perspective of a cloud provider. The next step is to understand how these services are provisioned and activated. Figure 10-5 illustrates the major process steps in one possible IaaS provisioning and activation cycle:

1. In the Manage Contact process, the cloud provider will typically manage the initial contact with the consumer through different channels and attempt to move the process along to the next step.
2. In the Sell Service process, the consumer might have trialed the service already or might be convinced of the overall business value and so wants to purchase the IaaS service. This can involve contracting for the service in the case of a large enterprise consumer or simply providing credit card details in the self-service portal in the case of a small consumer or individual.
3. In the Provision Service process, the consumer or provider technical user will request the resources to fulfill a specific design pattern. As long as these resources exist within the provider's infrastructure at that time, the user will be assigned to this specific service. The service is now provisioned, in that the consumer is happy with the configuration and the resources have been allocated.
4. In the Activate Service process, the provider systems begin to orchestrate the delivery of the service; logical concrete building blocks such as the VLANs, virtual machines, and session load balancers are created; and the any service inventory is updated to reflect the new service.
5. The consumer will now begin to use the service, provide access to the service end users, and perform operational functions, such as installing custom code/applications, backing up the VMs, and so on. These operational capabilities might be exposed through the portal as discussed in the previous section, or the end users might have to manually perform them.
6. The Obtain Payment process is the final step in the overall provisioning and activation cycle. In the background, the provider has been monitoring the portal actions and infrastructure usage and will generate an invoice.

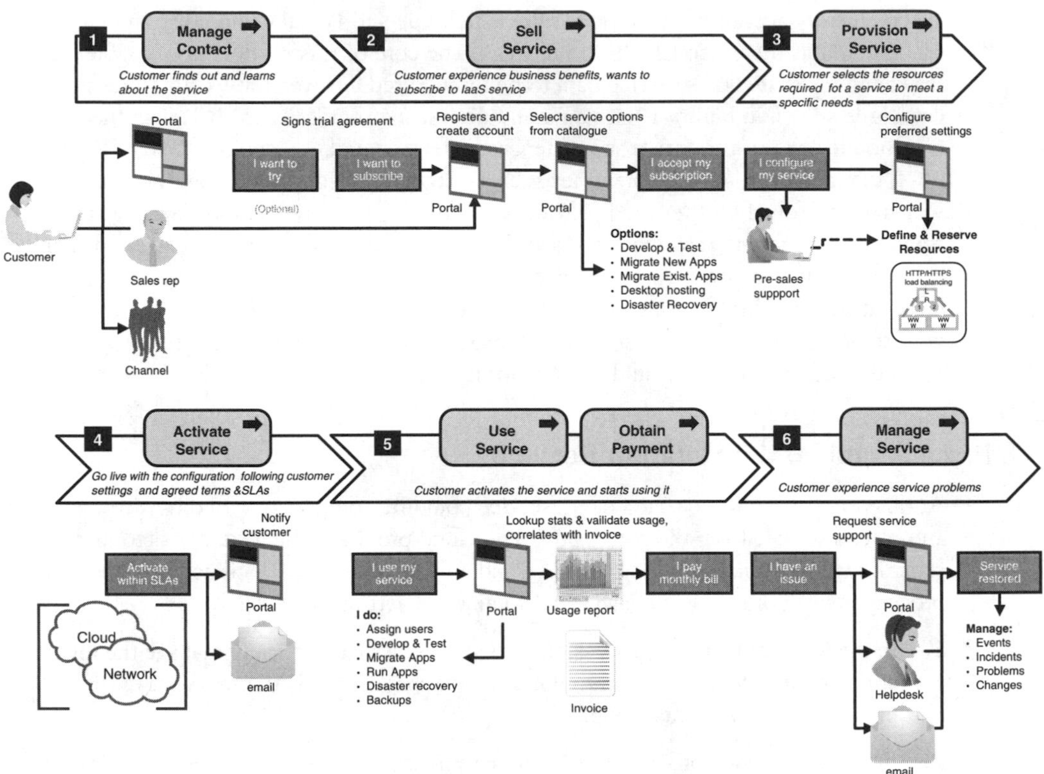

Figure 10-5 *Provisioning and Activating a Cloud Service*

One of the major advantages of the cloud is that should an incident/outage arise, the provider is responsible for fixing it; however, as discussed in Chapter 2, depending on the service model being consumed (SaaS, PaaS, or IaaS), the level of provider responsibility will vary. For example, if the consumer is using a concrete building block from the service catalogue to host his website, a LAMP stack for example, all aspects other than the content should be supported. If, on the other hand, the consumer chose a single OS and installed his own LAMP stack, it's likely that only the OS would be supported. The final process step, Manage Service, is responsible for handling all support issues from reporting and responding to the initial fault, resolving the fault, and providing any compensation for the outage.

The provisioning and activation process steps are critical components of the IaaS architecture; if implemented correctly, they can add significant value to a provider's solution. If implemented poorly, the cloud ecosystem will fail. The next two chapters take a detailed look at these areas; Chapter 11, "Automating and Orchestration Resources" dives more deeply into the provisioning and automation of these building blocks.

Persisting Service Data

As the cloud provider moves toward a more dynamic environment, the mechanisms for managing the relationship among the infrastructures, the service, and the SLA will become more complex, but also more critical for tracking usage and simplifying the assurance processes. Many service models are beginning to emerge from software vendors to try and address this. The high-level model for the VMware vCloud API is shown in Figure 10-6, and although it accurately represents the relationship among VMs, virtual networks, and an organization and its network "container" or VDC, it does not show any relationship between the physical infrastructure (servers, networking, or storage) or any other hypervisor technology.[3] Although it can be extended, it is not enough at present to represent a complete IaaS instance.

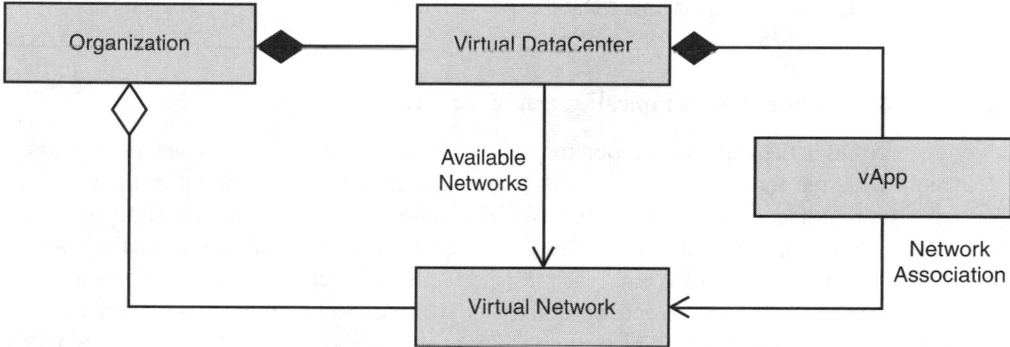

Figure 10-6 *vCloud Schema Fragment*

Looking at the components that exists in today's data center, you can see a cloud service could be made up of the following:

- Physical servers acting as either hypervisor hosts or supporting applications that cannot be virtualized or supported while being virtualized (for example, Oracle)
- Hypervisor technology
- A variety of physical and virtual networking switches/routers that provide connectivity from the servers to the data center core and to network-attached storage (NAS)
- A set of physical or virtualized network services such as firewalls and load balancers
- Storage switches and storage arrays providing both block and IP access

Maintaining the relationship between the physical and logical topologies accurately and in real time is a critical requirement of cloud or consumption-based services; however, this data is often distributed across the enterprise in different systems managed by different teams. These are typically called *systems of record* and represent the systems that are the single source of truth for a particular data area. Consider the following examples:

- Customer-centric data relating to the business/commercial service and the customer contract or technical limits will often be mastered in the Customer Relationship Management (CRM) systems or in a service catalogue.
- Data relating to the makeup of the technical service will be managed in real-time in a service inventory or in element managers such as vCenter. This data in a cloud or consumption-based service can be extremely dynamic in nature.
- The physical and logical instances that make up the tenant or infrastructure that are under change control and are typically less dynamic are maintained in a Configuration Management Database (CMDB) or Configuration Management System (CMS).

Figure 10-7 illustrates the typical system of records in a cloud provider.

The CMDB is the traditional repository for service inventory in IT; however, often in the more dynamic environments, a CMDB can struggle managing the amount of the updates that are required, as VMs are created, modified, and deleted in a relatively short period of time. This assumes that the CMDB update process is automatic; when a manual update process is used, the CMDB will cease to be effective as it takes too much time to update and maintain. Even if the process is automated, the reconciliation process used to move configuration items (CI) into an authorized space or dataset is normally a scheduled batch load so again real time use is limited.

Figure 10-8 illustrates this concept using IBM CCMDB, but the issue is prevalent across most CMDB vendors. In the IBM solution, CI are "discovered" by the discovery server, this discovery can be done through a set of sensors that interrogate the infrastructure and an API or bulk load feature. Once added to a list of discovered CIs, a reconciliation process to either move a specific CI or an entire model into the actual CI space of the CCMDB. Another process runs to promote the CIs into the authorized CI space, which are then subject to change the configuration management processes. It is not to say that this is not an important process—efficient and consistent change and configuration management process are the cornerstone of any good IT provider—but cloud is a dynamic environment and most traditional CMDBs are not built as real-time repositories; their role is to act as a single source of truth for the ITIL processes that use them.

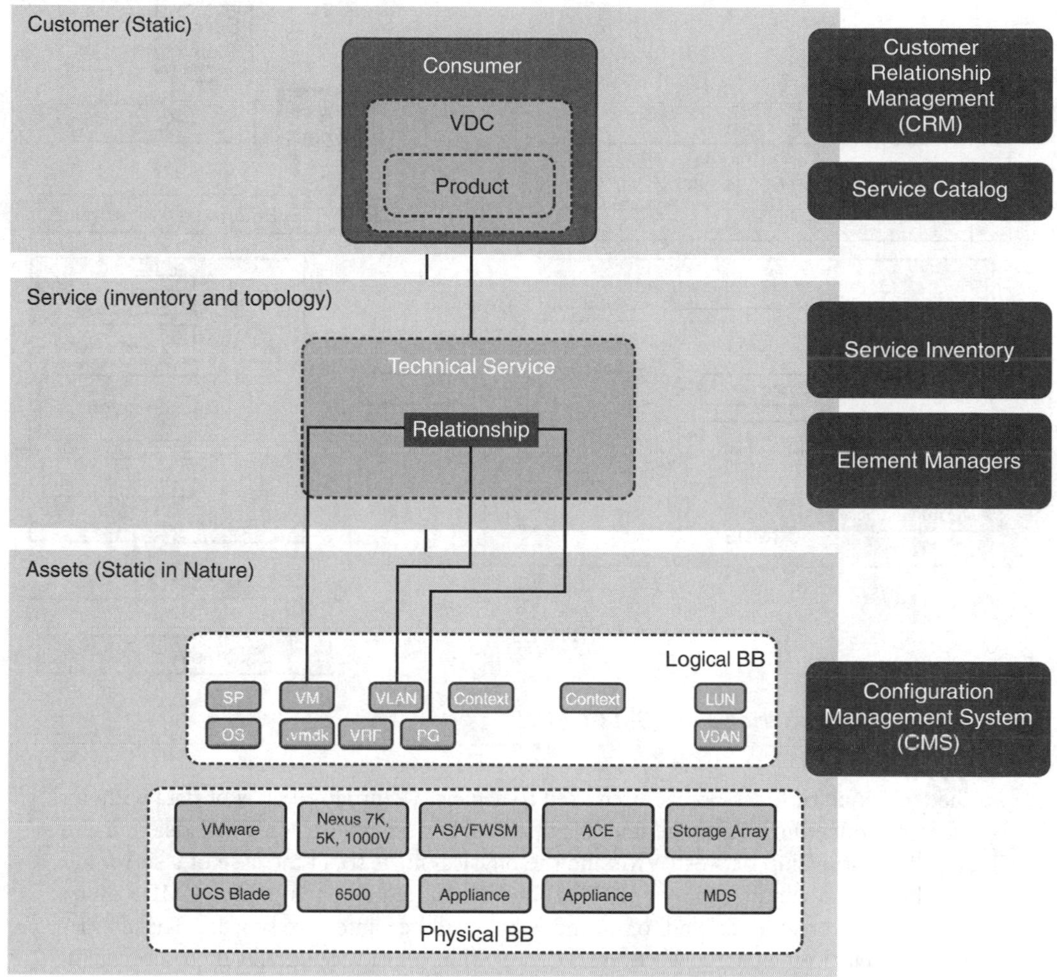

Figure 10-7 *Systems of Record in a Typical Cloud Provider*

Figure 10-8 also illustrates the two key components of the Cisco Intelligent Automation for Cloud (CIAC) solution: the Cloud Portal and Enterprise Orchestrator.[3] These two components maintain service data in a service items and service targets, respectively. A rough rule of thumb is that service data that needs to be exposed to the tenant, such as a VM configuration would be persisted as a service item in the cloud portal, service data that might not be exposed to the tenant such as a VLAN is persisted as a service target. Service items and service targets can be pushed into the CMDB, but they are mastered in the Portal and Orchestrator, respectively, which are built as real-time repositories, so they do reflect the service state in real time.

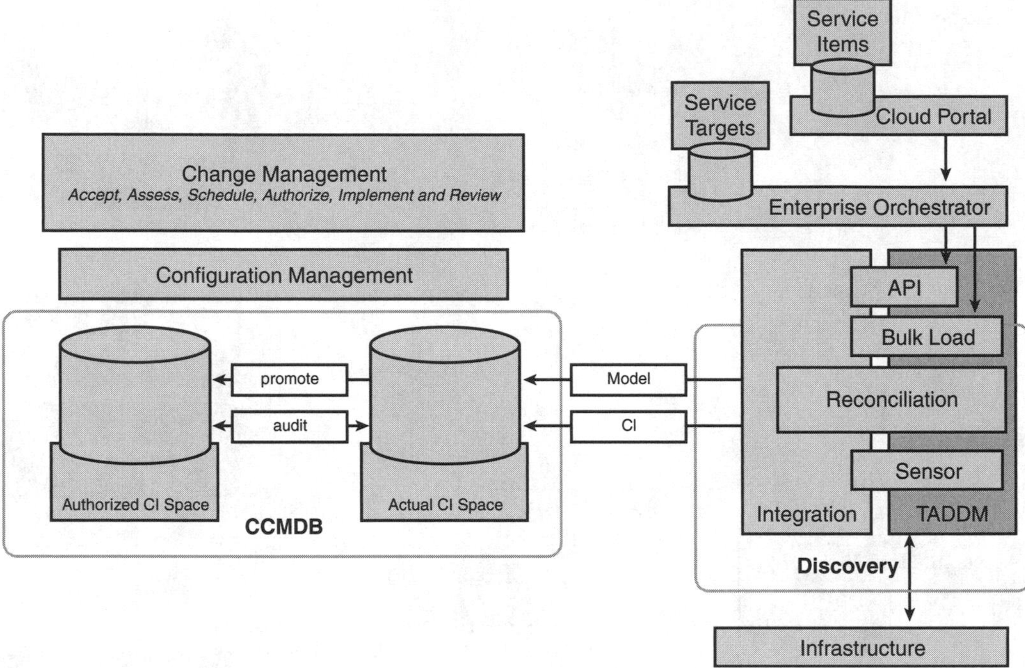

Figure 10-8 *Reconciliation with IBM CCMDB*

The technique of federation is often used to achieve a centralized view of data without necessarily needing to manage multiple updates. For example, it is a good idea to maintain the relationship between VMs and the physical hosts so, in the case of a server failure, the impact can be understood. This can be managed by updating the CMDB every time a VM is created, deleted, or moved, which will be a intensive process. The alternative is to use, in the case of VMware, vCenter which already maintains the relationship between virtual machines and the physical hosts and federate this relationship data into the CMDB.

This concept can be extended across the entire enterprise to provide a distributed data model that will scale to support more real-time dynamic services. Figure 10-9 illustrates an example of this model.

This list describes the components in Figure 10-9 in more detail:

- The CRM contains the definition of company Y and the virtual data center, Sydney.
- The Service catalogue contains a product which in turn is composed of a technical services maintained in the service inventory. (This can also be contained within the Service Catalogue.)

- The technical service contains a VM that is defined in an element manager, such as VMware vCenter, which also maintains the mapping between physical host and VM. This is an important point to recognize, managing this dynamic relationship in another system could mean potentially a lot of synchronization would need to occur to keep that service data accurate.
- Another element manager (VMware vCloud Director, for example) maintains the relationship between the VDC referenced in the CRM and instantiated in infrastructure and the VM held in vCenter.
- The CMS, which contains the CMDB, references the CIs for VM, physical host, and the linkage to the VDC referenced in the other systems

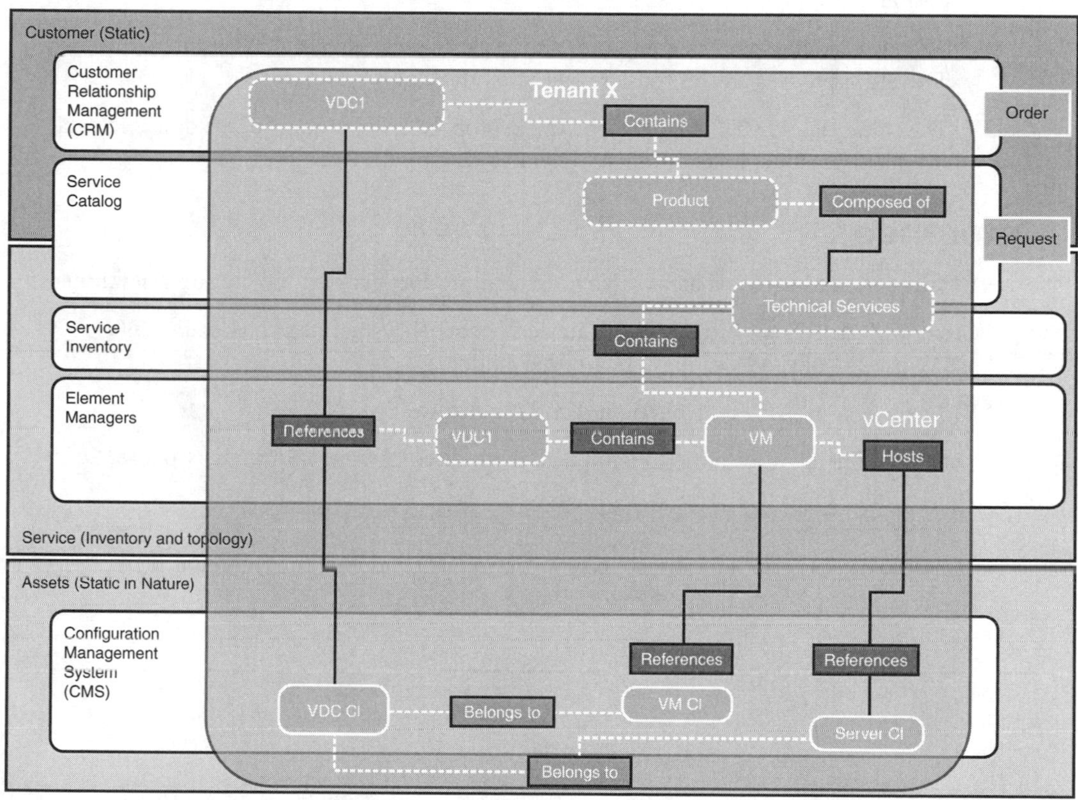

Figure 10-9 *Example Federated Service Inventory*

Determining how to manage all the cloud service data in real time is not a simple problem to solve and, in many ways, implementing a distributed data model that can federate/abstract between different sources offers an alternative to a large monolithic data model based on CIM.

Summary

The key to building a flexible and agile cloud ecosystem is the use of modular building block to build services many consumers want to buy, instead of monolithic services that only one consumer wants to buy:

- Building blocks come in two main forms: abstract (the things the provider or the market wants to provide) and concrete (the actual things that exist in the infrastructure).
- The service design should consider product requirements and technical capabilities when defining the building blocks that it will offer.
- The service catalogue is the system of record for all service and building block definitions.
- The provisioning process configures and reserves service resources, and then the activation process creates these resources in the cloud.
- The traditional CMDB might not be the appropriate vehicle to store the dynamic data prevalent in cloud; instead, a more federated data model is required.

References

[1] VMware vCloud Director, at www.vmware.com/products/vcloud-director/overview.html.

[2] Cisco VMDC Design Pattern, at www.cisco.com/en/US/solutions/collateral/ns340/ns517/ns224/solution_overview_c22-602978.html.

[3] VMware vCloud API, at http://tinyurl.com/3muzmwe.

[4] Cisco Intelligent Automation for Cloud, at www.cisco.com/en/US/products/ps11869/index.html.

Chapter 11

Automating and Orchestration Resources

Upon completing this chapter, you will be able to understand the following:

- How the basic resources are added to the cloud
- How services are added to the cloud
- The creation and placement strategies used within a cloud
- How services are managed throughout their life cycle

This chapter provides a detailed overview of how an Infrastructure as a Service (IaaS) service is orchestrated and automated.

On-Boarding Resources: Building the Cloud

Previous chapters discussed how to classify an IT service and covered a little bit about how to place that service in the cloud using a number of business dimensions, criticality, roles, and so on. So you know how to choose the application and how to define the components that make up those applications, but how do you decide where in the cloud to actually place the application or workload for optimal performance? To understand this, you must look at the differences between how a consumer and a provider look at cloud resources.

Figure 11-1 illustrates the differences between these two views. The consumer sees the cloud as a "limitless" container of compute, storage, and network resources. The provider, on the other hand, cannot provide limitless resources as this is simply not cost-effective nor possible. However, at the same time, the provider must be able to build out its infrastructure in a linear and consistent manner to meet demand and optimize the use of this infrastructure. This linear growth is archived through the use of Integrated Compute Stacks (ICS), which will often be referred to as a point of delivery (POD). A POD has been described previously. However, for the purposes of this section, consider a POD as a collection of compute, storage, and network resources that conform to a standard operating footprint that shares the same failure domain. In other words, if something catastrophic happens in a POD, workloads running in that POD are affected but neighboring workloads in a different POD are not.

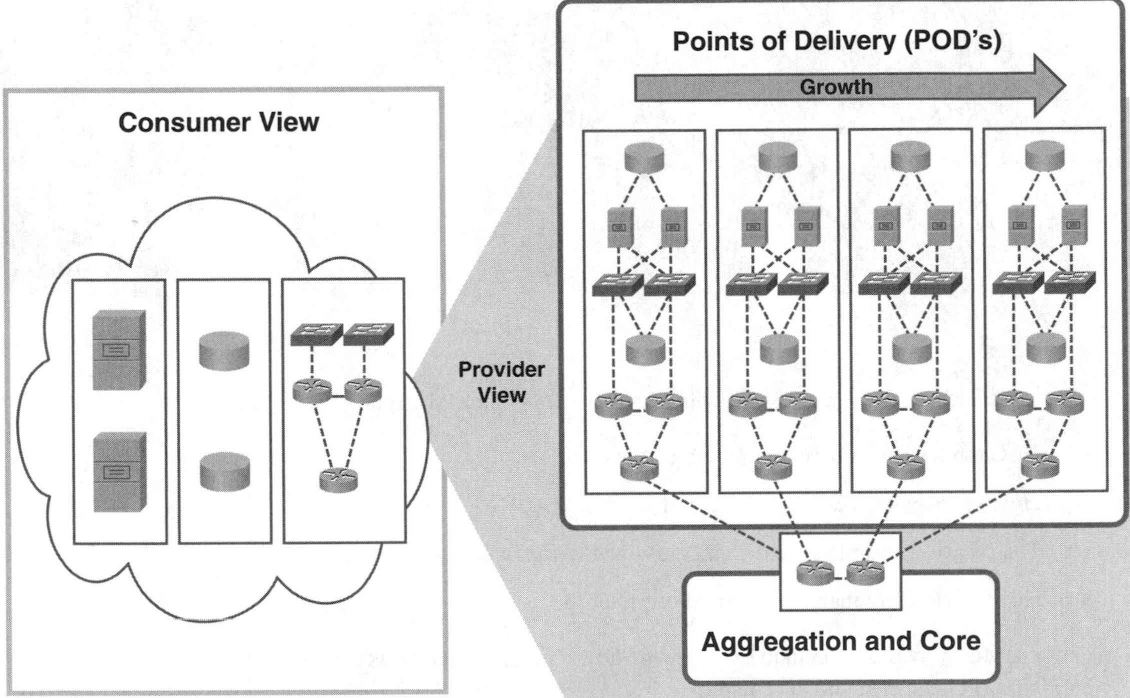

Figure 11-1 *Cloud Resources*

When the provider initially builds the infrastructure to support the cloud, it will deploy an initial number of PODs to support the demand it expects to see and also lines up with the oversubscription ratios it wants to apply. These initial PODs, plus the aggregation and core, make up the initial cloud infrastructure. This initial infrastructure now needs to be modeled in the service inventory so that tenant services can be provisioned and activated; this process is known as *on-boarding*.

Clearly at the concrete level, what makes up a POD is determined by the individual provider. Most providers are looking at a POD comprised of an ICS that offers a pre-integrated set of compute, network, and storage equipment that operates as a single solution and is easier to buy and manage, offering Capital Expenditure (CAPEX) and Operational Expenditure (OPEX) savings. Cisco, for example, provides two examples of PODs, a Vblock[1] and a FlexPod,[2] which provide a scalable, prebuilt unit of infrastructure that can be deployed in a modular manner. The main difference between the Vblock and FlexPod is the choice of storage in the solution. In a Vblock, storage is provided by EMC, and in a FlexPod, storage is provided by NetApp. Despite the differences, the concept remains the same; provides an ICS that combines compute, network, and storage resources; and enables incremental scaling with predictable performance, capability, and facilities impact. The rest of this chapter assumes that the provider has made a choice to use Vblocks as its ICS. Figure 11-2 illustrates the relationship to the conceptual model and the concrete Vblock.

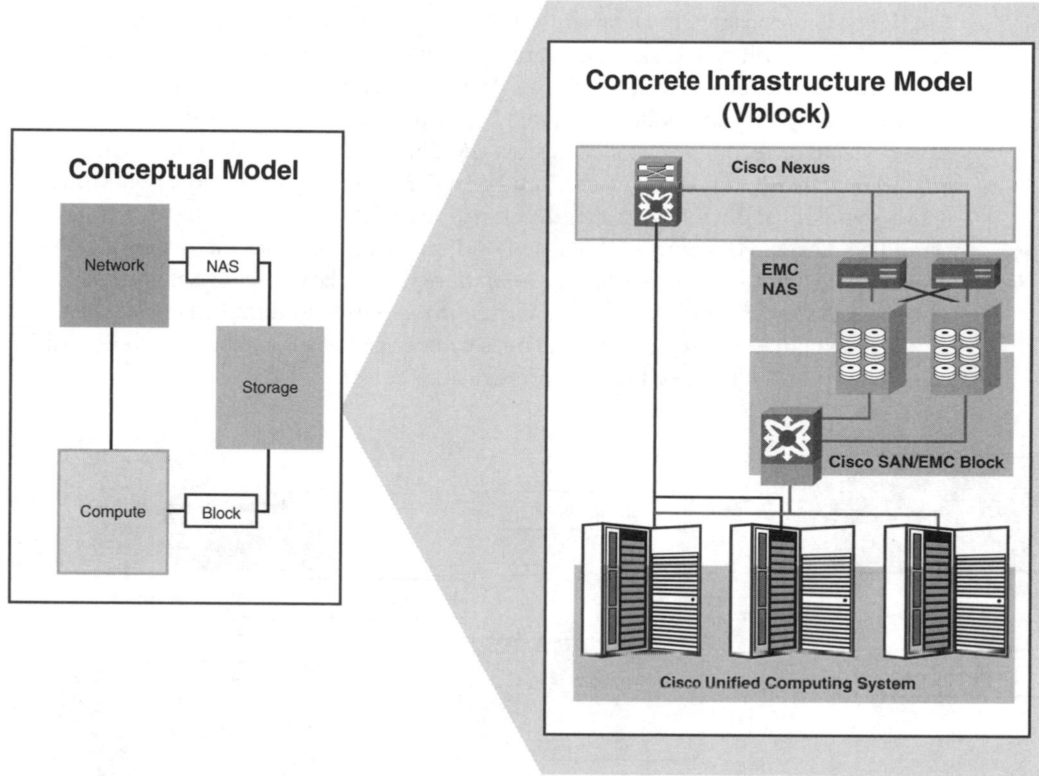

Figure 11-2 *Physical Infrastructure Model*

A Vblock can be specified by many different packages that provide different performance footprints. A generic Vblock for this example is comprised of

- Cisco Unified Computing System (UCS) compute
- Cisco MDS storage-area networking (SAN)
- EMC network-attached storage (NAS) and block storage
- VMware ESX Hypervisor
- Not strictly part of a Vblock, but the Cisco Nexus 7000 will be used as the aggregation layer and used to connect the NAS

A FlexPod offers a similar configuration but supports NetApp FAS storage arrays instead of EMC storage, and as it is typically NAS using Fibre Channel over Ethernet (FCoE) or

Network File System (NFS); then, the SAN is no longer required. Also, note that the Vblock definition is owned by the VCE company (Cisco, EMC, and VMware coalition), so it will be aimed at VMware Hypervisor-based deployments, whereas FlexPod can be considered more hypervisor neutral.

To deliver services on a Vblock, it first needs to be modeled in the service inventory or Configuration Management Database (CMDB), as the relationships between the physical building blocks will be relatively static, that is, cabling doesn't tend to change on the fly; the CMDB is a suitable place to store this data. The first choices in terms of modeling are really driven by the data model supported by the repository that has been chosen to act as the system of record for the cloud. Most CMDBs come with a predefined model based around the Distributed Management Task Force (DMTF) Common Information Model (CIM) standard, and where possible, the classes and relationships provided in this model should be reused. For example, BMC, an ITSM[3] company, provides the Atrium CMDB product, which implements the *BMC_ComputerSystem* class to represent all compute resources. An attribute of that class, *isVirtual=true*, is used to differentiate between physical compute resources and virtual ones without needing to support an additional class. Figure 11-3 illustrates a simple infrastructure model.

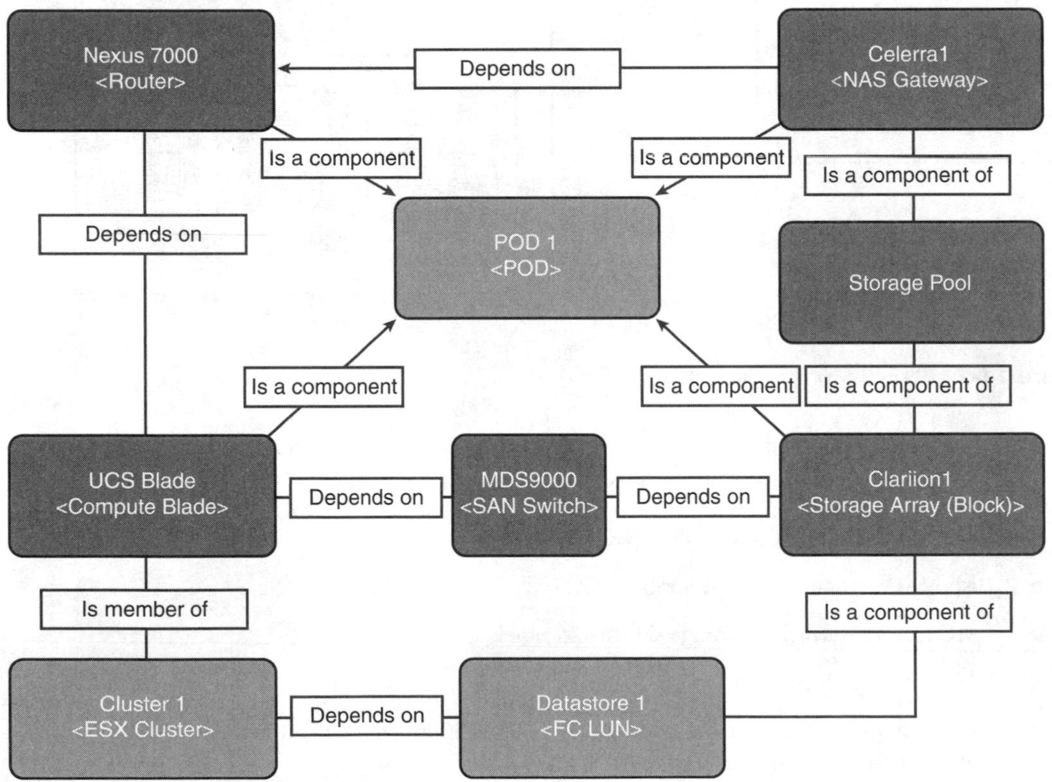

Figure 11-3 *Infrastructure Logical Model*

The following points provide a summary of the relationships shown in Figure 11-3:

- A compute blade instance depends on the router for connectivity and on the SAN switch for access block–based storage; a compute blade is also a member of an ESX cluster. The ESX cluster depends on a data store to access the storage array.
- The NAS gateway instance depends on the router for connectivity, and the storage pool is a component of the NAS gateway.
- The storage array instance depends on the SAN switch for access, and the storage pool is also a component of the NAS gateway.
- The POD acts as a container for all physical resources.

With this basic infrastructure model added to the CMDB or service inventory, you can begin to add the logical building blocks that support the service and any capabilities or constraints of the physical POD that will simplify the provisioning process. Does this seem like a lot of effort? Well, the reason for this on-boarding process is threefold:

- The technical building blocks discussed in the previous chapter need to exist on something physical, so it's important to understand that there is a relationship between physical building blocks and the building blocks that make up the technical service. Provisioning actions that modify or delete a technical service need to be able to determine which physical devices need to be modified so that they will consult the CMDB or service inventory for this information.
- The physical building blocks have a limit to how many concrete building blocks they can support. For example, the Nexus 7000 can only support a set number of VLANs, so these capacity limits should be modeled and tracked. (This is discussed in more detail in the next chapter.)
- From a service assurance perspective, the ability to understand the impact of a physical failure on a service or vice versa is critical. Figure 11-4 provides an example of the relationship between a service, the concrete building blocks that make up the service, and the physical building blocks that support the technical building blocks.

One important point to note is that we introduced the concept of a network container in the tenant model. A network container represents all the building blocks used to create the logical network, the topology-related building blocks. A network topology can be complex and can potentially contain many different resources, so using a container to group these elements simplifies the provisioning process.

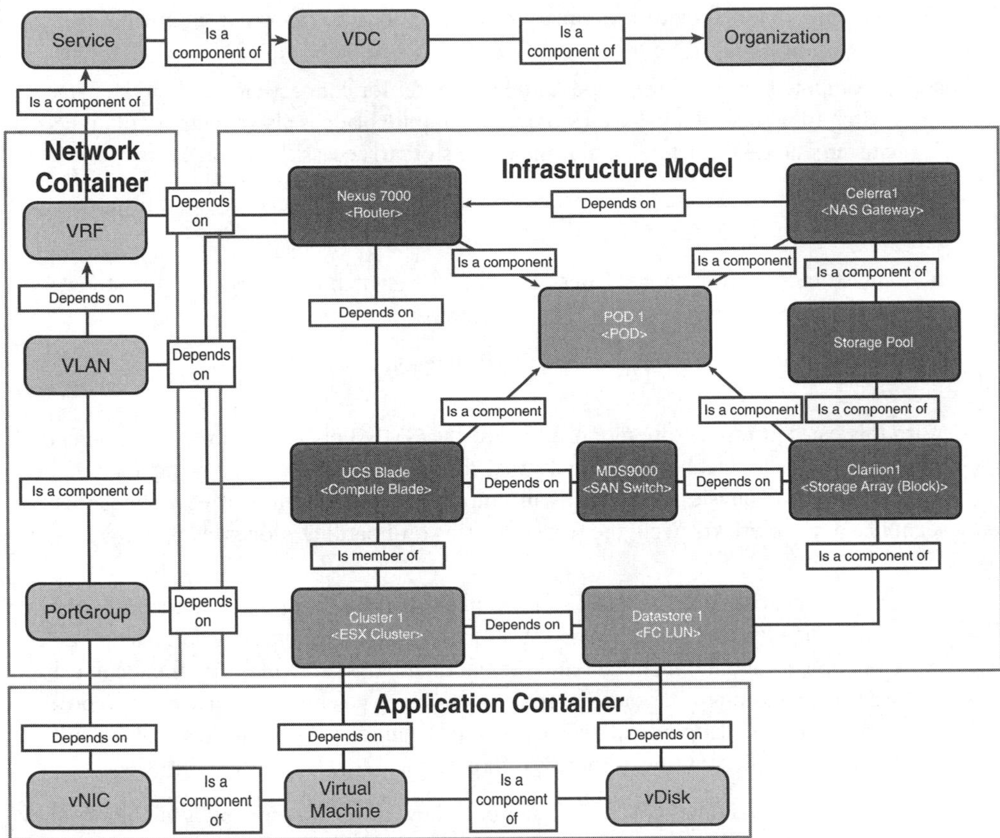

Figure 11-4 *Tenant Model*

The following points provide a summary of the relationships shown in Figure 11-4:

- The virtual machine (VM) contains a virtual disk (vDisk) and a virtual network interface card (vNIC). The VM is dependent on the ESX cluster, which in turn is dependent on the physical server. It is now possible to determine the impact on a service if a physical blade fails, even if it simply means that the service is just degraded.
- The vDisk depends on the data store in which it is stored. The vNIC depends on the port group to provide virtual connectivity, which in turn contains a VLAN that depends on both the UCS blade and Nexus 7000 to provide the Layer 2 physical connectivity. The VLAN depends on Virtual Routing and Forwarding (VRF) to provide Layer 3 physical connectivity. In the case of a physical failure of the Nexus, we can determine the impact on the service.

- The VRF is contained in a service, which is contained in a virtual data center (VDC), which is contained in an organization. These relationships mean that it is possible to understand the impact of any physical failure at a service or organization level and, when modifying or deleting the service, what the logical and physical impacts will be.
- The VRF, VLAN, and PortGroup are grouped in a simple network container that can be considered a collection of networking infrastructure, can be created by a network designer, and is part of the overall service.
- The VM, vNIC, and VDisk are grouped in a simple application container that can be considered a collection of application infrastructure, can be created by an application designer, and is part of the overall service.

Hopefully, you can begin to see that there can be up to five separate provisioning tasks to create the model shown in Figure 11-4:

1. The cloud provider infrastructure administrator provisions the infrastructure model into the CMDB or service inventory as new physical equipment is added.
2. The cloud provider customer administrator creates the outline tenant model by creating the organizational entity and the VDC.
3. The tenant service owner creates the service entity.
4. The network designer creates the network container to support the application and attaches it to the service.
5. The application designer creates the application container to support the application user's needs, connects it to the network resources created by the network designer, and attaches it to the service.

Modeling Capabilities

Modeling capabilities are an important step when on-boarding resources as they have a direct impact on how that resource can be used in the provisioning process. If you look at the Vblock definition again, you can see that it will support Layer 2 and Layer 3 network connectivity as well as NAS and SAN storage and the ESX hypervisor, so you can already see that it won't support the majority of the design patterns discussed earlier as they require a load balancer. If you were looking for a POD to support the instantiation of a design pattern that required a load balancer, you could query all the PODs that had been on-boarded and look for a *Load-Balancing=yes* capability. If this capability doesn't exist in any POD in the cloud infrastructure, the cloud provider infrastructure administrator would need to create a new POD with a load balancer or add a load balancer to an existing POD and update the capabilities supported by that POD.

Taking this concept further, if you configure the EMC storage in the Vblock to support several tiers of storage—Gold, Silver, and Bronze, for example—you could simply model these capabilities at the POD level and (as you will see in the next chapter) do an initial check when provisioning a service to find the POD that supports a particular tier of storage. Capabilities can also be used to drive behavior during the lifetime of the service. For example, if you want to allow a tenant the ability to reboot a resource, you can add a *reboot=true* capability, so this could be added to the class in the data model that represents a virtual machine. You probably wouldn't want to add this capability to a storage array or network device as rebooting one of these resources would affect multiple users and should only be done by the cloud operations team.

However, if a storage array supported a data protection capability such as NetApp Snapshot, a *snapshot=true* capability could be modeled at the storage array as well as the hypervisor level, allowing a tenant to choose whether he wants to snapshot at the hypervisor or storage level. The provider could offer these two options at different prices, depending on the resources they consume or the cost associated with automating this functionality.

Modeling Constraints

Modeling constraints are another important aspect of the on-boarding process. No resource is infinite, storage gets consumed, and memory gets exhausted, so it is important to establish where the limits are. Within a Layer 2 domain, for example, you only have 4096 VLANs to work with; in reality, after you factor in all infrastructure connectivity per POD, you will have significantly fewer VLANs to work with. So adding these limits to the resource and tracking usage against these limits give the provisioning processes a quick and easy way of checking capacity. Constraint modeling is no replacement for strong capability management tools and processes, but it is a lightweight way of delivering a quick view of where the limits are for a specific resource.

Resource-Aware Infrastructure

Modeling capabilities and constraints in the service inventory or CMDB are needed as these repositories act as the single source of truth for the infrastructure. As discussed in previous chapters, these repositories are not necessarily the best places to store dynamic data. One alternative method is the concept of an infrastructure that is self-aware that understands what devices exist within a POD, how the devices relate to each other, what capabilities those devices have, and what constraints and loads those devices have. This concept will be addressed further in the next chapter, but it is certainly a more scalable way of understanding the infrastructure model. These relationships could still be modeled in the CMDB, but the next step is simply to relate the tenant service to a POD and let the POD worry about placement and resource management. Figure 11-5 illustrates the components of a resource-aware infrastructure.

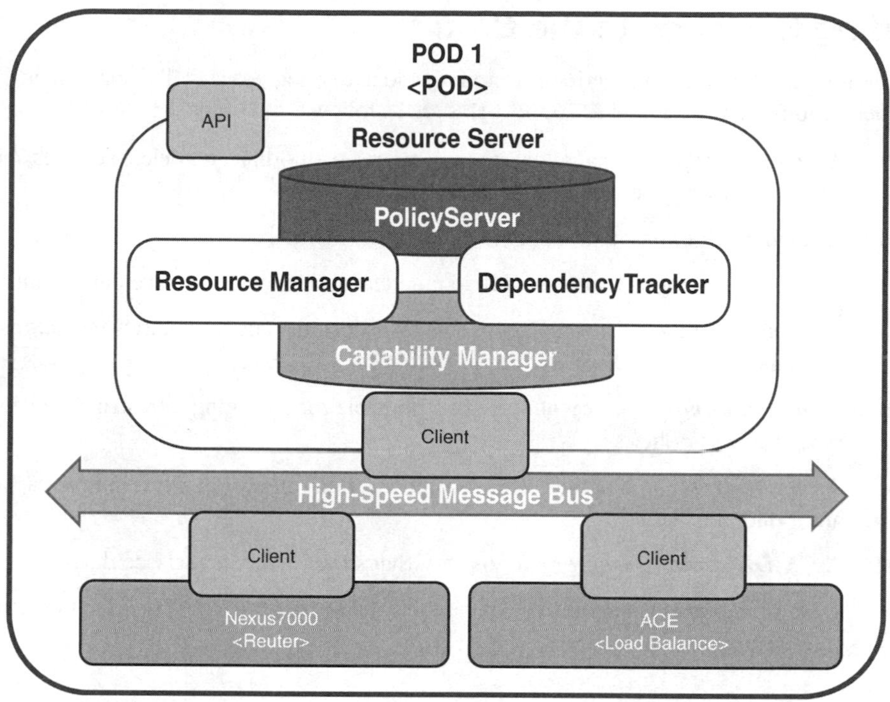

Figure 11-5 *Resource-Aware Infrastructure*

The following points provide a more detailed explanation of the components shown in Figure 11-5:

- A high-speed message bus, such as Extensible Messaging and Presence Protocol (XMPP), is used to connect clients running in the devices with a resource server responsible for a specific POD.
- The resource server persists policy and capabilities in a set of repositories that are updated by the clients.
- The resource server tracks dependencies and resource utilization within the POD.
- The resource manager implements an API that allows the orchestration system to make placement decisions and reservation requests without querying the CMDB or service inventory.

The last point is one of the most critical. Offloading the real-time resource management, constraint, and capabilities modeling from the CMDB/service inventory to the infrastructure will mean a significant simplification of the infrastructure modeling is needed going forward.

Adding Services to the Cloud

Figure 11-6 illustrates a generic provisioning and activating process. The major management components required to support this are as follows:

- A *self-service portal* that allows tenants to create, modify, and delete services and provides views or service assurance and usage views
- A *security manager* that manages all tenant credentials
- A *service catalogue* that stores all commercial and technical service definitions
- A *change manager* that orchestrates all tasks, manual and automatic, and acts as a system or record for all tenant requests that can be audited
- A *capacity and/or policy manager* responsible for managing infrastructure capacity and access policies
- An *orchestrator* that orchestrates technical actions and can provide simple capacity and policy decisions
- A *CMDB/service inventory* repository that stores asset and service data
- A set of *element managers* that communicate directly with the concrete infrastructure elements

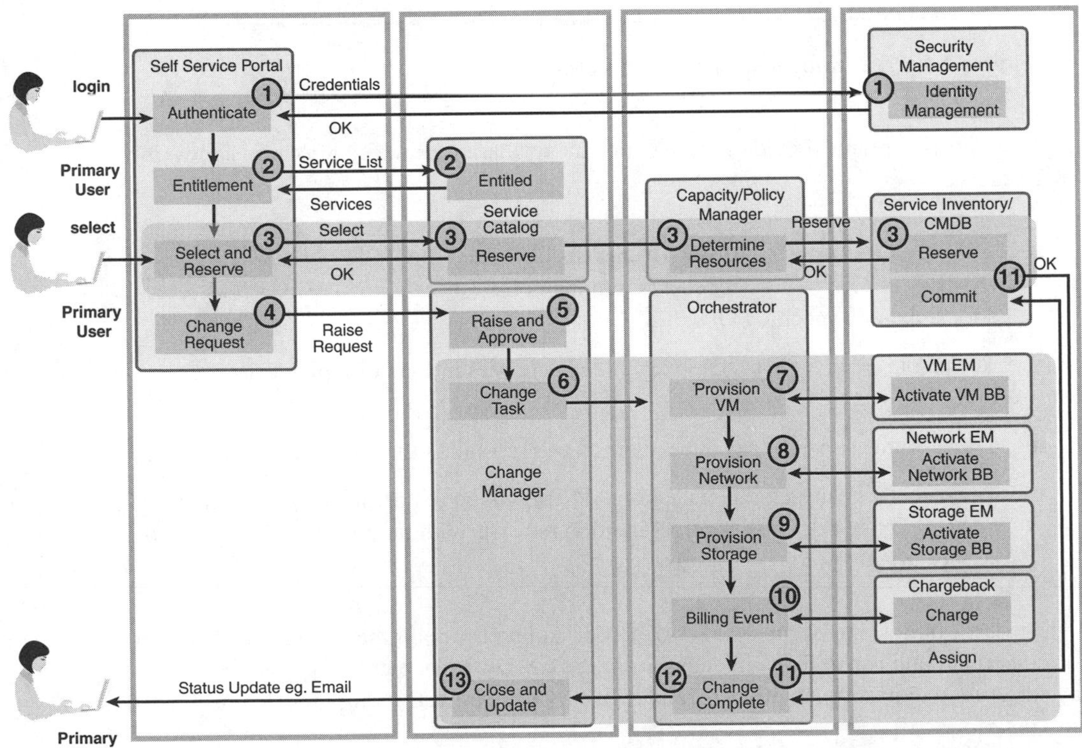

Figure 11-6 *Generic Orchestration*

The orchestration steps illustrated in Figure 11-6 are as follows:

Step 1. The tenant connects to the portal and authenticates against the security manager, which can also provide group policy information used in Step 2.

Step 2. A list of entitled services is retrieved from the service catalogue and displayed in the portal, along with any existing service data and the assurance and usage views.

Step 3. The provisioning process begins with the tenant selecting the required service and ends with the technical building blocks that support the service being reserved in the service inventory or CMDB. Depending on the management components deployed, the validation that the service can be fulfilled based on the constraints and capabilities provided by the POD will be done in a separate capacity or policy manager or can be performed by the orchestrator.

Note that the orchestrator/capacity manager is not necessarily making detailed placement decisions for the activation of the service. For example, on which blade in a vSphere/ESX cluster to place a resource, these will typically be made in the element manager that maintains detailed, real-time usage data.

Step 4. The portal will create a change request to manage the delivery of the request or order.

Step 5. The change will be approved. This could simply be an automatic approval, or it can be passed into some form of change process.

Step 6. The activation process begins. A change is decomposed into at least one change task that is passed to the orchestrator.

Step 7, 8, 9. These processes are being managed by the orchestrator to instantiate the concrete building blocks based on the service definition. The orchestrator will communicate with the various element managers. For example, in the case of a Vblock, the orchestrator would communicate with VMware vCenter to create, clone, modify, or delete a virtual machine. Up until this point, the data regarding the service has been abstracted away from the specific implementation. At this point, the orchestrator will extract the relevant data and pass it to the element manager using its specific APIs.

Step 10. A billing event is created that will be used to charge for fixed items such as adding more vRAM or another vCPU.

Step 11. The orchestration has completed successfully, so all resources are committed in the service inventory and the change task closed. This flow represents the "happy day" scenario in which all process steps are completed successfully. A more detailed process would have rollback and compensations steps documented as well, but this is beyond the scope of this chapter.

Step 12. The flow of control is passed back into the change manager, and this marks the end of the activation process. This might start another task or might close the overall change request if only one task is present.

Step 13. A notification is passed back directly to the tenant, indicating that the request has been completed. Alternatively, this notification could be sent to the portal if the portal maintains request data.

As discussed previously, there might be several provisioning steps, so you might need to iterate through this process several times.

Provisioning the Infrastructure Model

We now look at the steps needed to provision the tenant model shown in Figure 11-4, this assumes that the actual physical building blocks have been racked, stacked, cabled and configured in the datacenter already:

1. The cloud provider infrastructure administrator (CPIA) will log in to the self-service portal and be presented with a set of services that he is entitled to see, one of which is *On-board a New POD*. The CPIA will select this service; complete all the details required for this service, such as management IP addresses, constraints, and capabilities; and submit the request. The reservation step is skipped here because this service is creating new resources.
2. As this is a significant change, this service will go through an approval process that will see infrastructure owners and cloud teams review and approve the request.
3. After it is approved, as the infrastructure already exists, a single change task will be created to update the CMDB, and this will be passed to the orchestrator.
4. The orchestrator has little to do but simply call the CMDB/Service Inventory and create the appropriate configuration items (CI) and their relationships. Optionally, the orchestrator can also update service assurance components to ensure that the new resources are being managed, but in most cases, this has already been done as part of the physical deployment process.
5. A success notification is generated up the stack, and the request is shown as complete in the portal.

Provisioning the Organization and VDC

The same process used by the CPIA is followed by the cloud provider customer administrator (CPAD), but a few differences exist:

- The CPAD will be entitled to a different set of services than the CPIA.
- The approval process will now be more commercial/financial in nature, checking that all the agreed-upon terms and conditions are in place and that credit checks have been done.
- Orchestration activities will manage interactions with the CMDB to create the organization and VDC CIs to add user accounts to the identity repository so that the tenant can log in to the portal, and to add VDC resource limits to the capacity/policy manager and set up any branding required for the tenant in the portal.

Creating the Network Container

The same process is followed by the tenant network designer, but a few differences exist:

- The network designer (ND) logs in to the portal using the credentials set up by the CPIA and is presented with a set of services orientated around creating, modifying, and deleting the network container. The network designer could be a consumer or a provider role depending on the complexity of the network design.
- The ND selects the virtual network building blocks he requires and submits the request. As this is a real-time system, the resources are reserved so that they are assigned (but not committed) to this request. The capacity manager will make sure that sufficient capacity exists in the infrastructure and that the organization has contracted enough capacity before reserving any resources.
- The approval process is skipped here if the organization has contracted enough capacity and there is enough infrastructure capacity; then the change will be preapproved.
- Orchestration activities will manage interactions with the element managers responsible for automating and activating the configuration of the virtual network elements in a specific POD and generating billing events so that the tenant can be billed on what he has consumed.
- A success notification is generated up the stack, and the request is shown as complete in the portal. The resources that were reserved are now committed in the service inventory and/or CMDB.

Creating the Application

The same process used by the network designer is followed by the tenant application designer, but a few differences exist:

- The cloud consumer application designer (CCAD) logs on to the portal using the credentials set up by the CPIA and is presented with a set of services orientated around creating, modifying, and deleting the application container.
- The CCAD selects the application building blocks he requires and submits the request. The network building blocks created by the network designer will also be presented in the portal to allow the application designer to specify which network he wants the application elements to connect to. As this is a real-time system, the resources are reserved.
- Orchestration activities will manage interactions with the element managers responsible for automating and activating the configuration of the virtual machines, deploying software images, and generating billing events so that the tenant can be billed on what he has consumed.
- A success notification is generated up the stack, and the request is shown as complete in the portal. The resources that were reserved are now committed in the service inventory and/or CMDB.

Workflow Design

The workflow covered in the preceding sections will vary. Some will be based on out-of-the-box content provided by an orchestration/automation vendor such as Cisco and some will be completely bespoke; most workflow will be a combination. It is important to balance flexibility and supportability. On the one hand, you don't want to build a standardized, fixed set of workflows that cannot be customized or changed; on the other hand, you don't want to build technical workflows that are completely bespoke and unsupportable. One potential solution is to use the concept of moments and extension points to allow flexible workflows but at the same time introduce a level of standardization that promotes an easier support and upgrade path. Figure 11-7 illustrates these concepts.

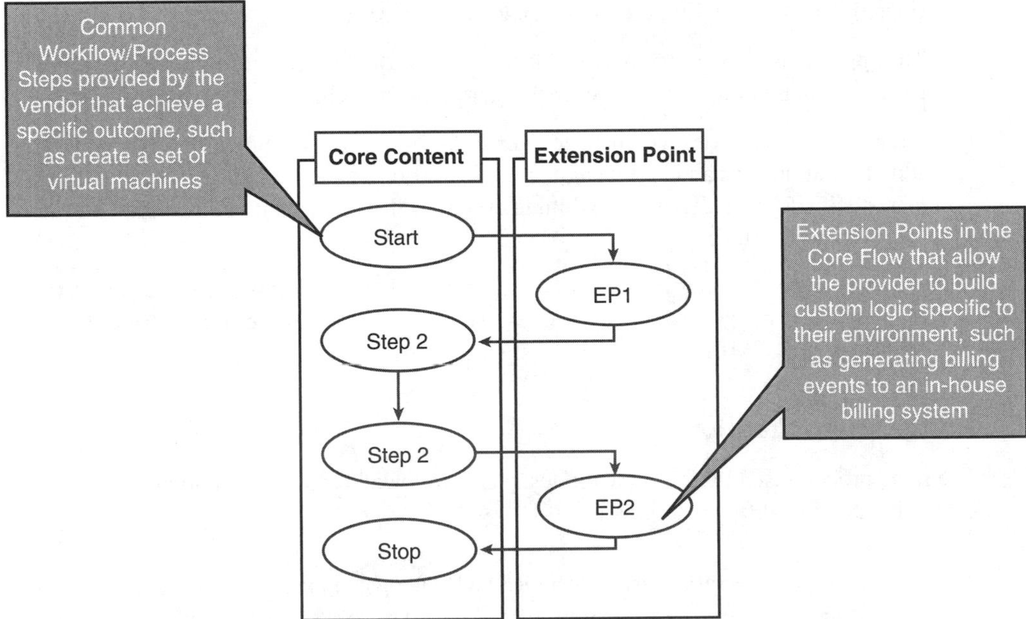

Figure 11-7 *Workflow Design*

The core content is comprised of workflow moments; the moment concept is applied to points in time of the technical orchestration workflow. Some example moments are as follows:

1. **Trigger and decomposition:** This moment is where the flow is triggered and decomposes standard payload items to workflow attributes, for example, the action variable, which is currently used to determine the child workflow to trigger but might also be required to be persisted in the workflow for billing updates and so on.
2. **Workflow enrichment and resource management:** This moment is where data is extracted from systems using standard adapters and any resource management or ingress checking is performed.

3. **Orchestration:** This is the overarching orchestration flow.
4. **Standard actions:** These are the standard automation action sequences provided by the vendor.
5. **Standard notifications and updates:** This step will update any inventory repositories (CMDBs) provided with the solution, such as the cloud portal, change manager, and so on.

The core consent can be extended to support bespoke functions using extension points. The concept here is that all processes would contain a call or dummy process element that can be triggered after the core task had completed to handle customized actions without requiring changes to the core workflow. An example set of extension points are as follows:

1. **Trigger and decomposition:** This extension point is where custom service data received from the calling system/portal is decomposed into variables used in the rest of the workflow. This will allow designers to quickly add service options/data in the requesting system and handle this data in a standard manner without changing the core decomposition logic.
2. **OSS enrichment and resource management:** This extension point is where custom service data is requested through custom WS* calls or other nonstandard methods and added to the workflow runtime data. This will allow designers to integrate with clients' specific systems without changing the core enrichment logic.
3. **Actions:** This extension point is where custom actions are performed using WS* calls or other nonstandard methods. This will allow designers to integrate with clients' specific automation sequences without changing the core automation logic.
4. **Notifications:** This extension point is where custom notifications are performed using WS* calls or other nonstandard methods. This will allow designers to integrate with clients' specific automation systems without changing the core notification logic.

Creation and Placement Strategies

The previous sections discussed that any form of activation would require a placement decision; these decisions are typically made on the following grounds:

- **Maximizing resource usage:** The provider wants to ensure that it gets the maximum workload density across its infrastructure. This means optimizing CAPEX (the amount of money spent on purchasing equipment).
- **Maximizing resilience:** The provider chooses to spread workloads across multiple hosts to minimize failures; this typically means hosts are typically underutilized.
- **Maximize usage:** This is similar to maximizing resource usage, but this requires a point-in-time decision to be made about what host is least loaded now and in the time span of the workload. Think of Amazon's Spot service.

- **Maximize facilities usage:** The provider wants to place workloads based on facilities usage and to reduce energy consumption.
- **Maximize application performance:** Place all building blocks in the same domain or data center interconnect.

Figure 11-8 illustrates these concepts.

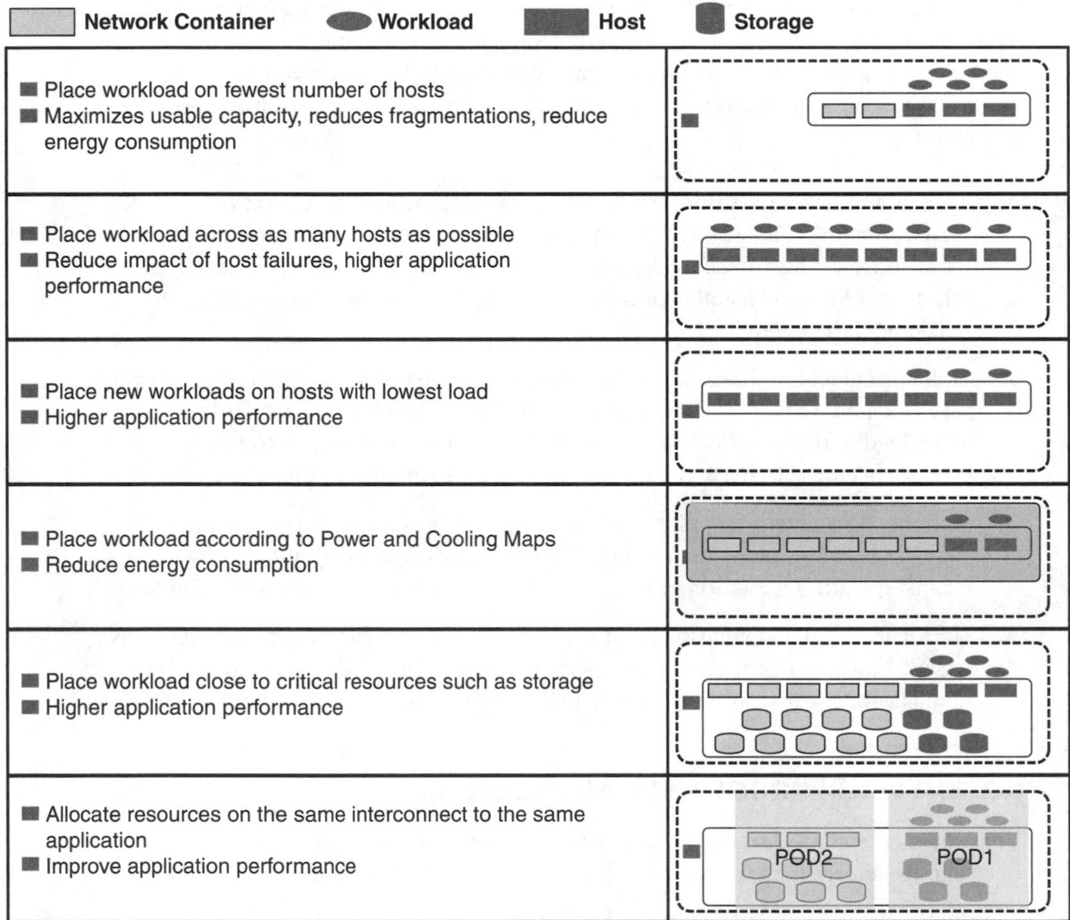

Figure 11-8 *Generic Resource Allocation Strategies*

Certain placement strategies are simpler to implement than others. For example, placing workloads based on current load can be done quite simply in a VMware environment because the API supports it if Distributed Resource Scheduling (DRS) is enabled. The orchestrator can query vCenter to determine DRS placement options or simply create a

VM in a cluster and let DRS decide placement. Maximizing facilities usage is substantially more difficult based on the following needs:

- A system that understands all this usage
- An interface to query this system
- The creation of an adapter that queries this system in the orchestrator and the logic associated with this query

A single placement strategy can be adopted, or the provider can adopt multiple strategies with prioritization. Typically a provider of public clouds will look to optimize its resource usage and reduce its energy consumption ahead of application performance unless the consumer chooses to pay for better application performance, in which case this will affect the placement or migration of the service to a POD that supports the placement requirement. A public cloud provider might prioritize resilience and application performance over resource optimization.

Choosing which POD supports a particular placement strategy will mean combining dynamic data such as vCenter DRS placement options with the capabilities and constraints that are modeled when the POD was on-boarded and making a decision based on all this data. The choice can be complicated as the underlying physical relationship within the POD needs to be understood. For example, assume that a provider has purchased two Vblocks and connected them to the same aggregation switches; each Vblock has 64 blades installed, four ESX clusters in total. Two clusters are modeled with high oversubscription capability and two with lower oversubscription capability. A tenant requests an HTTP load balancer design pattern that needs the web servers to run on Gold tier storage but on a low-cost (highly oversubscribed) ESX cluster.

If the orchestrator/capacity manager simply looks at the service inventory/CMDB, it will determine that two clusters can support low cost through the *oversubscription_type=high* capability modeled in the inventory. The orchestrator/capacity manager can also identify which ESX cluster of the two can support the workloads required by consulting DRS recommendations, but this simply identifies which compute building blocks will support the workload. As this design pattern requires a Gold storage tier, the service inventory must be queried to understand which storage is attached to that ESX cluster and whether it has enough capacity to host the required number of .vmdk files. In addition, as the design pattern requires a session load balancer and neither Vblock supports a network-based session load balancer, the compute and associated storage must also be able to support an additional VM-based load balancer. If there was a third POD that did contain a load balancer but was connected to different compute and storage resources, would this POD make a better choice for the service? As more infrastructure capabilities are modeled, it is likely that the need for a true policy manager will evolve as the capabilities of the orchestrator/capacity manager are overhauled.

Service Life Cycle Management

Previously, we discussed how a service could be designed and, in this chapter, how a service is instantiated and transitioned into an operational state. Viewing this from an Information Technology Infrastructure Library (ITIL)[4] perspective, these sections could be viewed as the service design and service transition phases of the ITIL V3 model, respectively. Of course, they don't cover the entire best-practice recommendations of ITIL V3, but the essence is there. This section covers service life cycle management, which is a term often used to refer to the complete ITIL V3 framework, from service strategy to service operations, including continual improvement. However, this section refers to service life cycle management as the management of an operational service throughout its remaining lifetime until the tenant chooses to decommission and/or delete the service. The reason for this is that depending on the overall cloud operations model that is chosen by the provider and the type of cloud service offered, there will often be a division of responsibility between the provider and consumer at the service operational level, whereas the provider is normally fully responsible for the strategy, design, and transition process areas. Service life cycle management from the consumer's perspective begins when the service is operational.

Making the distinction between decommission and delete is important because the tenant might simply choose to decommission the service (that is, not have the service active) rather than to delete it. Consider the example of the development and test environments. While development is taking place, the test environment might not be needed and vice versa. If those environments incur costs while active, it might be more cost-effective to decommission a service with the view that it will be commissioned again when it is required. Deleting a service obviously removes all the building blocks of the service, releases any resources, and deletes the service definition so that the service can no longer be recovered.

The service operations phase consists of a number of key process areas:

- Incident and problem management
- Event management
- Request fulfillment
- Access management
- Operations management
- Service desk function

ITIL V3 also expects some form of service improvement framework to be in place to support continual improvement, and this is never more important in the operational phase. This chapter is concerned with orchestrating and automating cloud services, and this doesn't stop simply because the service is operational. The following sections will discuss in more detail the impact that the cloud and, in particular, orchestration and automation have on each of the ITIL V3 areas.

Incident and Problem Management

The primary focus of the incident management process is to manage the life cycle of all incidents, an *incident* being defined as an unplanned outage or loss of quality to an IT/cloud service. The primary objective of incident management is to return the IT service to users as quickly as possible. If services are being deployed into a multitenant environment, a single incident might affect many different tenants or users, so this becomes a critical process. The primary objectives of problem management are to prevent incidents from happening and to minimize the impact of incidents that cannot be prevented. Both incident and problem management processes are typically managed by the service desk function, which is typically implemented in IT Service Management (ITSM) service desk software. All workflow and coordinating activities are managed in the service desk software, and this won't change when a service is hosted in a cloud, although the service desk software itself might need to support a different usage.

Event Management

The primary focus of event management is to filter and categorize events and to decide on appropriate actions. *Event management* is one of the main activities of service operations. Within the cloud, event handling and categorization will become a major task, the event manager must receive, categories, enrich and correlate alarms from virtual machines and the infrastructure but also alarms need to be processed from provisioning and activation systems, in fact alarms need to be processed form any operational activity that is being automated. Combine this complexity with the exponential demand and rate of change that cloud offers and the need to have operational awareness of any issues to do with service provisioning or operations, and you have identified one of the major operational challenges of a cloud platform. Orchestration can play a major part in linking event handling to problem and incident resolution, as illustrated in Figure 11-9.

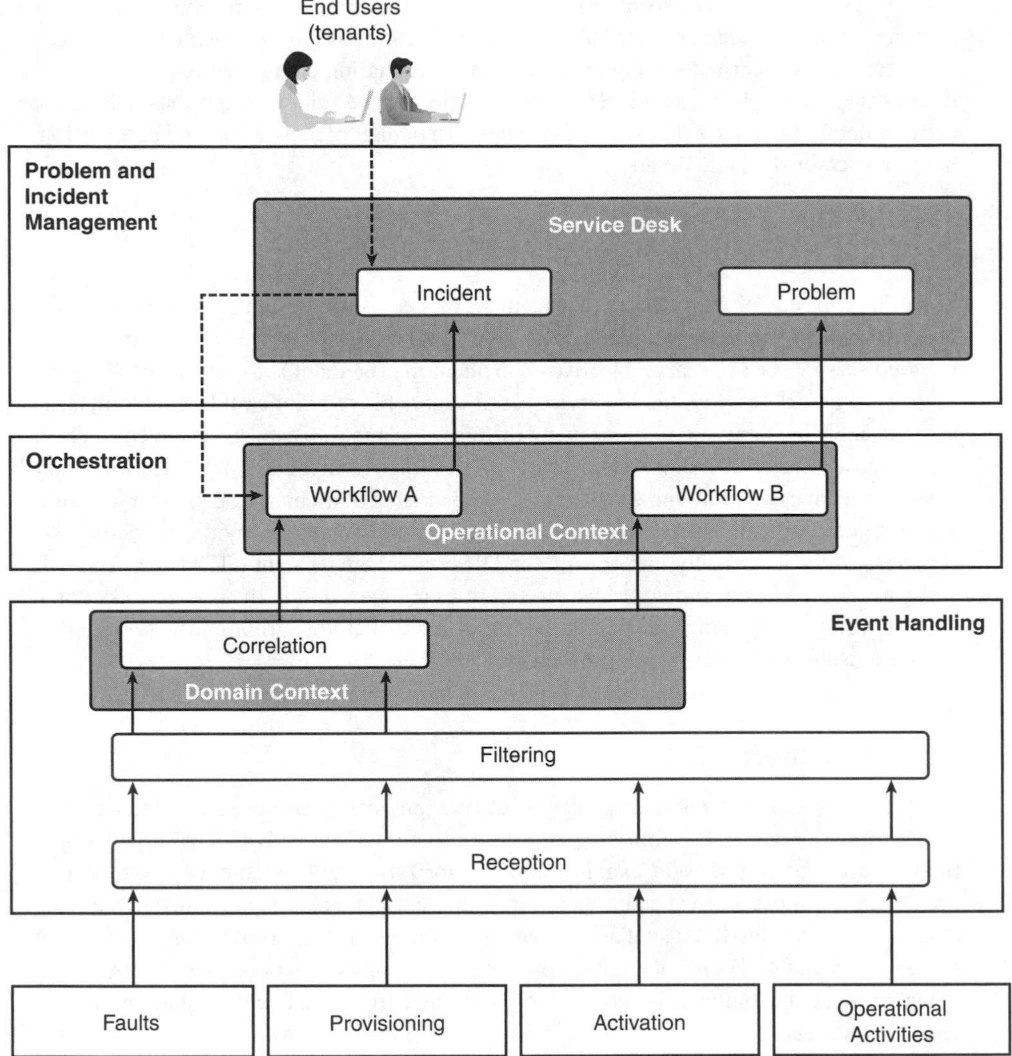

Figure 11-9 *Orchestration for Incident and Problem Management*

As the number and variety of alarms grow, the need to understand the operational context of an event becomes paramount. Is this event impacting multiple tenants or cloud users or just a single user? Does this event affect a service-level agreement (SLA) or not? Given the potential volume of events and the fact that a cloud is effectively open for business 24 hours a day, this analysis cannot be performed by operators any longer. The systems that perform event management can do event correlation; however, that is normally done by looking at the event data itself or applying the event data within a domain. For example, network faults can be correlated based on which device they occur on, that is, multiple failures can be correlated to the fact that an uplink on a device has failed or using a network topology model can be correlated against an upstream device failure.

Where event management systems are often weak is looking across domains, applying that operational context to a number of events. This is where orchestration can help. Orchestration can be used to process correlated and uncorrelated events within an operational context by querying other systems and relating different domain events together. Unfortunately, this will not happen "out of the box." The experience of senior support staff is required to build the orchestration workflows, and in effect, what you are doing is automating the investigation and diagnostic knowledge of engineers, or the ***known problem database*** in ITIL speak. Many years ago, Cisco launched a tool called MPLS Diagnostic Expert (MDE) that took the combined knowledge of the Cisco Technical Assistance Center (TAC) and distilled it into a workflow for deterring connectivity for IP-VPN. One of the first case studies involved rerunning a major service provider outage that took one full day to troubleshoot manually through the tool and resolving the problem in ten minutes (with the correct determination that the culprit, a network operator, had removed a Border Gateway Protocol [BGP] connectivity statement). The workflow was only successful because the subject matter expert responsible for its content really understood the technical context. Now expand that across multiple domains and include an understanding of the real-time state of the operational environment, and you begin to see the scope of the problem; however, the cloud is transformational, and this is one of the major areas that need to be considered by the provider when adopting the cloud. Consumers will normally be unaware of the underlying process and will typically only see the output of the event management and incident/problem management processes. When the incident is raised directly by the customer, orchestration can still assist with investigation and resolution within the operational context, but the trigger is the incident rather than an event.

Request Fulfillment

The primary focus of the request fulfillment process is to fulfill service requests, which in most cases are minor (standard) changes (for example, requests to change a password) or requests for information. Depending on the type of request, the orchestrator can forward the request to the required element manager to process or simply raise a ticket in the service desk to allow an operator to respond to a request for information. Given the self-service nature of the cloud, most standard changes will be preapproved and simply fulfilled by the appropriate element manager.

Access Management

The primary focus of the access management process is to grant authorized users the right to use a service while preventing access to non-authorized users. The access management process essentially executes policies defined in IT security management and, as such, is a critical process within cloud operations. From a Software as a Service (SaaS) perspective, this is relatively simple as the provider is responsible for all aspects of the application. Access management, therefore, is focused on simply providing access to the application, and the application provides access to the data. In IaaS, access must be granted at a more granular level:

- Access to the virtual machine
- Out-of-band access to the virtual machine, in the case of a configuration
- Access to backups and snapshots
- Access to infrastructure consoles such as restore consoles

All this access needs to be provided in a consistent and secure manner across multiple identity repositories. Orchestration and automation can ensure that as users are added to the cloud, their identity and access rights are provisioned correctly and modified in a consistent manner.

Operations Management

The primary focus of the operations management process is to monitor and control the IT services and IT infrastructure—in short, the day-to-day routine tasks related to the operation of infrastructure components and applications. Table 11-1 defines typical operational tasks and shows where orchestration and automation have a role to play. The task of facilities management is not covered because of the size and breadth of this subject.

Table 11-1 *Operational Tasks*

Task	Role of Orchestration
Patching	Typically, this function is carried out by element managers, but if the portal allows the consumer to upload specific patches and apply them, orchestration will be involved to coordinate the automated deployment and installation of the patches.
Backup and restore	Typically, a backup is scheduled to occur on a regular basis, so this would be handled by the cloud scheduler application, but the initial creation, modification, and deletion of the backup job would be automated and coordinated by the orchestration system.
Antivirus management	The orchestration system would coordinate the deployment of antivirus agents (if required), but typically the scanning, detection, and remediation of viruses and worms will be handled by the antivirus applications.

Table 11-1 *Operational Tasks*

Task	Role of Orchestration
Compliance checking	As with antivirus, the orchestration system would coordinate the deployment of compliance policies, but typically the scanning, detection, and reporting of compliance will be handled by the compliance applications.
Monitoring	While monitoring is a key component of Continuous Service Improvement from the provider perspective, this data is normally exported to the cloud portal to allow the tenants to see how their services are performing, so there is little orchestrator involvement here, apart from setting up the policy defining which data should be exported.

The Cloud Service Desk

The cloud service desk is the single point of contact between the consumer and provider. As such, it is typically a view within the overall cloud portal that provides access to the support functions and standard change options. The following features are typically required for a cloud-enabled service desk:

- Support multiple tenants
- Support a web-based user interface and be Internet "hardened"
- Allow content to be embedded in another portal
- Support a single sign-on

Continued Service Improvement

A dynamic, self-service demand model means that the IT environment and the services that run in the environment need to be continually monitored, analyzed, and optimized. The CSI process should implement a monitoring framework that is continually measuring performance against an expected baseline and optimizing the infrastructure to ensure that any deviation from the baseline is managed effectively. It is in the optimization step that orchestration and automation can play a significant part in coordinating and performing the actions that bring the cloud platform performance back in line with the expected baseline.

Summary

To create new services, the orchestration and automation systems need to work together to provision and activate the technical building blocks that make up the overall cloud service. There are a number of steps that need to take place in any fulfillment activity:

- An infrastructure model needs to build which represents the physical building blocks, capabilities, and constraints that make up cloud infrastructure deployed by the cloud provider.
- This infrastructure model is typically mastered in the service inventory or CMDB, but in the future, it is likely in the future it will be held in the infrastructure itself.
- After an infrastructure model is in place, tenant services can be overlaid on top, first by reserving a set of resources that support the logical building blocks and then by activating the resources on the various physical building blocks.
- The orchestration and automation tools not only play a part in the provisioning and activation process but also have a significant impact in service life cycle management.

References

[1] Vblock, at www.vce.com/solutions/Vblock.

[2] FlexPod, at www.netapp.com/us/technology/flexpod.

[3] ITSM, at www.itsmf.co.uk.

[4] ITIL, at www.itil-officialsite.com.

Chapter 12

Cloud Capacity Management

This chapter provides a detailed overview of how Infrastructure as a Service (IaaS) capacity can be measured and managed. Upon completing this chapter, you will be able to understand the following:

- The basic challenges and requirements for managing capacity in an IaaS platform
- How to model and manage capacity
- The importance of demand management
- The role of the procurement process in cloud

Tetris and the Cloud

As discussed throughout this book, the cloud consumer views the cloud as an infinite set of resources that it can consume as required. This clearly is not the case from the provider's point of view, nor is it a sustainable business model. So, the cloud provider (either an IT department or telco) must provide the illusion of infinite resources while continually optimizing and growing the underlying cloud platform in line with capital expenditure (CAPEX) and service-level agreement (SLA) targets. There is often debate within IT organizations as to whether a formal capacity management process is needed, as hardware costs have continued to fall. This is based on the premise that capacity management is purely a CAPEX management function; however, with the introduction of the cloud, capacity management also becomes an SLA management function. This stems from the possibility of SLA breaches because of oversubscribed equipment or lack of resources to support the bursting of existing services or the instantiation of new services, which will inversely impact the user experience of a cloud service. The self-service nature of the cloud and the increase in virtualization and automation make capacity management more complex as providers can no longer over dimension their infrastructure to support peak usage, as peak usage will vary dramatically based on consumer requirements. To visualize this, think of a typical data center as the game Tetris, as illustrated in Figure 12-1.

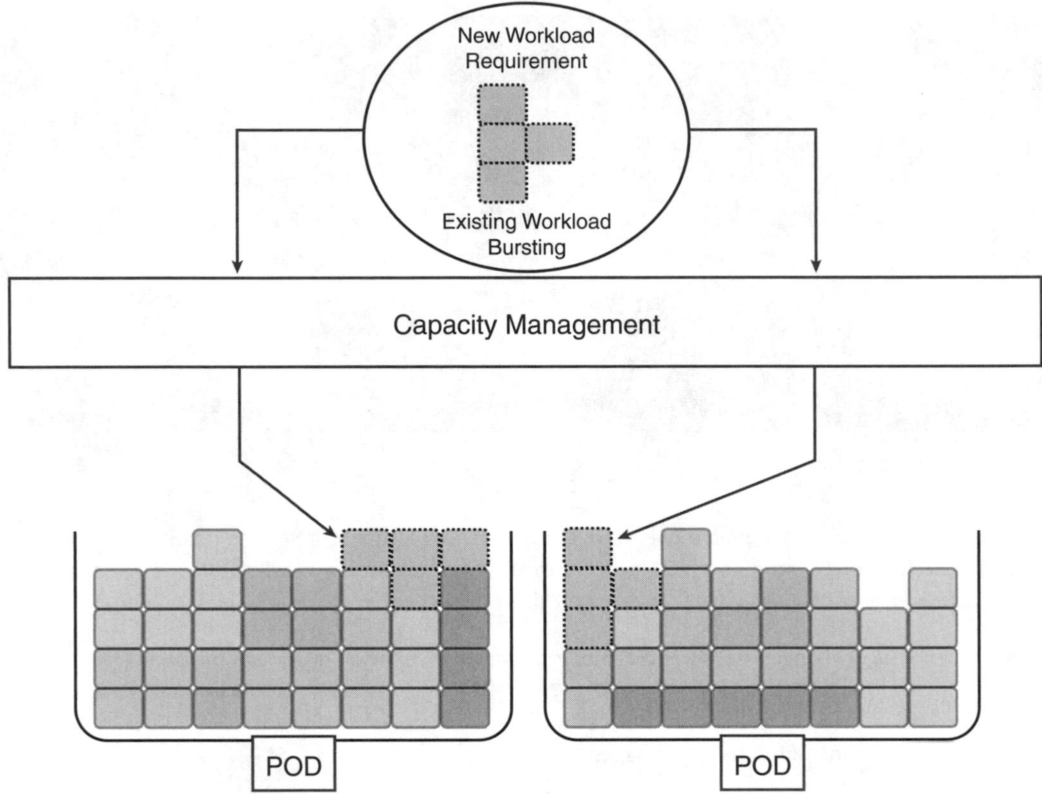

Figure 12-1 *Tetris*

A finite number of colored shapes (workloads) fall down into a clearly defined area (infrastructure point of delivery [POD]), and the position and orientation of the shape are optimized to fit that area. If the optimization process is successful, more shapes fall down; if not, they build up and until they fill the hole. Now, increase the speed and have an infinite number of shapes and colors (as workloads will have different resource dimensions), and you have a true cloud. Somewhere in the middle will be the cloud that is available today from most providers. There aren't an infinite number of workloads, but the demand is still much higher.

Capacity management, as defined by Information Technology Infrastructure Library Version 3 (ITIL V3), is seen as an ongoing process that starts in service strategy with an understanding of what is needed and then evolves into a process of designing capacity management into the services, ensuring that all capacity gates have been met before the service is operational, and finally managing and optimizing the capacity throughout the service lifetime. You can view capacity management as the process of balancing supply against a demand from a number of different dimensions, the main two being cost and SLA.

Referring to Table 12-1, you can see that Forrester defines a number of maturity levels for capacity management. We think it's clear from the preceding passage that providers need to have a maturity of at least the Defined level, which mandates a capacity model of some sort.

Table 12-1 *Capacity Management Maturity (Forrester)*

	Initial	Repeatable	Defined	Managed	Optimized
Capacity management	No responsibility defined; process works informally.	Capacity is managed on an individual system base, done through, for example, expert judgment.	Capacity modeling happens and follows a defined process. Prediction is not working 100%.	Prediction works well, and capacity-related problems almost never occur. Automation is high.	Full synchronization of capacity plans with business.

Cloud Capacity Model

The traditional capacity-planning process is typically achieved in four steps:

Step 1. Create a capacity model that defines the key resources and units of growth.

Step 2. Create a baseline to understand how your server, storage, and network infrastructure are used by capturing secondary indicators such as CPU load or global network traffic.

Step 3. Evaluate changes from new applications that are going to run on the infrastructure and the impact of demand "bursting" because of increased activity in given services.

Step 4. Analyze the data from the previous steps to forecast future infrastructure requirements and decide how to satisfy these requirements.

The main challenge with this approach is that it is very focused on the technology silos, not the platform as a whole. For example:

- It views all workloads as equal and doesn't focus on the relative value of a mission-critical workload over a noncore application.
- It is not optimized to cope with variable demand.
- It typically will not factor in emerging data center costs such as power consumption.

A new capacity-planning process should attempt to provide data that can be used to deliver more business value to the provider and optimize the existing infrastructure and growth. Figure 12-2 illustrates the component parts of the cloud platform forecast model that define a model for all the component parts and then factor in demand and forecasts for all silos before aggregating this for the cloud platform model.

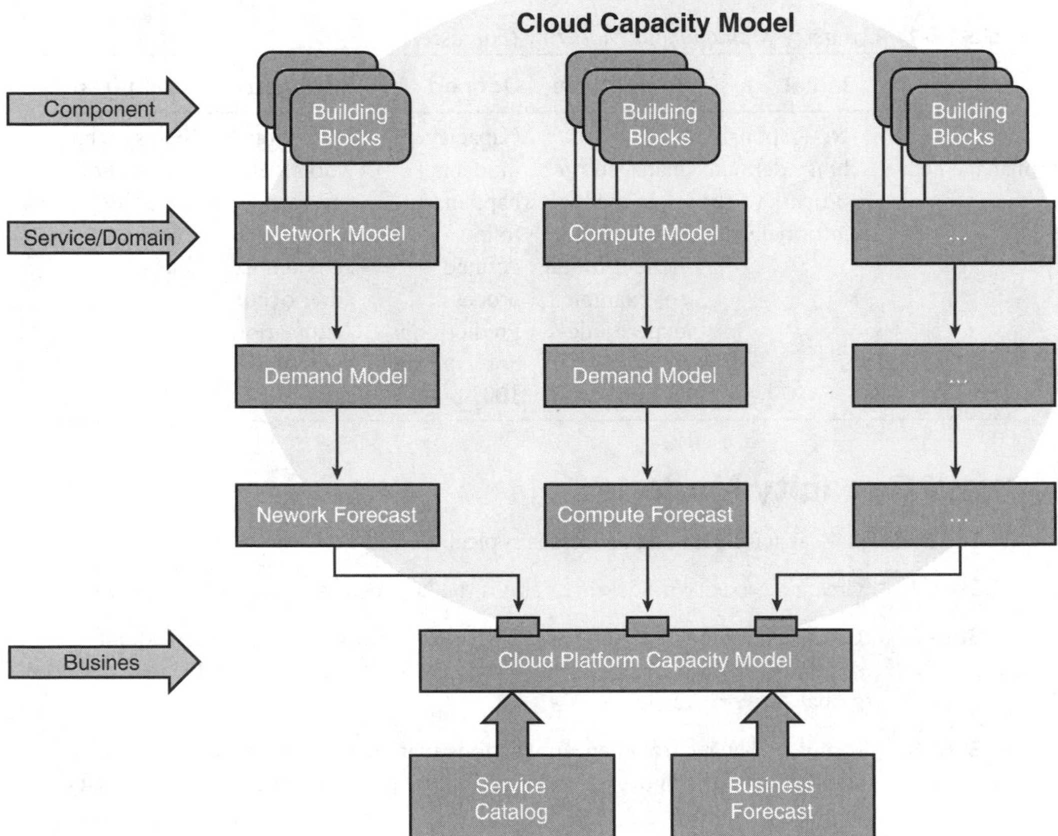

Figure 12-2 *Cloud Platform Forecast*

The following sections will focus on the demand and forecast models, so let's look at the capacity models. ITIL V3 focuses on capacity in three planes:

- Business
- Service
- Components

Chapter 10, "Technical Building Blocks of IaaS," discussed the concept of technical building blocks that are the basic reusable blocks that make up a service. From a capacity-planning perspective, we will consider these as components in the overall capacity plan and we will typically group them by technology services or domains within the cloud platform. Each technology service will have its own demand and forecast model applied to it, as the services will be consumed at different rates. Typically, the storage domain will grow exponentially, whereas compute and networking will fluctuate.

Business capacity is slightly harder to map, so you can refer to this as the cloud platform view, (that is, the capability for the cloud platform to support the services available in the service catalogue). It's important to view cloud capacity from a tenant services perspective to allow the business to step away from the technology silo view discussed previously and to understand the quantity of services they can deliver.

Network Model

The network model provides a view of the capacity from the perspective of the building blocks that make up the topology-related aspects of the tenant's service. For example, Chapter 10 introduced the Layer 2 separation building block. In the network model, this will be implemented as a VLAN. From an Ethernet standards perspective, you know that you have a maximum of 4096 VLANs (although this is being addressed with a recently announced Cisco/VMware VXLAN proposal) that can be used in any Layer 2 domain. If you chose to implement a vBlock with Cisco Nexus 7000 acting as the aggregation layer, any Unified Compute System (UCS) that connects to that Nexus 7000 connects to the same Layer 2 domain and so must share this pool of 4096 VLANs.

The previous limits can be seen as a capacity limitation from a provisioning point of view; the provisioning systems can only create 4096 VLANs. The performance of the Nexus 7000, CPU and throughput for example, is also a capacity limit, but from the perspective of service assurance, you can continue to add load to the Nexus until at a certain threshold the performance of all resources will be impacted. We will refer to provisioning and capacity limitations as static and dynamic limitations, respectively. The network itself is also continuing to be virtualized within the hypervisor with applications such as the Cisco Nexus1000v Distributed Virtual Switch (DVS) and VMware vShield (to name two), which means that the traditional boundary between compute and network is disappearing from a capacity management perspective.[1] Table 12-2 illustrates a capacity model for some example network building blocks.

Chapter 2, "Cloud Design Patterns and Use Cases," presented the HTTP/HTTPS load balancer design pattern. To provision and activate a single instance of this pattern that is accessed through the Internet, we would need one VLAN, one port profile, a single load balancer context, and the use of shared Internet Virtual Routing and Forwarding (VRF). Based on a performance baseline, collected by a hypothetical performance management system, you see that each instance will "typically" introduce a 1 percent load on the Nexus 7000 across both the backplane and the CPU (this is just an illustration). This means that the main limiting factor for new service is the load balancer, so only 30 new service instances can be created as the load balancer is shared across multiple tenants. From a bursting perspective, however, given that the two performance building blocks that have been chosen are well within their limits, there should be no issue supporting existing services' SLAs.

Table 12-2 *Example - Network Model Capacity Model*

Physical Building Block	Logical Building Block	Limitation*	Used/Available
Nexus 7000	Layer 2 separation (VLAN)	4096	3096/1000
Nexus 7000	Layer 3 separation (VRF)	200	100/100
Nexus 7000	Performance (CPU)	75%	40%/100
Nexus 7000	Performance (backplane throughput)	75%	20%/100
Cisco Application Control Engine (ACE)	Virtual session load balancer (context)	250	220/30
Nexus 1000v	Layer 2 separation (port profile)	2048	2000/48

*Limitation of devices at time of publication; current documentation should be consulted to determine current limitations.

Adding a new Cisco Application Control Engine (ACE) would allow the network domain to support an additional 18 services as this is the next capacity limit (Nexus 1000v). If a new Nexus 1000v was added at the same time, the network domain could potentially support another 250 services (the ACE is the limiting factor). Adding this amount of services would potentially impact SLAs as the performance thresholds for the Nexus 7000 CPU and backplane could be exceeded, so careful thought must be given to oversubscription of those two building blocks.

In this example, the ACE and the Nexus 1000V can be considered growth units; more can be added as more services are needed. The Nexus 7000 is not a growth unit; it is the central switch that interconnects all components. When it hits a static of dynamic limitation, a new POD would need to be deployed.

Compute Model

The compute model provides a view of the capacity from the perspective of the building blocks that make up the virtual and physical machines related to the tenant's service. You will have the same mix of static and dynamic building blocks used for the fulfillment and assurance processes; however, the boundary between these becomes less clear in this domain. For example, although you can say that, as a rule of thumb, a UCS B200 blade should support 30 virtual machines, it of course depends on the resources that those virtual machines consume that will make the difference. Thirty virtual machines implementing database servers will be different than 30 virtual desktops. As you begin to factor in control plane mechanisms, such as VMware Distributed Resource Scheduler (DRS), which can balance workloads within an ESX cluster based on load, the complexity of managing some of the values outlined in Table 12-3 becomes apparent. Table 12-3 illustrates a capacity model for some example compute building blocks.

Table 12-3 *Example - Compute Model Capacity Model*

Physical Building Block	Logical Building Block	Limitation*	Used/Available
Cisco UCS B200 Blade	Virtual machines	30	15/15
Cisco UCS B200 Blade	Performance (CPU)	75%	—
Cisco UCS	Layer 2 separation (VLAN)	1024	1000/24
ESX Cluster	Virtual machines per ESX cluster	1280	60/1220

*Limitation of devices at time of publication; current documentation should be consulted to determine current limitations.

Rather than focus on all these attributes, consider the Layer 2 separation building block. Cisco UCS extends the VLAN into the compute chassis, but currently supports only 1024 VLANs. After you factor in internal VLANs and any used for storage VSANs, you probably have 900 workable VLANs that can be used in ESX port groups. The previous examples stated that the network topology could support an additional 30 services; however, you can see that, in fact, you can only support an additional 24 services, because this is the limit that the UCS system will support, unless another UCS system is added. Adding another UCS system is not the solution here, unless it connects to a separate Layer 2 domain. In which case, the VLANs can be reused, but you cannot share services at Layer 2 because the VLANs will conflict. The same service running on both UCS systems, in this case, must be interconnected at the IP subnet level. You can see that there is a complex relationship between some of the compute and network models, and this is managed in the cloud platform capacity model.

Storage Model

The storage model provides a view of the capacity from the perspective of the building blocks that make up the storage-related aspects of the tenant's service. Storage building blocks can be complex to manage, because they might present different views depending on which element you look at. For example, viewing a Fibre Channel logical unit (LUN) that has been provisioned with "thin" provisioning from the ESX server perspective will show a different level of consumption than looking at the same LUN from the storage array perspective. So, it's important to understand what element will provide the most accurate view. Table12-4 illustrates a capacity model for some example storage building blocks.

Table 12-4 *Example - Storage Model Capacity Model*

Physical Building Block	Logical Building Block	Limitation*	Used/Available
EMC CLARiiON storage array	LUN (FC)	16384	300/16084
EMC CLARiiON storage array	LUN performance (IOPS)	20 ms	—
EMC CLARiiON storage array	Gold LUN	16384	100/16084
EMC CLARiiON storage array	Gold LUN .vmdk	15	14/1

*Limitation of devices at time of publication, current documentation should be consulted to determine any current limitations.

Focusing again on the HTTP/HTTPS load balancer design pattern described in Chapter 2, you can assume that the web server virtual machines could require a Gold LUN to store the operating system virtual disks and a Silver LUN for the data virtual disk. You can see that a single Gold LUN has a limit imposed on it of 15 virtual disks per Gold LUN to preserve I/O requirements. Fortunately, the CLARiiON will support a large amount of LUNs (depending on sizing), so the storage should not be a limiting factor. However, unless storage is reclaimed, the need for new storage continues to grow exponentially and therefore can be a considerable factor later in the cloud platform's lifetime.

Data Center Facilities Model

The facilities model provides a view of the capacity from the perspective of the building blocks that make up the physical facilities that support the physical data center equipment and tenant services. Traditionally, the capacity of the data center facility, in terms of the consumption and generation of power, heating, cooling, and so on, is modeled at the rack level and aggregated up into a room view and then the data center itself; however, in recent years, the "green" data center view has started to look at the total input/output of the data center. Table 12-5 illustrates a capacity model for some example facilities building blocks.

Table 12-5 *Example - Facilities Model Capacity Model*

Physical Building Block	Logical Building Block	Limit	Used/Available
Space	Available rack units in DC	N/A	2000/500
Cooling	Rack Cooling Index	75%	—
Connectivity	Number of available 10-GB ports	100	75/25

The Data Center Maturity Model proposed by Green Grid (www.thegreengrid.org/en/Global/Content/white-papers/DataCenterMaturityModel)[2] proposes some dynamic building blocks for general green IT. The Rack Cooling Index (RCI), for example, is a numerical value for air inlet temperature consistency and can be high or low (if applicable). For example, if every server is receiving air at the desired temperature, the result is an RCI of 100 percent. If half of the servers receive inlet air that is above the desired temperature, the RCI (high) is 50 percent. A Level 2 maturity suggests an RCI of 75 percent across all racks, which in turn drives the physical placement of servers, their efficiency, and the overall design of the cooling system. Making capacity-planning decisions without understanding the RCI metric desired will inversely impact the overall efficiency of the data center and that value/cost balance discussed previously. Placing workloads on a physical server will increase the load and therefore the heat output and the cooling required, so again we see a complex relationship between compute and facilities capacity.

Cloud Platform Capacity Model

The Cloud Platform Capacity model provides a holistic view of the capacity and demand forecast across the entire platform. Using the demand forecasts from the "business" for cloud service adoption and the service catalogue as primary inputs, it will aggregate the data from all domains that are considered part of the cloud platform and identify where capacity issues exist, which is easy to say but not easy to implement. It's fair to say that today, this type of complex capacity management is only available to those with large budgets and resources available to them; however, like all technology issues, time will simplify the solution and provide a more cost-effective solution. So, the principles outlined in this chapter should be viewed as guidance rather than explicit recommendations. Tools such as VMware Capacity IQ or EMC Unified Infrastructure Manager can provide domain views, whereas tools from performance management companies like Infovista or Netuitive[3] can give a broader "cloud platform" view.

Demand Forecasting

Demand forecasting is the activity of estimating the quantity of IT services that consumers will purchase or use. This data is then used to ensure that capacity can be met both in the short and long term. Demand forecasting typically involves quantitative techniques and methods such as trending to determine future demand. Trends describe capacity activity that has taken place in the past through to the present. A trend might show that demand is increasing, decreasing, or remaining the same. One of the biggest challenges in the cloud is that because of the on-demand nature of cloud requests, demand can be viewed as totally nondeterministic, that is, it is driven by a consumer's needs, which in a public cloud at least has no relationship to other consumers' demands. What is seen as a trend one month might simply be a never-repeated pattern. This means that additional analysis is required on top of the trending data to understand the actual patterns of cloud usage and to demand management.

Demand forecasting looks at capacity from two perspectives, managing in-flight peak capacity and expected demand. In-flight capacity can be viewed as the usable capacity of a domain, which is comprised of active and idle/spare capacity. Active capacity can be viewed as the average usage of a domain, the average bandwidth consumed through a Nexus 7000, the average CPU of an ESX host, and so on. Idle/spare capacity is the remaining capacity that hasn't been stranded or allocated as safety buffer; Figure 12-3 illustrates these concepts.

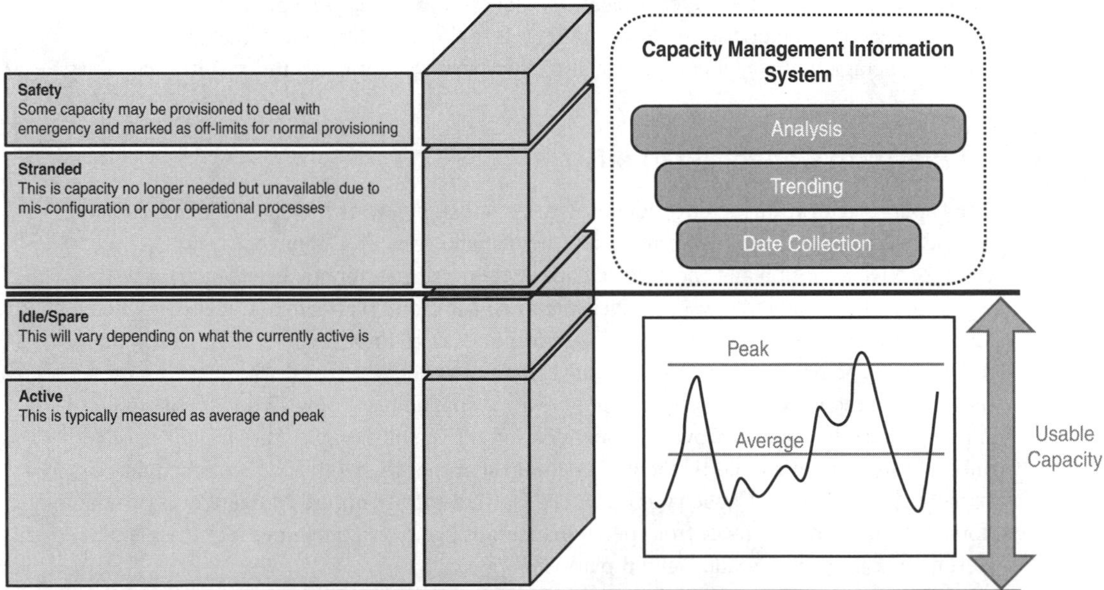

Figure 12-3 *Demand- and Forecast-Based Capacity Management*

Good operational and capacity management procedures should remove the need for a safety buffer and also highlight and reclaim any stranded resources. However, in reality, these types of capacity limits can take up a large proportion of the usable capacity, and many platform owners today simply "live with it." From a cloud provider's perspective, this is simply too high a cost to bear and will really impact the optimization. From an ITIL perspective, all this data is stored and managed in the Capacity Management Information System (CMIS), which acts as the system of record for all resource details. The CMIS can be comprised of many different systems, and in this case, the data in these systems will be federated to provide the capacity manager with a holistic view of all the data relating to capacity of the cloud.

Capacity management can be looked at from a proactive and reactive perspective. The goal of proactive in-flight capacity management is really to ensure that peak demands can always be met without compromising SLAs and maximizing the usable capacity, therefore minimizing spare and stranded capacity. Meeting the peak demand is done by looking at the trends, extrapolating the average peak, and forecasting what the future peak "might" be. Determining the average peak is relatively simple and really just part of statistical analysis. As long as you have enough usable capacity to support the average peak or your SLAs can cope with oversubscribed capacity, this might be the only metric you need. If you take a look at how VMware CapacityIQ[4] calculates the amount of remaining virtual machines for a given cluster, you can see an example of how this statistical baseline can be implemented. CapacityIQ calculates the remaining virtual machine capacity by using the remaining physical capacity divided by the average virtual machine demand for CPU and average memory consumed:

Remaining VM CPU = Remaining CPU Capacity / CPU Demand for Average VM

Remaining VM Memory = Remaining Memory Capacity / Memory Consumed for Average VM

Whichever of these two values is smaller determines how many more virtual machines can be deployed. For example, consider the following scenario for a cluster. An ESX cluster has the following:

- Idle/spare (remaining) CPU capacity of 6 GHz.
- Idle/spare (remaining) memory capacity is 9 GB.
- The average virtual machine has 1.5 GHz CPU demand and 4 GB memory consumed. We can make the assumption that these values represent the average new virtual machine's configuration that will be deployed in this cluster.

If two virtual machines exist in the cluster, there is enough CPU capacity for four virtual machines, but only enough memory capacity to support two virtual machines. The problem with this view is that, although it does provide some level of forecasting, it will be far more accurate where the demand is consistent and less so when demand is variable (that is, driven by a self-service model). CapacityIQ attempts to address this problem by aggregating data into what VMware call rollups. A *rollup* is an average value across a time period. A daily rollup is a number representing the average of the averages for a particular day. A weekly rollup represents the average across all seven days in the week. CapacityIQ provides rollups based on daily, weekly, monthly, quarterly, and yearly time periods. An alternative approach is to start applying more advanced models such as predictive analysis. An example of this is Netuitive, which builds on performance data and adds what it calls a behavioral learning engine to provide the context and trends to this raw data. Unfortunately, neither of these solutions will help the provider if a sudden demand spike means that it runs out of available physical capacity (even if it has safety capacity). Providers should expect this to occur and streamline their procurement process to ensure that these issues are handled as quickly and efficiently as possible.

Expected demand is typically a more qualitative measure coming from a product development group in telecommunications companies or from a business relationship manager in an ITIL-aligned IT department. Expected demand is a view of what is believed to be the uptake of a service prior to or after it is made available in the service catalogue. This data can be factored into the overall demand forecast, but care should be taken to ensure that the values provided are accurate as they can skew the overall capacity requirements.

From a reactive point of view, the provider now has a capacity issue. The proactive capacity management processes have, to some extent, failed, and now the provider is in danger of breaching its SLAs and impacting new requests. If the provider has spare resources such as some safety capacity, this can be used to provide a short-term respite to the problem, but if there is no additional capacity, some workloads must be prioritized over other workloads to ensure that some customers' SLAs are still met. For example, if tenant 1 has a high SLA or service grade, its workloads need to be prioritized over tenants that have a lower SLA or service grade when there is contention and no available spare capacity. This prioritization exercise can occur automatically. For example, in a VMware environment, resource pools can be used to manage resources within a cluster, physical host, or at the VM level, and prioritization is done by the Vsphere control plane without external intervention. For other resources, such as storage- or network-based components, some manual intervention will be required. Clearly, reactive capacity management will have an impact, so when possible, reactive management should be the exception and not the norm.

Procurement in the Cloud

The capacity model has identified that additional fixed capacity is required, and this means that, for example, additional compute blades are required. This will typically require capital expenditure, which in turn will require the procurement process to adjust fixed capacity to meet the expected demand. We say *typically* because many vendors, Cisco included, are looking at different financial models to support a public or private cloud that involves operational expenditure rather than CAPEX; however, for the purposes of this section, we will consider only the CAPEX model. Figure 12-4 illustrates the general impacts of capacity management. In an ideal world, fixed capacity meets the demand. If the expected demand is set too high, there will be a lot of waste. If the expected demand is set to low, there are peaks of resource requirement that cannot be met, which will impact SLAs and the experience of new customers. If there is zero procurement time, that is, the physical resources are in stock and already installed, it is possible to cope with demand seamlessly. However, the reality is that typically the hardware can take between three weeks and several months to be procured and be made available for service, in which case, SLAs and new cloud services will be impacted.

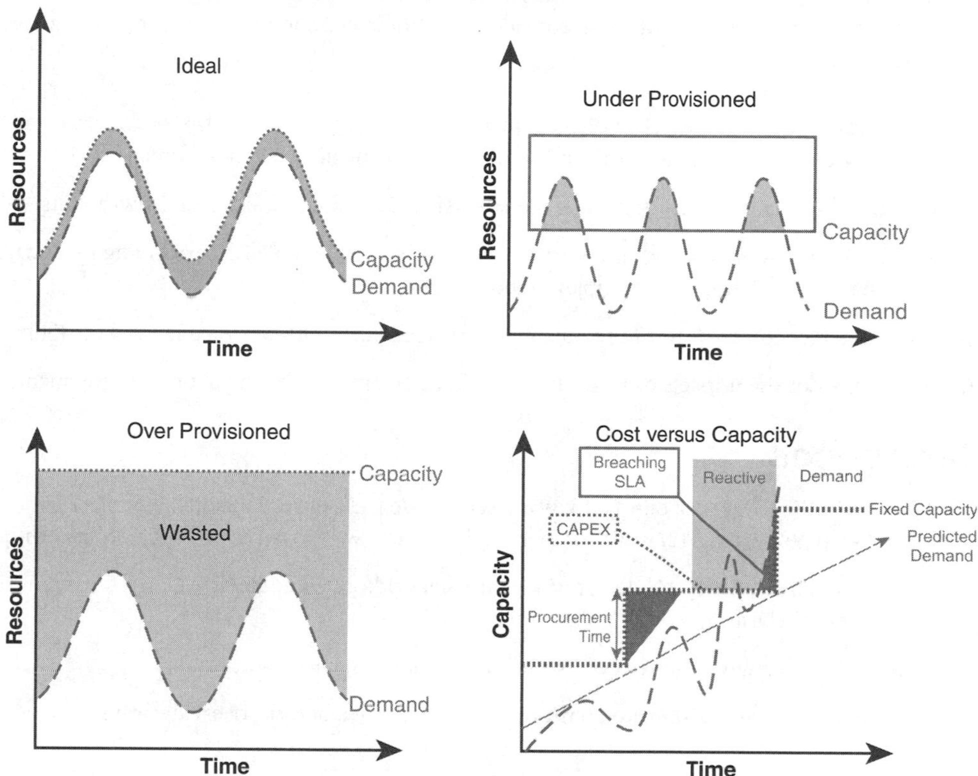

Figure 12-4 *Consequences of Capacity Management*

The cost-versus-capacity model shown in Figure 12-4 summarizes the main issues with capacity management in a cloud environment:

- The predicted demand is drawn from the business forecast and trends based on current usage.
- If the fixed capacity is built in line with predicted demand, as actual demand exceeds both the predicted demand and the fixed capacity, SLAs will be breached and the provision and activation of new services will be impacted. If the procurement time for new equipment is too long, this might incur SLA penalties or the loss of tenant contracts.
- Reactive capacity management is not a good thing as it leads to SLA breaches and poor user experience, and so should it be minimized when possible.

Summary

There is no silver bullet for capacity management in a typical data center, so when cloud services are deployed that require a self-service, real-time, on-demand provisioning approach, it gets harder as the demand model is much more challenging to understand. A number of key aspects need to be considered in implementing capacity management for a cloud solution:

- Implement strong capacity management processes that consider the entire platform service capacity from a holistic manner but also consider business forecasts.
- Build domain models that track the key service building blocks and growth units.
- Build measurement and monitoring systems that are capable of performing predictive analysis to extrapolate complex trends.
- Consider forecasts from the business, but treat them with reasonable level of doubt.
- Consider the impacts of poor demand management and the impact on procurement.

References

[1] Nexus 7000 VDC scalability, at www.cisco.com/en/US/prod/collateral/switches/ps9441/ps9402/ps9512/White_Paper_Tech_Overview_Virtual_Device_Contexts.html.

[2] Data Center Maturity Model, at www.thegreengrid.org/~/media/Tools/DataCenterMaturityModelv1_0.ashx?lang=en.

[3] Netuitive, at www.netuitive.com/solutions/capacity-management.html.

[4] CapacityIQ, at www.vmware.com/products/vcenter-capacityiq/overview.html.

Chapter 13

Providing the Right Cloud User Experience

Upon completing this chapter, you will be able to understand the following:

- The basic challenges, requirements, and building blocks for the cloud user interface
- How to provide user self-care
- Best practices around integration with other systems
- Providing an open API

This chapter provides a detailed overview of how Infrastructure as a Service (IaaS) capacity can be measured and managed.

The Cloud User Interface

One of the differentiators of a cloud service, as opposed to a traditional hosted or IT service, is the self-service characteristic. Cloud consumers are provided with an interface that allows them to design, approve, use, and monitor their cloud services. One thing to bear in mind is that the people who design, approve, use, and monitor a cloud service for any given consumer will probably be different, with different skill levels and different interface requirements. If the user interface is poor, the user experience is poor and the more likely the user will require additional support or will choose to look elsewhere. Figure 13-1 illustrates the major roles involved in the buying, designing, and use of the cloud service.

A *buyer* can be defined as someone who is involved in the procurement of a cloud service. The *designers* are involved in designing and releasing the service. The *users* are the end users of the service and/or the cloud portal. The portal itself can, depending on its complexity, simply expose Fulfillment, Assurance, and Billing (FAB) content, or it could contain additional functionality, such as a service catalogue and process engines that implement supporting FAB processes. The oval "service" icon in Figure 13-1 refers to the application service that is being presented in the portal rather than the cloud service that is being designed and used by the cloud consumer. Table 13-1 defines the consumer roles in more detail.

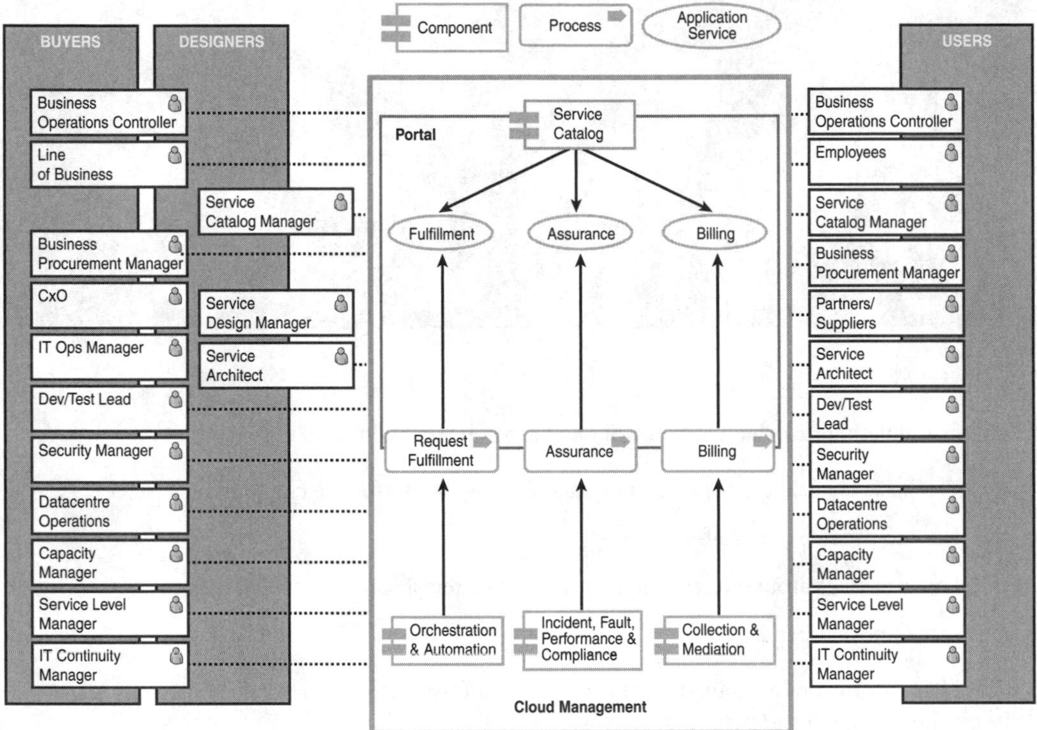

Figure 13-1 *Cloud Portal Buyers, Designers, and Users*

Using Table 13-1, you can see that many views can to be provided by the portal:

- A commercial view that provides business users with data regarding assets, costs, and performance
- An operational view that provides IT staff with access to view and modify the service instance, service data, and access to any related assurance systems
- A tenant view that provides users access to create, modify, and delete the service instance and associated service data
- A design view that allows direct access to the service data (that is, service catalogue) that is normally available only to IT operations and the service design community

Some of this capability might exist in systems today. For example, incident management systems will exist in an IT organization, and so should the interface and data of the existing systems be exposed in the cloud portal? Clearly, there is a requirement for users of a service to see data related to that service, either directly or indirectly; however, at the same time, not all data should be shown, so there is a need to filter the data being presented.

Table 13-1 *Cloud Consumer Roles*

Role	Primary Involvement	Description
Line of Business (LOB)	Purchasing	This is effectively the end user of the service and the group responsible for "paying" for the services.
Business operations controller	Purchasing/using	The business controller is part of the LOB and is responsible for managing the business process associated with the cloud service. Can use the portal API interface to integrate directly with the Business Process Execution Language (BPEL) engine and run on service performance.
Business procurement	Purchasing/using	The business procurement is part of the LOB and is responsible for managing cost and capacity from the business service perspective. Can use the portal to generate reports on assets and costs and can act as an approver for new requests.
CxO	Purchasing	The CxO (CIO, CFO, CTO) has overall responsibility for the strategic direction, sourcing, and investment models.
IT operations manager	Purchasing	Overall responsibility for all IT services running in the private or public cloud.
Dev/test lead	Purchasing/using	Overall responsibility for all development and test environments. Can use the portal to generate reports on development and test assets, compliance, and performance.
Security manager	Purchasing/using	Overall responsibility for all service data and system security. Can use the portal to generate reports on compliance and posture.
IT continuity manager	Purchasing/using	Overall responsibility for all service availability. Can use the portal to generate reports on availability and run continuity tests.
Data Center Operations	Purchasing/using	Overall responsibility for management of the service. Can use the portal to generate reports, update tickets, and perform simple operations on services.
Capacity manager	Purchasing/using	Overall responsibility for service and fixed capacity. Can use the portal to generate capacity and asset reports and reactive capacity processes.

Table 13-1 *Cloud Consumer Roles*

Role	Primary Involvement	Description
Service-level manager	Purchasing/using	Overall responsibility for meeting service levels agreed with the LOB. Can use the portal for Service Level Management (SLM)reporting and reactive processes.
Service design manager	Designing	Overall responsibility for the design of all aspects of the service, prior to it being "in service."
Service architect	Designing/using	Overall responsibility for building the service definition by combining business requirements and technical building blocks. Can use the portal to build initial services.
Service catalogue manager	Designing/using	Overall responsibility for ensuring that the service catalogue accurately reflects the cloud services that can be offered and align with the overall service portfolio.
Employees	Using	Users of the service will use the portal to create service instances, to perform basic operations, and to perform monitoring and reporting of the service.
Partner/supplier	Using	Can use the service as well to add value to the overall business.

Providing User Self-Care

Providing the right level of self-care is critical if the user is to receive a good customer experience. Any self-service/care portal should be able to support the same sort of experience that users are provided with in the web generally. If you look at Yahoo! mail or iGoogle, a user can arrange different types of content in their web view. The same should be the case for the cloud portal, allowing tenants to add fulfillment, assurance, and billing content as long as they are entitled to see such content as a critical part of any solution. In most cases, providers have three options:

- Build a portal using a standard framework, such IBM Websphere
- Buy a cloud portal
- Use an aggregator/broker

Of course, the provider might already have a portal and if it can support more interactive usage and has built to allow additional cloud content to be added, this is indeed a cheaper solution; however, in most cases, the provider will choose to bring something new into this area as it is a massive differentiator. How a cloud provider offers its services and the ease at which tenants can order, manage, and view data about these services will often influence how long a tenant stays with a provider, so ultimately for a public cloud, this will affect revenues, and for private clouds, this will affect the influence an IT department has.

We don't consider building a cloud portal in this chapter, because there are many volumes that discuss building portals and it is beyond the scope of this book. Instead, we will focus on the second and third options, namely, buying a cloud portal and using an aggregator.

A cloud portal should promote two capabilities above all else: flexibility and security. In a public cloud, of course, the multitenancy capability must also be considered, but this is a fundamental requirement across all aspects of a public cloud. Figure 13-2 illustrates a summary screen from the Cisco Cloud Portal (CCP), a recent Cisco acquisition from NewScale. In the figure, you can see a summary of financial data across a tenant organization, giving an excellent summary for a business manager or a financial controller; however, not the right data is presented for a security manager. The various "bits" (portlets) of content are controlled through an entitlement policy, but the users are allowed to arrange their view as they see fit and can add, delete, and move content as required. This fulfills one of the key requirements of a cloud portal—flexibility, allowing the provider and tenant to build views that make sense to them rather than being offered a single view.

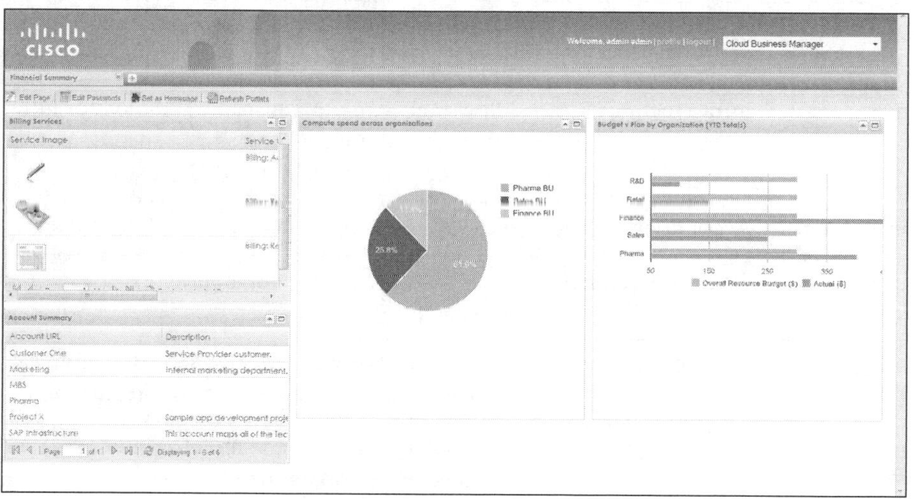

Figure 13-2 *Example Portal*

Content in CCP is provided in three ways:

- Cisco-authored service content such as service definitions, entitlement, and request orchestration logic that allows users to submit requests to perform standard cloud functions such as creating a virtual machine. This content comes preloaded in the catalogue and is exposed in the portal through a standardized set of portlets.

- By allowing the provider to build its own service definitions, entitlement, and request orchestration logic, which again is exposed through the same set of standardized portlets used for the Cisco-authored content.
- CCP supports the inclusion of Java Specification Review (JSR) 186 and 286 complement portlets. This allows not only third-party content to be easily added to the portal, but also allows those portlets to interact with the catalogue through the CCP API.

The second requirement of security is typically fulfilled through a combination of identity management and entitlement to ensure that the right content is available to the right user. In a multitenant environment, the identity component can be complicated by having to map roles from different organizations to a common set of "cloud" roles; however, in most cases, this is simpler to achieve if you identify who the users of the system are likely to be. After this has been done, the next step will involve identifying the policies that control what portal functionality is accessible for a given role. Table 13-2 illustrates some common policies.

Table 13-2 *Common Policies for Portal Functionality Control*

Role	Functionality	Description
All	Login	Allows a user to log in to the portal; not necessarily required for all portal API actions
All	Announcements	Allows a user to view all new announcements targeted at his user ID, organization, or all general users
Admin users	Infrastructures	Allows a user to view, manage, and monitor infrastructure components hosted in a specific virtual data center or point of delivery (POD)
Business users	Accounting/billing	Allows a user to view and monitor billing data
All users	Event management	Allows a user to view and monitor event/fault data associated to his services
All users	Service management	Allows a user to view, configure, and operate cloud services associated to his VDC or organization
All users	Task management	Allows a user to view and monitor tasks associated with his service operations
Admin and security managers	Compliance management	Allows a user to view and monitor service compliance across his organization, VDC, and/or services
Admin and service-level managers	Service-level management	Allows a user to view and monitor service levels across his organization, VDC, and/or services

CCP, for example, provides a Role-Based Access Control (RBAC) model that extends to individual portlets so that explicit allow/deny permission can be given to any portal or system, providing the administrator with very-fine-grained content control.

If the provider or consumer feels that portal development or purchasing is not what he is interested in, one alternative is to use an aggregator, which will provide all the portal aspects as well as support the key functions of fulfillment, assurance, and billing in a secure and flexible manner. RightScale, a cloud aggregator, for example, offers what it calls a multicloud engine. The solution, shown in Figure 13-3, allows cloud provider services (in this case, Amazon Web Services) to be offered from a central portal or a consumer to subscribe to multiple cloud providers.

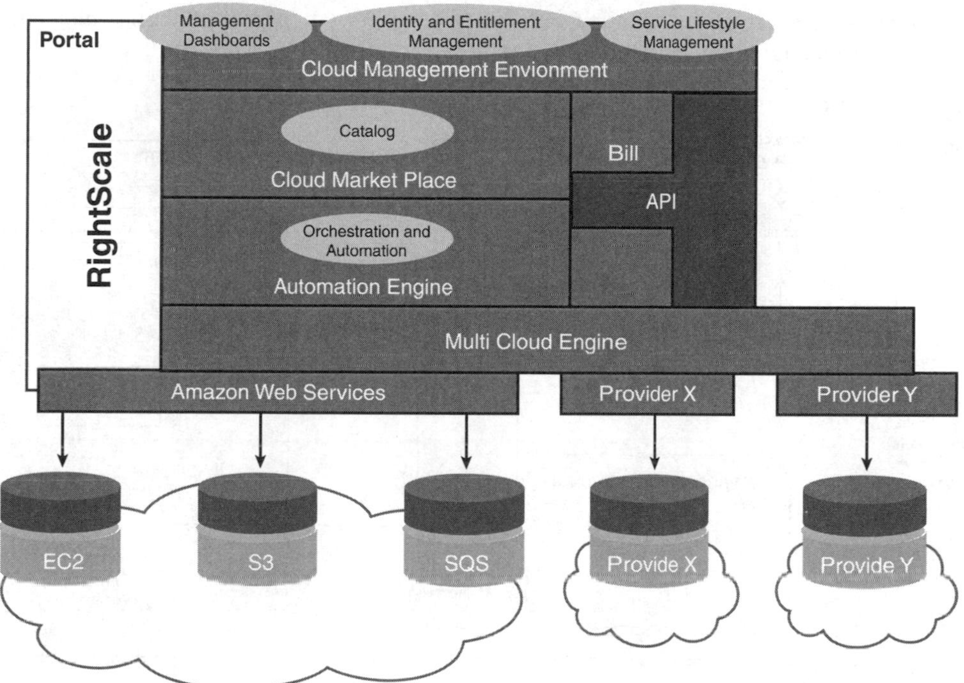

Figure 13-3 *RightScale Architecture*

At the time of publication, RightScale offer a premium service aimed at "single groups deploying business-critical applications in the cloud" for $1000/month, with a set-up fee of $4000, where all the user experience is centered on the RightScale portal using the previously shown architecture. This allows the consumer to consume services from different providers transparently, but it also means that as long as the provider offers a well-defined open API (more later), it they can leverage this solution.

The "integration tax" or cost of integration is something that any systems integrator or experienced architect/designer is familiar with, so adopting to use an aggregator from either the consumer or provider standpoint can be a strategy that not only provides a pleasant and consistent user experience, but also can be considerably cheaper.

Integration

If you must integrate as demonstrated throughout this book, there is a need to integrate many systems to provide consistent views to the cloud consumers and operational staff. There are many integrated design patterns. We have already discussed a few, but in many cases, the systems that make up a cloud solution are integrated through point-to-point interfaces, either open or in most cases using proprietary transport protocols and methods, as illustrated in Figure 13-4.

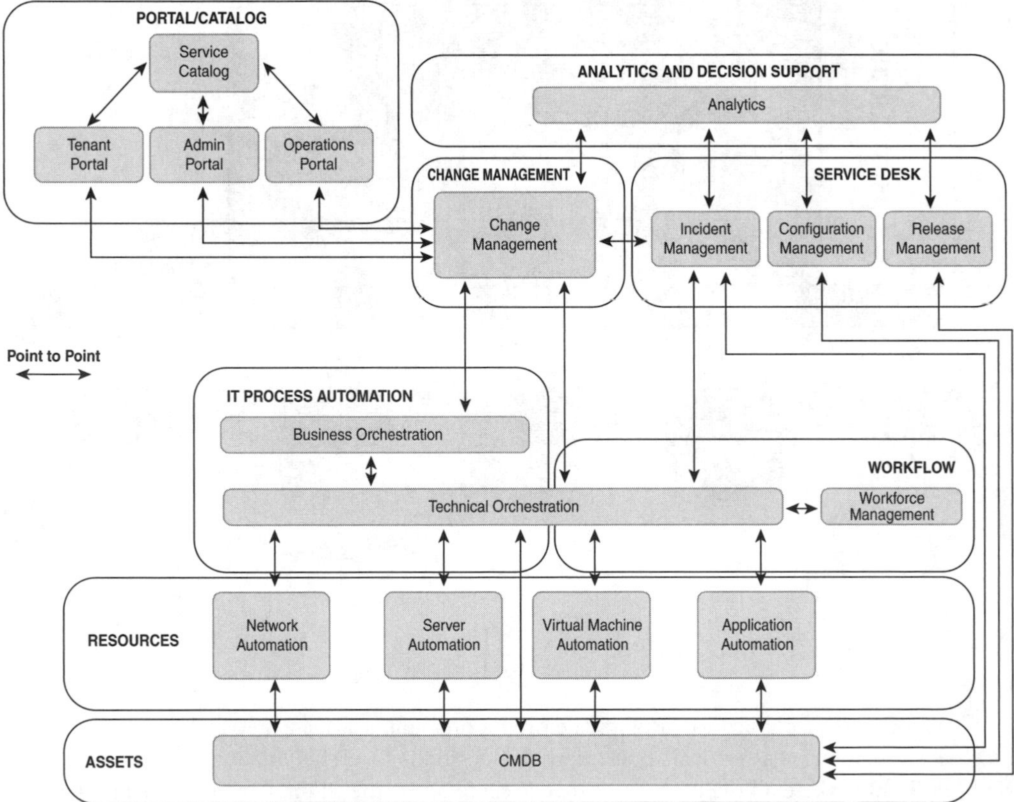

Figure 13-4 *Cloud Integration*

The main issue with integration in this manner is that as the underlying infrastructure or the management platform itself evolves, this impacts many systems. Consider changing the change management system shown in Figure 13-4; this impacts portals, automation, analytics, and service desk tools. If the change manager supports a different data model, some form of semantic integration is required to convert the data objects in the other systems to something that the new change manager can understand. This is an example of tightly coupled systems, each of which depend on as well as impact the other. Because a key capability of the cloud is agility, a key capability of the cloud management platform is loose coupling, removing the dependencies between systems.

Loose coupling, at least at the system/interface level, can be achieved through the deployment of an enterprise service bus (ESB) that will arbitrate between the various interfaces. In Figure 13-5, you can see that we have effectively decoupled the systems that manage the services from each other and the systems that manage the resources by implementing an ESB.

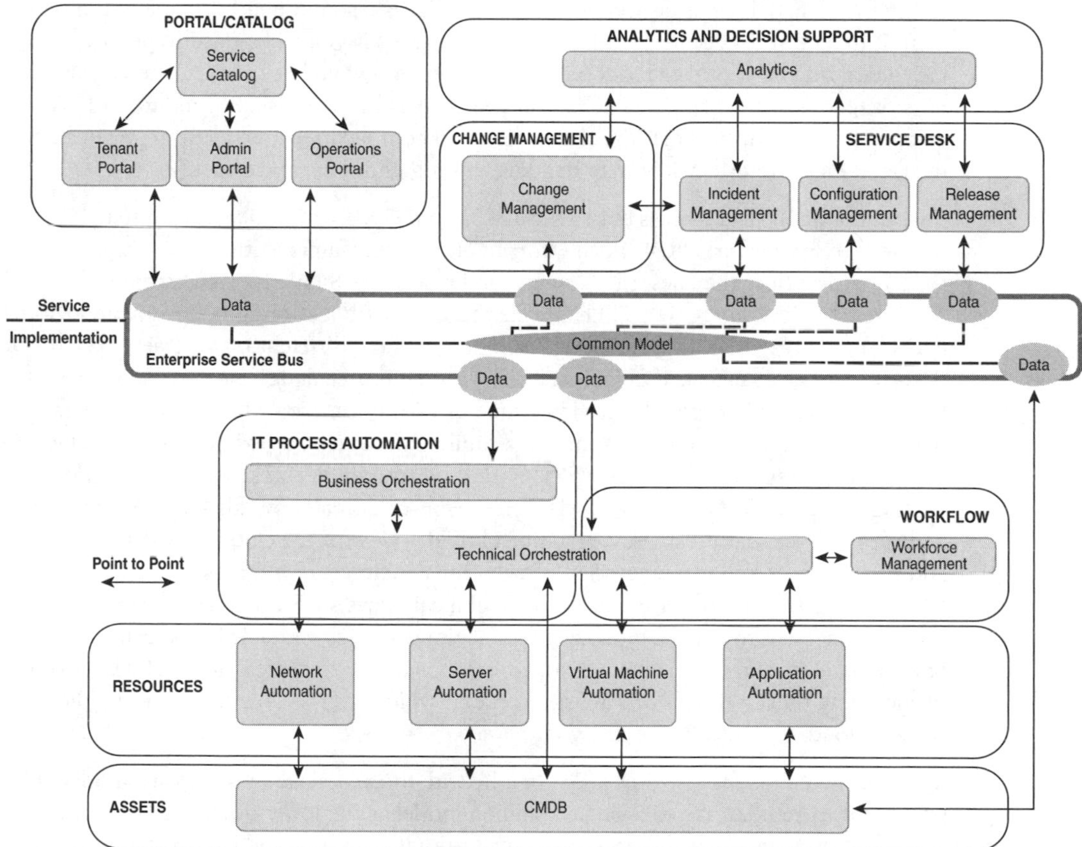

Figure 13-5 *Decoupling Service from the Implementation*

This means that if we now choose to replace the change manager, instead of having to modify/build multiple point-to-point interfaces, we can now simply change the interface between the change manager and the ESB and the other systems are not impacted. You could also add a new virtual machine manager, such as Red Hat Virtualization Manager, and it would not impact any of the service management tools. You could argue that it's the IT process automation layer that is providing the separation between the service management layer and the systems that implement specific technology solution; however, typically an ESB does much more than simply translate one interface to another. In this case, we chose to implement a common model that allows us to translate the data coming in and the data needed to go out using a common model as the translation mechanism. If, for example, a user creates a virtual machine (VM) with a high-availability (HA) option checked, the VM will be created on an ESX hypervisor cluster that supports HA. If the high-availability option is not selected, the VM will be deployed on a KVM hypervisor cluster. This decision as to which cluster to use could be done at the orchestration level. However, converting the service option to a set of XML data and presenting it to the right virtual machine manager could be a complex task, so it might be simpler to implement it in an ESB to do the translation. What happens if you add a third hypervisor or the underlying API, or data models change? Then, you would need to change your business or technical workflows, which again could be a complex task. So, adding an ESB and a common model means that the abstraction and complexity of the cloud service can be managed far more effectively than building this logic into complex workflows.

Several common data models exist. The TM Forum (TMF) introduced the System Integration Framework (SID)[1] in an effort to allow telecommunications service providers to standardize how they describe services and resources. Similarly, the Distributed Management Task Force (DMTF) has done the same with its Common Information Model (CIM) standard.[2] CIM was originally developed to allow different management systems to describe the same managed objects such as a server, router, and so on and is now one of the most commonly used schemas in commercial Configuration Management Databases (CMDB). CIM and SID contain some very similar concepts in terms of modeling logical and physical resources; however, SID is both broader and less prescriptive than CIM. SID in its entirety models customer, service, and resource domains but also markets, products, and suppliers so that it can provide a much broader view of the cloud provider/consumer and the products and resources they offer to the consumer. If you look at the current CIM schema (2.29), you have much more technical views such as devices, systems, application. That's not to say that you can't model cloud service with CIM. You can and we have done it, but any given cloud tends to touch many nontechnical areas. SID is capable of modeling these services in a holistic context, which is applicable for both a public or a private cloud.

Whether you chose to use SID, CIM, or a hybrid, or even make up your own model, it is important to standardize on a single common model as the lower down the stack you proceed, the more need you will find for point-to-point interfaces and to support proprietary data structures. This is mainly because of the lack of any standards at this level, which is a common issue. Several years ago, the TMF introduced the Multi-Technology Operations Systems Interface (MTOSI) standard, which attempted to provide a common interface across resource and service management.[3] It is fair to say that the TMF had limited success with this initiative as some vendors have adopted MTOSI whereas other have simply ignored it. Many telcos today mandate an MTOSI interface, which is increasing the adoption of this standard; however, below MTOSI still lurk proprietary nonstandard interfaces. There is a tendency in IT architecture to simplify, simplify, and simplify. However, the effort involved in this can be significant, and the results (other than something academically correct) can be underwhelming. A suggestion is to make sure that you abstract between the service and the resource layers, but accept that there will be a need to support proprietary point-to-point interfaces and architect/design your solution to provide the right level of flexibility and abstraction to the cloud consumers.

Providing an Open API

If you look at the success of Amazon Web Services (AWS) today, you can probably associate it with a number of things:

1. It was the first real commercial IaaS provider.
2. It continues to develop its service offerings as the market matures.
3. It offers an easy-to-use user interface.
4. It provides programmatic access to its services through an application programming interface (API).

You might argue the order of this list, but the fact that developers—both commercial and those consuming AWS services directly—can automate and manage services through an API has certainly helped establish AWS as one of, if not *the* premier cloud providers today. If we look at the AWS Elastic Compute (EC2) API,[4] you can see it roughly categorizes API actions in

- Actions to do with the configuration of an EC2 instance, such as creating, modifying, and deleting items
- Actions to do with operating the EC2 instance, such as monitoring, starting, stopping, and so on
- Actions to do with getting data about the EC2 instance, such as data on the snapshots or the DHCP configuration

So, while AWS provides a management console to manage EC2 instances, a whole host of developers have written applications to build and monitor EC2 instances with little effort. If you combine this with other Amazon services, such as Simple Queue Service (SQS) and its associated API, complete applications can be built and maintained without user interactions. Why is this important? This goes to the overall user experience; as users become more comfortable with cloud services, they want to do things more quickly and efficiently. This is what automation is really about, and if you provide a programmatic API to allow more efficient service provisioning, activation, and monitoring, the overall cloud platform will be more successful. As we begin to examine more advanced use cases such as cloud bursting, where workloads are dynamically added to meet demand, the use of an API is mandatory to allow a system to scale the application automatically without user intervention.

The standard for today's API is in the form of Representational State Transfer (REST or RESTful) calls. For many years, Simple Object Access Protocol (SOAP) was the preferred method. It uses HTTP/HTTPS and exposes a set of methods as URIs, and typical responses are in XML. RESTful APIs, on the other hand, add an element of using standardized URIs and give importance to the HTTP verb used (that is, GET/POST/PUT and so on). REST can be seen as a different architectural style rather than a new technology; nevertheless, many of the current cloud APIs provided by vendors are written in a RESTful style.

In 2010, VMware launched its vCloud Director (vCD) application to support the deployment of a private cloud on top of an ESX/ESXi infrastructure. vCD supported a RESTful API based on the VMware vCloud API and schema. The vCloud schema exposes numerous objects that have been discussed previously—an organization representing the cloud consumer, a virtual data center representing the container of services, and a virtual application (vApp) representing, in many cases, the service. A sample of the vCloud API methods relating to the service are as follows:

- POST <vapp-parent-element-uri>
- POST <vapp-uri>/power/action/{powerOn, powerOff}
- POST <vapp-uri>/power/action/{reset, suspend}
- GET <vapp-uri>

As with AWS, you can see there are operations to configure, operate, and retrieve data. So, whether you choose to implement a SOAP- or REST-based web service is probably more of an architectural decision. The key point is to make sure that your API allows the consumer to configure, operate, and retrieve data on his services, whatever building blocks the service might be comprised of.

Summary

The user's cloud experience can determine whether your platform is successful or fails. When considering how to provide the right level of content to your user, focus on the following areas:

- Understand who is using your platform and what they are likely to use it for.
- Loosely couple your cloud platform to provide maximum flexibility to your users and minimize the impact of changes.
- Abstract between the cloud "service" and the actual implementation details.
- Don't get caught up in which API style to implement; just ensure that the service can be configured, operated, and managed programmatically.

References

[1] TMF System Integration Framework (SID), at www.tmforum.org/InformationFramework/1684/home.html.

[2] DMTF Common Information Model, at www.dmtf.org/standards/cim.

[3] TMF Multi-Technology Operations Systems Interface, at www.tmforum.org/MultiTechnologyOperations/2319/home.html.

[4] AWS EC2 API, at http://docs.amazonwebservices.com/AWSEC2/latest/APIReference.

Chapter 14

Adopting Cloud from a Maturity Perspective

Upon completing this chapter, you will be able to understand the following:

- What a maturity mode is and how it can be used
- How to describe a maturity model for cloud
- How to use the maturity model to evaluate an organization

This chapter provides a detailed overview of how the maturity of an organization to adopt the cloud as an IT strategy can be assessed using a maturity model.

Maturity Models

Understanding whether your organization is ready to be a cloud provider or consumer is a critical part of the process. *Cloud* is a buzzword, and there are a lot of IT executives, engineers, and people in the business community who are jumping on the cloud hype train without thinking where it will take them or the cost of the journey. Any assessment needs to cover a number of dimensions, and one of the most recognized ways of assessing maturity is using a maturity model. Chapter 3, "Data Center Architecture and Technologies," discussed maturity models and a whole host of different models exists, but the grandfather of them all is the Capability Maturity Model Integration (CMMI) model, which is shown in Figure 14-1.

The CMMI model was designed to assess an organization's process maturity by assigning one of five levels, where

- Level 1 defines an organization as having limited processes that are unreliable.
- Level 2 defines an organization that has repeatable processes used in individual projects but in a reactive manner without a holistic view.
- Level 3 defines an organization that has evolved from simple project management to more proactive organization-wide processes but typically with limited ways of measuring success or failure of these processes.

- Level 4 defines an organization that has organization-wide processes that are well controlled and measured.
- Level 5 defines an organization as having a high standard of processes that are being continually optimized, and in most cases, this is more of an aspiration than an achievable. The other area to consider is that certain processes might be more mature than others, so this model doesn't need to consider the organization holistically. It can look at individual processes, and in many cases, this gives a more realistic view of an organization.

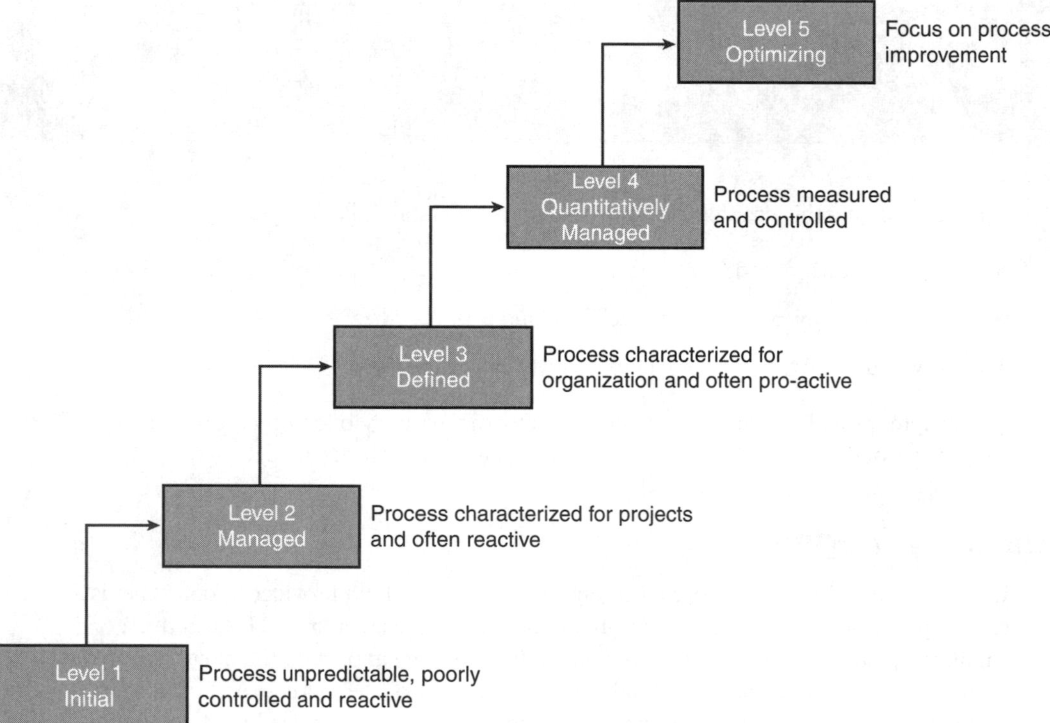

Figure 14-1 *Capability Maturity Model Integration (CMMI)*

A Cloud Maturity Model

Taking the maturity model concept and applying it to cloud have been taken further by a Cisco employee, James Urquhart,[1] and enhanced in this book. It considers six levels of maturity (described in Table 14-1) and five dimensions, which are as follows:

- The *processes* that a business run
- The *IT organization* itself
- The *infrastructure* used by the business encompassing the LAN, WAN, and data center

- The organization's *capability* to deliver IT expertise and experience
- The view of *IT by the consumer* within the business

This model is more aligned to a private cloud as a public cloud would not have the same view of the IT consumer; however, the remaining dimensions would be appropriate. Figure 14-2 illustrates the complete cloud maturity model.

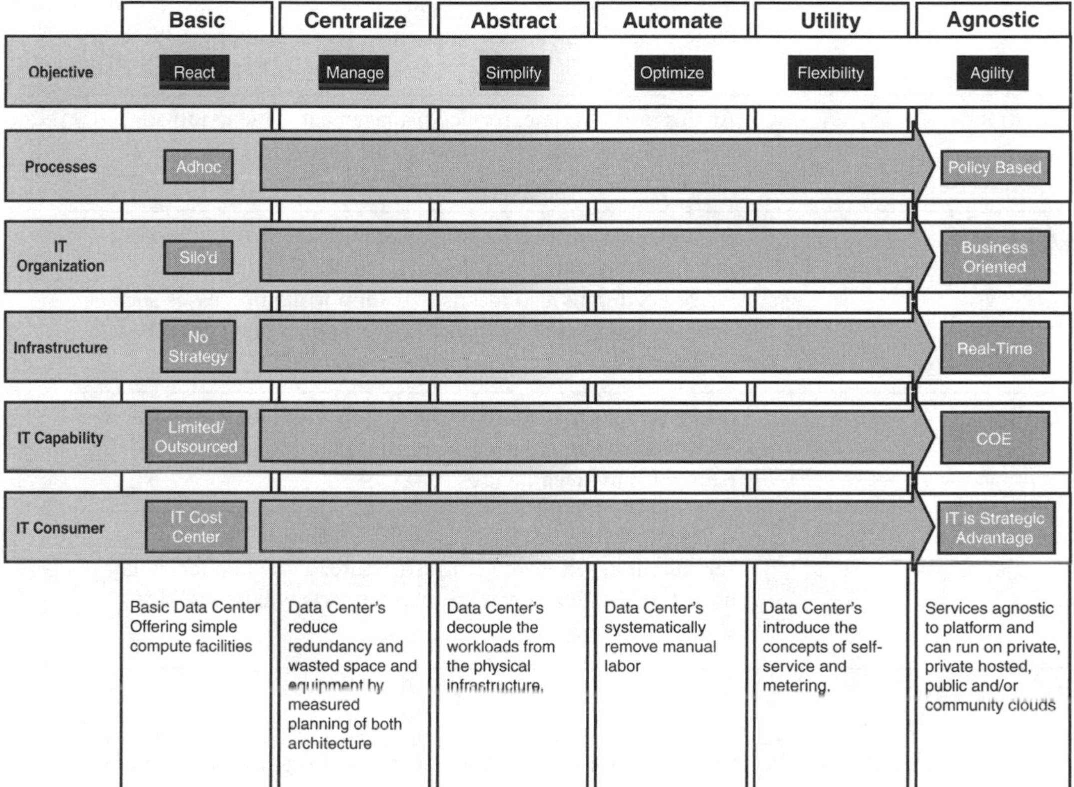

Figure 14-2 *Cloud Maturity Model*

Looking at how maturity typically evolves, you can see the role that the data center will play in the organization, which will shift over time from a distributed sprawl of physical hardware that is seen as a cost to business, to a more centralized, virtualized platform, and finally to a service delivery platform that is aligned to the business and provides real value. Table 14-1 details these stages.

Table 14-1 *Data Center Evolution*

Maturity Level	Description
Basic	At this level, IT is seen a utility providing little value to the business and the data center is just where the IT is hosted, but it is quite chaotic and reactive in nature.
Centralize	At this level, IT begins to manage the IT assets and bring order to chaos by centralizing around a core set of data centers, and more proactive management is introduced to support these efforts.
Abstract	At this point in time, service management is being introduced alongside virtualization as managing the relationship between the physical and virtual assets becomes critical.
Automate	As things become easier to provision through virtualization, more automation of fulfillment, assurance, and billing is introduced. This also means that supporting processes such as procurement, capacity management, and so on need to be optimized.
Utility	A cloud is born, resources can flex up and down, and no longer does the consumer have to pay a premium for his service—he pays for only what he uses.
Agnostic	Congratulations, we have reached IT heaven—the real-time, self-running, self-healing infrastructure, and while this might not be achievable in totality, certain parts will be and this should always be the "vision."

Criticism can be leveled at maturity models for oversimplifying the problem and the solution; however, they are certainly a good way to provide a high-level overview of the problem domains. Simply looking at the *as is* and *to be* states across multiple disciples is normally very helpful when starting a cloud transformation project/program. Table 14-2 illustrates an organization *as is* state, level 1-*basic*, and what its visionary *to be* state should look like, level 6-*agnostic*.

Table 14-2 *Cloud Current State to Future State Evolution*

Dimension	Current State (Basic)	Future State (Agnostic)
Process	Processes are ad hoc, used little, and manual.	Processes are fully automatic and align with business policy.
IT organization	Very organized around technology and IT disciplines (storage, network, security, and so on).	Business partner with a shared service model focused around ITIL processes (level 3) and siloed technical skills (levels 1–2).
Infrastructure	Disorganized set of resources, grown through cost-based purchasing decisions with no clear understanding of capabilities.	Real-time set of interrelated "platforms" where the capabilities and future road map are well understood and documented.
IT capability	Limited capability to deliver complex IT projects because of lack of funding and/or outsourcing constraints.	Center of excellence for the business in providing innovative business solutions to both internal and external consumers.
IT consumer	Views IT as a cost.	Understands the value of IT in today's business world and, more importantly, regularly discusses business issues with the COE.

Using the Cloud Maturity Model

So how do you use this model? To answer this question, you need to observe the following important principles:

- Define the dimensions that are relevant to you; perhaps you think you need to add a dimension looking at cost or governance.
- Don't overanalyze; this is a useful tool for articulating current and future/target state, but it won't replace good architecture or design.
- In the same token, make sure that you don't present a false picture by underanalyzing and basing your decisions on the opinions of too many people.
- Don't aim for the sun; set real expectations as to what the future state looks like.

As you can see from Figure 14-3, organization X specified its current state as predominantly *centralized*, with a more mature infrastructure that supports virtualization. Its overall vision is to move to a completely utility-based level of maturity, which is more realistic than the agnostic maturity level shown in the diagram. Organization X sees real value in IT being a center of excellence (COE) in the cloud as it has various partners that could utilize these skills. To get to its future state, the organization recognizes that there will be a need to deliver as a minimum one transitional architecture that addresses the maturity of the other dimensions and introduces a more automated infrastructure. Whether or not you buy into the concept of the maturity model, you can hopefully see the power of this tool as a communications vehicle.

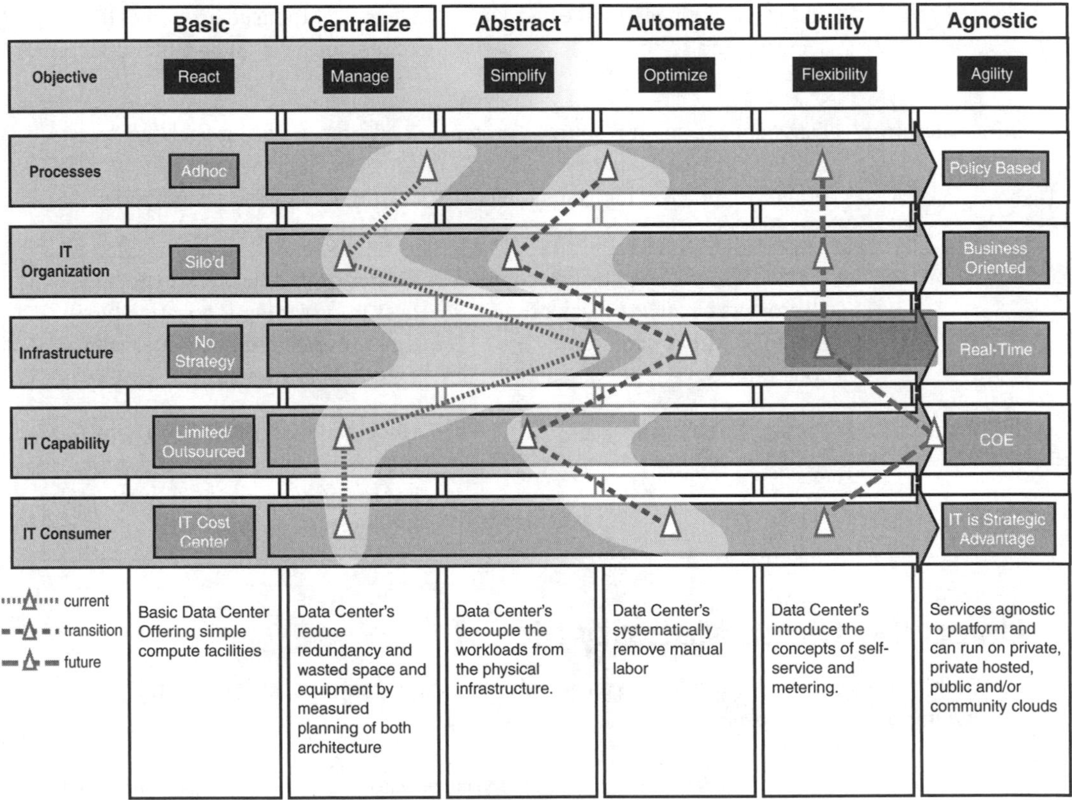

Figure 14-3 *Example of a Cloud Maturity Model*

Having established the current and future states, it's important to understand the transitional architectures that are likely to be needed. You need to start with the current state. Figure 14-4 illustrates the likely steps needed from the perspective of the current state.

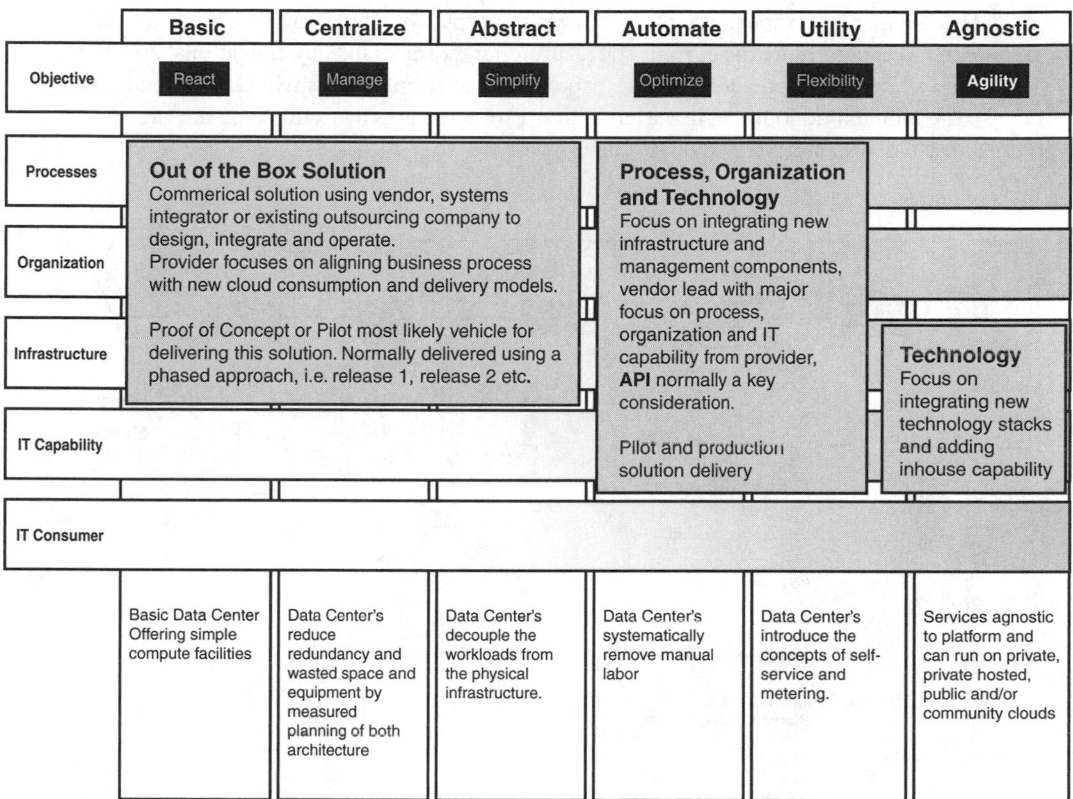

Figure 14-4 *Transitional Architectures*

If your starting point is the basic, centralized, or abstract maturity level, it's likely from a tools perspective that one of the major IT Service Management (ITSM) vendors, such as BMC, HP, IBM, and so on, will be able to supply a solution that will transition you into the automate phase. Using a vendor allows the organization to focus on aligning business processes and organizational structures to support the new IT delivery and consumption models being delivered by the tools. Often, a pilot or proof of concept is needed to understand the true impact on the process or organization. Cisco has partnered with BMC to deliver the Cloud Lifecycle Manager (CLM) solution, which automates the provision of cloud services on top of a Cisco infrastructure to address this need.

If your starting maturity level is automation, or if a fully ITSM ecosystem already exists, more of a point solution might be suitable. For example, VMware vCloud Director (vCD) offers a cloud-ready solution for managing cloud topologies and catalogues on top of VMware vSphere and vCenter. As the processes and organization mature, the vendor can lead more of the project as there are less organizational issues to address (hopefully).

Finally, if you already have a cloud, we're not sure why you're reading this book, because you've done an outstanding job; however, any technology that you are likely to add to your cloud will provide enhanced functionality to the infrastructure or management systems.

Using a maturity model has its advantages but typically won't provide a lot of detail. After you determine the current state, future/target state, and any transitional architectures, it's a case of defining a road map or enablement plan. This will vary depending on the overall cloud journey; however, Figure 14-5 illustrates an example of the Cisco Infrastructure as a Service (IaaS) view.[2]

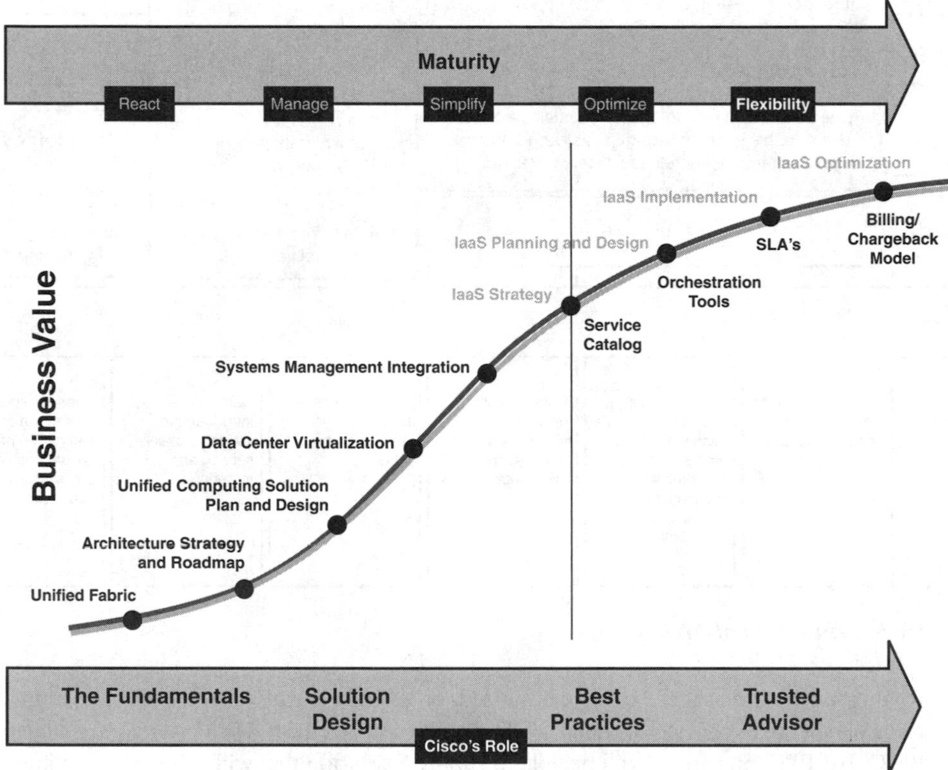

Figure 14-5 *Cisco IaaS Enablement*

There are some basic fundamentals that you should have, beginning with the following:

- A unified data center fabric.
- A clear definition of architecture, strategy, and road map; visualize this as maybe the first interaction of a TOGAF Architecture Development Method (ADM) cycle.[3]

Having clearly defined the *as is* and *to be*, you enter a solution design phase that looks at designing and implementing the core capabilities required by IaaS:

- The Cisco Unified Compute System
- Compute, network, and storage virtualization
- An integrated ITSM stack

After this is done, you begin to consider IaaS strategy, design, implementation, and optimization and the inclusion of management capabilities such as the service catalogue, chargeback, and so on.

Summary

Understanding the impact of the cloud on your business is just as important, if not more so, than undertaking how to implement a cloud. To understand this impact, you should

- Use a maturity model to understand the high-level problem domain and communicate your overall plane.
- Use strong architectural and design frameworks to underpin this maturity model to ensure that it provides a real view of the problem.
- Build a maturity model that makes sense for you.
- Understand how to implement your transitional architectures with or without vendor support.

References

[1] Cloud Maturity Model, by James Urquhart, at http://news.cnet.com/8301-19413_3-10122295-240.html.

[2] Cisco IaaS Solution, at www.cisco.com/en/US/netsol/ns995/networking_solutions_solution_category.html.

[3] The Open Group Architectural Framework (TOGAF), at www.opengroup.org/togaf.

Appendix A

Case Study: Cloud Providers - Hybrid Cloud

Throughout this book, we talked about areas of the cloud that need to be addressed to deliver a successful orchestration and automation solution. This case study, while fictional, brings together a lot of the subject areas addressed in this book in an attempt to provide an example of how to design, build, and automate a cloud. Cisco helps build public and private cloud for many organizations using Cisco products, services, and partners to provide services to end customers. This use case looks at the business challenges faced by a large enterprise end customer and describes how cloud services and technology can help meet the corporation's goals and reduce time to market. Although it is fictional, it is based on our experiences with production cloud deployments.

Cisco Cloud Enablement Services

Many telecommunications providers, which are already expert at monetizing, provisioning, managing, and scaling infrastructure-based services for existing customers, are starting with offerings based on Infrastructure as a Service (IaaS), a cloud utility architecture where the consumer uses a pay-as-you-go infrastructure from a provider. Many enterprises, on the other hand, have no or limited experience in defining or delivering these kind of services.

Given these market and IT challenges, cloud providers are asking some difficult, although highly relevant, questions about the value of cloud computing and IaaS:

- What new cloud services and capabilities will increase market share or business value?
- How do we grow the business and speed the time to market with cloud architectures?
- Is there a way to determine and justify the return on investment for a cloud?
- How can we define and deliver service-level or operational-level agreements (SLA/OLA) in cloud environments?
- How do we enable usage-based, per-customer costing in cloud environments?

Cisco provides services to address many of these questions and helps the customers through Cisco Advanced Services - Cloud Enablement Services. Figure A-1 shows the cloud services that Cisco can provide to its customers.

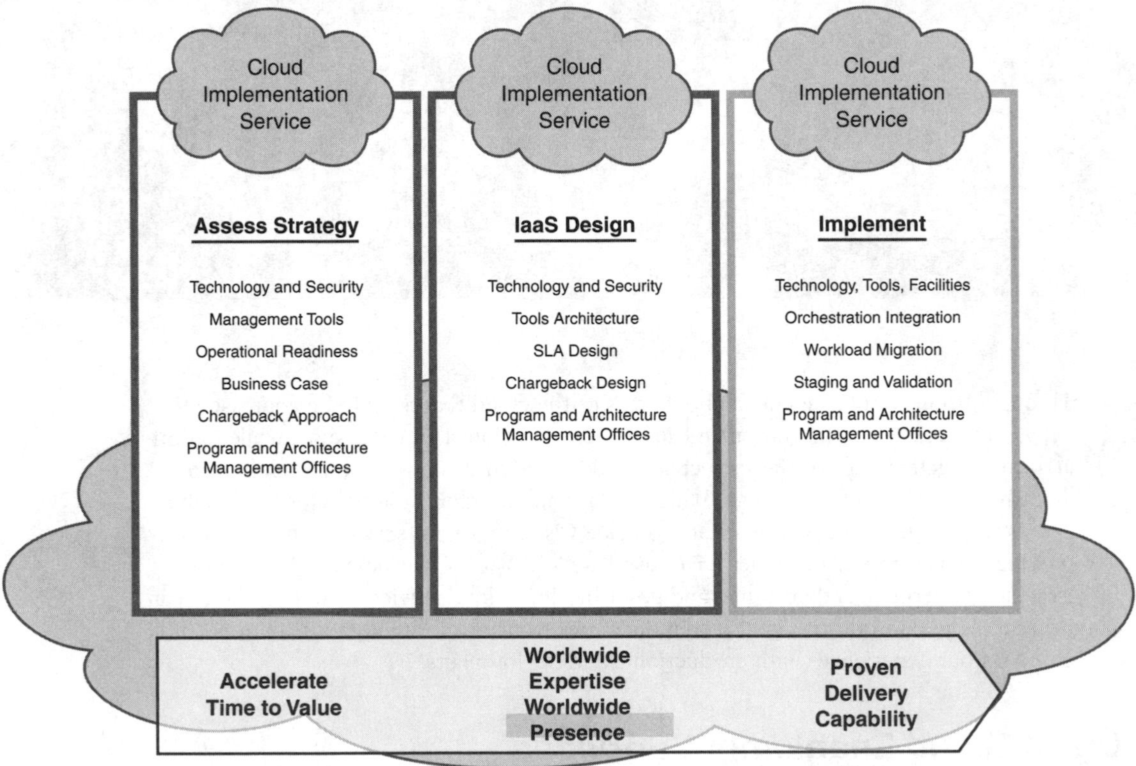

Figure A-1 *Cisco Cloud Enablement*

These cloud services align well with Information Technology Infrastructure Library (ITIL) phases: service strategy, service design, service implementation, service operate, and Continuous Service Improvement (CSI). The service operate phase is not addressed, because it is the phase where the customer takes ownership and operates the network. Cisco has a program called Build, Operate, and Transfer (BOT), however, where it could also operate the cloud for service providers. Chapter 7, "Service Fulfillment," and Chapter 8, "Service Assurance," detail the services that are important in all ITIL V3 phases. Based on those principles, Cisco enablement services for the service provider include the following:

- **Cloud Strategy Service:** Employs return on investment (ROI) tools and in-depth analysis of your current architecture and technology choices (with a primary focus on security) to help you determine the most appropriate cloud strategy and architectural options. It also helps assess your architectural options for various cloud uses, such as disaster recovery and computing as a service. Additionally, this service helps you evaluate data center applications and dependencies, as well as management tools and operations management approaches involved in a cloud transition. Cisco Cloud Strategy Service helps ensure that subsequent cloud architectural development, tools, and process integration and implementation are aligned with achieving business returns.

- **Cisco Cloud Planning and Design Service:** Provides a comprehensive, detailed design service encompassing network, computing, storage, network services, network security, management tools, and processes to realize the target IaaS architecture. The Cloud Planning and Design Service is crucial to linking strategic objectives with a secure overarching design, which prepares the foundations for the subsequent implementation and integration activities.
- **Cisco Cloud Implementation Service:** Helps enable the migration from your environment to an IaaS cloud architecture. Cisco manages the implementation and integration of the entire architecture by staging and delivering application migration, provisioning, and service orchestration of your desired cloud environment. Cisco and its partners provide the integration and staging of an IaaS cloud and provide you with a fully operational IaaS architecture, an automation tools architecture, and progressive implementation of new cloud-enabled IT services.

Company Profile

This case study describes a theoretical large enterprise called Diggit that is in the mining business. Diggit has a wide range of natural resource interests that include iron ore, rare earths, diamonds, and precious metals. As a consequence, mining and processing operations are scattered around the globe (Brazil, South Africa, China, and Australia), at which the company owns many tier 1 assets. (A *tier 1 asset* is defined as a large, expandable, long-life [20+ years] mine with a favorable mineralogy and geographic location.) Diggit has its headquarters in London, with further back office functions in New York; Figure A-2 illustrates the overall company distribution.

Diggit has chosen to contract Cisco to provide IaaS strategy and design services and a telecommunications service provider, ABCNet, for its public cloud offering. Although this case study is fictional, it represents the type of cloud engagements in which Cisco is involved.

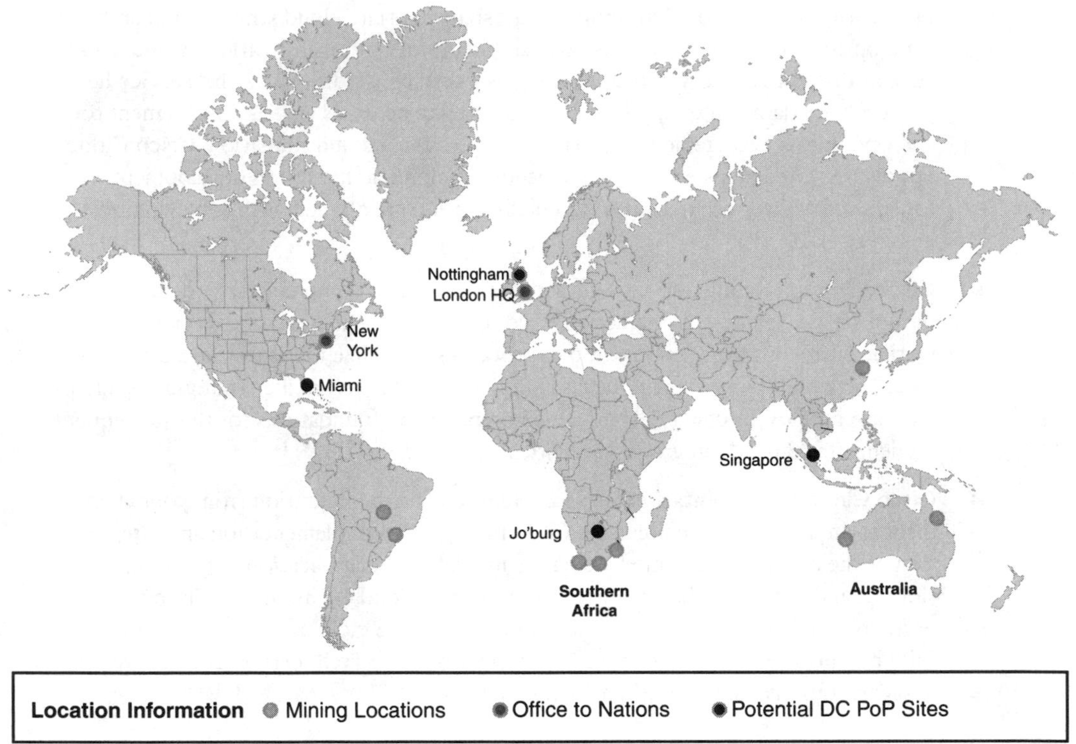

Figure A-2 *Diggit Organization*

Business Goals

Diggit's strategy is simple: to become the global leader in mining by investing in commodities that deliver superior returns over the long term. To achieve this business objective, Diggit's board of directors wants to improve its operational efficiency and speed of operations by part through the use of cloud technology–based products and services, but also through organizational restructuring. The idea is to create a leaner, meaner corporation that can outexecute its competition, providing superior α (alpha) measurements (outperforming industry benchmarks) and thus becoming the number one mining "natural resource" company in the world.

The following business and technology challenges apply to enterprises planning to consume cloud services:

- **Regulatory compliance and health safety:** Safety and security controls are a primary concern for the company, and any cloud service adopted would need to be able to uphold Diggit's stringent standards. The security concerns include end-to-end security, standards, and policy compliance. For example, health and safety operational records must be secure (that is, tamperproof and backed up to offsite locations). The company wants to increase its data security but at the same time save costs. A VDI (Virtual Desktop Infrastructure) is being considered.

- **Business process availability and assurance:** With recent events (for example, Amazon EC2 started April 21, 2011), it is necessary to have assurance systems monitoring the service and also have built-in redundancy so that there is always access to the applications. Mining operations need to continue 24x7 because of the high costs of equipment. Reliable global network connectivity with assured backup is required.

- **Information and knowledge-centric business:** The company wants to be far more interconnected with its mining operations. Remote telemetry from mining equipment, vehicles, and sensors needs to process in real time so that the business can respond faster to specific events. Diggit also wants to improve collaboration between its knowledge-based workers. Information sharing and quick access to key knowledge workers are essential to improve productivity and operating margins.

- **Service transparency:** This is an absolute must. Can the corporation understand the level of risk it is undertaking by consuming a service or a set of services from one or more cloud service providers?

- **Service platform strategy:** Build or buy? Should Diggit invest in building a cloud internally or partner with a provider who already has a cloud? Diggit's IT department has identified some key services that it needs to run on its next-generation service platform:

  - **Collaboration tools:** Office and mine locations
  - **Real-time telemetry and video:** From mine to office locations
  - **Development and test facilities:** Data center near offices
  - **High-performance computing (HPC), geological surveys, large floating-point calculations:** Data center near offices
  - **Enterprise Resource Planning (ERP), Business Automation (BA), Business Intelligence (BI) and customer Relationship Management (CRM):** Data center near office locations
  - **(New) Virtual Desktop Infrastructure (VDI) service:** Office and mine locations

Cloud Strategy

Working with Cisco, Diggit has defined its overall strategy as delivery of private cloud functionality to support collaboration and desktop services, as illustrated in Figure A-3. It has chosen to offload the development and test environments to a third-party provider, ABCNet, as this offers a far more flexible and, more importantly, a cost-effective way of managing these areas and to offload its customer relationship management and sales tools to Salesforce.com. This will allow Diggit's development and sales engineers to focus more on the High Performance Compute (HPC) and telemetry services that are actually systems of differentiation, whereas the sales tools are not. Remote clouds will be deployed that are built around a pod that can be deployed into any mine or research location. These remote clouds will offer a subset of IT services, namely, VDI and telemetry services. The HPC solution is too mission critical, so it will remain a technology island until the cloud has established a level of maturity that the business is happy with; then an HPC can be migrated into the private cloud. All services will be ordered through an internal, centralized portal and catalogue and the cloud broker, a component of the Diggit cloud platform, will be used to provide service transparency and implement business logic.

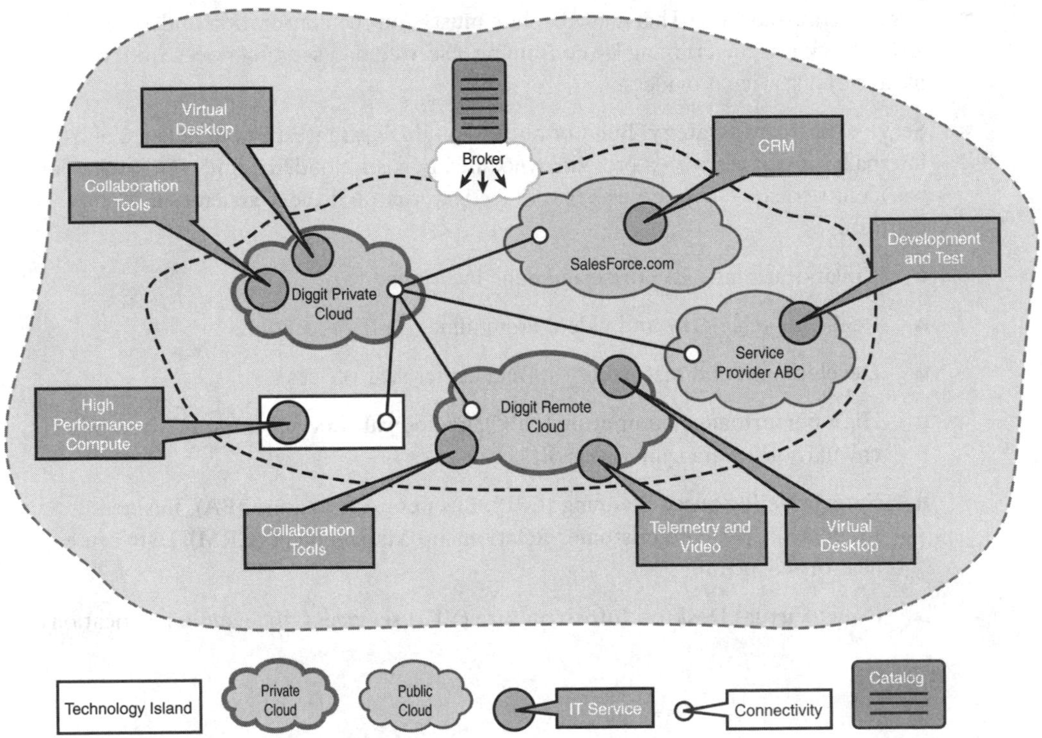

Figure A-3 *Diggit Cloud Strategy*

This strategy allows Diggit to realize its business goals and increase business agility by adopting both public and private clouds but without disrupting its key business services. This strategy also helps mitigate some of the risks seen with a pure public cloud strategy.

Cloud Maturity

As part of the strategy consultancy, Cisco has identified that while Diggit's current state is fairly advanced, it needs to significantly enhance its existing infrastructure to support its overall vision of a real-time cloud. Figure A-4 illustrates the overall maturity.

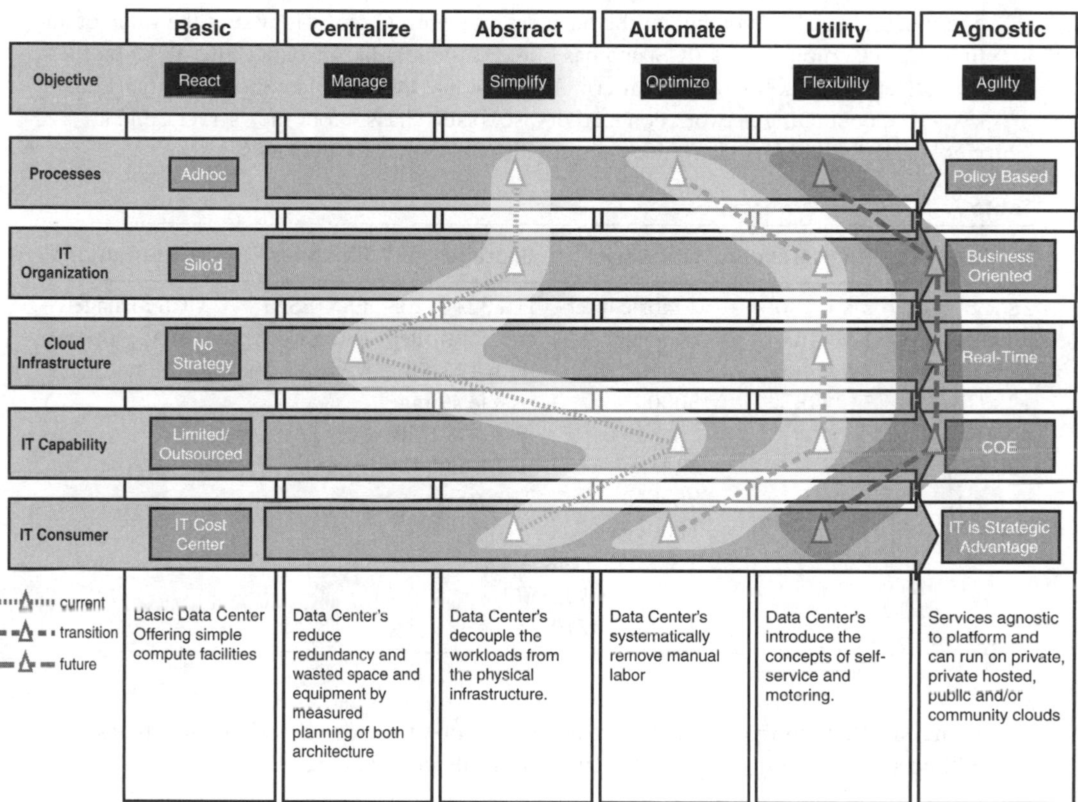

Figure A-4 *Diggit Cloud Maturity*

The transitional architecture that Diggit needs to deliver will consist of the following:

- A scalable, point of delivery (POD)–based IT platform that will support its existing applications and add greater flexibility to its execution platform
- A cloud framework that allows it to meet its overall strategy and vision

- An IT operational model that supports the dynamic cloud consumption and delivery of new cloud based IT Services
- An organization that uses IT to differentiate its services and so works closely with the IT department and vendors
- Automation and orchestration tools that can implement public and private cloud services in a timely and flexible manner

IT Platform

Diggit has traditionally spent its IT budget on separate compute, storage, and networking equipment, but after working on the business case with Cisco, it now sees the value of an Integrated Compute Stack (ICS) and has opted to standardize its data center POD on the Cisco/NetApp FlexPod design pattern. An individual POD would consist of three 12.5-kW racks containing network connectivity, six blade chassis, four rack servers, and a NetApp FAS 3240 HA filer. Table A-1 provides the details for the racks.

Table A-1 *POD Definition*

Blades (44)	Rack Servers	Network	Storage	Licenses	Management
28 x B200/ 96 GB 12 x B230/ 128 GB 4 x B460/ 128 GB	2 x C250/ 128 GB 2 x C460/ 512 GB	2 fabric interconnects 2 x Nexus 5000 2 x Nexus 2248 96 x Nexus 1000v licenses 2 x MDS 9148 SAN switches 2 x ACE 4710	HA 3240 storage controller with 125 TB usable storage, mix of 80-TB SATA and 45-TB SAS	ESX/ESXi enterprise and VMware View	UCS manager NetApp operations manager

Using this POD footprint enables the determination of what technical building blocks will be available from the new infrastructure, as illustrated in Figure A-5.

Table A-2 defines the entire building blocks that will be available to Diggit service architects.

Outside of the FlexPod, you can see that there is a need to offer some additional services around security, patching, and with the exception of the session load balancing, all the building blocks defined in the application support class. This is defined as a POD plus (POD+) architecture, because it encompasses an Integrated Compute Stack POD, plus a number of networking and network service components and is needed to meet the overall service requirements of Diggit. These additional network components will scale at different levels and will not be included in the POD itself.

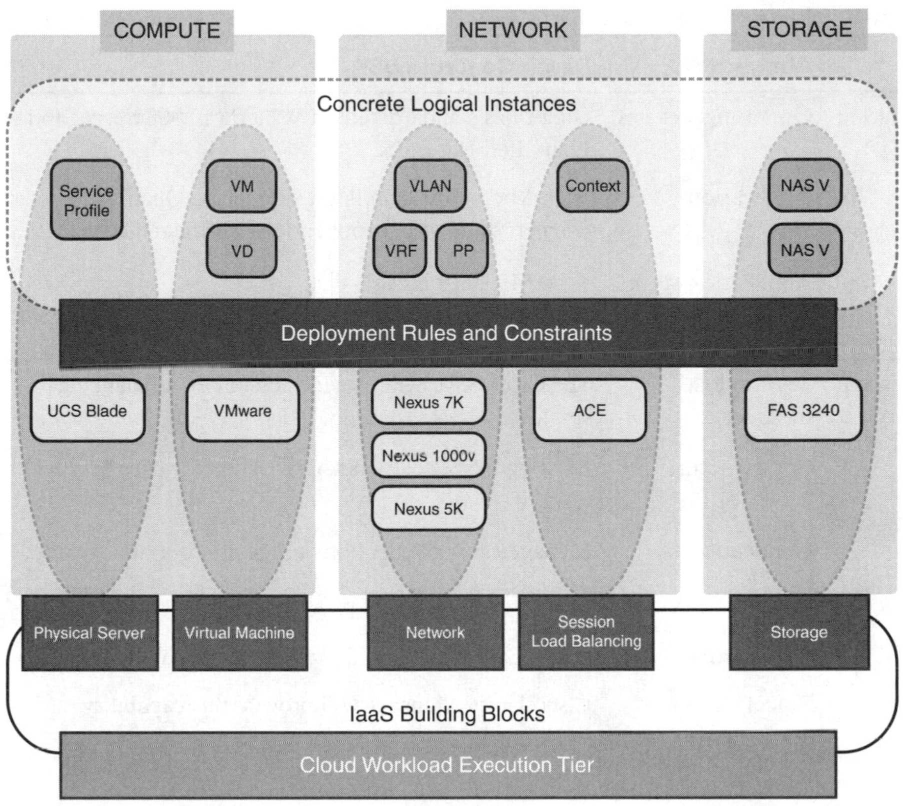

Figure A-5 *Diggit Cloud Technical Building Blocks*

Table A-2 *Concrete Building Blocks*

Class	Abstract BB	Diggit Concrete BB
Resource	Compute	UCS blades with a number of different operational tiers: Gold=B460, Silver=B230, and Bronze=B200.
	Storage	SAN and NAS volumes used to boot blades and provide different storage tiers: Gold=SAN and backup and Silver=NAS.
Topology	Service access	All access will be through the Diggit WAN or through the Internet for public cloud services.
	Perimeter security	This will utilize the existing Diggit security systems.
	Layer 3 separation	VRF Lite will be used to provide Layer 3 separation for remote clouds.
	Layer 2 separation	VLANs and private VLANs will be used to provide Layer 2 separation.

Table A-2 *Concrete Building Blocks*

Class	Abstract BB	Diggit Concrete BB
Application	Operating systems	Diggit has standardized on Windows 2008 Server and Linux Red Hat 5 ES.
	Application	VDI, Microsoft SharePoint, and Cisco Quad, proprietary telemetry and video applications for the remote cloud.
	Application stack	A LAMP stack is available.
	Patches	Existing patching services will be utilized.
Application support	Session load balancer	The Cisco ACE will provide session load-balancing services.
	Infrastructure	Existing DNS, NTP, and Active Directory services will be utilized.
	Connection broker	Manages user connections to the appropriate desktop.
	WAN acceleration	The Cisco WAAS will provide WAN acceleration.
	Call control server	Cisco CallManager will provide this capability.
	Voicemail server	Cisco Unity Manager will provide this capability.

BB = Building Blocks

Cloud Reference Model

Working with Cisco through the Cloud Strategy Service, Diggit has built a reference model that satisfies its strategic requirements, as illustrated in Figure A-6 and described in the list that follows.

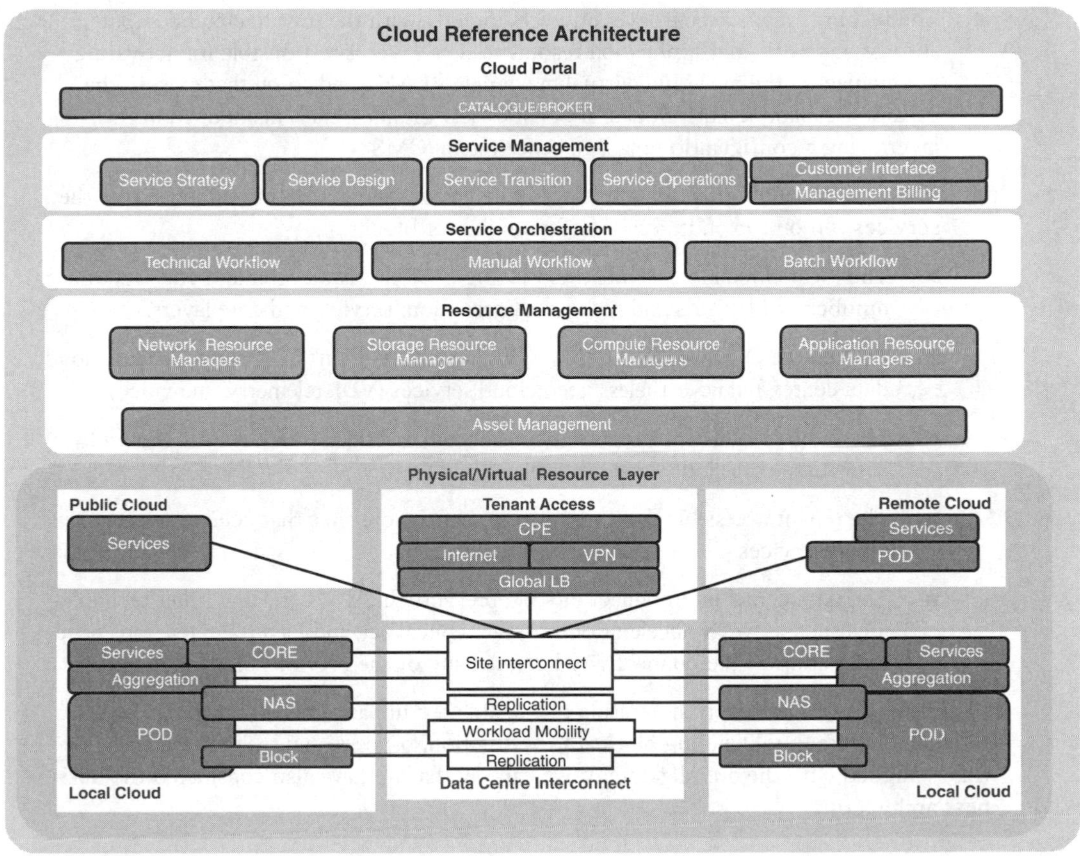

Figure A-6 *Diggit Cloud Reference Architecture*

- Starting at the top is the portal layer, which provides a number of different views (operation, business, tenant, and so on), provides a holistic view of all services (public and private cloud) through a service catalogue, and also provides the business routing or request through a broker component.
- The service management layer implements the core ITIL processes of strategy, design, transition, and operations for both public and private services, although private services will demand more than public services as these will be managed on the whole by the external service provider. In addition, some enhanced Telecom Operations Map (eTOM) process elements have been added around billing and customer interface management to support capabilities not typically considered in ITIL.
- The service orchestration layer acts as a conductor for the service management layer and supports a number of different types of workflow:
  - Technical/automation workflow for delivering and managing services
  - Manual workflow for actions that require operational intervention
  - Batch workflow where there is a scheduled or group aspect to a task such as backing up a service

- The resource management layer interacts directly with the private cloud compute, storage, network, and application resources. This layer is responsible for activating and managing the individual virtual machines, VLANs, and so on that exist in the private local and remote clouds. A holistic view of all assets is maintained in this layer using a configuration management system (CMS).
- The physical and virtual resource layer consists of the devices and software that the services run on top of. It consists of a number of blocks:
  - The local cloud block represents the Diggit cloud data center and consists of a number of FlexPods and network aggregation, service, and core layers.
  - The remote cloud block represents Diggit sites that don't/can't support a full cloud data center, but nevertheless need cloud services (VDI, telemetry, and video).
  - The public cloud block represents instances of service provider ABCNet and Salesforce.com clouds that are utilized by Diggit.
  - The tenant access block represents local or remote sites that need access to the cloud services.
  - The data center interconnect block represents the WAN and any other technologies such as WAN acceleration, storage replication, and Layer 2 extensions needed to support the connectivity between any of the previous blocks.

Figure A-6 represents the first iteration of the architecture and shows a simple view of the main architectural building blocks of the solution, process, and technology. Because this is aligned with the overall strategy, we can say that we have also considered the business architecture.

Private Cloud Services

As part of the Cisco Design Service, Cisco architects and Diggit stakeholders and architects have drawn up the design patterns shown in Figure A-7. These represent the actual service instances that need to be instantiated when a tenant requests a virtual desktop or the business deploys a new remote cloud with telemetry services. Clearly, a lot more design work is required to make these services "real," but the patterns at least can now be validated against what the infrastructure can support.

Using these patterns, it is possible to compare the technical building blocks defined in the POD+ and those required by the patterns shown in Table A-3. As part of the service definition, the initial service metrics have been added around availability and latency. This will allow IT to begin to establish service-level agreements or operational-level agreements with the various external and internal parties providing the service.

The Diggit business was also keen to see some measurement of cloud provisioning, so the time taken to provision a development/test and VDI service will also be measured as this is where previous issues arose. The time currently taken to deploy these types of environments adds significant delays to software development projects and impacts the ability of the business to deliver innovation.

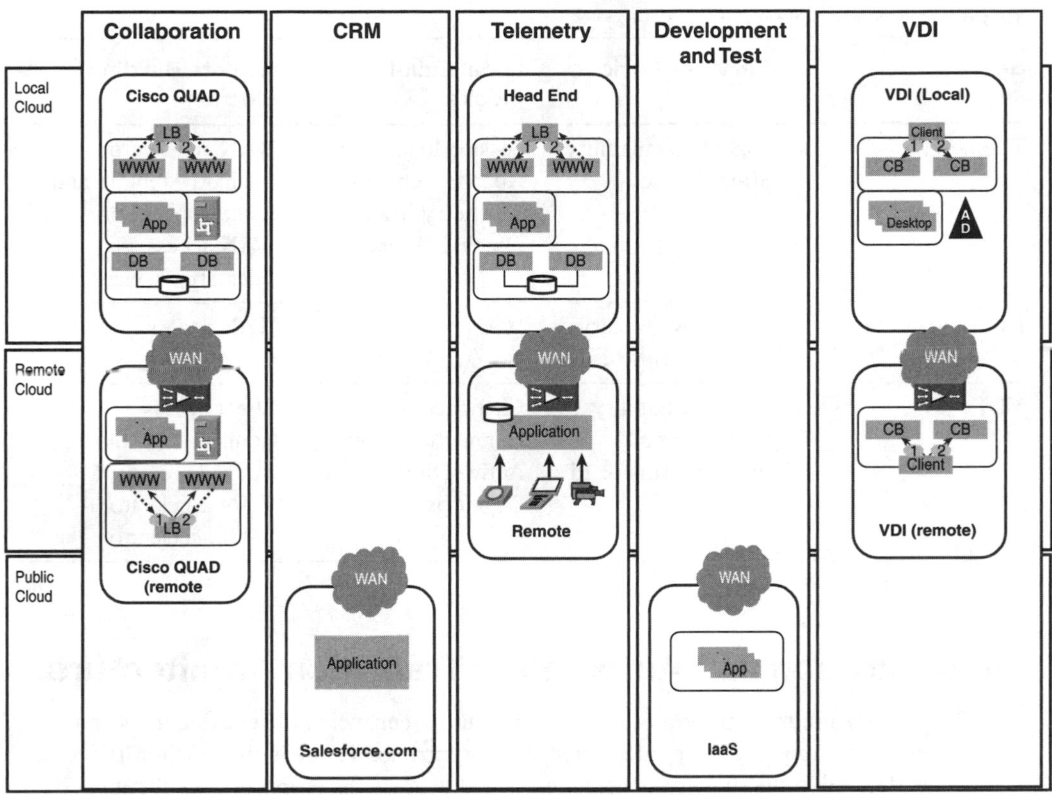

Figure A-7 *Diggit Cloud Design Patterns*

Table A-3 *Simple Service Catalogue*

Service	Service Metrics	Local Building Blocks	Remote Building Blocks
Collaboration	99.999% availability 50-ms latency	Session load balancer Apache web server Cisco quad application servers Oracle DB servers Call control servers Voicemail servers	Session load balancer Apache web server Cisco quad application servers WAN accelerator Call control servers Voicemail servers WAN access
CRM	99.95% availability	WAN access	WAN access

Table A-3 *Simple Service Catalogue*

Service	Service Metrics	Local Building Blocks	Remote Building Blocks
Telemetry	99.999% availability 50-ms latency	Session load balancer Apache web server Telemetry head end Oracle DB servers	WAN accelerator Telemetry remote and cache application WAN access Telemetry devices
Develop and test	99.95% availability Provision time < 1d	WAN access	WAN access
VDI	99.9% availability 80-ms latency Provision time < 1d	Client access Connection brokers Active Directory Desktops	Client access Connection brokers Active Directory WAN accelerator WAN accelerator

Orchestration and Automation Transition Architecture

The primary focus for this transitional architecture is enhancing the existing tools and processes to support greater automation and optimization in line with the maturity model defined in the strategy stage. Figure A-8 illustrates the proposed architecture.

The overall Diggit operational model will require enhancements to the following processes to support a more automated and on-demand provisioning process. The existing operational processes will be used where there is already a good level of maturity.

- New processes around service strategy and design
- More dynamic on-demand request fulfillment and configuration management
- Optimized capacity management
- Enhanced customer interface management
- New billing and chargeback processes

These processes will be supported by a new toolset that will automate the services delivered on both the public and private cloud and optimize the existing services delivered on top of the FlexPod or any additional infrastructure components.

Table A-4 illustrates the overall management functions and the tools that fulfill those functions.

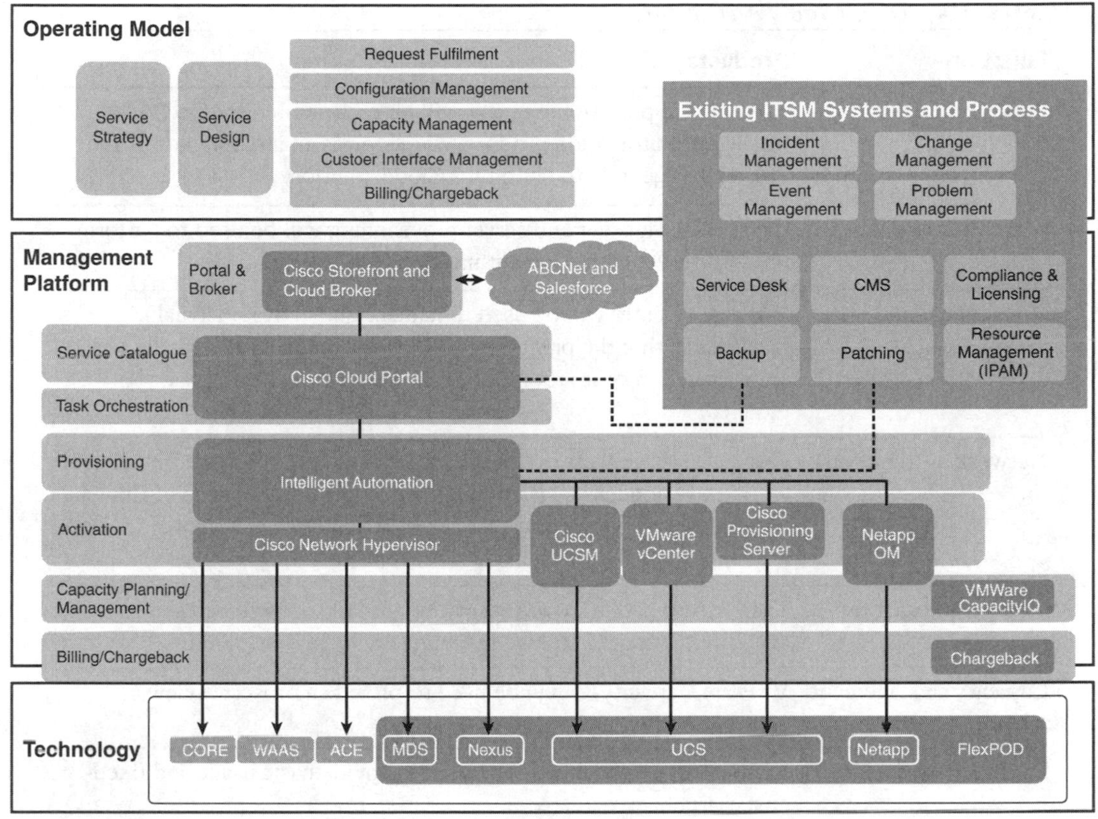

Figure A-8 *Orchestration and Automation Stack*

Table A-4 *Diggit Tools Architecture*

Function	Products
Global catalogue, portal, and broker	The cloud storefront and broker will be used to provide this function. This product is due for imminent release and is in trial with a variety of cloud providers today. The broker will interface with service provider ABCNet and Salesforce.com, as well as Cisco Cloud Portal, to provision new IaaS services.
Service catalogue	All private cloud services will be stored in Cisco Cloud Portal (CCP). The user requesting private cloud services can only use the CCP directly to order services. CCP is a recent acquisition and forms an integral part of the Cisco Intelligent Automation for Cloud solution.
Task orchestration	Any manual tasks or approvals will be automated in Cisco Cloud Portal.

Table A-4 *Diggit Tools Architecture*

Function	Products
Provisioning	All technical provisioning tasks will be orchestrated by the Cisco Intelligent Automation product, which forms an integral part of the Cisco Intelligent Automation for Cloud solution.
Server automation	Cisco UCS Manager and server provisioning will be used to perform physical server activation within the private cloud.
Virtual machine provisioning	VMware vCenter will be used to manage and activate virtual machines within the private cloud. As tenant details and catalogues are managed in other tools, VMware vCloud director was not required.
Network automation	Cisco Overdrive Network Hypervisor will be used to perform all network activation tasks within the private cloud. At the time of this writing, Network Hypervisor is a recent acquisition, so not all devices are supported, but this will change over time.
Storage automation	The NetApp Work Flow Automation (WFA) tool will be used to manage and activate the storage resources in the private cloud.
Capacity management	VMware CapacityIQ will be used to provide a proactive view of ESX capacity.
Billing/chargeback	VMware Chargeback will be used to provide basic usage and fixed-cost chargeback data.

The billing/chargeback and capacity management components will need to be enhanced to support the future state, but they provide enough capabilities to support the processes and requirements of the transitional architecture.

Integration with the existing Diggit systems and processes will typically occur in four places:

1. The cloud broker will interface with external third-party systems and catalogues and also the internal CCP.
2. The CCP will interface with the existing change management and incident management systems and processes.
3. Cisco Intelligent Automation will interface with the other technical systems to support IP address and license management, asset information, and so on.
4. The virtual and physical machines themselves will integrate with the existing systems management solutions such as compliance, patching, and backup to ensure that a consistent, secure service is delivered in the private cloud.

Telco Solution

Service provider ABCNet has decided that it needed to deliver cloud services to companies such as Diggit to generate additional revenues and differentiate itself in the telco markets where it is present. However, the company observed the following challenges with entering this market:

- **Security:** Security would be very important for any cloud environment. The security concerns include end-to-end security, standards, and policy compliance.
- **Availability and assurance:** With recent events at Amazon EC2 (system crashes in 2011), it is necessary to have assurance systems monitoring the service and have built-in redundancy so that there is always access to the applications.
- **Current offering:** Extend its current offerings, which include hosting, communications, media, and application services using cloud models.
- **New services:** Create new services through service portals, and tie these services to creative billing methods to charge for the services rendered.
- **Ease of integration:** Offer easy integration into the existing systems such as the service catalog and assurance systems.
- **Automation:** The end-to-end provisioning that includes network, compute, and storage that could take many hours to days and even weeks needs to be shortened to make cloud services a reality.
- **Scale/deployment:** The usage curve for cloud computing is like a hockey stick and needs to be prepared for the uptick by using an architecture that is modular and scalable.

Solution

To address these issues, service provider ABCNet approached Cisco for an out-of-the-box solution. Cisco proposed the Virtualized Multitenant Data Center (VMDC) solution with BMC Cloud Lifecycle Manager (CLM), which is a pretest, preintegrated solution for service providers. This solution is defined in two parts: the infrastructure architecture and the orchestration architecture.

Network Architecture

The network is a hierarchy reaching from a server farm to the core routers. The servers in the server farm are connected to the access layer through switches for redundancy. These switches aggregate in the aggregation layer. At the top of the hierarchy, core routers in the core layers carry the traffic at high speed into and out of the data center. The network architecture is built such that no single failure in the equipment can affect the customer service. Figure A-9 shows network architectures with devices at access, aggregation, service, and core layers, detailing the type of equipment needed along with the interconnections between the layers. This network architecture provides a platform to offer Infrastructure as a Service (IaaS). Network is sometimes referred to as infrastructure because it contains network, compute, and storage platforms.

Figure A-9 illustrates the cloud network architecture for the Cisco VMDC solution, and Table A-5 provides details on the device family and the actual devices. All the devices shown in Table A-5 for network, compute storage, and services, connected as shown in Figure A-9, make up the network architecture for offering cloud services.

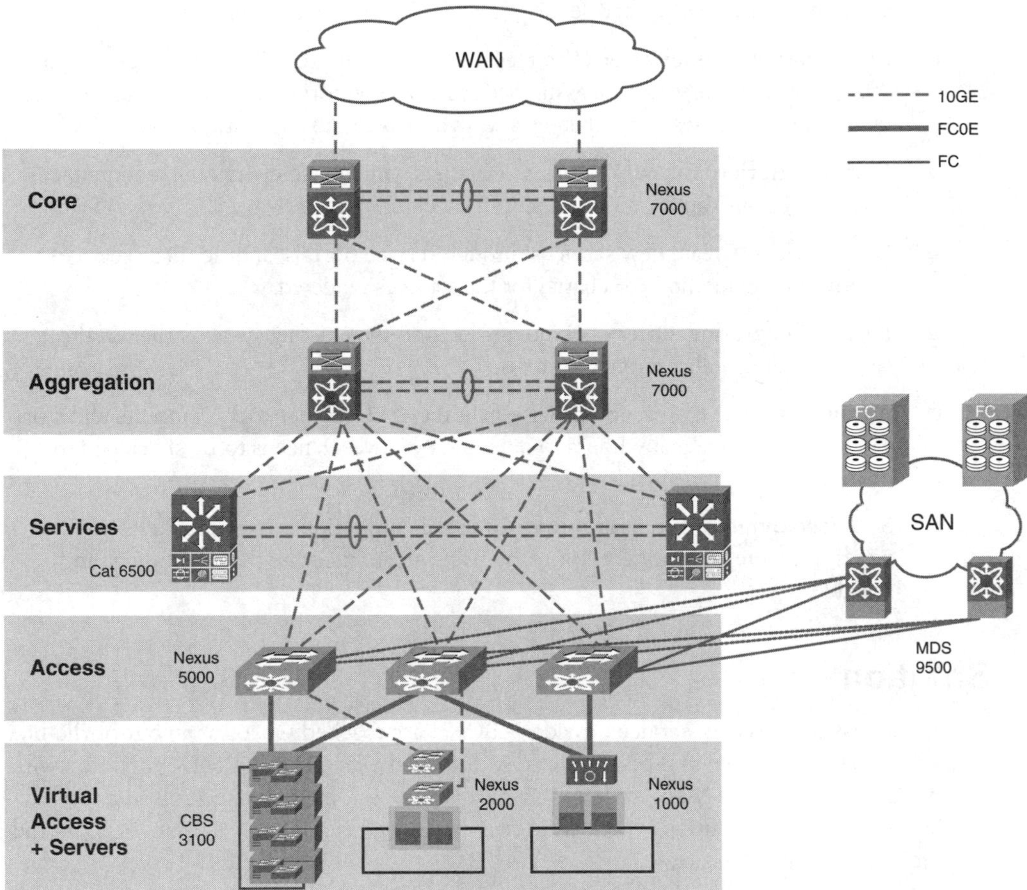

Figure A-9 *VMDC Network Architecture*

Table A-5 *VMDC Network Bill of Materials/Physical Network Building Blocks for IaaS*

Layer	Device Family	Devices
Core	Cisco Nexus switches	Cisco Nexus 7000 Series switches Cisco Nexus 5000 Series switches Cisco Nexus 2000 Series switches Cisco Nexus 1000 virtual switch
Aggregation	Cisco Catalyst switches	Cisco Nexus 4900 Series switches Cisco 6500 VSS/7600 switches/routers
Service	Firewall and load balancers	Cisco Firewalls (FWSM) Cisco ACE
Access	Cisco UCS	UCS B Series blade servers UCS 5100 Series Blade Server Chassis UCS C-Series Rack-Mount Servers UCS 6100 Series Fabric Interconnects UCS Manager
	Cisco Storage MDS	MDS 9500 Series Multilayer Directors MDS 9100 Multilayer Fabric Switches NX-OS for MDS 9000 Cisco Fabric Manager Cisco I/O accelerator

The core layer can use either Cisco 7000 Nexus switches or Catalyst 6500 E VSS switches. However, the Cisco premier switching platform for the data center core is the Nexus 7000 Series switch run by Cisco NX-OS. It was specifically designed for the most mission-critical place in the network the data center. The Nexus 7000 Series offers unique virtualization features, such as virtual device contexts (VDC) and virtual Port Channels (vPC). The Nexus 7000 Series switches also have excellent high-availability features, throughput, and 10-Gigabit Ethernet port densities.

The aggregation layer serves as the Layer 3 and Layer 2 boundary for the data center infrastructure. The aggregation layer also serves as the connection point for the data center firewalls and other services. Thus, it consolidates Layer 2 traffic in a high-speed packet-switching fabric and provides a platform for network-based services to reside at the interface between Layer 2 and Layer 3 in the data center.

Network and security services such as firewalls, server load balancers, intrusion detection systems, and network analysis modules are typically deployed at the data center services layer. Service modules, such as the Cisco Firewall Services Module (FWSM) and Application Control Engine (ACE) can be deployed on the Catalyst 6500 Series switches in the access layer. Multiple modules can be installed to support higher throughputs or to provide active/standby or active/active forms of high availability.

The access layer connects the server farm end nodes in the data center with the aggregation and services layers. The Cisco access layer also provides convergence of storage and IP traffic onto a common physical infrastructure, called a unified fabric. The Cisco Nexus 5000 Series of switches supports storage and IP traffic through support for Fibre Channel over Ethernet (FCoE) switching and 10-Gigabit Ethernet. Server nodes can be deployed with converged network adapters (CNA) supporting both IP data and FCoE storage traffic, allowing the server to use a single set of cabling and a common network interface. The Nexus 5000 Series also offers native Fibre Channel interfaces to allow these CNA-attached servers to communicate with traditional storage-area network (SAN) equipment.

Orchestration Architecture

The ability to successfully provide a cloud-computing service depends on a number of factors, including the ability to provide effective end-to-end management services and security, and the ability to quickly provision and monitor services for customers. However, provisioning frequently takes hours and days, as configuring even a simple virtualized data center can require hundreds of variables, parameters, and settings to be specified. The management architecture defined in this section addresses these challenges.

Figure A-10 shows the cloud management architecture for end-to-end provisioning that has been tested with the VMDC 2.0 infrastructure.

CLM is part of the BMC Cloud Lifecycle Management Suite that addresses fulfillment. In that context, ABCNet's existing request fulfillment and change management processes will be enhanced to support data center services, and CLM will provide the tools to support these enhancements. The ABCNet Operation Support Systems (OSS) and processes are very mature, as you would expect from a well-established telco, so CLM will be integrated into its existing portal and toolset to provide cloud fulfillment capabilities.

Table A-6 illustrates the overall management functions and the tools that fulfill those functions.

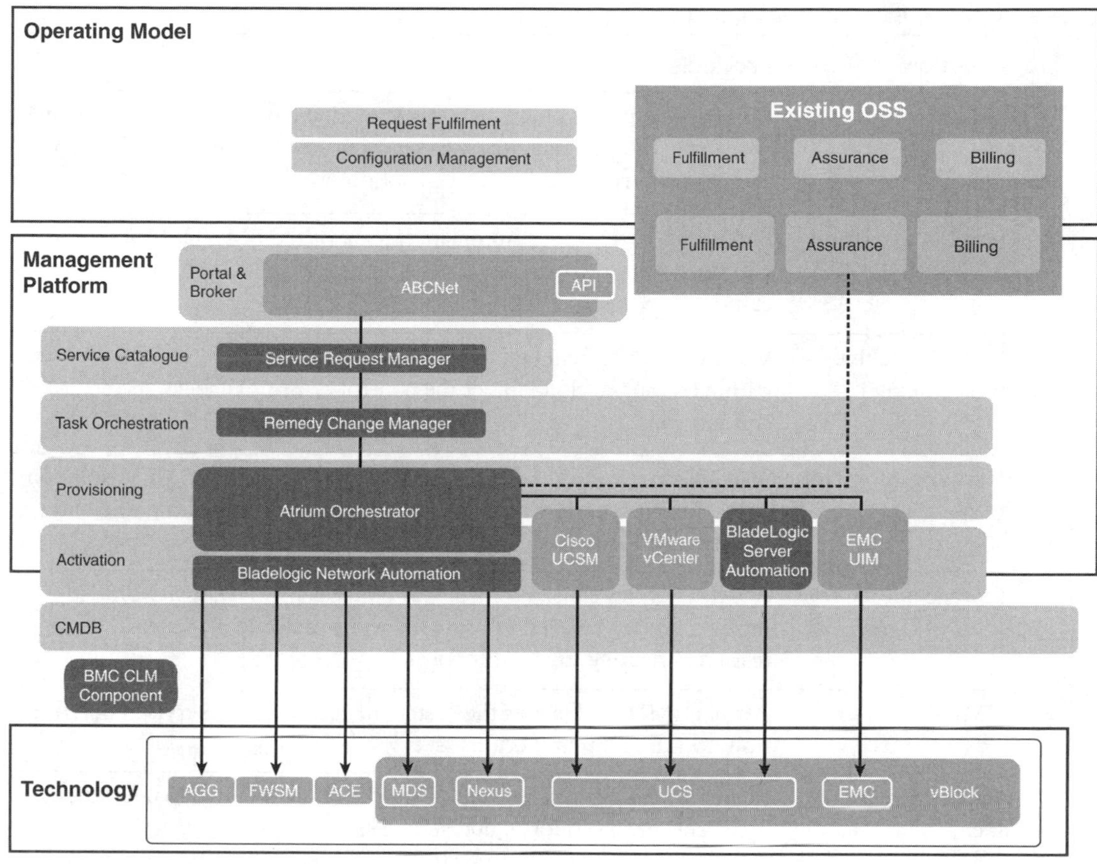

Figure A-10 *BMC Cloud Lifecycle Manager 1.x Architecture*

Table A-6 *ABCNet Tools Architecture*

Function	Products
Global catalogue, portal, and broker	The existing ABCNet Service Delivery Platform will provide this capability and will be enhanced to support cloud services. In addition, an Application Programming Interface (API) will be added to allow applications, such as the Diggit Cloud Broker, to provision and manage its development and test environments programmatically.
Service catalogue	The existing ABCNet Service Delivery Platform will provide this capability.
Task orchestration	The existing OSS workforce management tool will provide this capability.

Table A-6 *ABCNet Tools Architecture*

Function	Products
Provisioning	All technical provisioning tasks associated with cloud services will be orchestrated by the Remedy Change Management Module, which forms an integral part of the BMC CLM solution.
Server automation	BMC Bladelogic Server Automation (part of the BMC CLM solution) will be used to perform physical server activation within the private cloud.
Virtual machine provisioning	VMware vCenter will be used to manage and activate virtual machines within the public cloud under the control of BMC Bladelogic Server Automation.
Network automation	BMC Bladelogic Network Automation (part of the BMC CLM solution) will be used to perform all network activation tasks relating to cloud services.
Storage automation	As ABCNet has chosen to deploy Vblock as its POD, EMC Unified Infrastructure Manager will be used to manage and activate the storage resources relating to cloud services.
CMDB	Atrium CMDB will act as the system of record for all service configuration items and infrastructure assets.
Capacity management	The existing OSS systems will be used to provide this capability but will be enhanced to support cloud services.
Billing/chargeback	The existing OSS systems will be used to provide this capability but will be enhanced to support cloud services.

Out-of-the-Box Services

One of the main advantaged of CLM is that it supports the VMDC reference tenant services out of the box, so while these didn't fit ABCNet's long-term requirements, they did allow ABCNet to launch a cloud service relatively quickly. This, in turn, allowed ABCNet to capture Diggit's cloud business.

The VMDC reference services are based around the concept of a network container. The network container provides an abstraction of network resources that can be presented to users through a self-service portal. Providing users with a selection of predefined network containers practically eliminates the need for manually provisioning each network element in the underlying core, aggregation, and access layers, which in turn greatly reduces, if not outright eliminates, direct operator involvement in provisioning a virtualized data center. As a result, the network container approach can reduce service provisioning time from days and weeks to practically minutes. Further, when a user requests a given network container, the self-service portal can also allow users to specify and launch virtual machines inside their containers. As discussed in Chapter 10, "Technical Building Blocks of IaaS," and Chapter 11, "Automating and Orchestration Resources," the resource management and workflow mechanisms provided by such a system allow resource provisioning to be automated through the placement of variables in the physical data center systems. Figure A-11 illustrates these concepts.

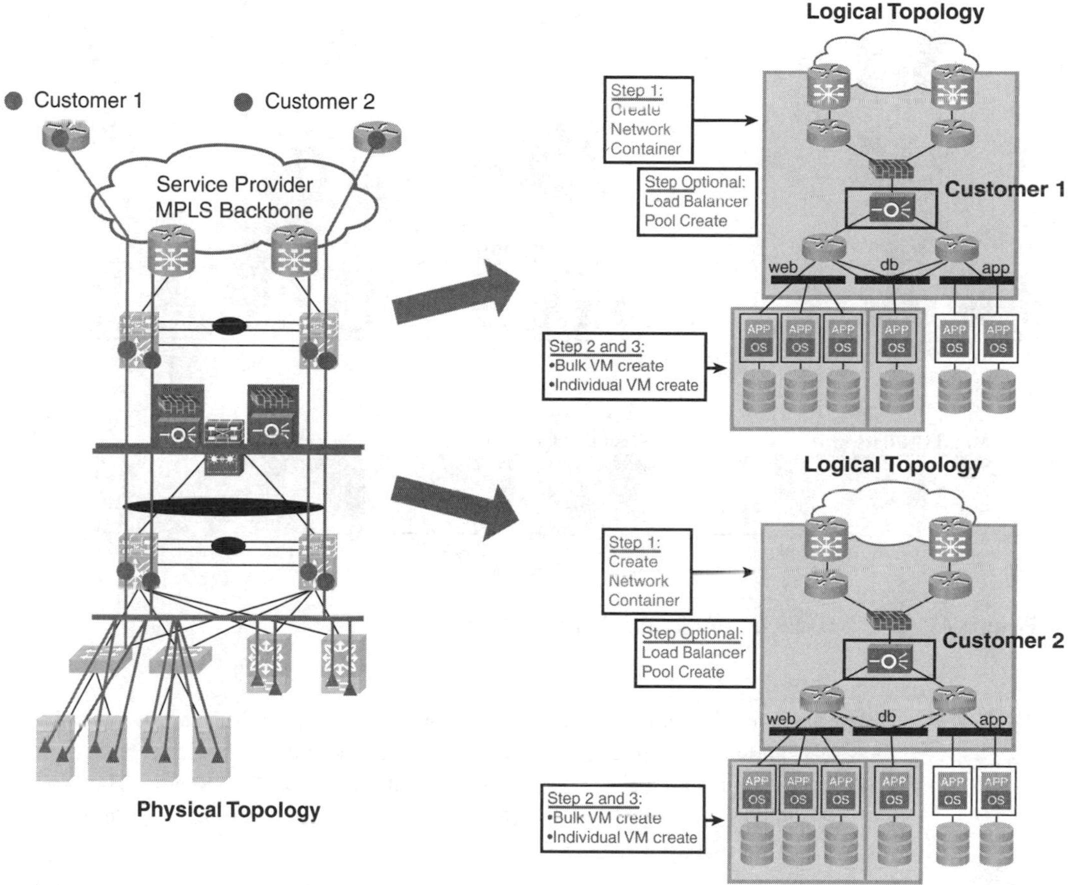

Figure A-11 *VMDC Network Container Described*

Figure A-12 illustrates the out-of-the-box network containers called Bronze, Silver, and Gold. A service provider might refer to them by different names, but the concept is the same. For cloud provisioning, the user will use the portal to request the services, and service providers typically want to have the services as package options so that it is easy to order the services. The services are described following Figure A-12.

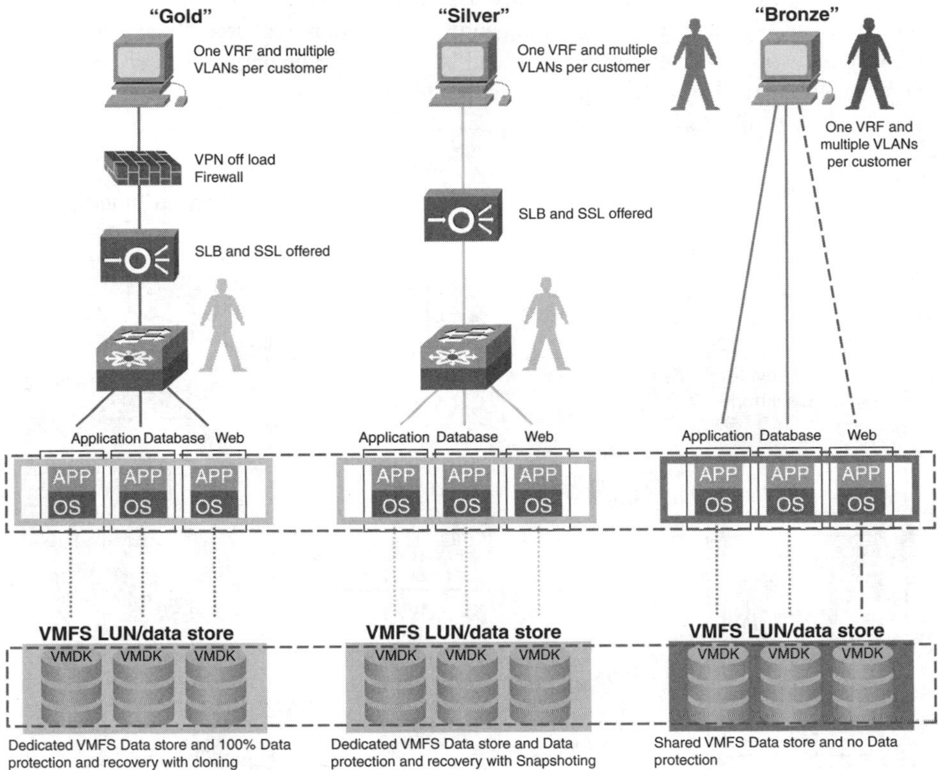

Figure A-12 *VMDC Out-of-the-Box Network Container*

- **Bronze service:** Provides customers with a private network, with the lowest level of SLA/QoS and no separate security through firewalls and no load balancers. Security is still provided through the Multiprotocol Label Switching (MPLS) core. The Bronze service will have a VM ratio of 4:1 and a queue bandwidth of 20 percent (dedicated VLAN and Virtual Routing and Forwarding [VRF]).
- **Silver service:** Provides isolated public and private connectivity, with a higher level of SLA/QoS than the Bronze service, and a separate security service is provided through firewalls. The users can specify security level (Low/Medium/High) during the service setup. The Silver service is comprised of a VM ratio of 2:1, FWSM, a queue bandwidth of 30 percent (dedicated VLAN and VRF), and local data protection and recovery using Snap. Remote replication exists to the disaster recovery (DR) site.

- **Gold service:** Provides isolated public and private connectivity, with the highest level of SLA/QoS, and a separate security service is provided through firewalls. The users can specify the security level (Low/Medium/High) during the service setup. In addition, a load-balancing service is provided through load balancers. The Gold service is comprised of a VM ratio of 1:1, ACE and FWSM, a queue bandwidth of 40 percent, and a dedicated VLAN, VRF, firewall, and load balancing. 100 percent local data protection and recovery exists using a clone (full copy). Remote replication exists to the DR site.

Diggit Service Requirements

Diggit has chosen to deploy Gold network containers to support its development and test environments to give it the greatest flexibility and security. Diggit is also working with ABCNet's product development teams to develop more flexible containers that will support its needs going forward as it believes it will ultimately migrate its remote cloud services to the public cloud to realize even more capital and operating expense savings.

Summary

The overall strategy of Diggit has been to adopt the cloud as a way to deliver more flexibility and cost savings to the business by offloading its testing and development platform to the public cloud and adopting a utility consumption model, pay as you use. The overall strategy of ABCNet has been to get to market quickly with a cloud solution that allows it to capture the business of early adopters such as Diggit and to continue to refine and enhance its cloud offerings over time.

Both organizations have recognized the value that the cloud brings as a business optimization and revenue generation vehicle. The changes on the Diggit side will be more significant as they are transforming IT into a service-orientated department, and while some IT organizations are well versed in an IT Service Management (ITSM) approach, Diggit is not one of those. On the other hand, ABCNet already understands how to create and monetize technical services, so the cloud for that company is very much more about extending its automation and orchestration know-how from the traditional telecommunications space into the IT data center.

This case study illustrated that although the technical challenges and solutions for a public and private cloud can be different, they are converging, and the cloud broker will be a key technical component in this integration. Additionally, most IT companies will benefit from leveraging telco experiences and work practices along with the more traditional IT ITIL/ITSM best practices as they become cloud providers or consumers.

Appendix B

Terms and Acronyms

This appendix provides a table that lists the acronyms and abbreviations related to cloud computing found throughout this book, along with the expansions and definitions.

Acronym/ Abbreviation	Expansion	Definition
AAA	Authentication, authorization, and accounting	AAA in some form is used by most users today. AAA is what keeps your network secure by making sure that only the right users are authenticated, that those users have access only to the right network resources, and that those users are logged as they go about their business.
ANSI	American National Standards Institute	ANSI oversees the creation, promulgation, and use of thousands of norms and guidelines that directly impact businesses in nearly every sector, from acoustical devices to construction equipment and from dairy and livestock production to energy distribution.
API	Application programming interface	An API allows computer programmers to access the functionality of prebuilt software modules. An API defines data structures and subroutine calls. Networking APIs are entry points to libraries that implement network and data communication protocols.

Acronym/ Abbreviation	Expansion	Definition
APM	Application Performance Management	Cisco APM enables service providers to extend application transaction visibility into the network and virtual machines running on physical servers to optimize the Quality of Experience (QoE) of the end user.
AWS	Amazon Web Services	AWS is a collection of web services that together make up a cloud-computing platform. The most well known of these services are Amazon EC2 and Amazon S3. Amazon Elastic Compute Cloud (Amazon EC2) is a web service that provides resizable compute capacity in the cloud. It is designed to make web-scale computing easier for developers. Amazon S3 is an online storage service offered by the Amazon web service.
BCP/DR	Business Continuity Process/Disaster Recovery	This is one of the common use cases in cloud computing. Business continuity is vital to many companies. However, the creation of a sound business continuity and contingency plan is a complex undertaking, involving a series of steps. Prior to creating BCP/DR, it is essential to consider the potential impacts of disaster and to understand the underlying risks.
BIOS	Basic Input/Output System	The primary function of the BIOS is to set up the hardware of a computer and load and start an operating system.
BN	Borderless networks	BNs connect anyone, anywhere, on any device, at any time.
CAB	Change Advisory Board	CAB is a group of people that advises the change manager in the assessment, prioritization, and scheduling of changes. This board is usually made up of representatives from all areas within the IT service provider, the business, and third parties such as suppliers.
CE	Customer edge	A customer router that connects the customer site to the service provider network is called a customer edge router (CE router). Traditionally, this device is called Customer Premises Equipment (CPE).
CI	Configuration item	Any component that needs to be managed to deliver an IT service. Information about each CI is recorded in a configuration record within the Configuration Management System and is maintained throughout its life cycle by Configuration Management.

Acronym/ Abbreviation	Expansion	Definition
CIM	Common Information Model	The CIM is an open standard that defines how managed elements in an IT environment are represented as a common set of objects and relationships between them.
CIO	Chief Information Officer	A CIO is a job title commonly given to the most senior executive in an enterprise responsible for the information technology that supports enterprise goals.
CLI	Command-line interface	The CLI is a mechanism for interacting with a computer operating system or software by typing commands to perform specific tasks. This text-only interface contrasts with the use of a mouse pointer with a graphical user interface (GUI) to click on options or menus on a text user interface to select options.
CMDB	Configuration Management Database	An ITIL term, the CMDB is a repository of information related to all the components of an information system.
CMMI	Capability Maturity Model Integration	CMMI is a process improvement approach that provides organizations with the essential elements of effective processes that will improve their performance. CMMI-based process improvement includes identifying your organization's process strengths and weaknesses and making process changes to turn weaknesses into strengths.
CMS	Configuration Management System	The evolution of the CMDB as a federated system that provides a holistic, process driven view of configuration management.
COBIT	Control Objectives for Information and Related Technology	COBIT is an IT governance framework and supporting tool set that allows managers to bridge the gap between control requirements, technical issues, and business risks.
CPU	Central processing unit	The CPU is the portion of a computer system that carries out the instructions of a computer program and is the primary element carrying out the functions of the computer or other processing device.

Acronym/ Abbreviation	Expansion	Definition
CRM	Customer Relationship Management	CRM is a widely implemented strategy for managing a company's interactions with customers, clients, and sales prospects. It involves using technology to organize, automate, and synchronize business processes—principally sales activities, but also those for marketing, customer service, and technical support.
CSA	Current-state architecture or Cloud Security Alliance	Typically, this is an assessment document of the provider environment containing the current state of technologies, people, processes, and so on. This CSA is done to determine the gaps between the current environment and the target environment, or target-state architecture (TSA). The CSA is a member-driven organization, chartered with promoting the use of best practices for providing security assurance within cloud computing.
CSI	Continuous Service Improvement	CSI is part of the ITIL V3 life cycle. It consists of the following processes: service evaluation, process evaluation, CSI initiatives, and CSI monitoring. Cisco uses the PPDIOO model, which is the equivalent of ITIL V3. The Cisco optimization phase in the PPDIOO life cycle is the equivalent of the ITIL CSI phase in the ITIL V3 life cycle.
CXO	Chief "X" officer	Where X can be Information, Executive, and so on.
DC	Data center	The DC is a facility used to house computer systems and associated components, such as telecommunications and storage systems. It generally includes redundant or backup power supplies, redundant data communications connections, environmental controls (for example, air conditioning and fire suppression), and security devices. A modern DC would have all the equipment necessary to create a cloud.

Acronym/ Abbreviation	Expansion	Definition
DC/V	Data Center/ Virtualization	In computing, virtualization is the creation of a virtual (rather than actual) version of something, such as a hardware platform, operating system, storage device, or network resources. *Hardware virtualization* or *platform virtualization* refers to the creation of a virtual machine that acts like a real computer with an operating system. Software executed on these virtual machines is separated from the underlying hardware resources. Other forms of virtualization are discussed in Chapter 1, "Cloud Computing Concepts."
DCB	Data Center Bridging	A set of IEEE 802.1 standards that provide enhancements to existing 802.1 bridge specifications to satisfy the requirements of protocols and applications in the data center and provide in part the foundation for "Unified I/O" data center network designs.
DCI	Data Center Interconnect	A general description of various apparatuses and methods to connect two geographically dispersed data center sites.
DCN	Data Center Network	A DCN connects various elements within the data center.
DMTF	Distributed Management Task Force	DMTF members collaborate to develop IT management standards that promote multivendor interoperability worldwide. (See www.dtmtf.org.)
DMZ	Demilitarized zone	In computer security, a DMZ is a physical or logical subnetwork that contains and exposes an organization's external services to a larger untrusted network, usually the Internet. It is sometimes referred to as a perimeter network.
DVS	Distributed virtual switch	A software-based OSI Layer 2 switch that extends its data, control, and management planes to two or more physical server hosts that are running hypervisor software.
EML	Element management layer	The EML of the TMN reference model manages each network element on an individual or group basis and supports an abstraction of the functions provided by the network element layer (see NML).

Acronym/ Abbreviation	Expansion	Definition
EMS	Element management system	The EMS is part of the element management layer: a management layer that is responsible for the management of network elements on an individual or collective basis.
EOL	End-of-life	Products reach the end of their life cycle for a number of reasons. This can be due to market demands, technology innovation, and development-driving changes in the product, or the products simply mature over time and are replaced by functionally richer technology. Cisco Systems recognizes that EOL milestones often prompt companies to review the way in which such end-of-sale and EOL milestones impact the Cisco products in their networks. With that in mind, we have set out the Cisco EOL policy to help customers better manage their end-of-life transition and to understand the role that Cisco can play in helping to migrate to alternative Cisco platforms and technology.
EOS	End-of-Sale	Access to the Cisco Technical Assistance Center (TAC) will be available 24 hours a day, seven days a week for a period of X years from the end-of-sale date for hardware and operating system software issues and for a period of X years from the end-of-sale date for application software issues. Here, "X" depends on the type of product.
ERP	Enterprise Resource Planning	ERP integrates internal and external management information across an entire organization, embracing finance/accounting, manufacturing, sales and service, CRM, and so on. ERP systems automate this activity with an integrated software application. Its purpose is to facilitate the flow of information between all business functions inside the boundaries of the organization and to manage the connections to outside stakeholders.
ESB	Enterprise service bus	A distributed software bus that interconnects multiple disparate systems.
eTOM	enhanced Telecom Operational Map	A catalogue of elements used to describe telco processes.

Acronym/ Abbreviation	Expansion	Definition
FAB	Fulfillment, Assurance, and Billing	The TMF define three vertical operational areas, fulfillment, assurance and billing that are collectively known as the FAB.
FCoE	Fibre Channel over Ethernet	FCoE is a mapping of Fibre Channel over selected full-duplex IEEE 802.3 networks. The goal is to provide I/O consolidation over DCB-based Ethernet.
HIPAA	Health Insurance Portability and Accountability Act	HIPAA regulates the availability and breadth of group health plans and certain individual health insurance policies.
IA	Information assurance	Data is broken down into a number of different impact levels to offer organizations guidance as to the level of IA (security) they might need.
IaaS	Infrastructure as a Service	Cloud infrastructure services, also known as IaaS, deliver computer infrastructure—typically, a platform virtualization environment—as a service. Rather than purchasing servers, software, data center space, or network equipment, clients instead buy those resources as a fully outsourced service. Suppliers typically bill such services on a utility computing basis; the amount of resources consumed (and therefore the cost) will typically reflect the level of activity.
IC	Intellectual capital	From a Cisco perspective, IC is defined broadly as the sum of the intellectual assets that Cisco has within the company—people, processes, methodologies, tools, and techniques that we accumulate and develop on a daily basis. IC is the unit of knowledge that is self-sufficient to define the problem at hand. It assumes that certain information is being provided by other ICs and is dependent on them.
IDM	Identity management	IDM relates to how humans are identified and authorized across computer networks. It covers issues such as how users are given an identity, the protection of that identity, and the technologies supporting that protection.

Acronym/ Abbreviation	Expansion	Definition
IEEE	Institute of Electrical and Electronics Engineers	IEEE, an association dedicated to advancing innovation and technological excellence for the benefit of humanity, is the world's largest technical professional society.
INCITS	International Committee for Information Technology Standards	INCITS serves as ANSI's Technical Advisory Group for the ISO/IEC Joint Technical Committee 1. JTC 1 is responsible for international standardization in the field of information technology.
IP	Internet Protocol	The network layer protocol for the TCP/IP protocol suite widely used on Ethernet networks, defined in STD 5, RFC 791. IP is a connectionless, best-effort packet-switching protocol. It provides packet routing, fragmentation and reassembly through the data link layer. IPv4 is the version in widespread use today, and IPv6 is the newer version starting to be more broadly deployed.
IPsec	IP Security	IPsec is a set of protocols developed by the IETF to support the secure exchange of packets at the IP layer. IPsec has been deployed widely to implement virtual private networks (VPN). IPsec supports two encryption modes: Transport and Tunnel. Transport mode encrypts only the data portion (payload) of each packet, but leaves the header untouched. The more secure Tunnel mode encrypts both the header and the payload. On the receiving side, an IPsec-compliant device decrypts each packet. For IPsec to work, the sending and receiving devices must share a public key. This is accomplished through a protocol known as Internet Security Association and Key Management Protocol/Oakley (ISAKMP/Oakley), which allows the receiver to obtain a public key and authenticate the sender using digital certificates.
ISO	International Organization for Standardization	ISO is the world's largest developer and publisher of international standards, being a network of the national standards institutes of 162 countries. ISO is a nongovernmental organization that forms a bridge between the public and private sectors.

Acronym/ Abbreviation	Expansion	Definition
ISP	Internet service provider	An ISP is a entity that supplies an Internet carriage service to the public. An Internet carriage service is a "listed carriage service" (under the Telecommunications Act of 1997) that enables end users to access the Internet. A "listed carriage service" is a carriage service between points in Australia, or with at least one point inside Australia (Telecommunications Act, Sect 16), while a "carriage service" indicates a service for carrying communications by means of guided and/or unguided electromagnetic energy.
ITIL	Information Technology (IT) Infrastructure Library	ITIL is the most widely adopted approach for IT service management in the world. It provides a practical, no-nonsense framework for identifying, planning, delivering, and supporting IT services to the business. ITIL advocates that IT services must be aligned to the needs of the business and underpin the core business processes. It provides guidance to organizations on how to use IT as a tool to facilitate business change, transformation, and growth.
ITU-T	International Telecommunications Union – Telecommunications Section	ITU-T is responsible for studying technical, operating, and tariff questions and issuing recommendations on them, with the goal of standardizing telecommunications worldwide. The ITU-T combines the standard-setting activities of the predecessor organizations formerly called the International Telegraph and Telephone Consultative Committee (CCITT) and the International Radio Consultative Committee (CCIR).
KPI	Key performance indicator	KPIs are provided on a report or a dashboard to give guidance to meet the business objectives.
KQI	Key Quality Indicator	KQIs provide a measurement of a specific aspect of the performance of the application or service. KQIs are derived from a number of sources, including performance metrics of the service or underlying support services such as KPIs. As a service or application is supported by a number of service elements, a number of different KPIs might need to be determined to calculate a particular KQI. More on SLAs, KPIs, and KQIs can be found in the TMF SLA Management Handbook.

Acronym/ Abbreviation	Expansion	Definition
LAMP	Linux, Apache, MySQL, and Perl/PHP/Python	LAMP is an acronym for a solution stack of free, open source software, originally coined from the first letters of Linux (operating system), Apache HTTP Server, MySQL (database software), and Perl/PHP/Python, principal components to building a viable general-purpose web server. The software combination has become popular because it is free, open source, and therefore easily adaptable, and because of the ubiquity of its components that are bundled with most current Linux distributions.
LAN	Local-area network	A local computer network for communication among computers, especially a network connecting computers, word processors, and other electronic office equipment to create a communications system between offices.
LISP	Locator Identifier Separation Protocol	LISP is a "map-and-encapsulate" protocol that is currently being developed by the Internet Engineering Task Force LISP Working Group.
MIB	Management Information Base	The MIB contains the name, object identifier (a numeric value), data type, and indication of whether the value associated with the object can be read from and/or written to. While the top levels of the MIB are fixed, specific subtrees have been defined by the IETF, vendors, and other organizations. Variables in MIB are named using Abstract Syntax Notation 1 (ASN.1), an international standard for representing data types and structures. For example, the MIB variable in the IP subtree that counts incoming IP datagrams is named internet.mgmt.mib-2.ip.iplnReceives.
MoM	Manager of Managers	In an ideal environment, the fault manager would collect both syslog and SNMP information, filter that information, and pass the filtered data to a MoM for further processing. This method helps decrease the amount of data that an end user needs to see or react upon. The MoM, in turn, can provide further analysis and automation based on the incoming event streams.

Acronym/ Abbreviation	Expansion	Definition
MPLS	Multi-Protocol Label Switching	MPLS is a highly scalable, protocol-agnostic data-carrying mechanism. In an MPLS network, data packets are assigned labels. Packet-forwarding decisions are made solely on the contents of this label, without the need to examine the packet itself. This allows one to create end-to-end circuits across any type of transport medium, using any protocol.
MTOSI	Multi-Technology Operations Systems Interface	MTOSI is an XML-based Operations System (OS)-to-OS interface suite defined by the Tele-Management Forum (TMF).
MTOSI	Multi-Technology Operations Systems Interface	A TMF standard defining the northbound API offered by a resource or service management system.
MySQL	My Structured Query Language	MySQL is a relational database management system (RDBMS) that runs as a server providing multiuser access to a number of databases. MySQL has made its source code available under the terms of the GNU General Public License, as well as under a variety of proprietary agreements. MySQL was owned and sponsored by a single for-profit firm, the Swedish company MySQL AB, now owned by Oracle Corporation.
NAND	Negated AND gate memory	NAND flash memory is a type of nonvolatile storage technology that does not require power to retain data. There are two types of flash memory: NAND and NOR. The names refer to the type of logic gate used in each memory cell. NAND has significantly higher storage capacity than NOR.

Acronym/ Abbreviation	Expansion	Definition
NAT	Network Address Translation	NAT is the translation of an IP address used within one network to a different IP address known within another network. One network is designated the inside network, and the other is the outside. Typically, a company maps its local inside network addresses to one or more global outside IP addresses and unmaps the global IP addresses on incoming packets back into local IP addresses. This helps ensure security because each outgoing or incoming request must go through a translation process that also offers the opportunity to qualify or authenticate the request or match it to a previous request. NAT also conserves the number of global IP addresses that a company needs, and it lets the company use a single IP address in its communication with the world. NAT is included as part of a router and is often part of a corporate firewall. Network administrators create a NAT table that does the global-to-local and local-to-global IP address mapping. NAT can also be used in conjunction with policy routing. NAT can be statically defined, or it can be set up to dynamically translate from and to a pool of IP addresses.
NCCM	Network Configuration and Change Management	Configuration and change management play a key role in the overall management. With DC/V and the cloud, the role of NCCM has expanded to not only network but also compute, storage devices, and applications. More on this is provided in Chapter 7, "Service Fulfillment."
NE	Network element	Typically, a network element that resides in the NML layer per TMN. A network element is generally a combination of a hardware and a software system that is designed primarily to perform a telecommunications service function. It is a piece of network equipment that can be managed through an element manager as part of a network management system.
NEL	Network element layer	Within the TMN framework, this is the logical layer responsible for the management of atomic units and functions within network elements.
NIST	National Institute of Standards and Technology	NIST, an agency of the U.S. Department of Commerce, was founded in 1901 as the nation's first federal physical science research laboratory. Over the years, the scientists and technical staff at NIST have made solid contributions to many technology areas including the cloud.

Acronym/ Abbreviation	Expansion	Definition
NML	Network management layer	As part of the TMN framework, the network management layer has the responsibility for the management of a network as supported by the element management layer. At this layer, functions addressing the management of a wide geographical area are located. Complete visibility of the whole network is typical and, as an objective, a technology-independent view will be provided to the service management layer.
NMS	Network Management System	The system responsible for managing at least part of a network. An NMS is generally a reasonably powerful and well-equipped computer, such as an engineering workstation. NMSs communicate with agents to help keep track of network statistics and resources. An element management system (EMS) manages one or more of a specific type of telecommunications network element (NE). Typically, the EMS manages the functions and capabilities within each NE but does not manage the traffic between different NEs in the network. To support management of the traffic between itself and other NEs, the EMS communicates upward to higher-level NMS as described in the telecommunications management network (TMN) layered model.
OA&M	Operations, Administration & Maintenance	The information transferred from the network element (NE) to OA&M equipment (typically OSS) can include customer usage and charging data, NE status indication, system resource utilization data, system performance measurements, alarms, and messages alerting operating personnel to the current state of the NE and other data.
OGC	Office of Government Commerce	The IT Infrastructure Library (ITIL) is a registered trademark of the OGC and maintains ITIL books.
OLA	Operational-level agreement	An OLA is an internal agreement between departments. An OLA defines how departments will work together to meet the service-level requirements (SLR) documented in an SLA. If you do not have formal SLAs in place, you are still delivering IT services, and a service catalog will do instead.

Acronym/ Abbreviation	Expansion	Definition
OS	Operating system	The most important program that runs on a computer. Every general-purpose computer must have an operating system to run other programs. Operating systems perform basic tasks, such as recognizing input from the keyboard, sending output to the display screen, keeping track of files and directories on the disk, and controlling peripheral devices such as disk drives and printers. For large systems, the operating system has even greater responsibilities and powers. It is like a traffic cop: It ensures that different programs and users running at the same time do not interfere with each other. The operating system is also responsible for security, ensuring that unauthorized users do not access the system.
OSI	Open Systems Interconnection (Model)	A model that subdivides a communications system into smaller parts called layers. Similar communication functions are grouped into seven logical layers. A layer provides services to its upper layer while receiving services from the layer below.
OSR	Operations Support and Readiness	TMF uses the term OSR. The core of the operations area is the Fulfillment, Assurance, and Billing (FAB) model. The OSR part was added to the original TOM FAB model (GB910). FAB operations are directly related to customer services, whereas OSR ensures that the operational environment is in place for FAB to be successful.
OSS	Operations Support Systems	Software applications used to support operational business processes. The term operations support system (OSS) generally refers to the system (or systems) that perform various management functions such as inventory, engineering, planning, and repair functions for communications service providers and their networks. OSSs help service providers maximize their return on investment (ROI) in one of their key assets—information. OSSs ultimately help enable next-generation service providers to reduce costs, provide superior customer service, and accelerate their time to market for new products and services.
OTV	Overlay Transport Virtualization	OTV is an industry-first solution that significantly simplifies extending Layer 2 applications across distributed data centers through dynamic encapsulation of OSI Layer 2 frames in OSI Layer 3 packets "MAC-in-IP."

Acronym/ Abbreviation	Expansion	Definition
P Router	Provider router	P routers are routers that are inside the core of the MPLS network. P routers are only aware of the PE routes, not the VPN or CE routes. This reduces complexity.
PaaS	Platform as a Service	PaaS is the delivery of a computing platform and solution stack as a service. PaaS offerings facilitate the deployment of applications without the cost and complexity of buying and managing the underlying hardware and software and provisioning hosting capabilities, providing all the facilities required to support the complete life cycle of building and delivering web applications and services entirely available from the Internet.
PCI	Peripheral Component Interconnect	PCI is an industry specification for connecting hardware devices to a computer's central processor.
PE	Provider edge	The designation for a router on the edge of a service provider network. PE routers maintain only the CE routes that are defined in their VRF tables, not the routes for all CE routers in the network.
PHP	Personal home page	PHP is a general-purpose scripting language originally designed for web development to produce dynamic web pages. For this purpose, PHP code is embedded into the HTML source document and interpreted by a web server with a PHP processor module, which generates the web page document.
PUE	Power usage efficiency	PUE = Total Facility Energy divided by the IT Equipment Energy. See www.thegreengrid.org.
QoE	Quality of Experience	QoE is related to but differs from quality of service (QoS), which attempts to objectively measure the service delivered by the vendor. QoE, sometimes also known as quality of user experience, is a subjective measure of a customer's experiences with a vendor. It looks at a vendor's offering from the standpoint of the customer or end user. To many service providers, this is most important, because the customer satisfaction comes from the user experience.

Acronym/ Abbreviation	Expansion	Definition
QoS	Quality of service	QoS refers to the ability of a network to provide better service to selected network traffic over various underlying technologies including Frame Relay, Asynchronous Transfer Mode (ATM), Ethernet and 802.1 networks, SONET, and IP-routed networks. In particular, QoS features provide better and more predictable network service by supporting dedicated bandwidth, improving loss characteristics, avoiding and managing network congestion, shaping network traffic, and setting traffic priorities across the network. In general, edge routers perform the following QoS functions: packet classification, admission control, and configuration management. In general, backbone routers perform the following QoS functions: congestion management and congestion avoidance.
RADIUS	Remote Authentication Dial-In User Service	RADIUS is the standard for centralized network authentication, authorization, and accounting of remote user access.
RAID	Redundant Array of Independent Disks	RAID refers to multiple independent hard drives combined to form one large logical array. The major objective of RAID is to improve data availability and security. RAID prevents downtime in the event of a hard disk failure.
RBIC	Rules-Based Intellectual Capital	Cisco RBIC allows consistent analysis across multiple devices in the network. The policy knowledge can be provided by Cisco network consulting engineers and other Cisco experts, or it can be provided in customer-specific custom policies that have been developed in conjunction with a CCIE certification.
ROI	Return on investment	A performance measure used to evaluate the efficiency of an investment or to compare the efficiency of a number of different investments. To calculate ROI, the benefit (return) of an investment is divided by the cost of the investment; the result is expressed as a percentage or a ratio.

Acronym/ Abbreviation	Expansion	Definition
SAA	Service assurance agent	Cisco IOS SAA is embedded software within Cisco IOS devices that performs active monitoring. Active monitoring is the generation and analysis of traffic to measure performance between Cisco IOS devices or between Cisco IOS devices and network application servers. Active monitoring provides a unique set of performance measurements: network delay or latency, packet loss, network delay variation (jitter), availability, one-way latency, website download time, as well as other network statistics. SAA can be used to measure network health, perform network assessment, verify service-level agreements, assist with network troubleshooting, and plan network infrastructure. SAA is supported on almost all Cisco IOS devices.
SaaS	Software as a Service	SaaS, sometimes referred to as "on-demand software," is a software delivery model in which software and its associated data are hosted centrally (typically in the [Internet] cloud) and are typically accessed by users using a thin client, normally using a web browser over the Internet.
SAN	Storage-area network	A SAN is a dedicated storage network that provides access to consolidated, block-level storage.
SID	Shared information/data	The TMF NGOSS SID model provides the industry with a common vocabulary and set of information/data definitions and relationships used in the definition of NGOSS architectures.
SIP	Strategy, Infrastructure, and Products	SIP is a TMF term. The Strategy and Commit Process grouping, Infrastructure Lifecycle Management grouping, and Product Lifecycle Management Process grouping are shown as three vertical, end-to-end process groupings. The Strategy and Commit processes provide the focus within the enterprise for generating specific business strategy and gaining buy-in within the business for this. The Infrastructure Lifecycle Management and Product Lifecycle Management processes drive and support the provision of products to customers.

Acronym/ Abbreviation	Expansion	Definition
SLA	Service-level agreement	SLAs define the quality of service expected by the user of the service from the provider. This can be an ISP, a telco providing WAN access, or an internal group providing infrastructure services to an enterprise. Whether you are the provider or customer, identifying and measuring service delivery are the only ways of assuring the quality of that delivery.
SML	Service management layer	As part of the TMN layered architecture, the service management layer is concerned with, and responsible for, the contractual aspects of services that are being provided to customers or available to potential new customers. Some of the main functions of this layer are service order handling, complaint handling, and invoicing. Customer-facing systems provide the basic point of contact with customers for all service transactions, including provision/cessation of service, accounts, QoS, fault reporting, and so on. The service management layer is responsible for all negotiations and resulting contractual agreements between a (potential) customer and the service(s) offered to this customer.
SNMP	Simple Network Management Protocol	The protocol governing network management and monitoring of network devices and their functions.
SOA	Service-Oriented Architecture	SOA defines how to integrate widely disparate applications for a web-based environment and uses multiple implementation platforms. Rather than defining an API, SOA defines the interface in terms of protocols and functionality.
SOAP	Simple Object Access Protocol	SOAP is a protocol specification for exchanging structured information in the implementation of web services in computer networks. It relies on eXtensible Markup Language (XML) for its message format, and usually relies on other application layer protocols, most notably Remote Procedure Call (RPC) and Hypertext Transfer Protocol (HTTP), for message negotiation and transmission.

Acronym/ Abbreviation	Expansion	Definition
SOX	Sarbanes-Oxley Act	The SOX is a United States federal law enacted on July 30, 2002, that set new or enhanced standards for all U.S. public company boards, management, and public accounting firms. The bill was enacted as a reaction to a number of major corporate and accounting scandals including those affecting Enron, Tyco International, Adelphia, Peregrine Systems, and WorldCom. These scandals, which cost investors billions of dollars when the share prices of affected companies collapsed, shook public confidence in the nation's securities markets.
SPOC	Single point of contact	A service desk is a primary IT capability called for in ITSM as defined by the ITIL. It is intended to provide an SPOC to meet the communications needs of both users and IT and to satisfy both customer and IT provider objectives.
TCP	Transmission Control Protocol	TCP is one of the main protocols in TCP/IP networks. Whereas the IP deals only with packets, TCP enables two hosts to establish a connection and exchange streams of data. TCP guarantees delivery of data and also guarantees that packets will be delivered in the same order in which they were sent.
TMF	Telecommunications Management Forum	An organization dedicated to Operations Support Systems (OSS) communication management issues.
TMN	Telecommunications Management Network	A management framework developed by the ITU T to facilitate interoperability among different network management systems and to meet the demand for a standard set of broadly defined network management functions.
TOGAF	The Open Group Architecture Framework	TOGAF is a detailed method and set of supporting resources for developing an enterprise architecture.
TRILL	Transparent Interconnection of Lots of Links	The IETF TRILL WG has specified a solution for shortest-path frame routing in multihop IEEE 802.1–compliant Ethernet networks with arbitrary topologies, using an existing link-state routing protocol technology and encapsulation with a hop count.

Acronym/ Abbreviation	Expansion	Definition
TSA	Target-state architecture	TSA is the one that the service provider wants to get to in order to support new services and fill any gaps in the current state. Typically current-state architecture (CSA) and target-state architecture (TSA) documents are done during the assessment phase of the engagement to understand the gaps in the current state and determine what it takes to get to the target state.
UC	Underpinning contract	An ITIL term, this is a contract between an IT service provider and a third party. The third party provides goods or services that support delivery of an IT service to a customer. The UC defines targets and responsibilities.
UUID	Universal Unique Identifier	A UUID is a 128-bit number used to uniquely identify some object or entity on the Internet. Depending on the specific mechanisms used, a UUID is either guaranteed to be different or is, at least, extremely likely to be different from any other UUID generated until 3400 A.D.
VCE	Virtual Computing Environment	The VCE coalition between VMware, Cisco, and EMC represents collaboration in development, services, and partner enablement that reduces risk in the infrastructure virtualization journey to the private cloud. VCE's Vblock infrastructure packages deliver a complete IT infrastructure that integrates best-of-breed virtualization, networking, compute, storage, security, and management technologies. The three companies have invested in industry-first collaborative delivery of seamless customer support with end-to-end vendor accountability.
VDC	Virtual Device Context	Cisco Nexus 7000 Series switches can be segmented into virtual devices based on business need. VDCs deliver true segmentation of network traffic, context-level fault isolation, and management through the creation of independent hardware and software partitions.
VIP	Virtual IP address	A virtual IP address can represent multiple virtual servers, and the correct mapping between them is generally accomplished by further delineating virtual servers by TCP destination port. So, a single virtual IP address can point to a virtual HTTP server, a virtual SMTP server, a virtual SSH server, and so on.

Acronym/ Abbreviation	Expansion	Definition
VLAN	Virtual LAN	A group of devices on one or more LANs that are configured (using management software) so that they can communicate as if they were attached to the same wire, when in fact they are located on a number of different LAN segments. Because VLANs are based on logical instead of physical connections, they are extremely flexible, a logical capability that allows physically separated LAN segments to operate on a common broadcast domain. See also LAN.
VM	Virtual machine	A VM is an environment, usually a program or operating system, that does not physically exist but is created within another environment. In this context, a VM is called a "guest" while the environment it runs within is called a "host." Virtual machines are often created to execute an instruction set that is different than that of the host environment. One host environment can often run multiple VMs at once. Because VMs are separated from the physical resources they use, the host environment is often able to dynamically assign those resources among them.
VMM	Virtual machine monitor	VMM is the software that creates a virtual machine environment in a computer. The term *hypervisor* is used to refer to the virtual machine monitor component nearest the hardware.
VPC	Virtual Private Cloud	A VPC is a private cloud existing within a shared or public cloud.
vPC	Virtual PortChannel	A vPC is a port channel that can operate between more than two devices. While multiple devices are used to create the virtual port channel, the terminating device sees the vPC as one logical connection/switch.
VPN	Virtual private network	Enables IP traffic to travel securely over a public TCP/IP internetwork by encrypting all traffic from one network to another. A VPN is essentially a collection of sites sharing common routing information, which means that a site can belong to more than one VPN if it holds routes from separate VPNs. This provides the capability to build intranets and extranets.

Acronym/ Abbreviation	Expansion	Definition
VRF	VPN routing and forwarding	VRF is a technology included in IP network routers that allows multiple instances of a routing table to exist in a router and work simultaneously. This increases functionality by allowing network paths to be segmented without using multiple devices. Because traffic is automatically segregated, VRF also increases network security.
VSAN	Virtual storage-area network	In computer networking, a VSAN is a collection of ports from a set of connected Fibre Channel switches that form a virtual fabric. Ports within a single switch can be partitioned into multiple VSANs, despite sharing hardware resources. Conversely, multiple switches can join a number of ports to form a single VSAN. VSANs were designed by Cisco, modeled after the VLAN concept in Ethernet networking. In October 2004, the Technical Committee T11 approved VSAN technology into the American National Standards Institute (ANSI) as the standard.
WAAS	Wide-area application service	Cisco WAAS solutions are deployed by more than 5000 customers to accelerate applications over the WAN, consolidate branch infrastructure, and empower cloud computing. Cisco WAAS appliances deliver comprehensive application, branch, and WAN optimization.
WAN	Wide-area network	The term WAN usually refers to a network that covers a large geographical area and uses communications circuits to connect the intermediate nodes. A major factor impacting WAN design and performance is a requirement that they lease communications circuits from telephone companies or other communications carriers. Transmission rates are typically 2 Mbps, 34 Mbps, 45 Mbps, 155 Mbps, and 625 Mbps (or sometimes considerably more).
WSDL	Web Services Description Language	WSDL is an XML format for describing network services as a set of endpoints operating on messages containing either document-oriented or procedure-oriented information.
XaaS	(Anything) as a Services	A catch-all term defining any service delivered using a consumption- or utility-based model.
XML	eXtensible Markup Language	A simple, flexible text format based on SGML (Standard Generalized Markup Language) designed specifically for large-scale electronic publishing.

Index

Numbers

A

B

D

G

H

I

J-K

L

M

N

O

P

Q

R

S

T

U

V

W

X-Y-Z